CREATIVE
MANAGEMENT

LEEDS !

The Open Business School

The Open Business School offers a three-tier ladder of opportunity for managers at different stages of their careers: the Professional Certificate in Management; the Professional Diploma in Management; and the MBA. If you would like to receive information on these open learning programmes, please write to the Open Business School, The Open University, Milton Keynes MK7 6AA, England.

This volume is a Course Reader for the Open Business School's MBA course *Creative Management* (B882).

A companion volume, also available from SAGE Publications, is:

Managing Innovation
edited by David Walker and Jane Henry

CREATIVE MANAGEMENT

edited by
Jane Henry
at the Open Business School

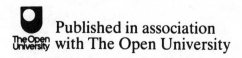

Published in association
with The Open University

SAGE Publications
London • Newbury Park • New Delhi

Selection and editorial matter © The Open University 1991

First published 1991
Reprinted 1992

SAGE Publications Ltd
6 Bonhill Street
London EC2A 4PU

SAGE Publications Inc
2455 Teller Road
Newbury Park, California 91320

SAGE Publications India Pvt Ltd
32, M-Block Market
Greater Kailash – I
New Delhi 110 048

British Library Cataloguing in Publication data

Creative management.
  1. Management. Creative thought
  I. Henry, Jane II. Open University
  658.403

  ISBN 0–8039–8490–1
  ISBN 0–8039–8491–X pbk

Library of Congress catalog card number 90–52934

Typeset by Fakenham Photosetting Ltd, Fakenham, Norfolk
Printed in Great Britain by J.W. Arrowsmith Ltd, Bristol

Contents

The Authors

Weston H. Agor	Professor of Public Management, University of Texas at El Paso
Vaune Ainsworth-Land	Formerly teacher and consultant
Richard Baker	Richard Baker and Company
David Bohm	Emeritus Professor of Theoretical Physics, Birkbeck College, London University
Edward de Bono	Author, consultant, previously held appointments at Oxford, Cambridge, London and Harvard Universities
Peter Drucker	Clark Professor of Social Science, Claremont Graduate School, California, Emeritus Professor of Management, Graduate Business School, New York University
Charles Handy	Author, Visiting Professor, London Business School
Jane Henry	Lecturer, Open Business School, Open University
David K. Hurst	Federal Industries Metals Group, Toronto, Canada
Daniel J. Isenberg	Assistant Professor, Harvard Business School
Geir Kaufmann	Senior Researcher in Cognitive Psychology, University of Bergen, Norway
Michael J. Kirton	Director, Occupational Psychology Unit, Hatfield Polytechnic
David Kolb	Professor, Department of Organizational Behaviour, Case Western Reserve University
Louis Kuhn	Chief Apparel Inc
Robert Lawrence Kuhn	Senior Fellow, IC^2 Institute of the University of Texas at Austin and Adjunct Professor, New York University
Ronnie Lessem	Reader in International Management, City University Business School, London
Stuart Lublin	Case Western Reserve University
John N.T. Martin	Lecturer in Systems, Open University
Neil McAleer	Journalist
Michael B. McCaskey	Formerly Harvard Graduate School of Business
Henry Mintzberg	Bronfman Professor of Management, Faculty of Management, McGill University, Canada

Gareth Morgan   Professor of Administrative Sciences, York
                       University, Toronto, Canada
Robert K. Mueller   Department of Management, Keller Graduate
                       School of Management, Chicago
F. David Peat   Theoretical physicist, previously with National
                       Research Council, Canada
John F. Rockart   Director, Centre for Information Systems, MIT
                       Sloan School of Management
James C. Rush   School of Business Administration, University of
                       Western Ontario, London, Canada
James E. Short   Center for Information Systems Research, MIT
                       Sloan School of Management
Juliann Spoth   Case Western Reserve University
Geoffrey Vickers   Posts included Directorship of Parkinson-Cowan,
                       Chairmanship of Coal Board
Roderick E. White   School of Business Administration, University of
                       Western Ontario, London, Canada

Acknowledgements

This book is one of two volumes originally prepared as part of the Open University course on Creative Management. I would like to thank those without whom this book would not have come to pass: in particular John Martin for involving me in this enterprise and suggesting the material on Winnicott and the Mueller paper; also John Scott for his support and comments, Eion Farmer and David Mayle for their comments, Judi Moore for locating papers without complaint and Debra Jetke for copying with a light heart.

The publishers are grateful to the following for permission to reprint: *Administrative Science Quarterly* (ch. 9), American Management Association (ch. 13), Edward de Bono (ch. 3), Paul Chapman Ltd and Jean Vickers (ch. 14), Creative Education Foundation (ch. 15), The Free Press and Robert Kirk Mueller (ch. 12), Gower Publishing (ch. 19), *Harvard Business Review* (chs 6 and 7), Heinemann Publishers (Oxford) Ltd (ch. 22), Jossey-Bass Inc. (ch. 21), MCB University Press (ch. 17), McGraw-Hill Book Company (ch. 8), Norwegian University Press (ch. 10), Omni Publications International Ltd and Neil McAleer (ch. 2), Pergamon Press plc (ch. 16), Random Century Ltd (ch. 20), Routledge (ch. 4), *Sloan Management Review* (ch. 23), John Wiley & Sons Ltd (ch. 18), and Winnicott Trust (ch. 5). Despite our best efforts we have been unable to trace the copyright holder of ch. 11: we should be glad to include an acknowledgement in any reprint.

Introduction

We live in remarkable times. The planet is faced with the spectre of catastrophic climatic changes. The old Satan of communism is no more. Information not industry rules our lives. New patterns emerge to meet the needs of our new order. We are one world, with a global economy, climate and increasingly similar cultural milieu, inextricably intertwined in interdependence.

This world needs a different form of perception, one that accepts change as a part of everyday life, that enables us to build on the opportunities change thrusts upon us, that co-operates with others, valuing the part we all play, and recognizes personal and organizational development, as a way of life. Change is occurring too fast for quantitative extrapolation, rather we will have to re-open the part of us that 'knows' in some other way: the sure judge with the courage to risk, the imagination to challenge, the sensitivity to know when to act and whom to involve. These are skills associated with creativity. Creativity is sometimes considered the antithesis of management; yet creative management is a growth area, as the quickening pace of change and shortening product life cycles make the need for procedures that deal with decision making under uncertainty and inspired judgement ever more critical. Creative management will also be vital in showing appropriate vision and strategy for the co-operative development so essential to our age.

This book offers a series of readings in the area of creative management that begin to address issues in creative perception, planning and action. It looks at the qualities attributed to the creative state and asks how these can be managed and developed. It examines the place of creative thinking and creative processes in management. It delineates styles of creative behaviour and paths of creative development and invites readers to apply creative practices to build a creative future. The main thrust of the book is about the impact of thought upon action, and attempts to change thought creatively so as to bring about creative action.

The book is divided into five sections. Section 1 offers a variety of viewpoints on creativity, representing management, cognitive, scientific and psychodynamic perspectives. Section 2 traces the relationship between thought and creativity in management. It includes classic accounts of the nature of management thinking and its non-rational character and explores the power of metaphor. Section 3 elaborates some key creative processes, including creative problem solving, mapping and networking, alongside intuition, judgement and imaging. Section 4 brings us back to the more psychological aspects of creativity, highlighting differences in personal styles via the Jungian-based MBTI and adaptor–innovator schemes and examining development over time through work on life phases and creative competencies. Section 5 looks forward to the future and asks students to contemplate the creative changes the 90s bring, through a consideration of the impact of key trends, the pervasive use of IT, the move to a more environmental consciousness, and accompanying changes in values and lifestyles.

Originally prepared for the Open University MBA option in Creative Management, the book is likely to appeal to managers, educators and others with an interest in developing and managing creatively.

SECTION 1

CREATIVE PERSPECTIVES

Creativity implies appropriate novelty. Many argue that the capacity for creative action seems to be a basic feature of life. This mysterious ability to transform our thoughts and actions to produce unique behaviour is far from understood. Recently scientists have started to take a renewed interest in this important area.

The opening section of this book presents a series of perspectives on creativity. These include accounts of lateral thinking, the cognitive angle, scientific opinion and a psychodynamic viewpoint. Henry places these in context with an overview of some of the main theories used to account for creativity and a résumé of some of the findings about creative people, processes, products and places.

Research has gone some way towards identifying common factors in the personality and approach to problems found in creative people from all walks of life. For example, many creative breakthroughs seem to have been made by people who have been working in a particular area and devoting considerable time and thought to a problem prior to discovering the creative solution. Perkins, a Harvard psychologist, is one of those who advocates a cognitive model of creativity which stresses the similarity of creative processes to other cognitive processes. He highlights personality factors that may account for the ability to maintain the sustained effort needed for many creative breakthroughs (Perkins 1981). The chapter by McAleer outlines some of the factors Perkins and others believe to be characteristic of both creative scientists and artists, including a personal aesthetic, problem finding ability, mental mobility, risk taking, objectivity and inner motivation.

Creativity is concerned with developing new ideas, and to do this we need to see the problem from a fresh perspective, which involves escaping from old ideas. The chapter by De Bono outlines the characteristics of lateral thinking, a term he coined and which along with his prolific writings on the topic has done much to popularize the idea of creative thinking. He spells out how lateral thinking differs from the more common evaluative thinking which he terms vertical thinking. Recognizing that the brain needs to organize information into patterns, he advocates lateral thinking as a means of escaping from set patterns to new perceptions and more productive approaches. De Bono and others argue that this kind of creative thinking is a skill that can be taught.

Bohm and Peat offer a scientist's view of creativity. Bohm, an eminent quantum physicist, bemoans the blocks to scientific advance wrought by barriers of the human mind, unable to perceive the assumptions that limit it. Bohm and Peat recognize the mind's preference for the comfort and security of familiar ideas. They argue that creative thoughts arise from a playfulness of mind. They illustrate how great scientific advances arise from creative perceptions formed out of an intense involvement that dares to question fundamental axioms. Like Perkins, Bohm and Peat are clear that it is those who have sufficient ability in and familiarity with the area being studied who are most likely to come up with useful creative insights. They argue that both science and society would benefit from a change of attitude that encourages the nurturing of new ideas.

The chapter by Martin on the work of Winnicott highlights the deeper aspects of creativity, relating the 'magical' engrossing side of creativity to play, and the centrality of owned, willed creative acts to satisfactory living. Like Bohm and Peat, Winnicott emphasizes the parallels between the creative thought and play, and recognizes the part played by passion. Winnicott believes the capacity for creative action to be synonymous with healthy living, and ascribes its absence to a faulty development of the concept of self, rooted in early childhood experience (Winnicott 1980).

References

Perkins D.N. (1981) *The mind's best work*. Cambridge MA: Harvard University Press.
Winnicott D.W. (1980) *Playing and reality*. Harmondsworth, Middlesex: Penguin Education.

1

Making sense of creativity

Jane Henry

Creativity is about the quality of originality that leads to new ways of seeing and novel ideas. It is a thinking process associated with imagination, insight, invention, innovation, ingenuity, intuition, inspiration and illumination. However, creativity is not just about novelty: for an idea to be truly creative it must also be appropriate and useful. The related term innovation is usually used to describe the process whereby creative ideas are developed into something tangible, like a new product or practice.

This chapter offers an introduction to thinking about creativity, first outlining some of the theories used to account for creativity and then discussing four aspects of creativity: the person, process, place and product.

Theories of creativity

There are a number of schools of thought as to the origin of creativity:

- Grace
- Accident
- Association
- Cognitive
- Personality

Grace

Creativity has something of a mysterious air about it, drawing forth images of wonderful insights, imaginative efforts, illumination and intuitions that come forth from nowhere. Archimedes shouts 'Eureka' in his bath at the realization that his body had displaced a volume of water and that a similar principle will allow him to measure the amount of gold in the King's crown; Kekulé sees two entwined snakes in a dream and realizes that this is the form of the benzene ring. This seems the work of magic, and one can understand the Greek idea of a 'creative' muse who granted a new idea, or the gift to compose or paint, as *grace* from the gods. The idea of genius may add force to this notion, since people like Mozart, Shakespeare or Leonardo da Vinci seem to be endowed with a superhuman creativity quotient. Insight experiences, in which creative ideas emerge unexpectedly from the unconscious in such a way that the creator is unable to explain how they got there, just add to the mystery.

Accident

In direct opposition to the idea of creativity as a gift from the gods is the notion that creativity may arise *accidentally* via serendipitous good fortune. Some writers go so far as to claim that many scientific discoveries can largely be accounted for on this basis. Van Andel (1989) offers various types of serendipitous discovery, such as those of immunization arising from an interruption in work, radioactivity from the wrong hypothesis and the smallpox vaccination from observation.

Association

The mechanism that allows such happy accidents is often thought to be an unanticipated connection. This *associationist* theory of creativity is perhaps the most popular; it suggests that applying procedures from one area to another can give rise to novel associations, and that such associations form the bedrock of creative ideas. This notion was popularized by Koestler (1970) under the term 'bisociation', and it underlies the justification for many divergent thinking techniques, such as lateral thinking and brainstorming. Whitfield (1975) gives the example of food and X-rays, neither new concepts, but connecting these two apparently unrelated ideas might suggest irradiating food. Sometimes we miss the potential in an idea. Freud, for instance, was a keen advocate of cocaine yet, despite recognizing its side-effect of numbing the mouth, he never spotted its potential commercial application as a dental anaesthetic. It is perhaps of some comfort to us lesser mortals that this highly creative man was obviously not open to the creative possibilities in all areas of life.

Cognitive

Another school of thought, championed by cognitively inclined investi-gators such as Perkins (1981) and Weisburg (1986), argues that there is nothing peculiarly special about creativity at all, and that it draws on perfectly normal *cognitive* processes like recognition, reasoning and under-standing. The crux of this view is the notion that chance favours a prepared mind. Sternberg,[1] for example, argues that insight depends on three pro-cesses: selective encoding of information, selective combination, ie synthe-sizing appropriate information, and selective comparison, relating new information to old.

The cognitive position on creativity stresses the part played by *appli-cation*. Many great inventors work at a problem for years: Edison, for instance, tried many different filaments before he obtained a functioning light bulb and Marie Curie showed similar application over many years in her study of radiation. Weisburg[2] points out that most supposed geniuses such as Freud, Picasso or Darwin were in fact very hard workers and highly productive. On the basis of a study of the achievements of exceptional individuals in various fields, including chess grandmasters and Mozart, Hayes[3] concluded that ten years of intense preparation was necessary for outstanding creative contributions.

The logic of the cognitive position is that deep thinking about an area over a long period leaves the discoverer informed enough to notice anomalies that might be significant. Perkins[4] acknowledges that there is something different in the character of the mind that is attracted to particularly difficult and complex problems. Highly creative people are strongly motivated and seem able to concentrate over a long period. (The chapter by McAleer reviews some of these characteristics.)

Personality

If I ask you to think of particularly creative individuals, many of you may cite the exceptional achievements of 'geniuses', naming artists such as Turner, musicians like Mozart and Beethoven, scientists like Einstein, and inventors such as Edison or Leonardo da Vinci. In the business world, Steve Jobs (the founder of Apple computers) or Clive Sinclair may come to mind. This may suggest the idea that creativity is a special *ability* possessed by a subset of the population. Yet we have all mastered the creative task of learning to walk and talk and utter unique sentences every day, so creative ability can be thought of as a human endowment that is common to us all, rather than the province of the isolated few. This view sees creativity as a natural human trait, an intrinsic part of life and growth.

Like most other attributes, creative ability seems to be distributed in varying 'strengths'. Perhaps the capacity for creative action is not so much a *personality trait* as a *state of mind* which can be learnt. Some people seem to have a facility for it and others do not, but as with running or any other skill we can all improve with training and practice. Viewing creativity as a natural talent directs attention towards removing mental barriers to creativity to allow an innate spontaneity to flourish. However, creative acts are not just isolated acts of perception; they require a certain emotional disposition too, for any new idea replaces and in effect destroys the previous order. It takes a certain courage and persistence to risk the wrath of those caught up in the old ideas and brave the resistance that any change seems to engender.

Aspects of creativity: person, process, place and product

A number of commentators have found it convenient to distinguish between creative persons, creative processes, creative places and creative products. The person angle focuses on creativity as an ability, process on creativity as a mental activity, place[5] on conditions that facilitate or inhibit creativity, and product on creative outcomes.

- Person
- Process
- Place
- Product

Person

Considerable energy has gone into trying to work out the characteristics of creative individuals. Whitfield (1975) offers a useful distinction between creative people, innovators and entrepreneurs. Creative people are usually seen as people who generate ideas, innovators as those who take an idea and develop it into something tangible, and entrepreneurs as those who take the product to market or implement the practice. Intrapreneurs fulfil a similar role to entrepreneurs within large organizations.

Studies of creative people have highlighted traits such as tolerance for ambiguity, independent thinking, not being inhibited by conformity pressures, good verbal communication skills, imagination, and a reasonable but not outstanding level of intelligence. Creative people are intrinsically motivated and work hard (this may be because working on something in which you are interested is more like play). Guildford (1959) highlights the importance of problem sensitivity, idea fluency, flexibility, originality and a capacity for redefining problems. Creative people are said to be better at asking the right questions, to be more sensitive to gaps in knowledge in their fields, and to opt to study more important problems than others. They appear comfortable with risk taking, are open to new experiences and exhibit a high degree of perseverance and discipline. (For a review see Sternberg 1988.)

Different personality styles may lead to different sorts of creativity. Kirton (1984) draws a distinction between 'adaptors', who are creative within the system, and 'innovators', who incline to more radical interventions such as transforming the system itself. The effect of upbringing has also been looked at. For example, Roe (1952) studied the background and character of eminent US physicists, biologists and social scientists. She found that the hard scientists such as physicists tended to have a history of being shy intellectuals, whereas the social scientists were involved in social groupings from a young age.

Recently, theorists have proposed more complex models which allow for an interaction between personality, ability and situation. For example, Amabile (1983) discusses the part played by domain-relevant skills, such as knowledge of the area, creativity skills, such as a thinking style favouring new perspectives, and intrinsic motivation to do the task, emphasizing that 'the love people feel for their work has a great deal to do with the creativity of their performances'.[6]

Process

Creative process suggests imaginative thinking, which is expansive in nature, as opposed to evaluative thinking, which is convergent in character.

Creative thinking has traditionally highlighted procedures that are supposed to aid the individual's capacity to think divergently – brainstorming, morphological analysis, lateral thinking and synectics for example. These procedures aim to develop participants' fluency, so that they generate large numbers of ideas, as well as variety, so that the ideas contain fundamentally different approaches. To ensure that such approaches have a practical outcome, this 'insight' phase of creative thinking is normally set within a wider framework which allows for alternating phases of expansive and convergent thinking.

Wallas (1926) stressed four stages: preparation, incubation, illumination and verification, in one of the earliest and most enduring conceptions of the creative process.

- Preparation
- Incubation
- Illumination
- Verification

Preparation involves gaining the necessary skills and knowledge, and refining your map of the area in question so that you are in a position to pose the right questions. It is also a stage at which the questioner puts in a lot of effort trying to find answers and may end up frustrated. At that point the questioner may temporarily give up and turn conscious attention elsewhere, leaving the problem to incubate in the unconscious mind, to return later with a fresh mind and attitude towards the problem. After *incubation* the lucky questioner experiences a period of *illumination* or insight when the way forward becomes clear. This is often accompanied by feelings of euphoria. Finally the insight needs to be developed and evaluated in the *verification* stage.

Much of the literature on creativity is devoted to creative problem solving. Clearly to solve problems effectively you need the flexibility to use both imaginative and evaluative thought. Most creative problem-solving models follow a similar sequence of separate stages of thinking (see Table 1). They begin with some kind of problem exploration phase and follow this with an idea generation phase and finally an implementation phase where the strategy for action is delineated. Within each of these stages there is an expansive phase where imagination is encouraged and 'anything goes', and a convergent phase where the output from the expansive phase is narrowed down and a selection made. Such procedures are particularly useful when you are stuck and need to challenge your assumptions.

Table 1   *Creative problem solving*

Stage	Function
Issue	Explore angle
Ideas	Generate alternatives
Implementation	Plan action

To begin with you need an issue to work on. This may be a problem you want to solve, an opportunity you want to explore or an area you feel confused by. The first stage involves exploring the problem, with a view to clarifying what is going on and, more important, considering the problem from different angles. Large, vague and messy problems may benefit from some kind of mapping process which allows the questioner to form a better idea of the elements in the problem and the relationship between them. Creative problem solving often involves reframing the problem from a number of angles, with the aim of reaching some kind of problem statement that encapsulates the nub of the issue to be addressed. The favoured approach to the problem is taken as the starting-point for the next stage of the process. In my experience about 70% of people opt to explore a question that is different from the one with which they started.

The second stage aims at generating as many ideas as possible, on the assumption that quantity breeds quality. This works on the principle of deferred judgement, an approach that demands a very different attitude from our usual thinking mode, since participants are encouraged to look for what is good in ideas rather than evaluate suggestions as they are raised. (De Bono expands on this point.) Brainstorming is the best-known procedure, involving pooling the ideas of a group of people. Classically, brainstorming encourages participants to accept any suggestion, whether wacky, improbable or obvious, and build on other people's ideas. Other more analytical procedures that can aid idea generation include the use of checklists, matrices and morphological analysis. (Kaufmann offers some examples.) Another group of techniques aims to provoke the mind into reaching ideas it would not normally reach, for instance the idea of reversing or distorting the problem in some way, or drawing ideas from a randomly introduced word. In each case participants end by relating the ideas they have generated back to the original problem. Analogies and metaphors offer other means of accessing different approaches to solving the problem at hand.

Needless to say, most of these procedures generate large numbers of ideas and some classification is usually required to aid people to sort out categories of ideas and examples of each. One way of doing this is to use the kind of mind map advocated by Buzan (1974), which moves out from a central starting point by means of radiating branches with sub-branches and twigs. Alternatively, each idea is written on a separate piece of paper or 'Post-it' note and may subsequently be clustered with related ideas. Ultimately some favoured ways forward need to be selected. These may be very obvious, be chosen on the basis of 'gut feel', be worked out via a system of criteria and/or hurdles that the solution must satisfy or be based on a computer-aided group decision support system.

The third stage involves considering the implementation process. This is an expansive phase where the question context is considered, and account is taken of the people, resources, policy, climate, etc., that will support the idea, and those factors that are likely to hinder its implementation. The action plan normally includes steps to engage this support, get round any expected opposition, and anticipate things that might go wrong. Finally the client or organization that initiated the problem-solving process needs to commit themselves to implementing the proposed plan.

As presented the procedure may sound very rigid, but in practice it is more iterative in character. It may emerge during the discussion that a further issue needs addressing, in which case the process would begin again with the second problem. Creative problem-solving procedures similar to that described above are in common use in organizations.

It is just as important to attend to the barriers that inhibit creative thinking as it is to teach procedures that aim to aid creative problem solving. Adams[7] lists a series of perceptual, intellectual, environmental and emotional barriers to creative thinking. The emotional blocks include the following:

> fear of failing, making a mistake or taking risks;
> an inability to tolerate ambiguity, an overriding need for security and no appetite for 'chaos';
> a preference for judging ideas;
> an inability to relax;
> lack of challenge and failure to engage with the task;
> excessive zeal;
> lack of access to imagination;
> lack of imaginative control;
> inability to distinguish reality from fantasy.

Such characteristics usually have deep psychological roots which make developing a more creative attitude more than a matter of learning a few creativity techniques. The effect of such attitudes on performance seems to be affected by the relative openness of the climate in which the work is being carried out.

Place

These days a good deal of management thinking argues that organizational and societal climate, culture and structure have a major impact upon creative output. The suggestion is that creative ideas flow where new ideas and challenges are welcomed and where people are encouraged to play, rather than controlled and threatened.

Structure

Structural changes designed to enhance creative performance have traditionally included the idea of autonomous departments specializing in new products or research, although such groups can sometimes be resented elsewhere in the organization. New products can be hived off into an enterprise that is effectively independent from the parent company. More radical structural changes may be needed if the intention is to raise the level of innovation throughout the enterprise. A common structural change in this situation is to introduce a much flatter organization in an attempt to reduce bureaucracy and speed responsiveness.

Climate

The immediate environment is also seen as an important factor. If a team of people are to be open to ideas, they need to have or develop a good deal of trust, feel comfortable enough to take risks and be free to fail. The task of managing a climate conducive to creative endeavours is not trivial, for the manager has to reconcile the need to provide direction with allowing employees enough freedom of expression to feel in control of their destiny, so that they are prepared to be active, participate fully, be focused, flexible and fast moving. It has been suggested that the leadership style that is most conducive to fostering creative endeavours is participative leadership, in which the leader becomes more of a facilitator and mentor.

Product

Creative products may arise from a radical breakthrough or a series of smaller incremental steps. Management methods in the West have emphasized the former while Japan has built much of its success with the latter. Such products have a novel form and/or level of performance and are perceived to be demonstrably useful and attractive. It is the province of the researcher, scientist, designer and engineer to turn ideas into tangible artifacts. The task of the manager is usually restricted to enthusing and co-ordinating multi-disciplinary teams working on product development and driving these processes along. The entrepreneur's or product champion's art is to judge correctly the potential in an innovation.

Ideally, invention leads to a process of innovation, but getting your idea taken up and acted upon is not easy. Indeed, many pundits argue that generating a good idea is the least difficult stage of the creative process; the problem lies in development and mastering the obstacle course of the innovation process. Simonton[8] and others have argued for a fifth p – persuasion, as individuals seen as creative are those who have managed to persuade others of the value of their work! (The art of managing innovation is expanded upon in the companion volume to this book.)[9]

Conclusion

Most commentators agree that neither creativity nor innovation happens in a flash. They place insight as a small part of a larger process in which the time spent planning, attempting to solve the problem and implement the solution is a very important part of the process. As the saying goes, it's 98% perspiration and 2% inspiration.

Creativity occurs in a social setting and it is the interaction between a creative organization and the creative people within it that produces innovation. By understanding the creative process and characteristics of a creative environment the creative manager is better placed to remove the barriers to creative action. At bottom this is a style of management that empowers others to live a more creative life.

Notes

1 Sternberg quoted in Perkins 1988, pp. 326–7.
2 Weisburg 1986, pp. 144–5.
3 Hayes 1989, pp. 293–7.
4 Perkins 1981, p. 100.
5 Place is more commonly referred to as press in the creative literature.
6 Hennessey and Amabile in Sternberg 1988, p. 11.
7 Adams 1974, pp. 52–3.
8 Simonton 1990, pp. 98, 99.
9 Walker and Henry 1991.

References

Adams, J. (1974) *Conceptual block busting*. San Francisco: W H Freeman.
Amabile, T. (1983) *The social psychology of creativity*. New York: Springer-Verlag.
Buzan, T. (1974) *Use your head*. London: BBC Books.
Guildford, J.P. (1959) 'Traits in creativity', in Anderson H.H. (ed.) *Creativity and its cultivation*. New York: Wiley.
Hayes, J.R. (1989) *The complete problem solver*, 2nd edition. Hillsdale NJ: Lawrence-Erlbaum Associates.
Hennessey, B. and Amabile, T.M. (1988) 'The conditions of creativity', in Sternberg 1988.
Kirton, M.J. (1984) 'Adaptors and innovators – why new initiatives get blocked', *Long Range Planning*, 17(3), pp. 137–43.
Koestler, A. (1970) *The act of creation*. London: Pan.
Perkins, D.N. (1981) *The mind's best work*. Cambridge MA: Harvard University Press.
Perkins, D.N. (1988) 'Creativity and the quest for mechanism', in R. Sternberg and E. Smith *The psychology of human thought*. Cambridge: Cambridge University Press. pp. 309–36.
Roe, A. (1952) *The making of a scientist*. New York: Dodd, Mead.
Simonton, D.K. (1990) 'History, chemistry, psychology and genius: an intellectual autobiography of historiometry', in M. Runco and R. Mark, *Theories of creativity*. Newbury Park CA: Sage Focus. pp. 92–115.
Sternberg, R.J. (1988) *The nature of creativity*. Cambridge, MA: Cambridge University Press.
Van Andel, M.V. (1989) Presentation to Second European conference on creativity and innovation: Learning from practice, Noordwijk, Holland, December.
Walker, D. and Henry, J. (eds) (1991) *Managing innovation*. London: Sage.
Wallas, G. (1926) *The art of thought*. New York: Franklin Watts.
Weisburg, R.W. (1986) *Creativity, genius and other myths*. New York: Freeman.
Whitfield, P. (1975) *Creativity in industry*. Harmondsworth: Penguin.

2

The roots of inspiration

Neil McAleer

Creativity is a passionate, exciting and challenging effort to make just the right connection amid the buffeting chaos of everyday reality. And in recent years the effort to understand humanity's imaginative quest has sprouted new wings. The reason for the renewed interest is the same today as it was 30 years ago: international competition.

Some scientists remain skeptical that we will ever fully understand the creative process. Nevertheless, many creativity researchers believe that a comprehensive psychology of creativity is within reach. And many hope to apply what we know about creativity to finding solutions to today's serious global problems. 'The idea that creativity spontaneously bubbles up from a magical well or gains a direct line to the Muses is just another myth among many about highly creative people and their work', says Harvard University psychologist David Perkins, co-director of Project Zero, a research project studying cognitive skills among scientists and artists. Momentary flashes of insight, often accompanied by images, make up only a small part of the creative continuum. At the heart of the process, personality and personal values shape an individual's intentional and sustained effort, often over a lifetime.

Creativity and genius have so often been considered bedfellows that creativity has been linked to intelligence. But intuition, much more than rational thought, appears to be vital to the creative thinking process. 'You don't have to have a high IQ to be intuitive,' says Frank Barron, a psychologist at the University of California at Santa Cruz who has measured and observed creativity for the last 40 years. 'Intuition depends less on reasoning and verbal comprehension [the main measure of IQ] than it does on feelings and metaphor.'

Scholastic skills do not predict whether a person can create something that will make a difference in society or even in his or her own life, Project Zero co-director Howard Gardner emphasizes. There are ample historical examples of creative individuals who had little interest in school or were poor students: Thomas Edison was at the bottom of his class; neither William Butler Yeats nor George Bernard Shaw was a very good speller; Benjamin Franklin was poor at maths.

Adapted from *Omni*, II, 7, 1989, pp. 44–102. Copyright 1989 by Neil McAleer, reprinted with the permission of Omni Publications International Ltd

Scrutinized and probed for some four decades, the creative personality has slowly revealed a number of common traits that are shared by artists and scientists – indeed, by all creative people. From the abundant laboratory data, as well as biographical evidence, Harvard's Perkins has developed what he calls the 'snowflake model of creativity.' Analogous to the six sides of the snowflake, each with its own complex structure, Perkins's model consists of six related but distinct psychological traits of the creative person. Creative people may not possess all six, Perkins points out, but the more they have the more creative they tend to be.

The first among the six traits is a strong commitment to a personal aesthetic, 'the drive to wrest order, simplicity, meaning, richness, or powerful expression from what is seemingly chaos,' Martindale says. Einstein's life, like his work, is full of examples of his powerful drive toward simplicity. Someone, for example, once asked him why he used hand soap for shaving instead of using shaving cream. 'Two soaps? That's too complicated,' Einstein replied.

As part of their personal aesthetic, creators have a high tolerance for complexity (some researchers call it ambiguity), disorganization, and asymmetry. They often enjoy the challenge of cutting through chaos and struggling toward a resolution and synthesis. 'In science very often the core challenge is to deal with a maze of ambiguities and forge a new identity,' Perkins says.

The second psychological trait, the ability to excel in finding problems, was demonstrated in studies involving art students. Through a battery of tests, University of Chicago researchers discovered that the students spent an unusual amount of time thinking about a problem and exploring all the options for solving it before they chose which solution to pursue.

Scientists value good questions because they lead to discoveries and creative solutions, to good answers. By asking the right question and finding the right problem, creators can define and 'see' the boundaries of their fields that can be extended or broken. A student once asked Nobel laureate Linus Pauling, for example, how he found good ideas. Pauling replied that 'you have a lot of ideas and throw away the bad ones.' Such a winnowing out of ideas, however, depends on the ability to apply critical judgment to work that is often extremely personal and emotionally charged.

Mental mobility, the third trait, allows creative people to find new perspectives on and approaches to problems. One example of such mental gymnastics is so-called Janusian thinking. Remember the Roman god Janus, who had two faces, each looking in a different direction? Well, creative people have a strong tendency to think in terms of opposites and contraries while they seek a new synthesis of ideas. They often think in analogies and metaphors and, as a matter of course, challenge assumptions. Pauling, for example, discovered the alpha helix (the most important way in which the polypeptide chains of proteins are folded) in large part because he questioned the assumption that all amino acids were not created equal. Pauling's idea, after years of frustrating work and dead ends, was that the amino acids are just one kind of unit, and, whatever their structures, they are equivalent to one another. By questioning the prevailing assumption he verified the helical structure in about two hours with a slide rule, a pencil, and a piece of paper. And he did it while in bed recuperating from a cold – before his vitamin C days.

The fourth psychological trait is the willingness to take risks. Psychologist Frank Farley has identified and studied risk takers and dubbed them Type T personalities for their thrill seeking. Creators as well as daredevils and criminals fit this criteria for Type T personalities, who, he says, constantly seek excitement and stimulation – physical thrills, mental thrills, or a mix of both. Farley explains that Type Ts may need more stimulation than other people because they have a low ability to become mentally aroused. In other words, they're not as responsive to stimuli as other personality types. The mental risk takers are the creators in whatever discipline or activity they pursue.

Along with risk taking, moreover, comes the acceptance of failure as part of the creative quest and the ability to learn from such failures. Many people believe that creative geniuses come up with ideas instantly, produce only masterpieces, never have any failures, and never take chances because they always know what they're doing. 'Such myths inhibit people from being as creative as they could be,' says psychologist Dean Simonton of the University of California at Davis. He argues that the odds of creative success depend on the number of attempts: The more you produce, the higher your chances of creating something really important. 'Posterity tends to ignore the failures and praise the successes,' Simonton says. 'Picasso, for example, produced some 20,000 works of art, but much of it was mediocre.'

By working at the edge of their competence, where the possibility of failure lurks, mental risk takers are more likely to produce creative results. For some, taking risks in uncharted territory is exciting. Others may not relish the risk, but they accept it as part of the way to reach creative goals.

'When I'm in the middle of fieldwork, there's a sense of terra incognita, of really being out on a frontier discovering absolutely untrod ground' says anthropologist Robert McCormick Adams, secretary of the Smithsonian Institution. 'You can also find terra incognita when you look into a microscope and other instrument-aided means of exploring the molecular or subatomic world or, for that matter, distant galaxies. Looking for new horizons is something that drives us. It's a particularly ingrained American trait because of the long influence of the frontier in the growth of the country.'

The popular image of creative individuals often highlights their subjectivity, personal insight, and commitment. But without objectivity, the fifth psychological trait, creative people simply construct a private world that has no reality. Creative people not only scrutinize and judge their ideas or projects, they also seek criticism. 'Contrary to the popular image, the creative person is not a self-absorbed loner,' said Perkins, who has studied professional and amateur poets. 'The poets who sought feedback produced poetry that a panel of experts judged to be better than the poetry of those who didn't seek criticism.' Objectivity, Perkins points out, involves more than luck or talent: it means putting aside your ego, seeking advice from trusted colleagues, and testing your ideas, as in scientific practice or market-place settings.

The driving force behind creative efforts, however, is inner motivation, the sixth side of Perkins's snowflake model of creativity. Creators are involved in an enterprise for its own sake, not for school grades or pay-checks. Their catalysts are the enjoyment, satisfaction, and challenge of the work itself. 'There are lots of people who have great potential for creativity,' says Brandeis University professor of psychology Teresa Amabile, who has conducted dozens of laboratory studies to verify the importance of intrinsic motivation in creativity. 'Many may have had some early success, but afterward they just dry up or are unable to produce, precisely because extrinsic constraints have taken over.' They were told, for example, that their work would or would not be evaluated. Amabile and her colleagues found ample evidence demonstrating that such factors as work evaluation, supervision, competition for prizes, and restricted choices in how to perform an activity undermine intrinsic motivation and inhibit creativity.

Words like love and passion frequently pop up when artists, scientists, and other creative people talk or write about their work. Such commitment is what motivates the scientist to discover, the artist to paint, or the writer to write. 'The emotional state which leads to such achievements resembles that of a worshipper or the lover,' Einstein wrote Max Planck in 1918. 'The daily struggle does not arise from a purpose or a program, but from an immediate need.'

As we delve deeper into the mysteries of creativity, learning more about its underlying nexus of biochemical, physiological, and psychological roots, we'll be able to increase creativity and instill more of it in more people. 'We are, in a perfectly real sense, creating creative thinking even as we study it,' Perkins says. And within the next 30 or 40 years, he believes, creative-thinking techniques will be used not just by artists, inventors, and scholars but by most of us.

The first step in that direction, University of California's Frank Barron suggests, is to think of creativity as the important human resource it really is. 'It is a unique force in the universe,' he says, 'a gift of life to the human species.'

References

Amabile, T.M. (1982) *The Social Psychology of Creativity*. New York: Springer Verlag.

Barron, F, (1968) *Creativity and Personal Freedom*. New York: Van Nostrand.

Gardner, H. (1983) *Frames of Mind: The Theory of Multiple Intelligences*. New York: Basic Books.

Perkins, D. (1981) *The Mind's Best Work*. Cambridge, MA: Harvard University Press.

Simonton, D.K. (1984) *Genius, Creativity and Leadership*. Cambridge, MA: Harvard University Press.

3

Lateral and vertical thinking

Edward de Bono

Difference between lateral and vertical thinking

Vertical thinking is traditional logical thinking. It is called vertical thinking because you proceed directly from one state of information to another state. It is like building a tower by placing one stone firmly on top of the preceding stone; or like digging a hole by making deeper the hole you already have. One of the characteristic features of vertical thinking is continuity. One of the characteristic features of lateral thinking is discontinuity.

Education concerns itself almost exclusively with vertical thinking. This is the type of thinking that is used all the time. To many people it is the *only* possible type of thinking. It was the type of thinking that was developed by the ancient Greeks, and we sometimes pride ourselves that we have done nothing to change or improve it. Many of the advantages of lateral thinking depend on the ability to escape from the rules of vertical thinking.

Some of the principles of lateral thinking directly contradict some of the traditional principles of vertical thinking. Although the principles of vertical and lateral thinking are quite distinct, the *end result* is not. By looking at a solution, it is quite impossible to tell whether it has been reached by vertical or lateral thinking. You can only tell this if you have an actual record of the thought processes involved. Once a solution has been reached by lateral thinking, it is always possible to see how that solution could have been reached by vertical thinking. For the same reason, what may be a brilliant lateral jump to one person may be a simple vertical progression to another.

Lateral and vertical thinking are two opposite poles but there is a spectrum between them. Any particular mental step may fall somewhere along the spectrum. It may be pure lateral thinking or pure vertical thinking, but it is usually something in between. In practice, the processes are usually intermingled. Nevertheless, the two types of thinking are quite distinct in nature.

First- and second-stage thinking

Most people are aware of the second stage of thinking. The first stage is taken for granted and often assumed not to be there at all. The second stage

Adapted from *Lateral Thinking for Management* (Harmondsworth, Middx: Penguin, 1984), pp. 4–13. Copyright © Edward de Bono 1970

is concerned with techniques of logic and mathematics. A computer is a second-stage thinking device. The first-stage thinking ends when the data and the program have been fed into the computer. Logical and mathematical techniques are never applied directly to a situation. They can only be applied when that situation has been divided into concepts, features, factors, effects, and other perceptual parcels. These perceptual parcels are not themselves created by the application of any special techniques, but by the natural patterning processes of mind with all their limitations and arbitrariness. We assume that these starting concepts are correct, and only pay attention to the validity of the second-stage algorithms which we use to process the concepts and arrive at a 'proved' solution. In other words, we assume that thinking only starts at the second stage. It is in the first stage of thinking that the concepts and perceptual parcels are put together. We are beginning to realize that most of the trouble with our thinking results from our inability to do anything about this first stage. We have very good techniques for the second stage of thinking and we are improving them all the time. But we have no techniques at all for the first stage. Paradoxically, it is the very excellence of the computer as a second-stage thinking device that has emphasized the importance of the first stage. It is the questions that are asked of the computer and the choice of data that is fed in that determine the usefulness and relevance of the output, not the excellence of the computer processing which we can now take for granted. No amount of excellence in the processing can, however, make up for deficiencies in the first stage. In closed mathematical systems, like getting a man to the moon or solving set problems, we can make good use of computers. But in open-ended problems and in situations where the whole problem is to *define* the problem, we can do little unless we get better at first-stage thinking.

It is not only a matter of what concepts we use but also of what values we give to them. By simply changing values without changing concepts, one can arrive at very different conclusions. Even more than concepts, values are the product of the natural perceptual patterning of mind. Choice of attention area, choice of entry point, choice of factors, these are all part of the first stage of thinking. And such choices will predetermine the final result of the thinking process.

Mathematics can get to work once we have chosen to look at things in a certain way. But mathematics cannot itself choose the way we are going to look at things.

For example, there are many ways in which one could approach the problem of absenteeism in industry. One could simply measure the man-hours lost or one could measure any change in the man-hours lost. One could measure the number of men out at any one time and note whether this was a steady number or whether there were any fluctuations. One could try to find out whether the same men were involved or whether absenteeism was evenly spread among all the men. One could try to see whether the absentee-ism was predictable at certain times of the year. These are all questions set up in the first stage of thinking. It would be possible to measure everything in sight and then generate the questions, but this approach becomes impossible because the number of things which can be measured and related can quickly become huge. For instance, in addition to the mere counting of man-hours one might want to see whether there was any way of telling which men were more likely to absent themselves. Or one might want to know what the cause of absenteeism was (illness, domestic organization, sports, and so on). Someone else might come along with a completely different approach, and instead of measuring man-hours lost be would want to know whether absenteeism did in fact affect production instead of *assuming* that it must do so. If it did not affect production, was this because there was overmanning anyway? Another person might turn up with a new concept of 'stretching.' This would mean the willingness or ability of work-mates to work a little harder for a short period of time to cover the absence of a fellow worker. Having generated such a concept, one might be able to do something positive with it – perhaps even by allowing a margin of absenteeism as part of 'job satisfaction.' It is clear that the mere counting of man-hours lost or the carrying out of mathematical correlations is only part of the process.

It is often assumed that it does not matter where you start in considering a problem because, if your second-stage processing techniques are correct, you will eventually reach the right answer. This is just not so. If you start off with certain concepts (for example, that absenteeism is an industrial crime and is bad for production), then you may never reach the right answer. This assumption that it does not matter where you start is responsible for many well-worked-out and supported errors. In fact, the solidity of the second-stage processing only worsens the error of first-stage patterning by giving it a spurious validity.

In the first stage of thinking, the emphasis is not on the manipulation of concepts but on the concepts themselves. This is the conceptual stage and one forms and re-forms concepts, cuts across them, introduces new concepts, and so on.

There are times when the sheer availability of second-stage processing techniques is an actual disadvantage. If one cannot easily find a suitable processing technique, then one has to spend far more time looking over the approach to the problem. But if a processing technique is obvious, then one settles for the first approach that comes to mind and moves ahead with the second-stage processing at once.

Consider the following simple problem. In a singles knock out tennis tournament, there are 111 entrants. What is the minimum number of matches that must be played? It is easy enough to start at the beginning and to work out how many first-round matches there must be and how many byes. But this takes much time. Yet in an audience of 100 people, there may not be anyone who tries a different approach. This different approach involves a change in the first stage of thinking. Instead of considering the players trying to win, consider the losers after they have lost. There is one winner and 110 losers. Each loser can only lose once. So there must be 110 matches. Had there been no other standard way of working out the matches, then this unusual approach might have been used more often, but the sheer availability of techniques leads one away too quickly from the first stage of thinking.

Skilled use of lateral thinking in the first stage can make things very much easier in the second stage. Far from detracting from the effectiveness of vertical thinking and second-stage processing, lateral thinking magnifies their usefulness, just as a gun is more effective the better it is aimed.

Lateral thinking changes. Vertical thinking chooses.

Lateral thinking is generative. There is change for the sake of change. The purpose of lateral thinking is movement – movement from one concept to another, from one way of looking at things to another. Lateral thinking recognizes no adequate solution but always tries to find a better one. Lateral thinking works with the hope that a better pattern can be arrived at by restructuring. Lateral thinking is never an attempt to prove anything but only to explore and to generate ideas.

Vertical thinking is selective. It seeks to judge. It seeks to prove and establish points or relationships. Where lateral thinking is concerned with change and movement, vertical thinking is concerned with stability – with finding an answer so satisfactory that one can rest with it. Vertical thinking is looking for answers, whereas lateral thinking is looking for questions.

Vertical thinking says: 'This is the best way of looking at things; this is the right way of looking at things.' Lateral thinking says: 'Let us try to generate other ways of looking at things; let us change this way of looking at things.'

Vertical thinking judges what is right and concentrates on it. Lateral thinking seeks alternatives. To *laterate* indicates this sideways movement for alternatives. Laterate and lateration replace *concentrate* and *concentration*.

Vertical thinking uses the YES/NO system. Lateral thinking does not.

The very basis of vertical thinking is that you are not allowed to be wrong at any stage. That is the most important characteristic that defines the system. Each step must be fully justified and rest soundly on the preceding step. Vertical thinking is a selective type of thinking and it uses judgment. This judgment is based on the YES/NO system, and selection is by exclusion of all those ideas to which the NO label can be attached. Without the YES/NO system vertical thinking could not work. Vertical thinking is looking for what is right.

Lateral thinking works outside the YES/NO system. Lateral thinking is not looking for what is right but for what is different. Lateral thinking uses information in a way that is quite different from vertical thinking and the question of right or wrong does not arise. In the course of lateral thinking, you may have to use an idea which everyone knows to be wrong and which you yourself know to be wrong. Nor do you hold it in the belief that it may eventually prove to be right. Right and wrong simply do not apply.

With lateral thinking the only 'wrong' is the arrogance or rigidity with which an idea is held. The nature of the idea itself does not matter at all.

Vertical thinking uses information for its meaning. Lateral thinking uses information for its effect in setting off new ideas.

Vertical thinking is analytical. Lateral thinking is provocative. Vertical thinking is interested in where an idea comes from: this is the backward use of information. Lateral thinking is interested in where an idea leads to: this is the forward use of information. A vertical thinker will try to find out why an idea will not work so that he can reject it. A lateral thinker will try to see what can be made of the idea even if he knows it to be inadequate in its present form. Instead of looking to see why an idea is wrong, a lateral thinker looks to see what can be got out of it. Lateral thinking uses ideas in a catalytic fashion in order to trigger off new ideas and to bring about repatterning.

Vertical thinking is used to *describe* what has happened in one's own thinking. Lateral thinking is used to *make* something happen.

In vertical thinking one thing must follow directly from another. In lateral thinking one can make deliberate jumps.

Vertical thinking seeks to establish continuity. Lateral thinking seeks to introduce discontinuity. In vertical thinking, one step follows directly from the preceding step in a logical sequence. In lateral thinking, one can make a completely unjustified jump. One does not have to make such a jump but one is allowed to. In vertical thinking there is a reason for saying something before it is said. In lateral thinking there may not be a reason for saying something until after it has been said. The point about the jumps in lateral thinking is that they are unjustified until *after* they have been made. In terms of the old pattern of ideas, the jump makes no sense but, once made, the jump can open up a new pattern which quickly justifies the jump.

In vertical thinking, one is uncomfortable if there is a gap. In lateral thinking, one may try hard to create such a gap in order to escape from the old ideas.

In vertical thinking, the conclusion must come after the evidence. In lateral thinking, the conclusion may come before the evidence. This is not to say that one adopts a conclusion and then seeks to justify it by rationalization. Such a procedure would imply an arrogant certainty in the conclusion that is the opposite of lateral thinking. The process is rather one of making a provocative jump to a new position and, once there, one is suddenly able to see things in a new way. The new way must of course prove itself by being effective.

Vertical thinking concentrates on what is relevant.
Lateral thinking welcomes chance intrusions.

Vertical thinking chooses what is to be considered. Anything else is rejected. This choice of what is relevant depends entirely on the original way of looking at the situation. Lateral thinking welcomes chance intrusions because it is difficult to change an idea from within itself. Lateral thinking encourages happy accidents because they can set off new patterns of ideas. Chance is one way of introducing that element of discontinuity that lateral thinking uses in order to bring about new ideas. In lateral thinking, nothing can be irrelevant. Even if something seems irrelevant in itself, it can still set off ideas when considered alongside the problem in hand.

Vertical thinking moves in the most likely directions.
Lateral thinking explores the least likely.

Vertical thinking proceeds along well-established patterns because it is seeking proof and proof is most easily found by using such patterns. Vertical thinking is not used to seek out new ideas, and there is no reason for avoiding the obvious. Lateral thinking, on the other hand, seeks to avoid the obvious. This is not because novelty has any value in itself, but because the very obviousness of an idea may obscure a better idea which lies just beneath. By making a habit of exploring beyond the obvious, lateral thinking can come up with such ideas. If no new ideas emerge, then you can always go back to the obvious idea. There is nothing to be lost by exploring beyond it. In the final stage, there is no point in choosing an odd idea just for the sake of its oddity, but in the exploratory stage such odd ideas can be more worthwhile to follow than the most obvious ones.

Vertical thinking is closed procedure. Lateral thinking is
open-ended.

Vertical thinking promises at least a minimal result. Lateral thinking increases the chances of a maximal result but makes no promises. You can work through vertical thinking procedures and you will come up with some sort of answer, for this answer is only a way of relating the concepts with which you started out. With lateral thinking, you may come up with a brilliant answer or you may come up with nothing at all. You can never guarantee that lateral thinking will produce an answer which is good enough or new enough. It is always an open-ended probabilistic system. With a skilled lateral thinker, the chances that some sort of solution will emerge are high; but there can never be certainty.

This does not mean that one cannot use a probabilistic system for practical problem solving. One can and should do so. If no new solutions turn up, then one can always go back to whatever solutions are turned up by vertical thinking. One is no worse off than if one had never used lateral thinking. But if a brilliant solution does turn up, then one may be considerably better off. Creativity is always open-ended but one can very much *increase the chances of success* by developing skill in lateral thinking. It is like having three black balls and one white one in a bag. The chances of drawing out the white ball are small at first. If you go on dropping additional white balls into the bag then the chances get better and better. But no matter how many white balls there are in the bag at the end, you can never be absolutely sure of picking out a white ball. Dropping white balls into the bag is equivalent to acquiring skill in lateral thinking.

The use of lateral and vertical thinking

Since lateral thinking is an open-ended procedure, it might be supposed that a lot of time could be wasted while one waited for a brilliant solution to come about. It might be argued that it was more sensible to get one with vertical thinking even if the results were less spectacular. Such an attitude shows a misunderstanding of the nature of lateral thinking. Lateral thinking is not something that is to be used all the time. Lateral thinking introduces discontinuity or a change in direction. You cannot get anywhere by changing direction at each pace. But by changing direction at one point and then striding on in the new direction you can 'go places.' The striding is equivalent to vertical thinking, and the change of direction to lateral thinking. To refuse to use lateral thinking is to condemn oneself to moving always in the same direction, or at least until so many other people have changed direction that obviously you must follow them.

In practice, one might use lateral thinking some 5 percent of the time and vertical thinking 95 percent of the time. Even this figure is high for lateral thinking. It depends a good deal on the nature of the situation. If you have to come up with a new product, or you cannot solve a problem with vertical thinking, then you might spend a lot of time thinking laterally. But in the normal course of events, one might spend no more than three minutes a day thinking laterally about some problem. That is an amount of time anyone can afford, especially when the payoff can be huge. The actual time spent thinking laterally is much less important than the availability of the tool. Because this thinking tool is available (if one has learned how to use it), then one can face situations in a different way. One is less inclined to be rigid, or arrogant, or dogmatic. One is inclined to listen to other people's ideas and even explore them for what they are worth. It is rather like having a jack in the back of the car. You may never need to use it, but merely having it there gives you more confidence and flexibility in your travels.

In practice, one uses lateral and vertical thinking in alternation. Lateral thinking turns up an idea, vertical thinking develops it. Vertical thinking comes to a dead end, lateral thinking changes the approach so that vertical thinking can proceed again. Rarely does lateral thinking actually provide a solution by itself. Usually, it simply provides an approach or rescues someone who has been blocked by a particular idea.

When lateral thinking casts doubt on a well-established idea or concept, the intention is not to make that idea unusable. One has to use what ideas one has, otherwise it is impossible to proceed at all. What lateral thinking does is to open up the possibility of restructuring the idea in order to bring it up to date. It is not so much a matter of creating chronic dissatisfaction with current ideas, but of creating the hope of restructuring them.

Once one has acquired the habit of lateral thinking, the actual use of it is not confined to formal occasions or techniques but mingles naturally with the use of vertical thinking. But before that stage can be reached, one does have to pay some attention to the principles of lateral thinking and also develop some skill through practice. Otherwise one must rest content with whatever natural skill one might have in this matter.

Lateral thinking is of course concerned with thinking, with the generating of new ideas and new approaches, and with the escape from old ones. It is not a method for decision or for action. Once the ideas have been generated, one has to satisfy oneself as to their *usefulness* before putting them into action. To do this one can use the full rigor of vertical thinking. But you do need to have the ideas first before you can examine them.

4

Science, order and creativity

David Bohm and F. David Peat

Science, like everything else, is in a constant process of evolution and change. In this process, the developments that are made in one area may sometimes have serious consequences for the foundations of theories and concepts in other areas. The overall context of science is constantly undergoing changes which, at times, are both deep and subtle. The result of this complex change is that the underlying tacit infrastructure of concepts and ideas may gradually become inappropriate or even irrelevant. But because scientists become accustomed to using their tacit skills and knowledge in subliminal and unconscious ways, there is a tendency of the mind to hold on to them and to try to go on working in old ways within new contexts. The result is a mixture of confusion and fragmentation.

As an example, consider the development of the theory of relativity. Before Einstein, the Newtonian concepts of absolute space and time had pervaded both the theory and the practice of physics for several centuries. Lorentz was able to explain the constancy of the velocity of light, independent of the relative speed of the observer, as an artifact produced by the measuring instruments themselves, without the need to question the fundamental nature of Newtonian ideas. It took the genius of Einstein to do this. But such was the strength of the tacit infrastructure of basic concepts that it required a long time before scientists could generally appreciate the meaning of Einstein's proposals. As with Lorentz, the general tendency was to hold on to basic ways of thinking in new contexts that called for fundamental changes.

Scientists attempt to press on by putting 'new wine in old bottles'. But why should this be? It involves a psychological factor, the mind's strong tendency to cling to what it finds familiar and to defend itself against what threatens seriously to disturb its overall balance and equilibrium. Unless the perceived rewards are very great, the mind will not willingly explore its unconscious infrastructure of ideas but will prefer to continue in more familiar ways.

One way of defending the subliminal structure of ideas is to overemphasize the separation between a particular problem and other areas. In this way the problem can be studied in a limited context and without the need to

Adapted from 'Revolutions, theories and creativity in science', in D. Bohm and F.D. Peat, *Science, Order and Creativity* (London: Routledge, 1987), pp. 15–62

question related concepts. But this only acts to prevent a clear awareness of the ultimate connections of the problem to its wider context and implications. The result is to produce artificial excessively sharp division between different problems and to obscure their connections to wider fields.

Creativity and metaphors

Scientific revolutions begin with a radical change, which then unfolds, through a long period of 'normal' science, into a whole new infrastructure of ideas and tacit assumptions. Of course, such long-term transformations within the largely unconscious infrastructure of ideas involve the operation of creativity on a continuous basis.

To begin an inquiry into creativity, consider the example of Newton's theory of universal gravitation. Newton's revolutionary step went far beyond the mere reordering of existing concepts, for it involved a radically new mental perception of nature. The idea that objects may attract each other did not actually originate with Newton. But his genius lay in realizing the full, explicit implications of what was already known within the scientific community. To understand the significance of Newton's perception, it is necessary to go back to the Middle ages, when science was strongly based on Aristotle's notion that earthly and heavenly matter are of two basically different natures. A great deal of experimental evidence began to accumulate after the Middle Ages which suggested that there is no fundamental difference between heavenly and earthly matter. But this knowledge tended to be kept in one compartment of scientists' minds, fragmented from another compartment which continued to cling to the notion that heaven and earth are separate. Thus scientists never raised the question as to why the moon does not fall, because it seemed evident that, as a result of its celestial nature, it naturally remains in the sky where it belongs.

It was Newton who first perceived the universal implications of the fall of the apple: As the apple falls towards the earth, so does the moon, and so does everything fall toward everything else. To see the universal nature of gravitational attraction, Newton had to become free of the habitual compartmentalization of earthly and celestial matter, a form of fragmentation that was implicit within the tacit infrastructure of the 'normal' science of his day. To break away from the habitual and commonly accepted modes of thought, which had been taken for granted for generations, required intense courage, energy, and passion. Newton had these in abundance, and at the height of his powers, he was always asking fundamental questions. The crucial factor in Newton's vision, and indeed in the creation of all new ideas, is this ability to break out of old patterns of thought. Indeed, once this has been done, new perceptions and novel ideas appear to arise naturally.

It is, of course, difficult for the nonscientist to obtain a direct experience of what it is like to create a new theory or scientific concept. This notion of metaphor can serve to illuminate the nature of scientific creativity by equating, in a metaphoric sense, a scientific discovery with a poetic metaphor. Newton's initial insight into the nature of universal gravitation can be expressed in metaphoric form as 'The moon is an apple', which is then extended to 'The moon is an earth'. At first, this use of language gives rise to a state of high creative and perceptive energy, which is not basically different from that arising in a poetic metaphor. At this point, therefore, it is sensed that the moon, an apple, and the earth are similar in a very important way, but as with the poetic metaphor, this is not yet expressed explicitly. However, almost immediately, scientific thought realizes that all these objects are basically similar in the sense that they attract each other and obey the same laws of motion. At this stage, while the insight is more explicit, it is still fairly poetic and qualitative in nature. The next step, however, is to transpose the unfolded metaphor into a mathematical language which renders the similarities and differences more explicit.

A second example of such metaphoric creation is given by the well-known story of how Archimedes was asked to determine the amount of gold in a crown. The philosopher was well aware that if he knew both the weight of the crown and its total volume, he could then calculate its density and determine if this was indeed equal to that of pure gold. If the crown proved to be too light for its particular volume, then Archimedes could conclude that its gold has been adulterated with some other metal. Weighing the crown posed no problem, but how was Archimedes to determine its volume? Greek geometry contained a series of rules for working out the volumes of various objects, provided that they were of simple, regular shapes. From such a rule, Archimedes could easily have calculated the volume of a cube. But how was he to proceed with such an irregular object as a crown, something that lay outside the whole system of Greek geometry?

Legend has it that Archimedes was resting in his bath when the solution occurred to him. The philosopher observed that the water level in his bath rose as his body sank, and he suddenly equated this process of displacement with the degree to which his body was immersed and then with the volume of another irregularly shaped object – the crown. A metaphor was therefore established between the irregular shape of the crown, the volume of his own body, and the rising water level in the bath. By immersing the crown in water and observing the rise in water level, its volume could be inferred. Archimedes' perception was, to some extent, a visual one, involving the rising of the bathwater. But the essence of his discovery lay in an internal perception of new ideas within the mind, which showed Archimedes how the volume of any object is equal to the volume of water it displaces. The state of high energy and vibrant tension inherent in this instant of creation is captured in the story that at the moment Archimedes saw the key point he cried out 'Eureka'. Archimedes' perceptive metaphor was later developed in more detail into a general method for the practical determination of irregular volumes and led to the new concept of specific gravity. Finally, with the creation of Newton's calculus, it became possible to place the notion of the volume of an irregular shape on a firm mathematical footing.

Metaphoric perception is, indeed, fundamental to all science and involves bringing together previously incompatible ideas in radically new ways. Creative perception in the form of a metaphor can take place not only in poetry and in science but in much broader areas of life. What is essential here is that the act of creative perception in the form of a metaphor is basically similar in all these fields, in that it involves an extremely perceptive state of intense passion and high energy that dissolves the excessively rigidly held assumptions in the tacit infrastructure of commonly accepted knowledge. The differences are in the modes and degrees of unfoldment from the metaphoric to the literal.

Thought as play

If science always insists that a new order must be immediately fruitful, or that it has some new predictive power, then creativity will be blocked. New thoughts generally arise with a play of the mind, and the failure to appreciate this is actually one of the major blocks to creativity. Thought is generally considered to be a sober and weighty business. But here it is being suggested that creative play is an essential element in forming new hypotheses and ideas. Indeed, thought which tries to avoid play is in fact playing false with itself. Play, it appears, is of the very essence of thought.

This notion of the falseness that can creep into the play of thought is shown in the etymology of the words illusion, delusion, and collusion, all of which have as their Latin root *ludere*, 'to play'. So illusion implies playing false with perception; delusion, playing false with thought; collusion, playing false together in order to support each other's illusions and delusions. When thought plays false, the thinker may occasionally recognize this fact, and express it in the above words. Unfortunately, however, our English language does not have a word for thought which plays true. Perhaps this is a reflection of a work ethic which does not consider the importance of play and suggests that work itself is noble while play is, at best, recreational and, at worst, frivolous and nonserious. However, to observe children at play is to realize the serious intensity of their energy and concentration.

Within the act of creative play, fresh perceptions occur which enable a person to *propose* a new idea that can be put forward for exploration. As the implications of this idea are unfolded, they are *composed* or put together with other familiar ideas. Eventually the person *supposes* that these ideas are correct; in other words, he or she makes an assumption or hypotheses and then acts according to the notion that this is the way that things actually are. The movement from *propose* to *compose* to *suppose* enables everyday actions to be carried out with little or no conscious thought. For example, if you *suppose* that a road is level, then you are *disposed* to walk accordingly. After a number of successful trips, you will be further disposed to take it for granted that the supposition or assumption that the road is level is indeed correct, and you will no longer have to think about this point. However, if some part of the road later turns out to be uneven so that you trip, you will be obliged to change your assumption and, through this, a disposition which is no longer appropriate. Taking certain assumptions for granted may be a useful way of freeing the mind to consider other questions, provided it always remains sensitive to evidence that the assumptions may, at times, be wrong.

What happens in this relatively simple case may also occur as the mind operates with the theories of science. If, for example, one set of ideas works for a long time, within a particular context, then scientists are disposed to take them for granted and are able to free their minds to focus on other ideas that may be relevant. But this is appropriate only as long as the mind remains sensitive to the possibility that, in new contexts, evidence may arise that shows that these ideas are wrong or confused. If this happens, scientists have to be ready to drop the ideas in question and to go back to the free play of thought, out of which may emerge new ideas.

The above account shows the appropriate relationship between thought and experience. Within such a relationship, creative new perceptions take place when needed. Such perceptions emerge through the creative play of the mind. It is the very nature of this play that nothing is taken for granted as being absolutely unalterable, and that its outcome and conclusions cannot be known beforehand. In other words, the creative person does not strictly know what he or she is looking for. The whole activity, therefore, is not regarded as a problem that must be solved but simply as play itself. Within this play it is not taken for granted that new things must always be different or that they can never in any significant way be related to what came before. Indeed, it could be suggested that the more different things are, the greater may be the value in perceiving their difference. Science, according to this argument, is properly a continuous ongoing activity. Through creative play and fresh perception there is a constant movement of similarities and differences, with each new theory differing in some subtle but significant fashion from what came before. To sustain this creative activity of the mind, it is necessary to remain sensitive to the ways in which similarities and differences are developing, and not to oversimplify the situation by ignoring them or minimizing their potential importance.

Unfortunately, however, this process, in which experience and knowledge interweave with creative insight, is not generally carried out in the way described above. Indeed it might therefore be called a kind of ideal that is seldom attained or approached. It is not generally carried out because of the common tendency toward unconscious defense of ideas which are of fundamental significance and which are assumed to be necessary to the mind's habitual state of comfortable equilibrium. As a result, there is instead a strong disposition to impose familiar ideas, even when there is evidence that they may be false. This, of course, creates the illusion that no fundamental change is required, when in fact the need for such a change may be crucial. If several people are involved, collusion will follow, as they mutually support one another in their false responses.

This often takes place in subtle ways that are extremely difficult to notice. Thus the cases of creative insight discussed all involved becoming aware of certain assumptions that everyone else had, hitherto, taken for granted. Newton's insight into universal gravitation, for example, involved questioning the fundamental difference between earthly and heavenly matter. Indeed, since medieval times evidence had been accumulating which should have suggested that heavenly matter and earthly matter were indeed basically similar. So to go on treating the motion of the moon and planets as if it was of a different order from the motion of apples and cannonballs was, in fact, a false play of thought within the mind. However, the deception involved was a particularly subtle one and most scientists were not consciously aware of its operation. Indeed, another form of false play, which enables people to continue in their habitual patterns of thought, is to assume that only a person of considerable genius is capable of a truly creative act. The cases explored in this chapter, however, suggest that genius in fact involves sufficient energy and passion to question assumptions that have been taken for granted over long periods. Of course geniuses must also have the necessary talent and ability to follow through and unfold the implications of their perceptions and questionings. Most people, however, tacitly suppose that they do not have the necessary passion and courage to act in a truly creative way and are doomed to forever 'play false' with the more subtle features of their knowledge. They believe that, not being geniuses, they are restricted to the tacit infrastructures of subliminally held ideas. But suppose that this assumption is false, and that everyone is potentially capable of truly creative acts in various fields that accord with his or her particular abilities, skills, and knowledge. Clearly a prerequisite for this creativity is that we must cease to take for granted that we are incapable of creativity.

It should now be clear that the mind's disposition to play false in fragmentation and the blockage of free creative play are intimately related. For example, to cling rigidly to familiar ideas is in essence the same as blocking the mind from engaging in creative free play. In turn, it is this very absence of such creative free play that prevents the mind from having the vibrant tension and passionate energy needed to free it from rigidity in the tacit infrastructure of familiar ideas. Indeed, a mind that is forced to cling to what is familiar and that cannot engage in free play is in fact playing false. It has already been compelled to take for granted that it cannot do otherwise. The question of which comes first, the false play or the blocking of free play, like that of the chicken and the egg, is not relevant. They are just two sides of one and the same process.

Closer consideration suggests that it is of the very nature of thought always to engage in some form of play, whether this is free and creative or not. Indeed, even thought that is excessively rigid, and therefore uncreative, is in fact still playing, for it is pretending that certain things are fixed, which in fact are not. Moreover such rigid thought is also at play when it pretends that no pretense is taking place, and that it is being absolutely 'serious' and based only on truth and fact. Hence, at the origin of thought, the activity of play cannot be avoided. The only question is whether this play is to be free or false.

It is being suggested that the basic problems of both science and society originate in a general disposition of the mind to engage in a false kind of play, in order to maintain a habitual sense of comfort and security. But this also implies that these problems, at their root, arise through inadequacies in society's current approach to creativity. The great significance of inquiring into the nature of creativity, and what impedes it, is thus evident.

Science as fundamentally creative

Paradigms clearly involve the process of taking ideas and concepts for granted, without realizing that this is in fact going on. Since this process takes place as the mind attempts to defend itself against what it believes to be a severe disturbance, a paradigm tends to interfere with that free play of the mind that is essential for creativity. Instead it encourages the process of playing false, especially in deep and subtle areas.

A paradigm, as Kuhn points out, is not simply a particular scientific theory but a whole way of working, thinking, communicating, and perceiving with the mind. It is based largely on the skills and ideas that are tacitly transmitted during what could be called a scientist's apprenticeship, in graduate school for example. The main force of Kuhn's idea is that the tacit infrastructure, mostly unconsciously, pervades the whole work and thought of a community of scientists.[1]

Up to now a paradigm has been discussed in a negative sense, but it must also be realized that a paradigm has the power to keep a whole community of scientists working on a more or less common area. In a sense, it could be taken as an unconscious or tacit form of consent. At first sight the paradigm would be of obvious use to the scientific community. However, it also exacts a price in that the mind is kept within certain fixed channels that deepen with time until an individual scientist is no longer aware of his or her limited position. The end result is that each scientist becomes caught in a process of playing false as he or she attempts to maintain this fixed position in situations that call for fundamental change. However, none of this will be apparent to the scientists who work within the paradigm, for they have a common feeling that, within this framework, everything will eventually be solved.

Nevertheless, as time passes, unsolved problems within a given paradigm tend to accumulate and to lead to an ever-increasing confusion and conflict. Eventually some scientists, who are generally spoken of as geniuses, propose fundamentally new ideas and a 'scientific revolution' results. In turn, these new ideas eventually form the basis of a new paradigm, and sooner or later this rigidifies into 'normal' science. In this way the cycle of revolution and 'normal' science continues indefinitely. Throughout the few centuries of its existence, science has proceeded in this fashion until today it is taken as perfectly normal for revolution to succeed revolution, interspersed by periods of relative stability. But is this whole strategy for doing science inevitable or even desirable?

It is certainly true that, without any established limits, ideas do tend to diverge from each other. However, there is also a natural tendency within scientific thinking for ideas to converge as well. Intelligent and creative perception of the different theories may, for example, give rise to new metaphors in which ideas are gathered together and the similarities and differences between them are explored and unfolded.

Clearly this tendency, to convergence within divergence, is very different from the sort of convergence that is brought about through a paradigm, in which arbitrary pressures and boundaries are imposed by the, largely unconscious, consensus of the scientific community. Instead it would be as a result of the intelligent perception of the whole situation that a degree of convergence would occur.

The major part of scientific activity is not at all concerned with direct sensation. Much of what could be called 'perception' takes place within the mind, in terms of theories: interaction with the external world is mediated through elaborate instruments that have been constructed on the basis of these theories. Moreover, the very questions that science asks arise not from sense data but out of an already existing body of knowledge. So the subjective element in our knowledge of reality comes about not through the sense but through the whole social and mental way that science is carried out.

The essential activity of science consists of thought, which arises in creative perception and is expressed through play. This gives rise to a process in which thought unfolds into provisional knowledge which then moves outward into action and returns as fresh perception and knowledge. This process leads to a continuous adaption of knowledge which undergoes constant growth, transformation and extension. Knowledge is therefore not something rigid or fixed that accumulates indefinitely in a steady way but is in a continual process of change. Its growth is closer to that of an organism than a data bank.

As a simple example, think of the worldview held by Europeans living in the Middle Ages. This did not include a particularly strong interest in sanitation; indeed sanitation was not very relevant to their worldview. Nevertheless vast numbers of people were killed by plague, in spite of what society happened to believe about the origin and nature of the disease. People did not notice the connection between their suffering and their view, or lack of it, on sanitation. Indeed they probably took it for granted that there could be no such relationship. However, as soon as the true connection was perceived, it became possible to change things in a positive way so that the new worldview led to revolutionary improvements in the prevention of disease and epidemics. The development of this worldview eventually led to the current notion that all disease is related to external causes, such as bacteria and viruses. Disease in the twentieth century is, therefore considered in terms of causes and cures, a view which is in accord with the general scientific infrastructure of analysis and fragmentation. Only relatively recently have some doctors begun to question the exclusiveness of this current approach and ask: Why is it that, exposed to similar causes, some people catch a disease and others do not? In this way, new perceptions of the nature of disease and the environment, in terms of lifestyle, stress, diet and neuroimmunology will begin to make themselves felt and may, someday, transform the current view of how it is that people get sick.

Clearly the well-being of society is intimately connected with the particular worldview it happens to hold. It is not simply a matter of 'constructing a reality that gratifies us' but of a whole cycle of thought, action, and experience that leads in the long run to the order or disorder of society. This cycle tends to be blocked, not only during periods of 'normal science', when people are insensitive to subtle but important changes, but also during revolutions, when they overemphasize changes and fail to see continuity. Unless a proper sensitivity and clarity about similarities and differences, change and continuity is maintained, rigidity of thought will set in and lead to confusion and inappropriate action – all signs that thought is caught up in 'playing false'.

Science consists of a two-way movement of confirmation and falsification. Fundamental ideas need to be sheltered for a while in a spirit of free creative 'play'. This should be acknowledged within the scientific community as being a necessary period in which the new idea can be discussed openly and refined. Indeed, it will be argued that this very communication is an essential phase in the creative action of science. If an individual scientist cannot talk about a new idea seriously until he or she has proposed a definite experiment that could falsify it, then science will be caught up in a rather 'workaday' attitude in which free play is discouraged unless it can rapidly be put to the test.

Once, however, a period of nurturing is allowed for a new theory so that several theories can exist side by side, theories need no longer be considered as rivals, and the problem of determining criteria for choosing between them becomes less urgent. It is even possible that the same scientist may entertain several alternatives in the mind at once and engage in a free creative play to see if they can be related, perhaps through a creative metaphor.

The key point here is not therefore to search for a method that is somehow supposed to prevent scientists from being caught up in playing false. Rather it is to face the fact that this whole problem arises because the mind does not wish to become unduly disturbed. It cannot, in such circumstances, act creatively but is impelled to play false in order to defend the ideas to which it has become so attached. What is needed, therefore, is to press on with this inquiry into the whole nature of creativity and what impedes its operation.

Summary and outlook

The current mode of doing science has evolved in such a way that certain of its features seriously discourage creativity. Among these, one of the most important is the development of paradigms. Clearly it is desirable at all times, and not merely during periods of scientific revolution, that there be the possibility of free play of the mind on fundamental questions so that a properly creative response is possible. Paradigms, especially after they have been established for some time, hold the consensual mind in a 'rut' requiring a revolution to escape from. Such excessive rigidity amounts to a kind of unconscious collusion, in which scientists unconsciously 'play false together' in order to 'defend' the currently accepted bases of scientific research against perceptions of their inadequacy.

The main form of creativity considered was that of the metaphor. What is essential to this form is that, in equating two very different kinds of things, the mind enters a very perceptive state of great energy and passion, in which some of the excessively rigid aspects of the tacit infrastructure are bypassed or dissolved. In science, as in many other fields, such a perception of the basic similarity of two very different things must further unfold in detail and lead to a kind of analogy which becomes ever more literal.

Naturally, not every scientific metaphor will be fruitful any more than every attempt at poetic metaphor is worthy of serious attention. Moreover it is clear that only a person who has gone into a field with great interest and diligence and who has the requisite skills and abilities will be capable of creating a useful metaphor. Even with such people this does not happen very frequently.

Given that the focusing of work in any given field, through the action of a paradigm, gives rise to an excessive rigidity of mind, it was suggested that a better approach is to allow for a plurality of basic concepts, with a constant movement that is aimed at establishing unity between them. Free creative play with ideas would aid in this process and could help scientific thinking to move in fresh and original ways. If this were the case, science would no longer become so rigid that a revolution would be required to bring about basic changes. Indeed this whole process would represent a significant move toward liberating the surge of creativity that is needed if science is to help in confronting the deeper problems of humanity.

Note

1 Thomas S. Kuhn, *The Structure of Scientific Revolutions*, Chicago: University of Chicago Press, 1962.

5

Play, reality and creativity

John N.T. Martin

Donald Winnicott considered that adult creativity and problem solving was in many respects similar to the creative activity that he observed in the small children he treated (some 60,000 children with their parents over 40 years as a hospital paediatrician and psycho-analyst). He wrote: 'It will be observed that I am looking at the highly sophisticated adult's enjoyment of living or of beauty or of abstract human contrivance, and at the same time at the creative gesture of the baby who reaches out for her mother's mouth and feels her teeth, and at the same time looks into her eyes, seeing her creativity. For me, playing leads on naturally to cultural experience and indeed forms its foundation.'

Though Winnicott did not himself write about managers, much of what he has to say is of direct relevance to organizational life and problem solving, and his ideas have influenced a number of writers on organizations.[1]

The nature of play

Because he worked with children, Winnicott was particularly concerned with those aspects of creative problem solving that are to do with *play*. Though we tend to take play for granted in children, Winnicott realized that it is actually a rather remarkable state.

Firstly, it is neither practical work for an external purpose, nor purely internal imagination. It is an *intermediate* condition in which an imaginary inner world is projected out onto a part of the external world; in many ways it is a precursor of adult metaphor. The objective playthings are used to serve the ends of the subjective imagination, and are given special meanings and feelings. So the child sees in an apparently neutral collection of bits and pieces their possibilities as 'a shop', 'a park', etc. This ability to use external objects to serve internal imaginings helps to develop the child's sense of independence: 'I made it be as I wanted it to be.'

Secondly, though play involves what is clearly an *illusion*, we do not challenge this as we normally would. We collude with the child; we know not

Donald Winnicott died in 1971. This chapter is based on his book, *Playing and Reality* (Harmondsworth, Mddx: Penguin, 1980). Passages are reprinted by permission of Mark Paterson and Associates for the Winnicott Trust

to say 'but that's not really a shop, it's only an old box'. However if the child were to *insist* that the play shop *really was* a shop, then we would begin to feel that something was seriously amiss. So on the one hand play is accepted as desirable and healthy behaviour, but on the other it is very close to behaviour we consider 'mad'. In a similar way adults in a brainstorming session are actually encouraged to produce ideas that in other circumstances would be worryingly bizarre.

Thirdly, play clearly involves *a special state of mind*. The child is often totally preoccupied by the game – 'lost in play' – and finds it hard to get out of this state or accept intrusions into it. This is a precursor of the adult's ability to become absorbed in solving a problem.

Fourthly, it operates *within certain emotional limits*. Play allows the child to dare to make its imagination become real. This is intrinsically exciting and satisfying, even when it leads to quite high levels of anxiety (eg ghost games). However, play is usually only possible against a background of relative safety and trust, such as the familiar play-room with known adults somewhere around; a child won't play when insecure or threatened. And the emotions stirred up by the game (either anxiety or excitement) must not be *too* great – *the child must feel able to contain the experience*. Adult creativity can also involve the same anxious excitement, and need for safety and containability.

Fifthly, *shared play is a major form of communication*. Playing together is obviously a central feature of children's lives; they make friends and enemies during play, and don't easily make friends apart from play. Like-wise in adults, as Winnicott pointed out, one of the natural roots of human groupings is for people with similar 'illusory' experiences (culture, values, myths, etc.) to come together – though *forcing* your illusions on others who don't share them is quite another matter. Indeed Winnicott went as far as to say: 'Only in playing is communication possible', because it is only in play that we interact unselfconsciously as ourselves.

Clearly Winnicott does not use 'play' in its trivial sense as, for instance, 'something that keeps the kids out of your hair while you get the supper' or 'a bit of fun as a reward for being good' or 'what I do in my time off, or when I want to relax and enjoy myself' or 'playing football'. Play can certainly fill time, be a wonderful source of pleasure and delight and many other things; but Winnicott's interest in it was for its potential for helping the child to develop its grasp of the confusing and complex world it lives in.

Play and problem solving

Winnicott regarded the 'strain' due to the mismatch between on the one hand our inner wants and expectations, and on the other what is actually happening, as a permanent feature of our lives from very early infancy onwards. Play (and its adult equivalents) is part of our response to that, and it has two functions. Firstly, it provides a temporary 'protected area' – a socially acceptable side-step into a special state of mind in which the direct pressures of the mismatch are not felt (or pressed) as strongly, perhaps analogous to the manager who gets a temporary breathing space from a group of irate customers by saying: 'Yes, we are working on it – come back later'. Secondly, it can lead towards a more substantial resolution of the strain by acting as a trial-and-error 'laboratory' in which you can try out various ways of making your outer reality match your inner expectations or vice versa.

Two phases of early development show particularly clearly how play can serve these functions. The first is the point at which the tiny infant begins to have a vague sense that the arms that hold it and the face that looks at it are not part of its own expectations and wishes, but something else – that unexpected events can happen, and that wishes are not always met; Winnicott refers to this is the appearance of the 'me/not-me' split. The second is the point at which some children develop a very special attachment to one particular toy (e.g. the security blanket of the little boy Linus in Schultz's 'Peanuts' cartoon series); Winnicott called this a 'transitional object'.

The me/not-me split and the first games

Finding that part of your world is unpredictable is uncomfortable and stressful, and trying to resolve this is the infant's very first 'problem'. What start as simple innate reflexes begin to turn into very simple 'games' with the 'not-me' – exchanges of eye-contact and smiles, peekaboo, reaching out to touch, and so on.

These are intrinsically pleasurable, so that the child becomes momentarily engrossed in them (immediate strain relief), and in due course, if all goes well, they lead to a feeling that the 'not-me' is reasonably reliable and can be influenced (rudimentary practical understanding).

So the successful invention of these games begins to 'solve' the 'problem' of the me/not-me split, and has the elements of a genuinely creative problem-solving; for instance the 'solution' is not wholly pre-programmed, but can take many different forms, and some forms work better than others.

As well as becoming aware of the 'not-me' the infant also becomes aware of itself – it learns about the choice-making 'me' that can make the 'not-me' less confusing and more rewarding. Winnicott believed that early failure to learn how to find yourself through play can limit later ease with, and capacity for, creative activity. Successfully tackling difficult problems at the limits of your ability can teach you a lot about yourself!

Transitional objects

For the slightly older child, there is often a teddy, or piece of blanket, that becomes a very special play thing. Three features of this stand out.

Firstly its value for *strain relief* is very clear – it is a device used particularly when the child feels insecure ('not-me' too much for 'me') or distraught ('me' too much for 'not-me').

Secondly the *power of this illusion* for the child is remarkable – Teddy has become a 'magic talisman' that tides the child over until development or changing circumstances provide a better solution.

Thirdly, Teddy acts as *a continuing reminder* that worrying situations have been successfully handled in the past, so that this one may be solvable too: 'We coped together last time – we can do it again'. It is not just a question of having something to cuddle. Teddy forms a half-way house between earlier stages where physical comforting by a parent was needed to provide strain relief, and later stages where a completely internalized capacity for *self-*comforting emerges.

Transitional behaviour in adults and society

Adults have their own equivalents to Teddy. For instance, most of us have a whole range of comforting, reassuring and self-reaffirming routines such as having a cup of coffee, sorting our mail, using familiar check-lists, playing music, etc., that we use as interim activities when we feel stuck and need 'something to hold on to' until we can see how to proceed. Many of these have strong echoes of those very earliest problem-solving settings: food, warmth, continuity, reliability and the need to regain control.

Because the me/not-me gap is always there for all of us, most human societies develop major cultural institutions such as religion and the arts that can support the strain-relief function. For instance, the strong and cohesive culture found in many traditional mining or fishing communities serves as a source of collective *emotional* support against the many uncertainties and dangers of that way of life – the many conventions and social institutions built into it can act as a 'collective teddy bear' when crisis strikes, providing a vital emotional breathing space that helps people to 'remain themselves' until the community's collective *practical* support can be mobilized to provide more objective solutions. An organization's culture can also serve this role.

On the 'magical' in creativity

An important feature of Winnicott's theory is that it suggests that one can go too far in attempting to de-mystify creativity, to reduce it to mere technicality. There is clearly an important sense in which play is a 'magical' activity, *and must be allowed to be felt as such if it is to be of value*. The problem-supporting capacity of cuddling Teddy, or of playing shop, or of participating in the social life of a mining village, or of following the cultural traditions of a particular organization, depend on their illusory nature not being challenged. Once the totem-pole is taken away from its original village and neatly labelled and explained in a museum, it loses its power to provide valuable support; it begins to look as pointless as the 'playing shop' cardboard box when the children have left. There is therefore an important sense in which creativity requires a proper respect for the role of the 'magical' in ordinary living, and an awareness of how 'magical' and 'rational' behaviour need to be fitted together.

Implications for creative problem-solving methods

Winnicott saw his basic therapeutic method as being one of allowing the client and the therapist to 'play' together and, when he had a client who was unable to 'play' in this setting (child or adult), the first requirement was to deal with this symptom. In much the same way, his ideas imply that creativity in general requires adults to be able to play – and that some people may need to re-learn how to do this.

Many published creativity techniques involve elements that reflect this 'magical' 'playful' element, but often they fail to work because they are treated as technical devices, rather than being allowed to take on the 'magical' 'playful' quality of Winnicott's 'intermediate area'. They emphasize objective 'reality-testing' and under-emphasize the subjective, engrossed periods of willingly shared 'illusion' that are equally necessary.

Metaphor is also a key element in many techniques, and involves subjective imagery superimposed on real situations, just as the child's subjective imagery may be superimposed on, say, a cardboard box when playing shops. Metaphor only works, like play, when its 'madness' is for the time being accepted and not challenged, and when you can become engrossed in it, and 'play' with it 'magically'.

Winnicott's description of the nature and conditions for play provides an excellent specification for the conditions required for brainstorming and related techniques, and in some respects goes beyond conventional specifications. For instance, it implies that as well as avoiding conditions of threat and insecurity (or selecting group members resilient enough not to be inhibited by it), one should also avoid the group going 'over the top' as sometimes happens when new groups over-react to the sudden removal of conventional inhibitions; the optimum condition is often one of contained energy rather than wild excitement.

Winnicott on creativity and health

This is how Winnicott himself saw creativity:

'I am hoping that the reader will accept a general reference to creativity, not letting the word get lost in the successful or acclaimed creation by keeping it to the meaning that refers to a colouring of the whole attitude to external reality.

'It is creative apperception more than anything else that makes the individual feel that life is worth living. Contrasted with this is a relationship to external reality which is one of compliance, the world and its details being recognized but only as something to be fitted in with or demanding adaptation. Compliance carries with it a sense of futility for the individual and is associated with the idea that nothing matters and that life is not worth living. In a tantalizing way many individuals have experienced just enough of creative living to recognize that for most of their time they are living uncreatively, as if caught up in the creativity of someone else, or of a machine.

'This second way of living in the world is recognized as illness in psychiatric terms. In some way or other our theory includes a belief that living creatively is a healthy state, and that compliance is a sick basis for life.

'For many individuals external reality remains to some extent a subjective phenomenon. There exist all sorts of expressions for this state ("fey", "not all there", "feet off the ground", "unreal"). They may see the world subjectively and be easily deluded. In a psychiatric sense, they are ill because of a weak sense of reality. Conversely, there are others who are so firmly anchored in objectively perceived reality that they are ill in the opposite direction of being out of touch with the subjective world and with the creative approach to fact.

' "Fey" people out of touch with reality are not satisfied with themselves any more than are extroverts who cannot get into touch with dream. Both have a sense that something is wrong and that there is a dissociation in their personalities.

'It is probably wrong to think of creativity as something that can be destroyed utterly. But when one reads of individuals dominated at home, or spending their lives in concentration camps or under lifelong persecution because of a cruel political regime, one first of all feels that it is only a few of the victims who remain creative. These, of course, are the ones that suffer. It appears at first as if all the others who exist (not live) in such pathological communities have so far given up hope that they no longer suffer, and they must have lost the characteristic that makes them human, so that they no longer see the world creatively. These circumstances concern the negative of civilization. This is looking at the destruction of creativity in individuals by environmental factors.

'But one has to allow for the possibility that there cannot be a complete destruction of a human individual's capacity for creative living and that, even in the most extreme case of compliance and the establishment of a false personality, hidden away somewhere there exists a secret life that is satisfactory because of its being creative or original to that human being. Its unsatisfactoriness must be measured in terms of its being hidden, its lack of enrichment through living experience.

'Let us say that in the severe case all that is real and all that matters and all that is personal and original and creative is hidden, and gives no sign of its existence.

'The creative impulse is therefore something that can be looked at as a thing in itself, something that of course is necessary if an artist is to produce a work of art, but also as something that is present when anyone – a baby, child, adolescent, adult, old man or woman – looks in a healthy way at anything or does anything deliberately. It is present as much in the moment-by-moment living of a backward child who is enjoying breathing as it is in the inspiration of an architect who suddenly knows what it is that he wishes to construct, and who is thinking in terms of material that can actually be used so that his creative impulse may take form and shape, and the world may witness.' (Adapted from *Playing and Reality*, pp. 76–81)

Note

1 A more general introduction to Winnicott's work is M. Davis and D. Wallbridge, *Boundary and Space – An introduction to the work of D.W. Winnicott*, Penguin, 1983.

SECTION 2

CREATIVE MANAGEMENT

We begin our analysis of creative management with two classic chapters pointing out the inadequacies of a purely rational approach to management thinking and the importance of intuitive processes. Isenberg pictures senior management thinking as being focused round a few overriding concerns rather than precise goals and attending more to how things are to be achieved than the final objective. He highlights how managers use intuition, and points out that managers check whether problems are solvable or not before giving them any attention; their intuition allowing them to act first and think later. Isenberg mentions features that are reminiscent of the creativity research findings, for instance high performers' tolerance of ambiguity. His stress on thinking and acting cycles draws attention to the messy iterative nature of creative problem solving in practice. In a later paper on the tactics of strategic opportunism, Isenberg (1987) takes up the senior manager's challenge of how to maintain flexibility and direction. He suggests that the way to achieve an optimum balance may be through an incremental and iterative approach that is non-linear and dynamic.

Mintzberg uses the metaphor of right and left brain processes to expound on the relational and holistic character of much management practice, and comments on the absence of a significant amount of analysis and planning by the senior managers he studied. He too points out how little attention has been paid to the dynamic, intuitive factors associated with management, such as judgement, timing and irregularities, factors that he suggests may take the lead at the level of policy. Elsewhere Mintzberg has described a form of emergent strategy that he has likened more to crafting, in the way that potters sense the way forward as they act, through involvement, experience and dedication. Mintzberg claims most organizations have clearly separate periods of stability and change, but interestingly that creative organizations exhibit a more balanced pattern of cycles of convergence and divergence (Mintzberg 1987: 72).

The Kuhns outline a place for creativity in the central management role of decision making and sketch some of the practical implications of adopting a creative attitude to management and decision making, including attention to the psychological motivation of others.

In his excellent book *Images of Organization*, Morgan (1986) describes eight metaphors that provide very different ways of thinking about organizations. The eight metaphors are the organization as machine, organism, brain, culture, political system, psychic prison, flux and transformation, and instrument of domination. The ramifications of these ways of thinking about organizations are too numerous to document here, but a few examples may give a flavour of this line of thought. The machine metaphor suggests the idea of unintelligent parts acting as cogs and an organization that is slow to adapt, whereas the organic metaphor emphasizes relationships and responding to the environment, and suggests an organization that is evolving all the time. Morgan argues that the machine metaphor has dominated classical management theory, whereas organismic metaphors underlie both systems and contingency theories. The organization as brain metaphor highlights the distributed nature of many of the organism's functions. The idea of flux and transformation inherent in some of the new physics and new biology (Maturana and Varela 1980), and espoused by Bohm and others, along with the up and coming science of chaos and ideas of self transformation alert us to the idea of the interconnectedness of all things, and with this the implication that strategic development is 'dependent on complex patterns of reciprocal connectivity that can never be predicted or controlled'. Morgan is keen to stress that all these perspectives have merit, and an organization is neither one nor the other but many different things simultaneously.

In the demanding paper featured here Morgan traces the assumptions that underlie much organizational thinking, through an examination of four very different paradigms. Like Bohm, Morgan spells out how the world view and dominant metaphors used limit the kind of insight that is possible and are reflected in the strategy and approach adopted. Metaphors are central to the creative process, for new metaphors offer novel insights and ideas, which can lead to new actions and different ways of managing and doing research.

References

Isenberg, D.J. (1987) 'The tactics of strategic opportunism', *Harvard Business Review*, no. 4, July–August.
Maturana, H. and Varela, F. (1980) *Autopoeisis and cognition: the realization of living*. London: Reisl.
Mintzberg, H. (1987) 'Crafting strategy', *Harvard Business Review*, no. 4, July–August.
Morgan, G. (1986) *Images of organization*. London: Sage.

6

How senior managers think

Daniel J. Isenberg

It is not enough to have a good mind
The main thing is to use it well.
                    René Descartes

Jim LeBlanc phoned Steve Baum, who formerly worked in his division, to ask about the CEO's new corporate task force on quality control that wanted to meet with Jim. Jim, the head of the industrial equipment division of Tanner Corporation, thought that Steve, now director of technology, could help him figure out why the task force wanted to meet with him in two weeks.

'It's because you're doing so damn well down there, boss!' Steve replied.

'Gee, thanks. By the way, Steve, what's the agenda for Singer's staff meeting for next week?' (Singer was the president and Jim's boss.)

'Well, we're going to talk about the reorganization and look at the overhead reduction figures for each division. Then Singer's going to report on last week's executive committee meeting and his trip to Japan.'

'How did it go?'

'His telex from Osaka sounded enthusiastic, but he just got in last night and I haven't seen him yet.'

'Well,' said Jim, 'I guess we'll just have to see, but if you hear something, call me right away because if Osaka comes through I'm going to have to hustle to get ready, and you know how Bernie hates to shake it. Now, about the task force . . .'

In the space of three minutes, Jim LeBlanc got a lot done. In addition to collecting critical information about a task force that the CEO, with unusual fanfare, had personally commissioned one month ago, he also began to plan his approach to the upcoming staff meeting. He decided *not* to try to get a presentation by his marketing people on opportunities in the Far East on the agenda. Sensing that Singer *was* optimistic about the Osaka trip, Jim decided that he should get his people ready for the possibility that the deal would materialize, which meant pulling engineers off another project for a while.

Reprinted by permission of *Harvard Business Review*, November–December 1984, pp. 81–90. Copyright © 1984 by the President and Fellows of Harvard College; all rights reserved

What were the thinking processes that allowed Jim to get so much done so pointedly and so rapidly? What was going on in his mind during his conversation with Steve? How, given the incomplete and uncertain information that Steve gave him, did Jim conclude that the Japan deal was imminent?

For the past two years I have studied the thought processes used by more than a dozen very senior managers while on the job.[1] The managers that I studied ranged in age from their lower 40s to their upper 50s, in managerial experience from 10 to 30 years, and in current job tenure from 4 months to 10 years. Their companies ranged from $1 billion divisions in *Fortune* '100' companies to $10 million entrepreneurial companies just beginning to take hold in the marketplace. Company products included low- and high-technology goods, and markets ranged from rapidly expanding to precipitately deteriorating. All but two of the executives were responsible for the overall performance of their business units. As all had been frequently promoted throughout their careers and were considered excellent performers across the board, they were a representative sample of today's successful business executives.

Two findings about how senior managers do *not* think stand out from the study. First, it is hard to pinpoint if or when they actually make decisions about major business or organizational issues on their own. And second, they seldom think in ways that one might simplistically view as 'rational', i.e., they rarely systematically formulate goals, assess their worth, evaluate the probabilities of alternative ways of reaching them, and choose the path that maximizes expected return. Rather, managers frequently bypass rigorous, analytical planning altogether, particularly when they face difficult, novel, or extremely entangled problems. When they do use analysis for a prolonged time, it is always in conjunction with intuition.

Let me make myself clear. Obviously, decisions *do* get made in organizations and these *are* frequently justified by data and logic. In particular, when viewed retrospectively over a long time period, effective executives often appear quite rational. Yet when studying their concurrent thinking processes, being 'rational' does not best describe what the manager presiding over the decision-making process thinks about nor *how* he or she thinks.

I have a fourfold purpose in this article. First, I want to present a more accurate and empirically grounded description of what goes on inside the minds of senior managers. (See the insert, pp. 46–7, on the good and bad news about cognition.) Second, I hope to offer a more accurate description of managerial thinking that should help provide a beginning language for talking about these elusive mental phenomena. Third, I hope that this language will also help to relieve some managers of the inconsistency between their view of how they are 'supposed to' think and the thinking processes that, through experience, they have learned are actually quite effective. Fourth, I want to take advantage of successful senior managers' experiences to explore the managerial implications of their thinking processes.

What senior managers think about

Senior managers tend to think about two kinds of problems: how to create effective organizational processes and how to deal with one or two overriding concerns, or very general goals. These two domains of thought underlie the two critical activities that John P. Kotter found general managers engaged in: developing and maintaining an extensive interpersonal network, and formulating an agenda.[2]

A focus on process

The primary focus of on-line managerial thinking is on organizational and interpersonal processes. By 'process' I mean the ways managers bring people and groups together to handle problems and take action. Whether proposing a change in the executive compensation structure, establishing priorities for a diverse group of business units, consolidating redundant operations, or preparing for plant closings, a senior executive's conscious thoughts are foremost among the processes for accomplishing a change or implementing a decision: 'Who are the key players here, and how can I get their support? Whom should I talk to first? Should I start by getting the production group's input? What kind of signal will that send to the marketing people? I can't afford to lose their commitment in the upcoming discussions on our market strategy.'

During the first months of his tenure, one area general manger I studied asked all of his business unit management teams to evaluate their own units. Subsequently, the area manager and his staff spent a day or more with each team discussing the whole area, each business unit within it, and how the two interrelated. Although he was concerned with the substance of the business-unit priorities, uppermost in his mind was a series of process concerns: How could the review process help managers be increasingly committed to their goals? How could the process help managers to become increasingly aware of the interdependencies among business units? How did his business unit managers use their people in reviewing their business units? How much management depth existed in the units?

In addition to thinking about organizational processes, successful senior managers think a lot about interpersonal processes and the people they come in contact with. They try to understand the strengths and weaknesses of others, the relationships that are important to *them*, what *their* agendas and priorities are.

For example, the CEO of a small high-technology company spent over an hour with his personnel director, a woman he rated as having performed excellently so far and whom he saw as having great potential although still inexperienced. At the time of the discussion, the CEO was considering adopting a new top-management structure under which the personnel director would report to another staff member rather than directly to him.

The CEO explained the proposed change to the personnel director, pointing out that it was not definite and that he was soliciting her reactions.

Some good and bad news about cognition

Although the study of cognition is not new, in the past 30 years the popularity and practical importance of the 'cognitive sciences' have increased dramatically, adding to our knowledge of the capabilities and limitations of the human mind. The news is both 'good' and 'bad' in terms of our accuracy as judges and decision makers.

Some good news
The good news is that each of us possesses a wide range of cognitive capabilities, including many that even the most powerful computers cannot match. For all intents and purposes the long-term storage capacity of the human memory is unlimited, capable of storing perhaps trillions of bits of information. Furthermore, much of this memory is almost immediately accessible.

The human mind is also capable of performing very complicated simulations such as giving directions to someone on how to get to an office from an airport or rehearsing an upcoming meeting. We are also capable of making huge inferential leaps with rarely a hitch. Try interpreting the following sentences: 'The manager prepared the forecast using an accepted inflation estimate. He knew that it was imprecise but figured that it was better than no projection at all.' Who is 'he'? What is 'it'? What does 'projection' refer to? We know what these sentences mean, yet to interpret them correctly required the reader to make a number of inferences, which he or she usually makes with unhesitating accuracy.

Finally, we are capable of using our unlimited memory, our rapid retrieval system, and our unconscious rules of inference to attain extremely high levels of skill, such as playing chess, analyzing stocks, conducting performance appraisals, or speaking a language. These skills do not come easily, requiring years of experience and many thousands of hours of practice. Nevertheless, when we use them we compress years of experience and learning into split seconds. This compression is one of the bases of what we call intuition as well as of the art of management.

Managers' 'maps' of people provide them with guides to action. In this case, because of his sense of the personnel director's needs, the CEO slowed the reorganizing process so that the people who reported to him could deal with the various issues that arose.

The CEO elaborately described to me his awareness of the personnel director's concern at being new and at being a woman, and her desire to be in direct contact with him. He also understood her worry that if she reported to someone lower than him, people would perceive that the new personnel function was not very important and she would lose power.

The overriding concern

The stereotypical senior executive pays a great deal of attention to the strategy of the business, carefully formulates goals, lays out quantified and

Some bad news

The same cognitive processes that underlie our greatest mental accomplishments also account for incorrigible flaws in our thinking. For instance, we easily believe that salient events occur more frequently than they really do: for example, despite the fact that dozens of examples exist where missed budgets did not lead to termination, managers interpret Sam's being fired for not making a budget as 'There is a good chance that division heads who do not meet the budgeted profit objectives will get axed.'

A second family of flaws arises from our overconfidence in our own expertise at making complex judgments. Various cognitive biases such as the 'hindsight bias,' our retrospective confidence in judgments that we hesitated about making at the time ('I *knew* it wouldn't work when she first proposed it'), and our tendency to search for confirming but not for disconfirming evidence of our judgments, conspire to exaggerate that belief.

And finally, research has shown that, when presented with data, we are not very good at assessing the degree of relationship among variables – even though this skill is critical for successful management. Unless the relationships are very obvious, we tend to rely on preconceptions and perceive illusory correlations.

A number of excellent books on human cognition are in print. For a nontechnical discussion of the good news, Morton Hunt's *The Universe Within* (Simon & Schuster, 1982), is a good starting place. A more technical discussion of human cognition is Stephen K. Reed's *Cognition: Theory and Applications* (Brooks/Cole, 1982). A somewhat technical but very comprehensive presentation of the bad news can be found in Daniel Kahneman, Paul Slovic, and Amos Tversky's edited volume, *Judgment Under Uncertainty: Heuristics and Biases* (Cambridge University Press, 1982).

---

clear objectives, and sets about achieving these objectives in the most efficient way. Whereas senior executives certainly attend to specific strategies and objectives some of the time, in their day-to-day reality specific objectives lurk in the background, not in the forefront of their thoughts.

Approximately two-thirds of the senior managers I studied were preoccupied with a very limited number of quite general issues, each of which subsumed a large number of specific issues. This preoccupation persisted for anywhere from a month to several years and, when in effect, dominated the manager's attention and provided coherence to many of his or her chaotic and disorganized activities.

The general manager of one large division of an automotive company, for example, used the word 'discipline' over a dozen times in the course of a two-hour interview. For him, this concept embodied his deep concern for creating order and predictability in a division that, in his view, had become too loose before he took it over. His concern for discipline appeared in a number of diverse actions – strongly discouraging his subordinates' fire-fighting mentality, criticizing their poor preparation for corporate reviews, introducing rigorous strategic planning, encouraging time management, putting out a yearly calendar with divisional and corporate meetings printed on it, publishing agendas for many of these meetings up to a year in advance, and, by keeping recent reports in the top drawer of his desk, forcing himself to review frequently the division's activities and performance.

Regardless of its substance, the overriding concern weaves its way in and out of all the manager's daily activities, at times achieving the dimensions of an all-consuming passion.

After his first 100 days in office, an area general manager described his experience turning around a subsidiary in these words:

'The personal cost of achieving our top priorities has been huge. I dropped all outside activities. Now I have a feeling of just having emerged, like a chap who's been taken by a surf wave and rolled. Suddenly he comes up and can look at daylight again. It has been like a single-minded rage or madness. At the end of the 100 days, somehow I have awakened. It was overwhelming.'

Of course senior managers do think about the content of their businesses, particularly during crises and periodic business reviews. But this thinking is always in close conjunction with thinking about the process for getting *others* to think about the business. In other words, even very senior managers devote most of their attention to the tactics of implementation rather than the formulation of strategy.

How senior managers think

In making their day-by-day and minute-by-minute tactical maneuvers, senior executives tend to rely on several general thought processes such as using intuition; managing a network of interrelated problems; dealing with ambiguity, inconsistency, novelty, and surprise; and integrating action into the process of thinking.

Using intuition

Generations of writers on the art of management have recognized that practicing managers rely heavily on intuition.[3] In general, however, people have a poor grasp of what intuition is. Some see it as the opposite of rationality, others use it as an excuse for capriciousness, and currently some view it as the exclusive property of a particular side of the brain.

Senior managers use intuition in at least five distinct ways. First, they intuitively sense when a problem exists. The chief financial officer of a leading technical products company, for example, forecast a difficult year ahead for the company and, based on a vague gut feel that something was wrong, decided to analyze one business group. 'The data on the group were inconsistent and unfocused,' he said after doing the analysis. 'I had the sense that they were talking about a future that just was not going to happen, and I turned out to be right.'

Second, managers rely on intuition to perform well-learned behavior patterns rapidly. Early on, managerial action needs to be thought through carefully. Once the manager is 'fluent' at performance, however, and the behavior is programmed, executives can execute programs without conscious effort. In the words of one general manager:

'It was very instinctive, almost like you have been drilled in close combat for years and now the big battle is on, and you really don't have time to think. It's as if your arms, your feet, and your body just move instinctively. You have a preoccupation with working capital, a preoccupation with capital expenditure, a preoccupation with people, and one with productivity, and all this goes so fast that you don't even know whether it's completely rational, or it's part rational, part intuitive.'

Intuition here refers to the smooth automatic performance of learned behavior sequences. This intuition is not arbitrary or irrational, but is based on years of painstaking practice and hands-on experience that build skills. After a while a manager can perform a sequence of actions in a seamless fabric of action and reaction without being aware of the effort.

A third function of intuition is to synthesize isolated bits of data and experience into an integrated picture, often in an 'aha!' experience. In the words of one manager: 'Synergy is always nonrational because it takes you beyond the mere sum of the parts. It is a nonrational, nonlogical thinking perspective.'

Fourth, some managers use intuition as a check (a belt-and-suspenders approach) on the results of more rational analysis. Most senior executives are familiar with the formal decision analysis models and tools, and those that occasionally use such systematic methods for reaching decisions are leery of solutions that these methods suggest that run counter to their sense of the correct course of action.

Conversely, if managers completely trusted intuition, they'd have little need for rigorous and systematic analysis. In practice, executives work on an issue until they find a match between their 'gut' and their 'head.' One manager explained to me, 'Intuition leads me to seek out holes in the data. But I discount casual empiricism and don't act on it.'

Fifth, managers can use intuition to bypass in-depth analysis and move rapidly to come up with a plausible solution. Used in this way, intuition is an almost instantaneous cognitive process in which a manager recognizes familiar patterns. In much the same way that people can immediately recognize faces that were familiar years ago, administrators have a repertoire of familiar problematic situations matched with the necessary responses. As one manager explained:

'My gut feel points me in a given direction. When I arrive there, then I can begin to sort out the issues. I do not do a deep analysis at first. I suppose the intuition comes from scar tissue, getting burned enough times. For example, while discussing the European budget with someone, suddenly I got the answer: it was hard for us to get the transfer prices. It rang a bell, then I ran some quick checks.'

By now it should be clear that intuition is not the opposite of rationality, nor is it a random process of guessing. Rather, it is based on extensive experience both in analysis and problem solving and in implementation, and to the extent that the lessons of experience are logical and well-founded, then so is the intuition. Further, managers often combine gut feel with systematic analysis, quantified data, and thoughtfulness.

It should also be clear that executives use intuition during *all* phases of the problem-solving process: problem finding, problem defining, generating and choosing a solution, and implementing the solution. In fact, senior managers often ignore the implied linear progression of the rational decision-making model and jump opportunistically from phase to phase, allowing implementation concerns to affect the problem definition and perhaps even to limit the range of solutions generated.

Problem management

Managers at all levels work at understanding and solving the problems that arise in their jobs. One distinctive characteristic of top managers is that their thinking deals not with isolated and discrete items but with portfolios of problems, issues, and opportunities in which (1) many problems exist simultaneously, (2) these problems compete for some part of his or her immediate concern, and (3) the issues are interrelated.

The cognitive tasks in problem management are to find and define good problems, to 'map' these into a network, and to manage their dynamically shifting priorities. For lack of a better term, I call this the process of problem management.

Defining the problem. After learning of a state health organization threat to exclude one of their major products from the list of drugs for which the state would reimburse buyers, top executives in a pharmaceutical company struggled to find a proper response. After some time, the managers discovered that the real problem was not the alleged drug abuse the availability of the drug on the street caused. Rather, the problem was budgetary: the health services department had to drastically reduce its budget and was doing so by trimming its list of reimbursable drugs. Once they redefined the problem, the pharmaceutical executives not only could work on a better, more real problem, but also had a chance to solve it – which they did.[4]

In another case, a division general manager discovered that, without his knowledge but with the approval of the division controller, one of his vice presidents had drawn a questionable personal loan from the company. The division manager told me how he defined the problem: 'I could spend my time formulating rules to guide managers. But the real fundamental issue here was that I needed to expect and demand that my managers manage their resources effectively.' Although he recognized the ethical components involved, he chose to define the problem as concerned with asset management rather than cheating. Because asset management was an issue the division frequently discussed, the manager felt that it was more legitimate and efficacious to define the problem in this way.

Making a network of problems. By forming problem categories, executives can see how individual problems interrelate. For instance, a bank CEO had a 'network' of at least 19 related problems and issues that he was concerned about. Among these were: establishing credibility in international banking, strengthening the bank's role in corporate banking, increasing the range of financial services and products, being prepared to defensively introduce new products in response to competitor's innovations, developing systems to give product cost information, reducing operational costs, standardizing branch architecture, and utilizing space efficiently.

The bank CEO classified these problems in terms of broad issue categories. He found that many were related to the issue of expanding and broadening the bank's competence beyond consumer banking in which it was already firmly established. A second overarching issue was standardization of the bank's many branches with regard to architecture, physical layout, accounting systems, and so on.

Having an interrelated network of problems allows a manager to seize opportunities more flexibly and to use progress on one problem to achieve progress on another, related issue. The bank CEO likened himself to a frog on a lily pad waiting for the fly – the problem or issue – to buzz by. Having a mental network of problems helped him to realize the opportunities as they occurred.

Choosing which problem to work on. Although managers often decide to work on the problem that seems to offer the best opportunities for attack, determining which problems they ought to tackle can be hard. As one manager commented:

'I have to sort through so many issues at once. There are ten times too many. I use a number of defense mechanisms to deal with this overload – I use delaying actions, I deny the existence of problems, or I put problems in a mental queue of sorts. This is an uncomfortable process for me. My office and responsibility say I need to deal with all of these issues, so I create smoke or offer some grand theory as my only way to keep my own sanity. One of the frustrations is that I don't want to tell my people that their number one problems have lower priorities than they think they should get.'

In my observations, how managers define and rank problems is heavily influenced by how easy the problems are to solve. Very shortly after perceiving that a problem exists, managers run a quick feasibility check to see if it is solvable. Only if they find it is solvable will they then invest further energy to understand its various ramifications and causes. In other words, managers tend not to think very much about a problem unless they sense that it is solvable. Contrary to some management doctrines, this finding suggests that a general concept of what is a possible solution often precedes and guides the process of conceptualizing a problem.

Thus, the two stages of problem analysis and problem solving are tightly linked and occur reiteratively rather than sequentially. By going back and forth between these two cognitive processes, managers define the array of problems facing them in terms that already incorporate key features of solutions and that thus make it easier for them to take action.

One outcome of this process is that managers have an organized mental map of all the problems and issues facing them. The map is neither static nor permanent; rather, managers continually test, correct, and revise it. In the words of one CEO, the executive 'takes advantage of the best cartography at his command, but knows that that is not enough. He knows that along the way he will find things that change his maps or alter his perceptions of the terrain. He trains himself the best he can in the detective skills. He is endlessly sending out patrols to learn greater detail, overflying targets to get some sense of the general battlefield.'

Tolerating ambiguity.   The senior managers that I observed showed an ability to tolerate and even thrive on high degrees of ambiguity and apparent inconsistency. As one top executive said:

'I think ambiguity can be destroying, but it can be very helpful to an operation. Ambiguities come from the things you can't spell out exactly. They yield a certain freedom you need as a chief executive officer not to be nailed down on everything. Also, certain people thrive on ambiguity, so I leave certain things ambiguous. The fact is we tie ourselves too much to linear plans, to clear time scales. I like to fuzz up time scales completely.'

Because demands on a manager become both stronger and more divergent as responsibility increases, the need to tolerate apparent ambiguity and inconsistency also increases. For example, the top manager has to deal with stakeholders who may have adversarial roles. By responding positively to one set of demands, the manager automatically will create other conflicting sets of demands.

The reason I have called the inconsistency 'apparent' is that senior managers tend to have ways of thinking that make issues seem less inconsistent. For example, the president of a leading high-technology company was considering whether to exercise or forgo an option to lease land on which to build expensive warehouse space for one of the divisions at the same time as the division was laying off workers for the first time in its history. 'To spend a half million dollars on keeping the land and building warehouse space while the plant is laying off people looks terrible and makes no sense,' he said, 'but if next year is a good year, we'll need to be in a position to make the product.'

Perceiving and understanding novelty.   The managers I observed dealt frequently with novel situations that were unexpected and, in many cases, were impossible to plan for in advance. For example, one division general manager found himself with the task of selling his division, which was still developing a marketable product. In response to its shareholders, the corporation had shifted its strategy and thus decided to divest the fledgling division. How should the general manager look for buyers? If buyers were not forthcoming, would the corporation retain a stake to reduce the risk to potential new partners? How should he manage his people in the process of selling? Should he himself look for a new position or commit himself to a new owner? These were some of the unique questions the division head faced while selling his own division, and there was no industry experience to give him clear answers.

In general, the human mind is conservative. Long after an assumption is outmoded, people tend to apply it to novel situations. One way in which some of the senior managers I studied counteract this conservative bent is by paying attention to their feelings of *surprise* when a particular fact does not fit their prior understanding, and then by highlighting rather than denying the novelty. Although surprise made them feel uncomfortable, it made them take the cause seriously and inquire into it – 'What is behind the personal loan by my vice president of sales that appears on the books? How extensive a problem is it?' 'Why did the management committee of the corporation spend over an hour of its valuable time discussing a problem three levels down in my division?' 'Now that we've shown the health services department beyond a reasonable doubt that this drug is not involved in drug abuse, why don't they reinstate it on the list?'

Rather than deny, downplay, or ignore disconfirmation, successful senior managers often treat it as friendly and in a way cherish the discomfort surprise creates. As a result, these managers often perceive novel situations early on and in a frame of mind relatively undistorted by hidebound notions.

What to do about thinking

Having looked at the inner workings of the managerial mind, what insights can we derive from our observations? Literally hundreds of laboratory and field studies demonstrate that the human mind is imperfectly rational, and dozens of additional articles offering arguments based on every field of study from psychology to economics, explain why.[5] The evidence that we should curtail our impractical and overly ambitious expectations of managerial rationality is compelling.

Yet abandoning the rational ideal leaves us with two glaring problems. First, whether managers think in a linear and systematic fashion or not, companies still need to strive towards rational action in the attainment of corporate goals, particularly in their use of resources. Second, we still need to spell out what kinds of thinking processes are attainable and helpful to senior managers.

Program rationality into the organization

Of course, rationality is desirable and should be manifest in the functioning of the company. One alternative to the vain task of trying to rationalize managers is to increase the rationality of organizational systems and processes. Although organizational behavior is never completely rational, managers can design and program processes and systems that will approach rationality in resource allocation and employment.

Decision support systems are one source of organizational rationality. These generally computerized routines perform many functions ranging from providing a broad and quantitative data base to presenting that data base in easily understandable form, to modeling the impact of decisions on various financial and other criteria, to mimicking expert judgment such as in the diagnosis and repair of malfunctioning equipment or in oil field exploration.

Another rational process that many businesses employ is strategic planning. Nonrational or partly rational managers can devise, implement, and use a plan that systematically assesses a company's strengths and weaknesses, logically extrapolates a set of its competencies, proposes a quantitative assessment of environmental constraints and resources, and performs all these tasks in a time-sequenced, linear fashion.

Of course, companies have used rational systems for information gathering, strategic planning, budgeting, human resource planning, environmental scanning, and so forth for a long time. But I see these systems not only as useful but also as a necessary complement to a manager's apparent inability to be very systematic or rational in thought.

But is it possible for imperfectly rational managers to design even more perfectly rational systems? The answer is a qualified yes. There is evidence, for example, that with help people can design systems that are better than they are themselves at making judgments.[6] Creating organizational systems to improve on their own behavior is not new to managers. In order to still hear the beautiful sirens yet prevent himself being seduced by the music and throwing himself into the sea, Ulysses ordered his men to block their own ears with wax, bind him to the mast, and to tighten his bindings if he ordered them to let him go. Although Ulysses begged his sailors to release him, they obeyed his original orders and Ulysses succeeded in both hearing the sirens and surviving their perilous allure.[7]

Programming rationality into the organizational functioning is important for another reason: rational systems free senior executives to tackle the ambiguous, ill-defined tasks that the human mind is uniquely capable of addressing. Many senior managers today face problems – developing new products for embryonic markets, creating new forms of manufacturing operations, conceiving of innovative human resource systems – that are new to them and new to their companies and that they can deal with only extemporaneously and with a nonprogrammable artistic sense. In fact, it may even seem paradoxical that managers need to create rational systems in order to creatively and incrementally tackle the nonrecurrent problems that defy systematic approaches.

Hone intellectual skills

In the literature on managerial behavior there is disagreement as to how much or how often senior managers engage in thoughtful reflection. Many executives that I studied do make time for in-depth thinking, sometimes while they are alone, sometimes with their peers or subordinates, and sometimes in active experimentation.

Furthermore, most senior managers I studied constantly maintain and sharpen their intellectual abilities in order to better analyze their current or past experiences. Rigorous thinking is a way of life for them, not a task they try to avoid or to expedite superficially.

These senior managers read books outside their fields, engage in enthusiastic discussions of political and economic affairs, attend academic lectures and management seminars, and tackle brain teasers such as word problems, chess, and crossword puzzles. One company president I studied is a regular theatergoer who can discuss Shakespearean and contemporary plays at great length, while another often immerses himself in classical music and allows ideas about difficult work-related issues to float around in his consciousness. These activities are valuable not only for their content but also for the thinking processes that they establish, develop, and refine. Whether managers indulge in such 'blue sky' irrelevant activities at work or outside, they are developing critical mental resources that they can then apply to problems that arise in their jobs.

Think while doing

One of the implications of the intuitive nature of executive action is that 'thinking' is inseparable from acting. Since managers often 'know' what is right before they can analyze and explain it, they frequently act first and think later. Thinking is inextricably tied to action in what I call thinking/acting cycles, in which managers develop thoughts about their companies and organizations not by analyzing a problematic situation and then acting, but by thinking and acting in close concert. Many of the managers I studied were quite facile at using thinking to inform action and vice versa.

Given the great uncertainty of many of the management or business issues that they face, senior managers often instigate a course of action simply to learn more about an issue: 'We bought that company because we wanted to learn about that business.' They then use the results of the action to develop a more complete understanding of the issue. What may appear as action for action's sake is really the result of an intuitive understanding that analysis is only possible in the light of experience gained while attempting to solve the problem. Analysis is not a passive process but a dynamic, interactive series of activity and reflection.

One implication of acting/thinking cycles is that action is often part of defining the problem, not just of implementing the solution. Frequently, once they had begun to perceive the symptoms, but before they could articulate a problem, the managers I studied talked to a few people to collect more information and confirm what they already knew. The act of collecting more data more often than not changed the nature of the problem, in part because subordinates then realized that the problem was serious enough to warrant the boss's attention. Managers also often acted in the absence of

clearly specified goals, allowing these to emerge from the process of clarifying the nature of the problem.

Yet how often do managers push their subordinates to spell out *their* goals
clearly and specify *their* objectives? A creative subordinate will always be
able to present a plausible and achievable goal when pressed, but in the early
stages of a tough problem it is more helpful for managers to provide a
receptive forum in which their people can play around with an issue,
'noodle' it through, and experiment. Sometimes it will be necessary for
managers to allow subordinates to act in the absence of goals to achieve a
clearer comprehension of what is going on, and even at times to *discover*
rather than achieve the organization's true goals.

Manage time by managing problems

All managers would like to accomplish more in less time. One of the
implications of the process of mapping problems and issues is that when a
manager addresses any particular problem, he or she calls a number of
related problems or issues to mind at the same time. One by-product is that a
manager can attain economies of effort.

For example, when working on a problem of poor product quality, a
division manager might see a connection between poor quality and an
inadequate production control system and tackle both problems together.
To address the issues, she could form a cross-functional task force involving
her marketing manager, who understands customers' tolerance for defects.
(One reason for bringing him in might be to prepare him for promotion in
two or three years.) She might intend the task force to reduce interdepart-
mental conflicts as well as prepare a report that she could present to
corporate headquarters.

Managers can facilitate the process of creating a problem network in many
ways. They can ask their staff to list short- and long-term issues that they
think need to be addressed, consolidate these lists, and spend some time
together mapping the interrelationships. Or they can ask themselves how an
issue fits into other nonproblematic aspects of the company or business unit.
How does product quality relate to marketing strategy? To capital and
expenditure guidelines? To the company's R&D center with a budget
surplus? To the new performance appraisal system? To the company's
recent efforts in affirmative action? To their own career plans? Managers
should never deal with problems in isolation. They should always ask
themselves what additional related issues they should be aware of while
dealing with the problem at hand.[8]

Some suggestions

A number of suggestions on how managers can improve their thinking
emerge from my study of senior managers' thought processes:

☐ Bolster intuition with rational thinking. Recognize that good intuition requires hard work, study, periods of concentrated thought, and rehearsal.

☐ Offset tendencies to be rational by stressing the importance of values and preferences, of using imagination, and of acting with an incomplete picture of the situation.

☐ Develop skills at mapping an unfamiliar territory by, for example, generalizing from facts and testing generalities by collecting more data.

☐ Pay attention to the simple rules of thumb – heuristics – that you have developed over the years. These can help you bypass many levels of painstaking analysis.

☐ Don't be afraid to act in the absence of complete understanding, but then cherish the feelings of surprise that you will necessarily experience.

☐ Spend time understanding what the problem or issue is.

☐ Look for the connections among the many diverse problems and issues facing you to see their underlying relationships with each other. By working on one problem you can make progress on others.

☐ Finally, recognize that your abilities to think are critical assets that you need to manage and develop in the same way that you manage other business assets.

Notes

Among the many people who have helped my research I want to single out Paul Lawrence and John Kotter. I also extend thanks to the corporate managers who have given freely of their time and ideas. Miriam Schustack made very helpful comments on a previous version of this article.

1 In studying these dozen executives, I conducted intensive interviews, observed them on the job, read documents, talked with their colleagues and, in some cases, subordinates, and engaged them in various exercises in which they recounted their thoughts as they did their work. I also reported my observations and inferences back to the managers to get feedback. I spent anywhere from 1 to 25 days studying each manager (the mode was two and a half days in field interviews and observation).

2 John P. Kotter, *The General Managers* (New York: Free Press, 1982).

3 See, for example, Chester I. Barnard, *The Functions of the Executive* (Cambridge: Harvard University Press, 1938), also Henry Mintzberg, 'Planning on the Left Side and Managing on the Right,' *Harvard Business Review*, July–August 1976, p. 49 [also reprinted in this volume].

4 See my study, 'Drugs and Drama: The Effects of Two Dramatic Events in a Pharmaceutical Company on Managers' Cognitions,' Working Paper 83–55 (Boston: Harvard Business School, 1983).

5 Some of Herbert A. Simon's classic work on bounded rationality and 'satisficing' is collected in *Models of Thought* (New Haven: Yale University Press, 1979). More recently, Amos Tversky, Daniel Kahneman, and other psychologists have described the mechanisms producing imperfect judgment and nonrational choice. See, for example, Daniel Kahneman, Paul Slovic, and Amos Tversky, ed., *Judgment under Uncertainty: Heuristics and Biases* (Cambridge, UK: Cambridge University Press, 1982).

6 Louis R. Goldberg, 'Man vs. Model of Man: A Rationale, Plus Some Evidence, for a Method of Improving on Clinical Inferences' *Psychological Bulletin*, 1970, 73, p. 422.

7 Jon Elster, *Ulysses and the Sirens: Studies in Rationality and Irrationality* (Cambridge, Mass.: Cambridge University Press, 1979).

8 For an interesting application of these ideas to a different leadership setting, see my chapter 'Some Hows and Whats of Managerial Thinking: Implications for Future Army Leaders' in *Military Leadership on the Future Battlefield* (New York: Pergamon Press, 1984).

7

Planning on the left side and managing on the right

Henry Mintzberg

In the folklore of the Middle East, the story is told about a man named Nasrudin, who was searching for something on the ground. A friend came by and asked: 'What have you lost, Nasrudin?'

'My key,' said Nasrudin.

So, the friend went down on his knees, too, and they both looked for it. After a time, the friend asked: 'Where exactly did you drop it?'

'In my house,' answered Nasrudin.

'Then why are you looking here, Nasrudin?'

'There is more light here than inside my own house.'

This 'light' little story is old and worn, yet it has some timeless, mysterious appeal, one which has much to do with the article that follows. But let me leave the story momentarily while I pose some questions – also simple yet mysterious – that have always puzzled me.

First: Why are some people so smart and so dull at the same time, so capable of mastering certain mental activities and so incapable of mastering others? Why is it that some of the most creative thinkers cannot comprehend a balance sheet, and that some accountants have no sense of product design? Why do some brilliant management scientists have no ability to handle organizational politics, while some of the most politically adept individuals cannot seem to understand the simplest elements of management science?

Second: Why do people sometimes express such surprise when they read or learn the obvious, something they already must have known? Why is a manager so delighted, for example, when he reads a new article on decision making, every part of which must be patently obvious to him even though he has never before seen it in print?

Third: Why is there such a discrepancy in organizations, at least at the policy level, between the science and planning of management on the one hand, and managing on the other? Why have none of the techniques of planning and analysis really had much effect on how top managers function?

Adapted and reprinted by permission of *Harvard Business Review*, 54 (July–August), 1976, pp. 49–58. Copyright © 1976 by the President and Fellows of Harvard College; all rights reserved

What I plan to do in this article is weave together some tentative answers to these three questions with the story of Nasrudin around a central theme, namely, that of the specialization of the hemispheres of the human brain and what that specialization means for management.

The two hemispheres of the human brain

Let us first try to answer the three questions by looking at what is known about the hemispheres of the brain.

Question one

Scientists – in particular, neurologists, neurosurgeons, and psychologists – have known for a long time that the brain has two distinct hemispheres. They have known, further, that the left hemisphere controls movements on the body's right side and that the right hemisphere controls movements on the left. What they have discovered more recently, however, is that these two hemispheres are specialized in more fundamental ways.

In the left hemisphere of most people's brains (left-handers largely excepted) the logical thinking processes are found. It seems that the mode of operation of the brain's left hemisphere is linear; it processes information sequentially, one bit after another, in an ordered way. Perhaps the most obvious linear faculty is language. In sharp contrast, the right hemisphere is specialized for simultaneous processing; that is, it operates in a more holistic, relational way. Perhaps its most obvious faculty is comprehension of visual images.

What does this specialization of the brain mean for the way people function? Speech, being linear, is a left-hemispheric activity, but other forms of human communication, such as gesturing, are relational rather than sequential and tend to be associated with the right hemisphere. Imagine what would happen if the two sides of a human brain were detached so that for example, in reacting to a stimulus, a person's words would be separate from his gestures. In other words, the person would have two separate brains – one specialized for verbal communication, and the other for gestures – that would react to the same stimulus.

The 'imagining,' in fact, describes how the main breakthrough in the recent research on the human brain took place. In trying to treat certain cases of epilepsy, neurosurgeons found that by severing the corpus callosum, which joins the two hemispheres of the brain, they could 'split the brain,' isolating the epilepsy. A number of experiments run on these 'split-brain' patients produced some fascinating results.

In one experiment doctors showed a woman epileptic's right hemisphere a photograph of a nude woman. (This is done by showing it to the left half of each eye.) The patient said she saw nothing, but almost simultaneously blushed and seemed confused and uncomfortable. Her 'conscious' left hemisphere, including her verbal apparatus, was aware only that something had happened to her body, but not of what had caused the emotional turmoil. Only her 'unconscious' right hemisphere knew. Here neurosurgeons observed a clear split between the two independent consciousnesses that are normally in communication and collaboration.[1]

Now, scientists have further found that some common human tasks activate one side of the brain while leaving the other largely at rest. For example, a person's learning a mathematical proof might evoke activity in the left hemisphere of his brain, while his conceiving a piece of sculpture or assessing a political opponent might evoke activity in his right.

So now we seem to have the answer to the first question. An individual can be smart and dull at the same time simply because one side of his or her brain is more developed than the other. Some people – probably most lawyers, accountants, and planners – have better developed left-hemispheric thinking processes, while others – artists, sculptors, and perhaps politicians – have better developed right-hemispheric processes. Thus an artist may be incapable of expressing his feeling in words, while a lawyer may have no facility for painting. Or a politician may not be able to learn mathematics, while a management scientist may constantly be manipulated in political situations.

Eye movement is apparently a convenient indicator of hemispheric development. When asked to count the letters in a complex word such as 'Mississippi' in their heads, most people will gaze off to the side opposite their most developed hemisphere. (Be careful of lefties, however.) But if the question is a specialized one – for example, if it is emotionally laden, spatial, or purely mathematical – the number of people gazing one way or another will change substantially.

Question two

A number of word opposites have been proposed to distinguish the two hemispheric modes of 'consciousness,' for example: explicit versus implicit; verbal versus spatial; argument versus experience; intellectual versus intuitive; and analytic versus gestalt.

I should interject at this point that these words, as well as much of the evidence for these conclusions, can be found in the remarkable book entitled *The Psychology of Consciousness* by Robert Ornstein, a research psychologist in California. Ornstein uses the story of Nasrudin to further the points he is making. Specifically, he refers to the linear left hemisphere as synonymous with lightness, with thought processes that we know in an explicit sense. We can *articulate* them. He associates the right hemisphere with darkness, with thought processes that are mysterious to us, at least 'us' in the Western world.

Ornstein also points out how the 'esoteric psychologies' of the East (Zen, Yoga, Sufism, and so on) have focused on right-hemispheric consciousness (for example, altering pulse rate through meditation). In sharp contrast, Western psychology has been concerned almost exclusively with left-hemispheric consciousness, with logical thought. Ornstein suggests that we might find an important key to human consciousness in the right hemisphere, in what to us in the West is darkness. To quote him:

> Since these experiences [transcendence of time, control of the nervous system, paranormal communication, and so on] are, by their very mode of operation, not readily accessible to causal explanation or even to linguistic exploration, many have been tempted to ignore them or even to deny their existence. These traditional psychologies have been relegated to the 'esoteric' or the 'occult,' the realm of the mysterious – the word most often employed is 'mysticism.' It is a taboo area of inquiry, which has been symbolized by the Dark, the Left side [the right hemisphere] of ourselves, the Night.[2]

Now, reflect on this for a moment. (Should I say meditate?) There is a set of thought processes – linear, sequential, analytical – that scientists as well as the rest of us know a lot about. And there is another set – simultaneous, relational, holistic – that we know little about. More importantly, here we do not 'know' what we 'know' or, more exactly, our left hemispheres cannot articulate explicitly what our right hemispheres know implicitly.

So here is, seemingly, the answer to the second question as well. The feeling of revelation about learning the obvious can be explained with the suggestion that the 'obvious' knowledge was implicit, apparently restricted to the right hemisphere. The left hemisphere never 'knew.' Thus it seems to be a revelation to the left hemisphere when it learns explicitly what the right hemisphere knew all along implicitly.

Now only the third question – the discrepancy between planning and managing – remains.

Question three

By now, it should be obvious where my discussion is leading (obvious, at least, to the reader's right hemisphere and, now that I write it, to the reader's left hemisphere as well). It may be that management researchers have been looking for the key to management in the lightness of logical analysis whereas perhaps it has always been lost in the darkness of intuition.

Specifically, I propose that there may be a fundamental difference between formal planning and informal managing, a difference akin to that between the two hemispheres of the human brain. The techniques of planning and management science are sequential and systematic; above all, articulated. Planners and management scientists are expected to proceed in their work through a serious of logical, ordered steps, each one involving explicit analysis. (The argument that the successful application of these techniques requires considerable intuition does not really change my point. The occurrence of intuition simply means that the analyst is departing from his science, as it is articulated, and is behaving more like a manager.)

Formal planning, then, seems to use processes akin to those identified with the brain's left hemisphere. Furthermore, planners and management scientists seem to revel in a systematic, well-ordered world, and many show little appreciation for the more relational, holistic processes.

What about managing? More exactly, what about the processes used by top managers? (Let me emphasize here that I am focusing this discussion at the policy level of organizations, where I believe the dichotomy between planning and managing is most sharp.) Managers plan in some ways, too (that is, they think ahead), and they engage in their share of logical analysis. But I believe there is more than that to the effective managing of an organization. I hypothesize, therefore, that *the important policy processes of managing an organization rely to a considerable extent on the faculties identified with the brain's right hemisphere.* Effective managers seem to revel in ambiguity; in complex, mysterious systems with relatively little order.

If true, this hypothesis would answer the third question about the discrepancy between planning and managing. It would help to explain why each of the new analytic techniques of planning and analysis has, one after the other, had so little success at the policy level. PPBS, strategic planning, 'management' (or 'total') information systems, and models of the company – all have been greeted with great enthusiasm; then, in many instances, a few years later have been quietly ushered out the corporate back door. Apparently none served the needs of decision making at the policy level in organizations; at that level other processes may function better.

Managing from the right hemisphere

Because research has so far told us little about the right hemisphere, I cannot support with evidence my claim that a key to managing lies there. I can only present to the reader a 'feel' for the situation, not a reading of concrete data. A number of findings from my own research on policy-level processes do, however, suggest that they possess characteristics of right-hemispheric thinking.[3]

One fact recurs repeatedly in all of this research: the key managerial processes are enormously complex and mysterious (to me as a researcher, as well as to the managers who carry them out), drawing on the vaguest of information and using their least articulated of mental processes. These processes seem to be more relational and holistic than ordered and sequential, and more intuitive than intellectual; they seem to be most characteristic of right-hemispheric activity.

Here are ten general findings:

1   The five chief executives I observed strongly favored the verbal media of communication, especially meetings, over the written forms, namely reading and writing. (The same result has been found in virtually every study of managers, no matter what their level in the organization or the function they supervised.) Of course verbal communication is linear, too,

but it is more than that. Managers seem to favor it for two fundamental reasons that suggest a relational mode of operation.

First, verbal communication enables the manager to 'read' facial expressions, tones of voice, and gestures. As I mentioned earlier, these stimuli seem to be processed in the right hemisphere of the brain. Second, and perhaps more important, verbal communication enables the manager to engage in the 'real-time' exchange of information. Managers' concentration on the verbal media, therefore, suggests that they desire relational, simultaneous methods of acquiring information, rather than the ordered and sequential ones.

2 In addition to noting the media managers use, it is interesting to look at the content of managers' information, and at what they do with it. The evidence here is that a great deal of the manager's inputs are soft and speculative – impressions and feelings about other people, hearsay, gossip, and so on. Furthermore, the very analytical inputs – reports, documents, and hard data in general – seem to be of relatively little importance to many managers. (After a steady diet of soft information, one chief executive came across the first piece of hard data he had seen all week – an accounting report – and put it aside with the comment, 'I never look at this.')

What can managers do with this soft, speculative information? They 'synthesize' rather than 'analyze' it, I should think. (How do you analyze the mood of a friend or the grimace someone makes in response to a suggestion?) A great deal of this information helps the manager understand implicitly his organization and its environment, to 'see the big picture.' This very expression, so common in management, implies a relational, holistic use of information. In effect, managers (like everyone else) use their information to build mental 'models' of their world, which are implicit synthesized apprehensions of how their organizations and environments function. Then, whenever an action is contemplated, the manager can simulate the outcome using his implicit models.

There can be little doubt that this kind of activity goes on all the time in the world of management. A number of words managers commonly use suggest this kind of mental process. For example, the word 'hunch' seems to refer to the thought that results from such an implicit simulation. 'I don't know why, but I have a hunch that if we do x, then they will respond with y.' Managers also use the word 'judgment' to refer to thought processes that work but are unknown to them. 'Judgment' seems to be the word that the verbal intellect has given to the thought processes that it cannot articulate. Maybe 'he has good judgment' simply means 'he has good right-hemispheric models.'

3 Another consequence of the verbal nature of the manager's information is of interest here. The manager tends to be the best informed member of his organization, but he has difficulty disseminating his information to his

employees. Therefore, when a new manager overloaded with work finds a new task that needs doing, he faces a dilemma: he must either delegate the task without the background information or simply do the task himself, neither of which is satisfactory.

When I first encountered this dilemma of delegation, I described it in terms of time and of the nature of the manager's information; because so much of a manager's information is verbal (and stored in his head), the dissemination of it consumes much of his time. But now the split-brain research suggests that a second, perhaps more significant, reason for the dilemma of delegation exists. The manager may simply be incapable of disseminating some relevant information because it is removed from his verbal consciousness. (This suggests that we might need a kind of managerial psychoanalyst to coax it out of him!)

4 Earlier in this article I wrote that managers revel in ambiguity, in complex, mysterious systems without much order. Let us look at evidence of this. What I have discussed so far about the manager's use of information suggests that their work is geared to action, not reflection. We see further evidence for this in the pace of their work ('Breaks are rare. It's one damn thing after another'); the brevity of their activities (half of the chief executives' activities I observed were completed in less than 9 minutes); the variety of their activities (the chief executives had no evident patterns in their workdays); the fact that they actively exhibit a preference for interruption in their work (stopping meetings, leaving their doors open); and the lack of routine in their work (only 7% of 368 verbal contacts I observed were regularly scheduled, only 1% dealt with a general issue that was in any way related to general planning).

Clearly, the manager does not operate in a systematic, orderly, and intellectual way, puffing his pipe up in a mountain retreat, as he analyzes his problems. Rather, he deals with issues in the context of daily activities – the cigarette in his mouth, one hand on the telephone, and the other shaking hands with a departing guest. The manager is involved, plugged in; his mode of operating is relational, simultaneous, experiential, that is, encompassing all the characteristics of the right hemisphere.

5 If the most important managerial roles of the ten described in the research were to be isolated, *leader*, *liaison*, and *disturbance handler* would certainly be among them. (The other seven are *figurehead*, *monitor*, *disseminator*, *spokesman*, *negotiator*, *entrepreneur*, and *resource allocator*, and the last two are also among the most important roles.) Yet these three are the roles least 'known' about. *Leader* describes how the manager deals with his own employees. It is ironic that despite an immense amount of research, managers and researchers still know virtually nothing about the essence of leadership, about why some people follow and others lead. Leadership remains a mysterious chemistry; catchall words such as 'charisma' proclaim our ignorance.

In the *liaison* role, the manager builds up a network of outside contacts, which serve as his or her personal information system. Again, the activities of this role remain almost completely outside the realm of articulated knowledge. And as a *disturbance handler* the manager handles problems and crises in his organization. Here again, despite an extensive literature on analytical decision making, virtually nothing is written about decision making under pressure. These activities remain outside the realm of management science, inside the realm of intuition and experience.

6 Let us turn now to strategic decision-making processes. There are 7 'routines' that seem to describe the steps involved in such decision making. These are *recognition*, *diagnosis*, *search*, *design*, *screening*, *evaluation/choice*, and *authorization*. Two of these routines stand out above the rest – the *diagnosis* of decision situations and the *design* of custom-made solutions – in that almost nothing is known of them. Yet these two stand out for another reason as well: they are probably the most important of the seven. In particular, diagnosis seems to be *the* crucial step in strategic decision making, for it is in that routine that the whole course of decision making is set.

It is a surprising fact, therefore, that diagnosis goes virtually without mention in the literature of planning or management science. (Almost all of the later literature deals with the formal evaluation of given alternatives, yet this is often a kind of trimming on the process, insignificant in terms of determining actual outcomes.) In the study of the decision processes themselves, the managers making the decisions mentioned taking an explicit diagnostic step in only 14 of the 25 decision processes. But all the managers must have made some diagnosis; it is difficult to imagine a decision-making process with no diagnosis at all, no assessment of the situation. The question is, therefore, *where* did diagnosis take place?

7 Another point that emerges from studying strategic decision-making processes is the existence and profound influence of what can be called the *dynamic factors*. Strategic decision-making processes are stopped by interruptions, delayed and speeded up by timing factors, and forced repeatedly to branch and cycle. These processes are, therefore, dynamic ones of importance. Yet it is the dynamic factors that the ordered, sequential techniques of analysis are least able to handle. Thus, despite their importance, the dynamic factors go virtually without mention in the literature of management science.

Let's look at timing, for example. It is evident that timing is crucial in virtually everything the manager does. No manager takes action without considering the effect of moving more or less quickly, of seizing the initiative, or of delaying to avoid complications. Yet in one review of the literature of management, the authors found fewer than 10 books in 183 that refer directly to the subject to timing.[4] Essentially, managers are left

on their own to deal with the dynamic factors, which involve simultaneous, relational modes of thinking.

8 When managers do have to make serious choices from among options,
how do they in fact make them? Three fundamental modes of selection
can be distinguished – analysis, judgment, and bargaining. The first
involves the systematic evaluation of options in terms of their consequences on stated organizational goals; the second is a process in the mind
of a single decision maker; and the third involves negotiations between
different decision makers.

One of the most surprising facts about how managers made the 25
strategic decisions studied is that so few reported using explicit analysis;
only in 18 out of 83 choices made did managers mention using it. There
was considerable bargaining, but in general the selection mode most
commonly used was judgment. Typically, the options and all kinds of data
associated with them were pumped into the mind of a manager, and
somehow a choice later came out. *How* was never explained. *How* is never
explained in any of the literature either. Yehezkel Dror, a leading figure
in the study of public policy making, is one of the few thinkers to face the
issue squarely. He writes:

Experienced policy makers, who usually explain their own decisions largely in
terms of subconscious processes such as 'intuition' and 'judgment', unanimously
agree, and even emphasize, that extrarational processes play a positive and
essential role in policymaking. Observations of policymaking behavior in both
small and large systems, indeed, all available description of decisional behavior,
especially that of leaders such as Bismarck, Churchill, DeGaulle, and Kennedy,
seem to confirm that policy makers' opinion.[5]

9 Finally, in the area of strategy formulation, I can offer only a 'feel' for the
results since my research is still in progress. However, some ideas have
emerged. Strategy formulation does not turn out to be the regular,
continuous, systematic process depicted in so much of the planning
literature. It is most often an irregular, discontinuous process, proceeding
in fits and starts. There are periods of stability in strategy development,
but also there are periods of flux, of groping, of piecemeal change, and of
global change. To my mind, a 'strategy' represents the mediating force
between a dynamic environment and a stable operating system. Strategy
is the organization's 'conception' of how to deal with its environment for a
while.

Now, the environment does not change in any set pattern. For example,
the environment does not run on planners' five-year schedules; it may be
stable for thirteen years, and then suddenly blow all to hell in the
fourteenth. And even if change were steady, the human brain does not
generally perceive it that way. People tend to underreact to mild stimuli
and overreact to strong ones. It stands to reason, therefore, that strategies
that mediate between environments and organizational operations do not

change in regular patterns, but rather, as I observed earlier, in fits and starts.

How does strategic planning account for fits and starts? The fact is that it does not (as planners were made so painfully aware during the energy crisis). So again, the burden to cope falls on the manager, specifically on his mental processes – intuitional and experiential – that can deal with the irregular inputs from the environment.

10 Let me probe more deeply into the concept of strategy. Consider the organization that has no strategy, no way to deal consistently with its environment; it simply reacts to each new pressure as it comes along. This is typical behavior for an organization in a very difficult situation, where the old strategy has broken down beyond repair, but where no new strategy has yet emerged. Now, if the organization wishes to formulate a new strategy, how does it do so (assuming that the environment has stabilized sufficiently to allow a new strategy to be formulated)?

Let me suggest two ways (based on still tentative results). If the organization goes the route of systematic planning, I suggest that it will probably come up with what can be called a 'main-line' strategy. In effect, it will do what is generally expected of organizations in its situation; where possible, for example, it will copy the established strategies of other organizations. If it is in the automobile business, for instance, it might use the basic General Motors strategy, as Chrysler and Ford have so repeatedly done.

Alternatively, if the organization wishes to have a creative, integrated strategy which can be called a 'gestalt strategy,' such as Volkswagen's one in the 1950s, then I suggest the organization will rely largely on one individual to conceptualize its strategy, to synthesize a 'vision' of how the organization will respond to its environment. In other words, scratch an interesting strategy, and you will probably find a single strategy formulator beneath it. Creative, integrated strategies seem to be the products of single brains, perhaps of single right hemispheres.

A strategy can be made explicit, can be announced as what the organization intends to do in the future, only when the vision is fully worked out, if it ever is. Often, of course, it is never felt to be fully worked out, hence the strategy is never made explicit and remains the private vision of the chief executive. (Of course, in some situations the formulator need not be the manager. There is no reason why a manager cannot have a creative right-hand man -- really a left-hand man – who works out his gestalt strategy for him, and then articulates it to him.) No management process is more demanding of holistic, relational, gestalt thinking than the formulation of a creative, integrated strategy to deal with a complex, intertwined environment.

How can sequential analysis (under the label 'strategic planning' possibly lead to a gestalt strategy?

Another 'famous old story' has relevance here. It is the one about the blind men trying to identify an elephant by touch. One grabs the trunk and says the elephant is long and soft; another holds the leg and says it is massive and cylindrical; a third touches the skin and says it is rough and scaly. What the story points out is that:

Each person standing at one part of the elephant can make his own limited, analytic assessment of the situation, but we do not obtain an elephant by adding 'scaly,' 'long and soft,' 'massive and cylindrical' together in any conceivable proportion. Without the development of an overall perspective, we remain lost in our individual investigations. Such a perspective is a province of another mode of knowledge, and cannot be achieved in the same way that individual parts are explored. It does not arise out of a linear sum of independent observations.[6]

What can we conclude from these ten findings? I must first reemphasize that everything I write about the two hemispheres of the brain falls into the realm of speculation. Researchers have yet to formally relate any management process to the functioning of the human brain. Nevertheless, the ten points do seem to support the hypothesis stated earlier: *the important policy-level processes required to manage an organization rely to a considerable extent on the faculties identified with the brain's right hemisphere.*

This conclusion does not imply that the left hemisphere is unimportant for policy makers. I have overstated my case here to emphasize the importance of the right. The faculties identified with the left hemisphere are obviously important as well for effective management. Every manager engages in considerable explicit calculation when he or she acts, and all intuitive thinking must be translated into the linear order of the left if it is to be articulated and eventually put to use. The great powers that appear to be associated with the right hemisphere are obviously useless without the faculties of the left. The artist can create without verbalizing; the manager cannot.

Truly outstanding managers are no doubt the ones who can couple effective right-hemispheric processes (hunch, judgment, synthesis, and so on) with effective processes of the left (articulateness, logic, analysis, and so on). But there will be little headway in the field of management if managers and researchers continue to search for the key to managing in the lightness of ordered analysis. Too much will stay unexplained in the darkness of intuition.

Before I go on to discuss the implications for management science and planning, I want to stress again that throughout this article I have been focusing on processes that managers employ at the policy level of the organization. It seems that the faculties identified with the right-hemispheric activities are most important in the higher levels of an organization, at least in those with 'top-down' policy-making systems.

In a sense, the coupling of the holistic and the sequential reflects how bureaucratic organizations themselves work. The policy maker conceives the strategy in holistic terms, and the rest of the hierarchy – the functional departments, branches, and shops – implement it in sequence. Whereas the right-hemispheric faculties may be more important at the top of an organization, the left-hemispheric ones may dominate lower down.

Implications for the left hemisphere

Let us return to practical reality for a final word. What does all I've discussed mean for those associated with management?

For planners and management scientists

No, I do not suggest that planners and management scientists pack up their bags of techniques and leave the field of management, or that they take up basket-weaving or meditation in their spare time. (I haven't – at least not yet!) It seems to me that the left hemisphere is alive and well; the analytic community is firmly established, and indispensable, at the operating and middle levels of most organizations. Its real problems occur at the policy level. Here analysis must co-exist with – perhaps even take its lead from – intuition, a fact that many analysts and planners have been slow to accept. To my mind, organizational effectiveness does not lie in that narrow-minded concept called 'rationality'; it lies in a blend of clear-headed logic *and* powerful intuition. Let me illustrate this with two points.

First, only under special circumstances should planners try to plan. When an organization is in a stable environment and has no use for a very creative strategy – the telephone industry may be the best example – then the development of formal, systematic strategic plans (and main-line strategies) may be in order. But when the environment is unstable or the organization needs a creative strategy, then strategic planning may not be the best approach to strategy formulation, and planners have no business pushing the organization to use it.

Second, effective decision making at the policy level requires good analytical input; it is the job of the planner and management scientist to ensure that top management gets it. Managers are very effective at securing soft information; but they tend to underemphasize analytical input that is often important as well. The planners and management scientists can serve their organizations effectively by carrying out ad hoc analyses and feeding the results to top management (need I say verbally?), ensuring that the very best of analysis is brought to bear on policy making. But at the same time, planners need to recognize that these inputs cannot be the only ones used in policy making, that soft information is crucial as well.

For the teacher of managers

If the suggestions in this article turn out to be valid, then educators had better revise drastically some of their notions about management education, because the revolution in that sphere over the last fifteen years – while it has brought so much of use – has virtually consecrated the modern management school to the worship of the left hemisphere.

Should educators be surprised that so many of their graduates end up in staff positions, with no intention of ever managing anything? Some of the best-known management schools have become virtual closed systems in which professors with little interest in the reality of organizational life teach inexperienced students the theories of mathematics, economics, and psychology as ends in themselves. In these management schools, management is accorded little place.

I am not preaching a return to the management school of the 1950s. That age of fuzzy thinking has passed, thankfully. Rather, I am calling for a new balance in our schools, the balance that the best of human brains can achieve, between the analytic and the intuitive. In particular, greater use should be made of the powerful new skill-development techniques which are experiential and creative in nature, such as role playing, the use of videotape, behavior laboratories, and so on. Educators need to put students into situations, whether in the field or in the simulated experience of the laboratory, where they can practice managerial skills, not only interpersonal but also informational and decisional. Then specialists would follow up with feedback on the students' behavior and performance.

For managers

The first conclusion for managers should be a call for caution. The findings of the cognitive psychologists should not be taken as license to shroud activities in darkness. The mystification of conscious behavior is a favorite ploy of those seeking to protect a power base (or to hide their intentions of creating one); this behavior helps no organization, and neither does forcing to the realm of intuition activities that can be handled effectively by analysis.

A major thrust of development in our organizations, ever since Frederick Taylor began experimenting in factories late in the last century, has been to shift activities out of the realm of intuition, toward conscious analysis. That trend will continue. But managers, and those who work with them, need to be careful to distinguish that which is best handled analytically from that which must remain in the realm of intuition, where, in the meantime, we should be looking for the lost keys to management.

Notes

1 Robert Ornstein, *The Psychology of Consciousness* (San Francisco: W.H. Freeman, 1975), p. 60.
2 Ibid., p. 97.
3 These findings are based on (a) my observational study of the work of five chief executives reported in *The Nature of Managerial Work* (New York: Harper and Row, 1973) and in 'The Manager's Job: Folklore and Fact' (*Harvard Business Review* July–August 1975, p. 49); (b) a study of twenty-five strategic decision processes reported in 'The Structure of "Unstructured" Decision Processes,' coauthored with Duru Raisinghani and André Théorêt, *Admi-*

nistrative Science Quarterly 1976, 21, pp. 244–75; and (c) a series of studies carried out under my supervision at McGill University on the formation of organizational strategies over periods of decades, reported in 'Patterns in Strategy Formation,' *International Studies of Management and Organisation*, 1979, 9, 3: 67–86. See also 'Of Strategies, Deliberate and Emergent', *Strategic Management Journal* 6, July/Sept. 1985, pp. 257–72.

4 Clyde T. Hardwick, and Bernard F. Landuyt, *Administrative Strategy and Decision Making*, 2nd ed. (Cincinnati: South Western, 1966).

5 Yehezkel Dror, *Public Policymaking Re-Examined* (Scranton: Chandler, 1968), p. 149.

6 Ornstein (see note 1) p. 10.

8

Decision making and deal making: how creativity helps

Robert Lawrence Kuhn and Louis Kuhn

Executives are consumed by making decisions and making deals. If they're not wrestling with one, they're struggling with the other. It's virtually an executive job description. Managers make decisions constantly – from allocating company resources to apportioning personal time. They also make deals constantly – not only the flashy external kind (e.g., financial transactions) but the quiet internal kind (e.g., personnel shifts). Keeping subordinates and peers working well can demand negotiating skills as creative as those required for complex acquisitions. We seek to understand the process of decision making and deal making and then suggest ways to make each more creative.

Creative decision making

How do executives make large-scale decisions? Though attention in recent years has focused on tools of decision technology – data processing, information analysis, modeling, forecasting, expert systems – the real story is what happens next. How can enormously complex problems, involving competing and interwoven social, cultural, ethical, and personal issues, as well as economic ones, be integrated into coherent wholes? Considering the large numbers of people often involved and the compressed periods of time for finding solutions, the question becomes baffling.

Decision theory

Mechanisms and techniques of decision making are studied by psychologists, economists, mathematicians, and statisticians. The basic concept is a person's 'utility function,' a numerical representation of how individuals rank alternative choices. Decision making can be thought of as 'sequential choice behavior,' the phrase embodying cognitive processes such as encoding, chunking, and hypothesis testing. 'Probabilistic judgment,' or 'intuitive

Adapted from 'Decision making and deal making: how creativity helps', in R.L. Kuhn (ed.), *Handbook for Creative and Innovative Managers* (New York: McGraw-Hill, 1988)

statistics,' drives the personal decision-making process; the process is not, of course, simple arithmetic, considering the complex influence of risk adjustments, biases, and heuristics (nonspecific search and discovery).

Decision making by groups can follow predictable patterns, as emotional and task-related elements assume differential importance at different stages. Emotional elements predominate at the beginning and end of each problem discussed, while task-related elements predominate during the actual discussions themselves. As the group progresses two different kinds of leaders can emerge – one, the 'task leader,' assumes leadership during task-related discussions; and the other, the 'play leader,' takes over during emotional periods. These two leadership roles are quite distinct, are rarely filled by the same person, and can be even antagonistic toward each other.

Computer versus brain

Can computers help? Will they be making more creative decisions? For operational issues, computers are essential: record keeping and database management, minimizing costs of ingredients and inventory levels, maximizing efficiency in component scheduling and travel routes, and so on. Even for the organization and integration of long-range planning, computers are vital. The desk terminal or personal computer has become the new executive status symbol, symbolizing the control of data not money and representing the new wealth of a new world – information. But who wants all that data? Who needs all those numbers? Today's most critical need is not more information but less. We need data reduction techniques, systems of selection and discernment, the intelligent search for meaning. We have enough numbers; what we need is understanding. True creative decisions demand insight and imagination.

One theory associates ordinary thought with medium levels of overall brain activity or arousal and other kinds of consciousness (great mental excitement, ecstasy, meditative states, etc.) with very high or very low levels. Information is processed according to different rules at different levels of activity or arousal so that we are bound to specific states of consciousness as a result of specific states of activity or arousal. This theory associates creativity with an ability to shift or combine diverse levels of brain activity or arousal.

Alfred Adler, the Austrian psychiatrist, hypothesized that dreams are rehearsals or trial solutions to current problems. Common support for this belief comes from introspective observations, especially from writers. Some experimental evidence lends credence. Subjects scored higher on tests of both problem solving and creative thinking after sleep when 'rapid eye movement' (REM) was present than after sleep when REM was absent. REM is always associated with dreaming; but does dreaming actually 'cause' improvement in problem solving and creativity? Strict scientific logic cannot determine whether it was the dreaming per se or the psychophysiological state associated with REM that enhances subsequent problem solving and brings to mind creative new thought combinations that can be put to use the next morning.

Rational versus nonrational

Rational inquiry and nonrational insight should be complements, not antagonists, in seeking solutions to complex problems. Brain research has shown that one side of the cerebral hemisphere, usually the left, is logical and cognitive, while the other side, usually the right, is holistic and affective. The left brain, the one that speaks, dissects the pieces; the right brain, the one that visualizes, synthesizes wholes; the left operates deductively and rigorously, the right by patterns and images. Creative decision making involves the exquisite interweaving of programmable logic and nonprogrammable impression. An executive requires both hemispheres active; he or she must see forest and trees. (Although popular, the brain lateralization model is highly stylized and simplistically stark. In fact, both hemispheres of the brain are actively involved in most mental functions. Nonetheless, the left brain–right brain dichotomy is, at least, a good *metaphor* for representing contrasting modes of the life of the mind.)

Personal opinion and values used to be dismissed. 'Irrelevant' was its kindest appellation. Of course, executive desire could never be avoided. Now we take a different tack. We consider individual want a perfectly respectable input for decision makers. Intuition has come out of the closet. There is new appreciation for the art of conceptualizing decisions amidst the science of analyzing them. A manager's subjective feelings should not be intimidated by objective tests. Executives should not be afraid to contradict the computer. But neither should they leap to arbitrary conclusions with wild abandon.

Procedure for creative decision making

First assess the problem intuitively. One should not call expert advice too quickly or track traditional trains of thought too willingly. Isolation is vital: it allows the psyche minimum constraint and coercion, lessening the likelihood of interference from preset concepts and long-standing lines of logic. On the other hand, wholly intuitive decisions can be dangerous if quantitative input is ignored. Executives should make a nonrational decision – that is, a 'creative' one – only after they clearly understand rational alternatives and logical implications of the 'innovative' choice. Intuition and analysis must be tested against each other repetitively in a recursive process, with each iteration gaining greater confidence. But remember the key: never begin by checking the experts, and always use insight and intuition *before* logic and analysis.

Decision modifiers

What is creative management? More, to be sure, than external analysis and internal intuition. Psychological motivation and political positioning are also involved. 'Stakeholder analysis' is a qualitative technique that segregates out relevant parties and projects personal attitudes of each. What's everyone's driving motivation, his or her 'stake' in the matter? Crucial here is an assessment of individual feelings and hidden agendas. What's the private bottom line? Potential political standing and perceived career paths are often lurking beneath the surface and must be considered in all creative management decisions.

Are most executive decisions made rationally? If Yes, that's not necessarily good; if No, that's not necessarily bad. Decisions are made by people, and people are constrained by company traditions and manipulated by political bargaining. The inertia of functional departments to do things the way they have always done them, according to standard operating procedures, is a potent regulating mechanism, just as the influence of powerful personalities is a reality of the corporate hierarchy (Allison 1971). The pervasive strength and profound pressure of long-set bureaucracies – formal staffs, assists to's, budget directors – is more a focus of serious study than the butt of sarcastic humor. 'Networking' a company – discovering channels through which influence flows – often shocks top management. How real power patterns are structured can differ markedly from official organization charts. (Watch the executive secretary!)

Decision settings

Making creative decisions must take into account the nature of the organization. How to 'cut a company' is essential for understanding the creativity-generating process and making the innovation ring right. Numerous dimensions are involved. Decision making, especially when strategic, is a function of social structure and corporate culture. Is the sector profit-making or not for profit? The organization large or small? The product original or repetitive? The level of managerial decision top or middle? The personalities assertive or passive? The procedure individual or collective? For example, in a high-technology company, how should the chief operating officer direct the key research scientist? In a charitable foundation, what dollar value should be placed on subsidized concerts for poor children? In a manufacturing firm, what level of losses can be sustained before a division is dispatched? In the media, should a magazine publisher stop his or her editor from printing a story critical of a top advertiser? Each of these creative decisions, while similar in superficial form, differs in fundamental substance. The scientist is a creative sort, perhaps not receptive to close supervision. The artistic enrichment of the poor children defies quantification. The manufacturing division may become a vital resource in future years. The magazine may not exist without editorial freedom.

Compromise, said to be golden, is sometimes a weak manager's failure to choose between contradictory positions or people. As such, the 'in-between' solution can be worse than either of the extremes – and be no solution at all. To allocate to each of two competing projects half the money requested dooms both parties together, encouraging interaction and establishing conditions for innovation. The dialectic of dissent, carefully controlled, is a marvellous antidote for the poison of group-think.

Models can be used as classification frameworks, as long as one doesn't take them too seriously. For example, consider 'information required' and 'dimensions of thinking.' If decision makers use low information and think in only one dimension, they are decisive and independent, 'dictators.' If they use high information and think in one dimension, they're analytic and rigorous, 'computer programs.' If they use low information and think in many dimensions, they're flexible and fleeting, 'scatterbrains.' If they use high information and think in many dimensions, they're transformational and synthetic, 'alchemists.' (The integrated attitudes of the last type would seem to make the most effective executive under normal circumstances – although a company nearing bankruptcy might need a dictator, a mutual fund might want a computer program, and an advertising agency might fancy a scatterbrain.)

Creative versus strategic

Creative management decisions begin novel in character, vague in structure, open-ended in process, and ambiguous in context. Complex decisions in unfamiliar areas must be factored into simpler subdivisions in familiar areas. Only then can strategic routines and procedures be applied: problem recognition, diagnosis, solution search, alternative generation, alternative analysis, preliminary screening, serious evaluation, final choice, authorization, feedback, and review. The critical test of strategic management is *internal consistency*. Does the overall plan make sense? Does it resonate well with all issues and areas? Is, for example, the decision to launch a new product consistent with all functional departments: are production ready to make it, marketing ready to sell it, financing ready to pay for it? (How often do ever-eager sales forces promise delivery before plants can produce the stuff!)

One often associates 'creativity' with the arts and 'innovation' with science and technology. While wholly appropriate in these contexts, creative and innovative management attains its potential as a *strategy*-making mechanism even more than a decision-making one. Thus a difference emerges between strategy making and decision making, the former subsuming larger scope and complexity. More than traditional tradeoffs between 'optimizing' and 'satisficing' reside here. Corporate power and prosperity are the chips being bet. Creative and innovative management, desirable for decision making, becomes essential for strategy making.

Creative deal making

Business has but two parts, managing people and making deals. Deal making should be a means not an end, a mechanism to achieve goals not a showcase for advancing ego. All participants should be satisfied on signing, committed during execution, pleased on reflection. Solution sets optimizing nonconflicting objectives are always present and should be sought. Good deals enhance reputations of all deal makers.

Getting the edge

The popular press harangues us with predatory propaganda. If you're not a 'gamesperson,' you're a pushover; if you don't 'win through intimidation,' you're a pansy; if you don't 'look out for Number One,' you're a fool. Beating your customer, squeezing your supplier, pinning your partner – all too often these become goals. Too many business people pride themselves on besting their buddies; they must twist an advantage to enjoy success; they must feel the turn of the screw. You know the type. A fair price is never fair. Grinding never stops. Agreements are made to be broken. Power plays are always made. A done deal is altered on signing. Simple meaning is perverted by arcane language. Some like to bully, others prefer to hoodwink – the former want to see you squirm, the latter relish the painless kill. Priorities are inverted, objectives pulled inside out. An edge-getter is often vain, more turned on by clever kill than by extra meat. What counts is not the spending power of bigger payoffs but the puffing power of smoother strokes. It's the edge itself that's sought, not necessarily the amount.

But crafty deal makers fool themselves more often than opponents. Distorted egos make sure deals less sure, closed deals not closed. Playing the ego game is fugitive and short-sighted. Today's quick buck chokes off a thousand tomorrow. Streams of dollars that could flow in the future are never seen. The irony is that what is not seen is not known; no negative reinforcement ever occurs, no long-term consequences in short-term actions are ever appreciated. The edge-getting deal makers strut blithely on their pompous ways, smug that they've played the perfect games, won through intimidation, and looked after Number One – whereas, in reality, they have lost the game, flubbed the deal, and flattened Number One. What happens here happens often: new problems erupt, commitment drifts, time is lost, deals rupture, relationships tear, reputations ruin – all silly sacrifices on the altar of oneupmanship. Building the business takes a back seat when personal ego does the driving.

The good deal

Being a sharp business person means being a shrewd deal maker, someone who formulates, structures, and implements transactions and arrangements with skill and finesse, someone who plans, organizes, and executes the interchange of products, services, and monetary considerations. Such an animal, it is assumed, lives by wit and scheme, claw and fang, with only raw cunning providing cover. Yet the best business people live by reputation, the evidence of track record, and the image of integrity.

A good deal, of course, does not require each party to play an equal role or even to make money. Natural power is distributed according to pre-

existing patterns. For example, a liquidator may buy end-of-season mer-
chandise below cost; but although manufacturers lose money on these
particular lots, they convert unsalable inventory to cash, and if their overall
costs have been covered, the transactions, in a real sense, produce pure
profit.

Stages of deal making

Creative deal making involves understanding critical issues at each stage of
the process. Deal making can be dissected into sequential stages, and
although boundaries between them may be fuzzy, critical issues are usually
clear.

Deciding.   Too many people forget preliminaries and lose the ball game
before it begins. Determining *whether* and *what* to deal often controls more
of the outcome than all strategy and tactics. What are your long-term goals
and short-term objectives here? Verbalizing the 'obvious' often reveals it
wasn't so obvious.

Preparing.   Doing all your homework is essential. Complete, relevant
information should be generated early on – and then boiled down before
actual negotiations begin. Discern superficial stances and underlying
necessities. Get your hands on all numbers, public statements and reports,
private opinions, and interests. Treat both sides alike: do self-analysis from
your opponent's point of view.

Initiating.   Postures and positions are established up front. Power plays of
office venue, seating arrangements, first proposals, and immediate deadline
setting are all well-known. But such subliminal irritations are more disrup-
tive than useful. Effective deal makers establish people rapport at the
outset, trying to discern bottom-line needs of opponents. Often such needs
are not incompatible and win–win solution sets can be found.

Continuing.   Persistence and patience are assets in any deal-making situation. Progress will never be linear so don't expect smooth rides. Ratcheting
forward – two steps ahead, one step back, even one step sideways – is
terrific. Be satisfied to continue the process even if the direction appears
temporarily wrong. Overcoming frustration is important, impasses may be
surmounted by retreating to first principles. Why are we here? Sticking
points are almost always the result of artificial hindrances (e.g., face saving)
not fundamental fact barriers. Novelty is an effective win–win tactic; try
generating fresh sets of alternatives to overcome inertia, even in the middle
of protracted negotiations.

Concluding.   Have the sense to finalize when finished. Nothing is more
creative than to know when the deal is done. Many deals have broken down

after having been made because one side continued to press for advantage, which is invariably more psychological than substantive. Having an attitude of genuine pleasure at seeing your opponent achieve goals and fulfill needs is a marvellous test for the creative deal maker.

Deal-making strategies

The following principles produce good deals but not necessarily self-importance. They are creative in that they work, making the deal and enhancing the deal-maker's image.

1. *Show quiet self-confidence.* Personal faith is perhaps the most vital trait for deal makers. But self-confidence that is effective is self-confidence that is understated. Show your surety with unruffled composure. Fortitude and tenacity do not exude conceit and presumptuousness. Be circumspect and very careful: pomposity and arrogance are powerful turnoffs. Boasters and blowhards alienate more than they influence. Chips on shoulders cut opponents and splinter deals. Antagonizing the other side is a definite downer.

2. *Know what you want; don't worry what others get.* It's self-defeating to judge by comparison. Jealousy and envy are diversions and become obstacles to successful business. With proper preparation and self-confidence, a deal maker can segregate needs and wants from what others ask and get. For instance, if you sell your company with fair price and terms, you should have no gripe if the buyer makes more money over time.

3. *Understand the other side.* Project yourself into the place of those with whom you are dealing. What are their real requirements? Hopes? Plans? What are they looking for now, bottom line, and how important is it? Often, giving others what they want will not detract from what you get. If, say, the owner of a closely held firm wants to sell in order to retire or for estate-planning purposes, price can become secondary to terms and conditions. Such a person might well sell his or her business – his or her beloved baby – to a buyer offering a lower price if he or she believes that these new managers will take better care of his or her legacy (employees, products, reputation, customers, etc.)

4. *Seek win–win solutions.* Search for areas in which each side can achieve certain of its goals, desirably primary ones, without adversely affecting the other. These optimal regions of win–win intersection can be surprisingly broad if one has insight to seek them and perception to recognize them. When one structures deals with imagination and intelligence, win–win solutions emerge. For example, the purchase price of an acquisition often can be allocated so that a greater percentage of the proceeds are taxed at better rates for the seller without altering cash requirements from the buyer; or similarly, parts of the purchase price can be deferred to a time of lower tax bite. (The buyer can in fact pay less, and the seller can in fact receive more!)

5. *Be comprehensive in representation and conservative in projection.* Hype sometimes helps sell a first deal but never a second. If all you have is one deal to do, have at it. But if you plan a career not a caper, give heed. Hype always hinders subsequent deals. Exaggeration is a short-term, rapidly depleting asset – and a long-term, quickly accruing liability. Don't be afraid to admit uncertainty about parts of your package – nothing can be that 'perfect' and that 'precise' – honesty enhances credibility and such admissions can be most disarming. Develop alternative scenarios: allow the other side choices; give room and keep options open. Use sensitivity analysis to show what might happen 'if' various internal surprises or external shocks have an impact on the proposed transaction (such as sales up or down 10%, 20%, 30%; gross-margin problems; escalating interest rates). Make a conservative forecast of your most likely result; strive to exceed a somewhat pessimistic projection rather than fall behind a more optimistic one. Also, use sensitivity analysis to test the other side's options. Are they really at the breakpoint, or can they move a bit further?

6. *Answer questions nobody asked.* Nothing makes more impact than one side bringing up sensitive subjects about its own proposals that the other side never considered. For example, in negotiating bank financing a company should enumerate all assumptions, pointing precisely to areas of difficulty or ambiguity. The honesty shown will cause credibility to soar. Potential problems should be exposed by design, not hidden by default.

7. *Be fair but be frank.* Do not seek the upper hand – but do not play doormat either. Let others realize that you know game, rules, and players. Being fair does not mean being weak. (Weakness, in fact, encourages disruption by tempting the other side to expand its position.) Some of the toughest deal makers are also some of the fairest. If you decide to do business with certain suppliers even though their *prices* are not the lowest, be sure they know that you know the score.

8. *Act as if the other side will become your public relations agents.* Act this way because they *will*. No matter how confidential the negotiations, no matter how secret the deal, other people will hear about it. Word of your deeds and conduct will reach important ears. Regardless of how you envision yourself, what circulates is how others see you. Above all, never boast about besting. Reputation is the deal maker's most valuable asset. Protect it.

Bibliography

Allison, Graham T.: *Essence of Decision: Explaining the Cuban Missile Crisis.* Little Brown, Boston, 1971.
Kuhn, Robert Lawrence: 'Creative and Innovative Management – A Challenge to Academia,' in A. Charnes and W.W. Cooper (eds.), *Creative and Innovative Management: Essays in Honor of George Kozmetsky,* Ballinger, Cambridge, 1984.
'Negotiating,' in Lester R. Bittel and Jackson Ramsey (eds.), *Handbook for Professional Managers,* McGraw-Hill, New York, 1985.

9

Paradigms, metaphors, and puzzle solving in organization theory

Gareth Morgan

For the son of a peasant who has grown up within the narrow confines of his village and spends his whole life in the place of his birth, the mode of thinking and speaking characteristic of that village is something that he takes entirely for granted. But for the country lad who goes to the city and adapts himself gradually to city life, the rural mode of living and thinking ceases to be something to be taken-for-granted. He has won a certain detachment from it, and he distinguishes now, perhaps quite consciously, between 'rural' and 'urban' modes of thought and ideas. . . . That which within a given group is accepted as absolute appears to the outsider conditioned by the group situation and recognized as partial (in this case, as 'rural'). This type of knowledge presupposes a more detached perspective. (Mannheim, 1936)

Mannheim uses this example of the urbanization of a peasant boy as a means of illustrating how ways of thinking about the world are mediated by social milieu, and how the acquisition of new ways of thinking depends upon a departure from the old world view. Organization theorists, like scientists from other disciplines, often approach their subject from a frame of reference based upon assumptions that are taken-for-granted. To the extent that these assumptions are continually affirmed and reinforced by fellow scientists, and others with whom the organization theorist interacts, they may remain not only unquestioned, but also beyond conscious awareness. In this way the orthodox world view may come to assume a status as real, routine, and taken-for-granted as the world view of Mannheim's peasant boy who stayed at home. The partial and self-sustaining nature of the orthodoxy only becomes apparent to the extent that the theorist exposes basic assumptions to the challenge of alternative ways of seeing and begins to appreciate these alternatives in their own terms.

Paradigms, metaphors, and puzzle solving

In order to understand the nature of orthodoxy in organization theory, it is necessary to understand the relationship between specific modes of theorizing and research and the world views that they reflect. It is useful to start with

Adapted from *Administrative Science Quarterly*, 25, 4 (1980), pp. 605–22 the concept of paradigm made popular by Kuhn (1962). Kuhn himself used the paradigm concept in three broad senses: (1) as a complete view of reality, or way of seeing; (2) as relating to the social organization of science in terms of schools of thought connected with particular kinds of scientific achievements; and (3) as relating to the concrete use of specific kinds of tools and texts for the process of scientific puzzle solving (Figure 1).

Probably one of the most important implications of Kuhn's work stems from the identification of paradigms as alternative realities. The term 'paradigm' is therefore used here in its metatheoretical or philosophical sense to denote an implicit or explicit view of reality. Any adequate analysis of the role of paradigms in social theory must uncover the core assumptions that

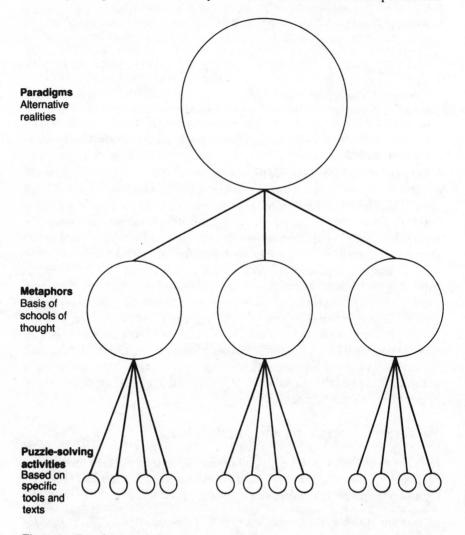

Paradigms
Alternative
realities

Metaphors
Basis of
schools of
thought

**Puzzle-solving
activities**
Based on
specific
tools and
texts

Figure 1   *Paradigms, metaphors, and puzzle solving: three concepts for understanding the nature and organization of social science*

characterize and define any given world view, to make it possible to grasp what is common to the perspectives of theorists whose work may otherwise, at a more superficial level, appear diverse and wide ranging.

Any metatheoretical paradigm or world view may include different schools of thought, which are often different ways of approaching and studying a shared reality or world view (the metaphor level of Figure 1). It will be argued in this article that schools of thought in social science, those communities of theorists subscribing to relatively coherent perspectives, are based upon the acceptance and use of different kinds of metaphor as a foundation for inquiry.

At the puzzle-solving level of analysis (Figure 1) it is possible to identify many kinds of research activities which seek to operationalize the detailed implications of the metaphor defining a particular school of thought. At this level of detailed analysis, many specific texts, models, and research tools vie for the attention of theorists, and much of the research and debate in the social sciences is focused at this level. This comprises what Kuhn (1962) has described as 'normal science.' In organization theory, for example, Thompson's (1967) book, *Organizations in Action*, has come to serve as a model statement and principal point of departure for theorists interested in contingency theory, which develops insights generated by the organismic metaphor (Burrell and Morgan, 1979). The numerous propositions offered in Thompson's book have generated a great deal of puzzle-solving research, in which the metaphorical assumptions underlying Thompson's model are taken-for-granted as a way of understanding organizations.

By appreciating how specific puzzle-solving activities are linked to favored metaphors, which are in accord with a favored view of reality, the theorist can become much more aware of the role which he or she plays in relation to the social construction of scientific knowledge. As in the case of Mannheim's 'urbanized' peasant boy, a cosmopolitan outlook in theorizing depends upon the theorist leaving, at some stage, the community of practitioners with whom he or she may feel at home, to appreciate the realms of theorizing defined by other paradigms, and the varieties of metaphors and methods through which theory and research can be conducted.

Paradigms as alternative realities

The role of paradigms as views of social reality was recently explored in detail by Burrell and Morgan (1979), who argued that social theory in general, and organization theory in particular, could be usefully analyzed in terms of four broad world views, which were reflected in different sets of metatheoretical assumptions, about the nature of science, the subjective–objective dimension, and the nature of society, the dimension of regulation–radical change (Figure 2). Each of these four paradigms – functionalist, interpretive, radical humanist, and radical structuralist – reflects a network of related schools of thought, differentiated in approach and perspective,

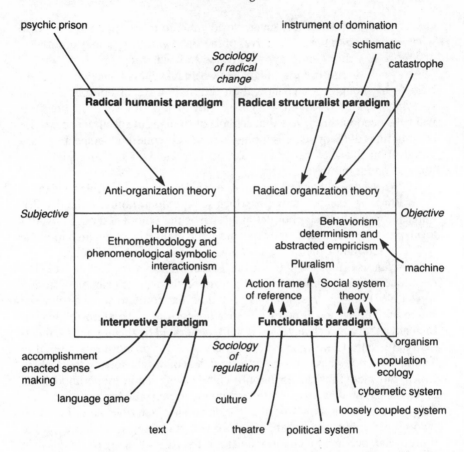

Figure 2   *Paradigms, metaphors, and related schools of organizational analysis*

but sharing common fundamental assumptions about the nature of the reality that they address.

The *functionalist* paradigm is based upon the assumption that society has a concrete, real existence, and a systemic character oriented to produce an ordered and regulated state of affairs. It encourages an approach to social theory that focuses upon understanding the role of human beings in society. Behavior is always seen as being contextually bound in a real world of concrete and tangible social relationships. The ontological assumptions encourage a belief in the possibility of an objective and value-free social science in which the scientist is distanced from the scene which he or she is analyzing through the rigor and technique of the scientific method. The functionalist perspective is primarily regulative and pragmatic in its basic orientation, concerned with understanding society in a way which generates useful empirical knowledge.

The *interpretive* paradigm, on the other hand, is based upon the view that the social world has a very precarious ontological status, and that what passes as social reality does not exist in any concrete sense, but is the product of the subjective and inter-subjective experience of individuals. Society is understood from the standpoint of the participant in action rather than the observer. The interpretive social theorist attempts to understand the process through which shared multiple realities arise, are sustained, and are changed. Like the functionalist, the interpretive approach is based on the assumption and belief that there is an underlying pattern and order within the social world: however, the interpretive theorist views the functionalist's attempt to establish an objective social science as an unattainable end. Science is viewed as a network of language games, based upon sets of subjectively determined concepts and rules, which the practitioners of science invent and follow. The status of scientific knowledge is therefore seen as being as problematic as the common sense knowledge of everyday life.

The *radical humanist* paradigm, like the interpretive paradigm, emphasizes how reality is socially created and socially sustained but ties the analysis to an interest in what may be described as the pathology of consciousness, by which human beings become imprisoned within the bounds of the reality that they create and sustain. This perspective is based on the view that the process of reality creation may be influenced by psychic and social processes which channel, constrain, and control the minds of human beings, in ways which alienate them from the potentialities inherent in their true nature as humans. The contemporary radical humanist critique focuses upon the alienating aspects of various modes of thought and action which characterize life in industrial societies. Capitalism, for example, is viewed as essentially totalitarian, the idea of capital accumulation molding the nature of work, technology, rationality, logic, science, roles, language and mystifying ideological concepts such as scarcity, leisure, and so on. These concepts, which the functionalist theorist may regard as the building blocks of social order and human freedom stand, for the radical humanist, as modes of ideological domination. The radical humanist is concerned with discovering how humans can link thought and action (praxis) as a means of transcending their alienation.

The reality defined by the *radical structuralist* paradigm, like that of the radical humanist, is predicated upon a view of society as a potentially dominating force. However, it is tied to a materialist conception of the social world, which is defined by hard, concrete, ontologically real structures. Reality is seen as existing on its own account independently of the way in which it is perceived and reaffirmed by people in everyday activities. This reality is viewed as being characterized by intrinsic tensions and contradictions between opposing elements, which inevitably lead to radical change in the system as a whole. The radical structuralist is concerned with understanding these intrinsic tensions, and the way in which those with power in society seek to hold them in check through various modes of domination. Emphasis is placed upon the importance of praxis as a means of transcending this domination.

Each of these four paradigms defines the grounds of opposing modes of social analysis and has radically different implications for the study of organizations.

Epistemological status of metaphor

Human beings are constantly attempting to develop conceptions about the world, and as Cassirer (1946, 1955) and others have argued, they do so symbolically, attempting to make the world concrete by giving it form. Through language, science, art, and myth, for example, humans structure their world in meaningful ways. These attempts to objectify a reality embody subjective intentions in the meanings which underwrite the symbolic constructs which are used. Knowledge and understanding of the world are not given to human beings by external events; humans attempt to objectify the world through means of essentially subjective processes. As Cassirer has emphasized, all modes of symbolic understanding possess this quality. Words, names, concepts, ideas, facts, observations, etc., do not so much denote external 'things,' as conceptions of things activated in the mind by a selective and meaningful form of noticing the world, which may be shared with others. They are not to be seen as a representation of a reality 'out there,' but as tools for capturing and dealing with what is perceived to be 'out there.' The scientist on this score, like others in everyday life, draws upon symbolic constructs to make concrete the relationships between subjective and objective worlds, in a process which captures only a pale and abbreviated view of either. For science, like other modes of symbolic activity, is built upon the use of imperfect epistemological tools, harboring what Cassirer (1946) described as the 'curse of mediacy,' and providing what Whitehead (1925) described as 'useful fictions' for dealing with the world.

In understanding the way in which scientific theory is constructed as a symbolic form, it is important to give attention to the role of metaphor. For the process of metaphorical conception is a basic mode of symbolism, central to the way in which humans forge their experience and knowledge of the world in which they live. Metaphor is often regarded as no more than a literary and descriptive device for embellishment, but more fundamentally is a creative form which produces its effect through a crossing of images. Metaphor proceeds through assertions that subject A is, or is like, B, the processes of comparison, substitution, and interaction between the images of A and B acting as generators of new meaning (Black, 1962).

The research work of different theorists contributes to a view of scientific inquiry as a creative process in which scientists view the world metaphorically, through the language and concepts which filter and structure their perceptions of their subject of study and through the specific metaphors which they implicitly or explicitly choose to develop their framework for analysis. Attention in this article is focused upon the latter use of metaphor, with a view to showing how schools of thought in organization theory are based upon the insights associated with different metaphors for the study of organizations, and how the logic of metaphor has important implications for the process of theory construction.

The use of a metaphor serves to generate an image for studying a subject. This image can provide the basis for detailed scientific research based upon attempts to discover the extent to which features of the metaphor are found in the subject of inquiry. Much of the puzzle-solving activity of normal science is of this kind, with scientists attempting to examine, operationalize, and measure detailed implications of the metaphorical insight upon which their research is implicitly or explicitly based. Such confinement of attention calls for a great deal of prior and somewhat irrational commitment to the image of the subject of investigation, for any one metaphorical insight provides but a partial and one-sided view of the phenomenon to which it is applied.

The creative potential of metaphor depends upon there being a degree of difference between the subjects involved in the metaphorical process. For example, a boxer may be described as 'a tiger in the ring.' In choosing the term 'tiger' we conjure up specific impressions of a fierce animal moving at times with grace, stealth, power, strength, and speed in aggressive acts directed at its prey. By implication, the metaphor suggests that the boxer possesses these qualities in fighting his opponent. The use of this metaphor requires that the tiger's orange and black striped fur, four legs, claws, fangs, and deafening roar be ignored in favor of an emphasis upon the characteristics that boxer and tiger have in common. Metaphor is thus based upon but partial truth; it requires of its user a somewhat one-sided abstraction in which certain features are emphasized and others suppressed in a selective comparison. Figure 3 illustrates the crucial significance of difference in a metaphor. If the two subjects brought together are perceived to be completely unalike, e.g., boxer and saucepan (Figure 3a), or are seen as almost identical, e.g., boxer and man (Figure 3c), the metaphorical process produces either nonsensical or weak imagery. The most powerful use of metaphor arises in instances typified in Figure 3b, in which the differences between the two phenomena are perceived to be significant but not total. Effective metaphor is a form of creative expression which relies upon constructive falsehood as a means of liberating the imagination.

The logic of metaphor thus has important implications for organization theory, for it suggests that no one metaphor can capture the total nature of organizational life. A conscious and wide-ranging theoretical pluralism rather than an attempt to forge a synthesis upon narrow grounds emerges as an appropriate aim. Different metaphors can constitute and capture the nature of organizational life in different ways, each generating powerful, distinctive, but essentially partial kinds of insight. The logic here suggests that new metaphors may be used to create new ways of viewing organizations which overcome the weaknesses and blindspots of traditional metaphors, offering supplementary or even contradictory approaches to organizational analysis.

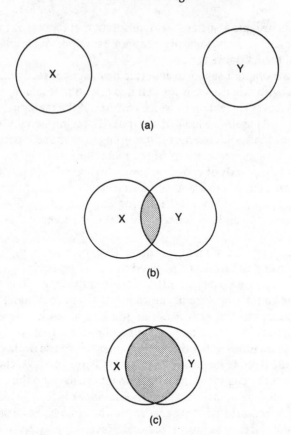

Figure 3   *The role of difference in metaphor*

To acknowledge that organization theory is metaphorical is to acknowledge that it is an essentially subjective enterprise, concerned with the
production of one-sided analyses of organizational life. This has important
consequences, for it encourages a spirit of critical inquiry and cautions
against excessive commitment to favored points of view. Traditional
approaches to organizational analysis are often based upon a few well-tried
concepts and methods, which are regarded as axiomatic insofar as an
understanding of organization is concerned. In such situations the metaphorical nature of the image which generated such concepts is lost from
view, and the process of organizational analysis becomes over-concretized
as theorists and researchers treat the concepts as a description of reality. To
return to the illustration presented earlier, the boxer is treated as a tiger, and
'tigerness' provides the focus of detailed theory and research, often to the
exclusion of all else. Such a perspective results in a premature closure in both
thought and inquiry. Schools of theorists committed to particular
approaches and concepts often view alternative perspectives as misguided,
or as presenting threats to the nature of their basic endeavor. The
approaches, techniques, concepts and findings which these alternative

perspectives generate are often interpreted and evaluated in inappropriate ways, with great loss of significant meaning. Misunderstanding, hostility, or calculated indifference often tends to follow, with the result that open and constructive debate becomes difficult or impossible. An awareness of the metaphorical nature of theory may help to break down the false and restricting compartmentalization of inquiry and understanding which characterizes the conduct of modern organization theory. In order to understand any organizational phenomenon many different metaphorical insights may need to be brought into play.

Metaphor in organization theory

The orthodox view in organization theory has been based predominantly on the metaphors of machine and organism. The metaphor of a machine underwrites the work of the classical management theorists (Taylor, 1911; Fayol, 1949) and Weber's specification of bureaucracy as an ideal type (Weber, 1946). Although the conceptions underlying the work of these very different theorists were intended to serve different ends, that is, the improvement of efficiency in classical management theory, and our understanding of society in Weber's theory, the two lines of thought have fused to provide the foundations of modern organization theory. And the mechanical imagery is very clear. Machines are rationally devised for performing work in pursuit of prespecified ends; the machine metaphor in organization theory expresses these ends as goals and the means–ends relationship as purposive rationality. Indeed, machine models of organization have been variously described in the literature on organization theory as 'rationality models' (Gouldner, 1959; Thompson, 1967) and 'goal models' (Georgiou, 1973; Etzioni, 1960). The details of these machine models are drawn from mechanical concepts. They attribute principal importance, for example, to the concepts of structure and technology in the definition of organizational characteristics. Machines are technological entities in which the relationship between constituent elements forms a structure. In classical and bureaucratic organization theory the principal emphasis is placed upon the analysis and design of the formal structure of an organization and its technology. Indeed, these theories essentially constitute blueprints for such design; they seek to design organizations as if they were machines, and the human beings expected to work within such mechanical structures are to be valued for their instrumental abilities. Taylor's conception of economic man and Weber's concept of the faceless bureaucrat extend the principles of the machine metaphor to define the view of human nature which best suits the organizational machine. Furthermore, the operation of the whole bureaucratic enterprise is judged in terms of its efficiency, another concept deriving from the mechanical conception of an organization as an instrument for achieving predetermined ends.

The other major metaphor in organization theory is that of the organism.

The term 'organism' has come to be used to refer to any system of mutually connected and dependent parts constituted to share a common life and focuses attention upon the nature of life activity. An organism is typically seen as a combination of elements, differentiated yet integrated, attempting to survive within the context of a wider environment (Spencer, 1873, 1876–1896). The links between this metaphor of an organism and much contemporary organization theory are strong and clear. The main emphasis of the open-systems approach, for example, is the close interactive relationship between organization and environment and how the continued life or survival of an organization is dependent upon an appropriate relationship being achieved. Emphasis is also placed upon the idea that the organization has needs or imperative functions, which must be satisfied for the organization to achieve this relationship with the environment. The Hawthorne studies (Roethlisberger and Dickson, 1939), the structural functionalist theories of Selznick (1948) and Parsons (1951, 1956), the sociotechnical systems approach (Trist and Bamforth, 1951), the general systems approach (Katz and Kahn, 1966), and much modern contingency theory (Burns and Stalker, 1961; Lawrence and Lorsch, 1967) are all based upon the development of the organismic metaphor. Whereas in the machine metaphor the concept of organization is as a closed and somewhat static structure, in the organismic metaphor the concept of organization is as a living entity in constant flux and change, interacting with its environment in an attempt to satisfy its needs. The relationship between organization and environment has stressed that certain kinds of organizations are better able to survive in some environments than others. The focus upon needs and imperative functions had allowed theorists to identify essential life-sustaining activities. The imperative of satisfying the psychological needs of organizational members (Trist and Bamforth, 1951; Argyris, 1952, 1957), and of adopting appropriate managerial styles (McGregor, 1960; Likert, 1967), technology (Woodward, 1965), modes of differentiation, integration and conflict resolution (Lawrence and Lorsch, 1967), and modes of strategic choice and control (Child, 1972; Miles and Snow, 1978), have all been incorporated into contemporary contingency theory, which, in essence, carries the implications of the organismic metaphor to their logical conclusion. For organizations are viewed from this perspective not only in terms of the network of relationships that characterize the internal structure or organisms, but also in terms of the relationships which exist between the organization (organism) and its environment.

The distinction between machine and organism has been the basis for a continuum of organizational forms (Burns and Stalker, 1961), and has influenced many attempts to measure organizational characteristics. Research on organizations since the late 1960s, for example, has been dominated by attempts to conduct detailed empirical studies of various aspects of the contingency approach. Although these studies have generated numerous detailed insights, which inform our understanding of organizations as machines and organisms, it is important to appreciate that the kind of insight generated is limited by the metaphors upon which they are based. In recent years organizational theorists have come to recognize this, and realized that viewing organizations on the basis of new metaphors makes it possible to understand them in new ways. Viewing organizations systematically as cybernetic systems, loosely coupled systems, ecological systems, theatres, cultures, political systems, language games, texts, accomplishments, enactments, psychic prisons, instruments of domination, schismatic systems, catastrophes, etc., it is possible to add rich and creative dimensions to organization theory.

The cybernetic metaphor encourages theorists to view organizations as patterns of information, and focuses attention upon the way in which states of homeostatic balance can be sustained through learning processes based on negative feedback. Some theorists have begun to explore the implications of this metaphor for organization and management (Buckley, 1967; Hage, 1974; Argyris and Schön, 1978), and cybernetics has been widely used as a technique for improving organizational control systems (Lawler and Rhode, 1976). The metaphor of a loosely coupled system, introduced to organization theory by Weick (1974, 1976), specifically attempts to counter the assumptions implicit in mechanical and organismic metaphors that organizations are tidy, efficient, and well-coordinated systems. The population–ecology metaphor (Hannan and Freeman, 1977) emphasizes the importance of focusing upon competition and selection in populations or organizations, instead of organization–environment adaption. The metaphor of theatre focuses upon how organizational members are essentially human actors, engaging in various roles and other official and unofficial performances (Goffman, 1959, 1961). The culture metaphor draws attention to the symbolic aspects or organizational life, and the way in which language, rituals, stories, myths, etc., embody networks of subjective meaning which are crucial for understanding how organizational realities are created and sustained (Turner, 1971; Pondy and Mitroff, 1979). The metaphor of a political system focuses attention upon the conflicts of interest and role of power in organizations (Crozier, 1964; Pettigrew, 1973; Pfeffer and Salancik, 1978).

These metaphors create means of seeing organizations and their functioning in ways which elude the traditional mechanical and organismic metaphors. Yet they can all be used in a functionalist manner, generating modes of theorizing based upon the assumption that the reality of organizational life rests in a network of ontologically real relationships, which are relatively ordered and cohesive. As a result, they may simply develop different approaches toward study of a common paradigm. The cybernetic, loosely-coupled system, and population–ecology metaphors all have their roots in the natural sciences, and all in one way or another emphasize the idea that organizations can be seen as adaptive systems. Negative feedback, loose coupling, and natural selection are the three different kinds of adaptive mechanisms highlighted by these different metaphors. Each of the theatre, culture, and political system metaphors introduces an explicitly social dimension to the study of organizations, and gives particular attention to the way in which human beings may attempt to shape organizational activities. Insofar as the dramaturgical, cultural, and political activities involved here are seen as occurring within a contextually defined and hence ontologically real setting, and viewed as a form of adaptive activity, these metaphors also develop a functionalist approach to the study of organizations. They attempt to capture and articulate aspects of an underlying view of reality but from different angles and in different ways.

Interpretive metaphors question the grounds upon which functionalist theory is built, focusing upon the way in which organizational realities are created and sustained. The metaphor of a language game (Wittgenstein, 1968), for example, denies organizations concrete ontological status and presents organizational activity as little more than a game of words, thoughts, and actions. It suggests that organizational realities emerge as rule-governed symbolic structures as individuals engage their worlds through the use of specific codes and practices, in order to vest their situations with meaningful form. Organizational realities from this point of view rest in the use of different kinds of verbal and nonverbal language. Language is not simply communicational and descriptive; it is ontological. Thus being a manager in an organization involves a particular way of being in the world, defined by the language game which a person has to play to be recognized and function as a manager. The organizational concepts which give form to notions of rationality, bureaucratic structure, delegation, control, etc., are managerial concepts (Bittner, 1965), which label and realize a world in which managers can act as managers. In a similar way, the concept and detailed language of leadership creates and defines the nature of leadership as an ongoing process (Pondy, 1978). Viewed in terms of the language game metaphor, organizations are created and sustained as patterns of social activity through the use of language; they constitute no more than a special form of discourse.

The metaphor of text (Ricoeur, 1971) suggests that the organization theorist should view organizational activity as a symbolic document, and employ hermeneutic methods of analysis as a means of unravelling its nature and significance. Texts give form to particular kinds of language games, explicate themes, and make use of metaphorical expressions to convey significant patterns of meaning. Once authored, the text is available for interpretation and translation by others, who may vest it with significance and meaning other than that intended by the author. All these qualities are evident in day-to-day organizational life where everyone is both author and reader, though some more significantly so than others. The organization theorist adopting the metaphor of text is concerned with understanding the manner in which organizational activities are authored, read, and translated, the way in which the structure of discourse may explore certain key themes and develop particular kinds of imagery. The metaphor can be utilized for the analysis of organizational documents (Huff, 1979), and organizational talk and action (Manning, 1979).

The metaphors of accomplishment (Garfinkel, 1967) and enacted sense making (Weick, 1977) provide two further interpretive approaches to the study of organization. Garfinkel's ethnomethodology focuses upon the way in which human beings accomplish and sustain social situations intelligible both to themselves and to others. Weick's sense making metaphor develops related insights, emphasizing how realities are enacted by individuals through after-the-event rationalizations as to what has been happening. Viewed in terms of these metaphors, organizational realities are to be seen as ongoing social constructions, emerging from the skillful accomplishments through which organizational members impose themselves upon their world to create meaningful and sensible structure. Like other interpretive metaphors, they emphasize that the routine, taken-for-granted aspects of organizational life are far less concrete and real than they appear.

When organizations are approached from the perspectives of the radical humanist paradigm, all the concepts and modes of symbolic action that sustain organizational life are scrutinized for their alienating properties. The guiding metaphor here is that of the psychic prison, an image which focuses upon the way human beings may be led to enact organizational realities experienced as confining and dominating. This metaphor is evident in a number of strands of social thought. In the critical theory stemming from the work of Marx (1844) and Lukács (1971), the emphasis is placed upon the process of reification through which individuals over-concretize their world, perceiving it as objective and real, and something independent of their own will and action. As developed in the work of the so-called Frankfurt School (Marcuse, 1955, 1964; Habermas, 1970, 1972), principal emphasis is placed upon how ideological modes of domination may be manipulated by those with power in pursuit of their own ends. Organizational members are effectively viewed as prisoners of a mode of consciousness which is shaped and controlled through ideological processes. Many specific aspects of organizational life have been examined from this point of view. Marcuse (1964) has addressed the alienating aspects of purposive rationality, Clegg (1975) the language of organizational life, Dickson (1974) the worship of technology, and Anthony (1977) the ideology of work itself. Life at work, when viewed from the critical theory perspective, constitutes an alienated mode of life in which individuals are shaped, controlled, and generally made subservient to the artificially contrived and reified needs of modern organization. The work of Freud (1922), Jung (1953–1965), and other psychoanalytic theorists also articulates perspectives consistent with the psychic prison metaphor, individuals being viewed as captives of unconscious processes. Organizations from the Freudian perspective may be seen as based upon the externalization of repressive tendencies operating within the human psyche (Marcuse, 1955), and from the Jungian perspective as the manifestation of some form of archetype expressing relationships between subjective and objective worlds. The psychic prison metaphor sets the basis for an 'anti-organization theory' (Burrell and Morgan, 1979) which challenges the premises of functionalist organization theory in many ways.

The radical structuralist paradigm generates a radical organization theory based upon metaphors such as the instrument of domination, schismatic system, and catastrophe. Weber's classic analysis of bureaucracy as a a mode of domination (Weber, 1946), Michels' analysis of the 'iron law of oligarchy' (Michels, 1949), and Marxist analyses of organization (Baran and Sweezy, 1966; Braverman, 1974; Benson, 1977), for example, are all informed by the image or organizations as powerful instruments of domination to be understood as an integral part of a wider process of domination within society as a whole. Although such analyses often utilize insights deriving from the machine metaphor, organizations as machines are studied for their oppressive qualities. This is clearly evident, for example, in Weber's work, which, stripped of its radical dimension, is the basis for much functionalist theory based upon the machine metaphor. Theorists who have used Weber's ideas from a functionalist point of view completely ignore the fact that Weber considered bureaucracy an 'iron cage.' The metaphor of instrument of domination devotes much attention to this neglected aspect of organization, and encourages an analysis of the means by which modes of domination operate and are sustained. This metaphor leads to an interest in understanding how the power structure within organizations is linked to power structures within the world political economy, and how societal divisions between classes, ethnic groups, men and women, etc., are evident in the work place. Insights generated by the psychic prison metaphor are often utilized within the context of radical structuralist theory as a means of articulating the nature of ideological domination as part of a more broadly based mode of socioeconomic domination. Those in control of organizations are viewed as utilizing ideological, political, and economic means of dominating their members (Friedman, 1977), and for dominating the wider context within which they operate. Study of the role of multinationals in the world political economy (Barnet and Muller, 1974), and the role of the modern state (Holloway and Picciotto, 1978), has provided a strong center of interest here.

The schismatic metaphor (Morgan, 1981) focuses attention upon how organizations may have a tendency to fragment and disintegrate as a result of internally generated strains and tensions. It specifically counters the functionalist premise that organizations are unified entities seeking to adapt and survive, by focusing upon processes through which organizations factionalize as a result of schismogenesis (Bateson, 1936) and the development of patterns of functional autonomy (Gouldner, 1959).

The 'catastrophe' metaphor has been used in Marxist theory to analyze internal contradictions of the world political economy (Bukharin, 1915, 1925) which set the basis for revolutionary forms of change. A somewhat different version is developed in the 'catastrophe theory' of René Thom (1975). Both have relevance for studying the role of organizations in the contemporary world economy, the labor process, and labor–management relations. While the metaphor has been used in many ways as a basis for detailed puzzle-solving models within a functionalist perspective, it has not been systematically used to develop a comprehensive radical structuralist analysis of organization.

Conclusions

Orthodoxy in organization theory has developed upon the basis of metaphors which reflect the assumptions of the functionalist paradigm. These assumptions are rarely made explicit and are often not appreciated, with the consequence that theorizing develops upon unquestioned grounds. The assumptions of interpretive, radical humanist, and radical structuralist paradigms challenge functionalist assumptions in fundamental ways. They generate a variety of metaphors for organizational analysis, resulting in perspectives that often contradict the tenets of orthodox theory. For example, whereas functionalist theory emphasizes that organizations and their members may orient action and behavior to the achievement of future states, interpretive theory emphasizes that action is oriented as much to making sense of the past as to the future. Whereas functionalist theory views organizations and their members interacting and behaving within a context or environment of some kind, interpretive theory questions the status and existence of such contextual factors, other than as the social constructions of individuals which have become shared. Functionalist theory builds upon premises which interpretive theory suggests are fundamentally ill conceived.

The radical humanist and radical structuralist paradigms offer a similar kind of challenge, which draws attention to the political and exploitative aspects of organizational life. From the perspective of these paradigms, both functionalist and interpretive theory fail to understand that the apparent order in social life is not so much the result of an adaptive process or a free act of social construction, as the consequence of a process of social domination. Organizations from this point of view oppress and exploit, and embody a logic which sets a basis for their eventual destruction. The order which interpretive theory seeks to understand, and which functionalist theory seeks to enhance, is from the radical humanist and radical structuralist perspectives a superficial order masking fundamental contradictions. The challenge to organization theory emanating from these paradigms is to penetrate beneath the surface appearance of the empirical world, and reveal the deep structure of forces which account for the nature, existence, and ongoing transformation of organizations within the total world situation. Organization theory from the radical humanist and radical structuralist perspectives cannot provide an adequate understanding of the nature or organization through an exclusive focus upon organizations and behavior in organizations. These paradigms suggest that the study of such phenomena must be linked to the wider mode of societal organization to which they give detailed empirical content and form.

The challenge presented to orthodox organization theory by these different paradigms is to rethink the very nature of the subject to which it is addressed. Different paradigms embody world views which favor metaphors that constitute the nature of organizations in fundamentally different ways, and which call for a complete rethinking as to what organization theory should be about. The challenge raised relates to the ground assumptions upon which theorizing is based, and can only be settled through a consideration of the appropriateness of these rival grounds as a basis for organizational analysis.

Note

I want to thank Richard Brown, Peter Frost, Walter Nord, and Linda Smircich for helpful comments on an earlier draft of this paper.

References

Anthony, P.D. (1977) *The Ideology of Work*. London: Tavistock.
Argyris, Chris (1952) *The Impact of Budgets Upon People*. New York: Controllership Foundation.
Argyris, Chris (1957) *Personality and Organization*. New York: Harper.
Argyris, Chris and Donald A. Schön (1978) *Organizational Learning: A Theory of Action Perspective*. Reading, MA: Addison-Wesley.
Baran, Paul, and Paul M. Sweezy (1966) *Monopoly Capital*. New York: Monthly Review Press.
Barnet, Richard J., and Ronald E. Muller (1974) *Global Reach: The Power of Multinational Corporations*. New York: Simon and Schuster.
Bateson, Gregory (1936) *Naven*. Cambridge: Cambridge University Press.
Benson, J. Kenneth (1977) 'Organizations: A dialectical view,' *Administrative Science Quarterly*, 22: 1–21.
Berggren, Douglas (1962) 'The use and abuse of metaphor: 1,' *Review of Metaphysics*. 16: 237–58.
Berggren, Douglas (1963) 'The use and abuse of metaphor: 2,' *Review of Metaphysics*. 16: 450–72.
Bittner, Egon (1965) 'On the concept of organization,' in Roy Turner (ed.), *Ethnomethodology*: 69–81, Harmondsworth: Penguin (1974).
Black, Max (1962) *Models and Metaphors*. Ithaca, NY: Cornell University Press.
Braverman, Harry (1974) *Labour and Monopoly Capital*. London and New York: Monthly Review Press.
Brown, Richard H. (1977) *A Poetic for Sociology*. Cambridge: Cambridge University Press.
Buckley, Walter (1967) *Sociology and Modern Systems Theory*. Englewood Cliffs, NJ: Prentice-Hall.
Bukharin, Nikolai (1915) *Imperialism and World Economy*. London: Merlin Press (1972).
Bukharin, Nikolai (1925) *Historical Materialism: A System of Sociology*. New York: Russell and Russell.
Burke, Kenneth (1945) *A Grammar of Motives*. New York: Prentice-Hall.
Burke, Kenneth (1954) *Permanence and Change: An Anatomy of Purpose*, 2nd ed. Los Altos, CA: Hermes.
Burns, Tom, and G.M. Stalker (1961) *The Management of Innovation*. London: Tavistock.
Burrell, Gibson, and Gareth Morgan (1979) *Sociological Paradigms and Organizational Analysis*. London, and Exeter, NH: Heinemann.
Cassirer, Ernst (1946) *Language and Myth*. New York: Dover.
Cassirer, Ernst (1955) *The Philosophy of Symbolic Forms, vols. 1–3*. New Haven and London: Yale University Press.

Child, John (1972) 'Organizational structure, environment, and performance: The role of strategic choice.' *Sociology*, 6: 1–21.

Clegg, Stewart (1975) *Power, Rule, and Domination*. London and Boston: Routledge and Kegan Paul.

Crozier, Michel (1964) *The Bureaucratic Phenomenon*. London: Tavistock.

Dickson, David (1974) *Alternative Technology and the Politics of Technical Change*. London: Fontana.

Etzioni, Amitai (1960) 'Two approaches to organizational analysis: A critique and suggestion.' *Administrative Science Quarterly*, 5: 257–8.

Fayol, Henri (1949) *General and Industrial Management*. Constance Storrs (trans.) London: Pitman.

Freud, Sigmund (1922) *A General Introduction to Psychoanalysis*. New York: Liveright.

Friedman, Andrew L. (1977) *Industry and Labour: Class Struggle at Work and Monopoly Capitalism*. London: Macmillan.

Garfinkel, Harold (1967) *Studies in Ethnomethodology*. Englewood Cliffs, NJ: Prentice-Hall.

Georgiou, Petro (1973) 'The goal paradigm and notes towards a counter paradigm.' *Administrative Science Quarterly*, 18: 291–303.

Glassman, R.B. (1973) 'Persistence and loose coupling in living systems.' *Behavioral Science*. 18: 83–98.

Goffman, Erving (1959) *The Presentation of Self in Everyday Life*. New York: Doubleday.

Goffman, Erving (1961) *Asylums*. New York: Doubleday.

Gouldner, Alvin W. (1959) 'Reciprocity and autonomy in functional theory.' In Alvin W. Gouldner (ed.), *For Sociology*: 190–225. Harmondsworth: Penguin (1973).

Habermas, Jurgen (1970) 'On systematically distorted communications.' *Inquiry*, 13: 205–18.

Habermas, Jurgen (1972) *Knowledge and Human Interests*. London: Heinemann.

Hage, Jerald (1974) *Communication and Organizational Control*. New York: Wiley.

Hannan, Michael T., and John H. Freeman (1977) 'The population ecology of organizations.' *American Journal of Sociology*, 82: 929–64.

Hesse, Mary (1966) *Models and Analogies in Science*. Notre Dame, IN: University of Notre Dame Press.

Holloway, John, and Sol Picciotto (1978) *State and Capital: A Marxist Debate*. London: Edward Arnold.

Huff, Anne (1979) 'A rhetorical analysis of argument in organizations.' Unpublished manuscript, University of Illinois.

Jakobson, Roman, and Morris Halle (1956) *Fundamentals of Language*. The Hague: Mouton.

Jung, Carl G. (1953–1965) *Collected Works*. London: Routledge and Kegan Paul.

Katz, Daniel, and Robert L. Kahn (1966) *The Social Psychology of Organizations*. New York and London: Wiley.

Kuhn, Thomas S. (1962) *The Structure of Scientific Revolutions*. Chicago: University of Chicago Press.

Kuhn, Thomas S. (1970) 'Reflections on my critics.' In Imre Lakatos and Alan Musgrave (eds.) *Criticism and the Growth of Knowledge*: 231–78. Cambridge: Cambridge University Press.

Kuhn, Thomas S. (1974) 'Second thoughts on paradigms.' In Frederick Suppe (ed.), *The Structure of Scientific Theories*: 459–82. Urbana, IL: University of Illinois Press.

Kuhn, Thomas S. (1977) *The Essential Tension*. Chicago, IL: University of Chicago Press.

Kuhn, Thomas S. (1979) 'Metaphor in science.' In Andrew Ortony (ed.), *Metaphor and Thought*; 409–19. Cambridge: Cambridge University Press.

Lakatos, Imre, and Alan Musgrave (eds.) (1970) *Criticism and the Growth of Knowledge*. Cambridge: Cambridge University Press.

Lawler, E.E., and J.G. Rhode (1976) *Information and Control in Organizations*. New York: Goodyear.

Lawrence, P.R., and J.W. Lorsch (1967) *Organization and Environment*. Cambridge, MA: Harvard Graduate School of Business Administration.

Likert, Rensis (1967) *The Human Organization*. New York: McGraw-Hill.

Lukács, George (1971) *History and Class Consciousness*. London: Merlin Press.

McGregor, Douglas (1960) *The Human Side of Enterprise*. New York: McGraw-Hill.

Mannheim, Karl (1936) *Ideology and Utopia*. New York: Harcourt, Brace and World.

Manning, Peter K. (1979) 'Metaphors of the field: Varieties of organizational discourse.' *Administrative Science Quarterly*, 24: 660–71.

Marcuse, Herbert (1955) *Eros and Civilization*. Boston, MA: Beacon Press.

Marcuse, Herbert (1964) *One Dimensional Man*. Boston, MA: Beacon Press.

Marx, Karl (1844) 'Economic and philosophical manuscripts.' In *Early Writings*: 279–400. R. Livingstone and G. Benton (trans.) Harmondsworth: Penguin (1975).

Masterman, Margaret (1970) 'The nature of a paradigm.' In Imre Lakatos and Alan Musgrave (eds.), *Criticism and the Growth of Knowledge*: 59–89. Cambridge: Cambridge University Press.

Michels, Robert (1949) *Political Parties*. Glencoe, IL: Free Press.

Miles, Raymond E., and Charles C. Snow (1978) *Organizational Strategy, Structure, and Process*. New York: McGraw-Hill.

Morgan, Gareth (1979) 'Response to Mintzberg.' *Administrative Science Quarterly*, 24: 137–9.

Morgan, Gareth (1981) 'The schismatic metaphor and its implications for organizational analysis.' *Organization Studies*:2: 23–44.

Morgan, Gareth, and Linda Smircich (1980) 'The case for qualitative research.' *Academy of Management Review*, 5: 491–500.

Muller, Max (1871) *Metaphor*. Lectures on the Science of Language 2nd Series: 351–402. New York: Scribners.

Ortony, Andrew (1975) 'Why metaphors are necessary and not just nice.' *Educational Theory*: 25: 45–53.

Ortony, Andrew (ed.) (1979) *Metaphor and Thought*. Cambridge: Cambridge University Press.

Parsons, Talcott (1951) *The Social System*. Glencoe, IL: Free Press.

Parsons, Talcott (1956) 'Suggestions for a sociological approach to the theory of organizations,' parts 1 and 11. *Administrative Science Quarterly*: 63–85: 225–39.

Pepper, Stephen C. (1942) *World Hypotheses*. Berkeley and Los Angeles: University of California Press.

Pettigrew, Andrew M. (1973) *The Politics of Organizational Decision Making*. London: Tavistock.

Pfeffer, Jeffrey, and Gerald R. Salancik (1978) *The External Control of Organizations: A Resource Dependence View*. New York: Harper & Row.

Pondy, Louis R. (1978) 'Leadership is a language game.' In Morgan W. McCall and Michael M. Lombardo (eds.), *Leadership: Where Else Can We Go*? 87–99. Durham, NC: Duke University Press.

Pondy, Louis, R., and Ian I. Mitroff (1979) 'Beyond open system models of organization.' *Research in Organizational Behavior*, 1: 3–39. Greenwich, CT: JAI Press.

Ricoeur, Paul (1971) 'The model of the text: Meaningful action considered as a text.' *Social Research*, 38: 529–62.

Roethlisberger, F.J., and W.J. Dickson (1939) *Management and the Worker*. Cambridge, MA: Harvard University Press.

Schön, Donald (1963) *Invention and the Evolution of Ideas*. London: Tavistock.

Selznick, Philip (1948) 'Foundations for the theory of organizations.' *American Sociological Review*, 5: 25–35.

Spencer, Herbert (1873) *The Study of Sociology*. London: Kegan, Paul and Tench.

Spencer, Herbert (1876) *Principles of Sociology*, Vols. 1 and 2. New York: Appleton and Company.

Suppe, Frederick, ed. (1974) *The Structure of Scientific Theories*. Urbana, IL: University of Illinois Press.

Taylor, Frederick W. (1911) *The Principles of Scientific Management*. New York: Harper.

Thom, René (1975) *Structural Stability and Morphogenesis*. New York: Benjamin.

Thompson, James D. (1967) *Organizations in Action*. New York: McGraw-Hill.

Trist, E.L., and K.W. Bamforth (1951) 'Some social and psychological consequences of the longwall method of coal getting.' *Human Relations*, 4: 3–38.

Turner, Barry A. (1971) *Exploring the Industrial Subculture*. London: Macmillan.

Weber, Max (1946) *From Max Weber: Essays in Sociology*, H.H. Gerth, and C.W. Mills, eds. New York: Oxford University Press.

Weick, Karl E. (1974) 'Middle-range theories of social systems.' *Behavioral Science*, 19: 357–67.

Weick, Karl E. (1976) 'Educational organizations as loosely coupled systems.' *Administrative Science Quarterly*, 21: 1–19.

Weick, Karl E. (1977) 'Enactment processes in organizations.' In Barry M. Staw and Gerald R. Salancik (eds.), *New Directions in Organizational Behavior*: 267–300. Chicago: St. Clair Press.

Whitehead, Alfred North (1925) *Science and the Modern World*. New York: Macmillan.

Wittgenstein, Ludwig (1968) *Philosophical Investigations*. G.E.M. Anscombe (trans.) Oxford: Blackwell.

Woodward, Joan (1965) *Industrial Organization: Theory and Practice*. London: Oxford University Press.

SECTION 3

CREATIVE PROCESSES

This section explores six creative processes – problem solving, mapping, networking, intuition, judgement and imaging – from different angles.

Creative thinking and problem solving are closely related. Creative thinking is about being sensitive to important problems that are worth addressing, seeing the gaps and incongruities that exist and coming up with appropriate new ideas. Kaufmann opens this section with an excellent review of work on problem solving and its relationship to creativity. He distinguishes between different types of problem, from the well-structured to the ill-structured. He suggests ill-structured problems can be differentiated further in terms of their novelty, complexity and ambiguity. He argues that creative thinking is most useful with 'constructed problems' or opportunities. He discusses three stages of problem solving – preparation, production of solutions and judgement, and reviews problem-solving work on capacity, strategy, symbolic tools, expertise and conditions. Arguing from a conventional, cognitive viewpoint he questions whether there is anything special about the processes that are supposedly unique to creativity, such as incubation and intuition. He believes more attention should be given to constructed problems, where the present is compared to a hypothetical future, as opposed to presented problems, where a present crisis needs solving. Kaufmann points out that this is reminiscent of Mintzberg's opportunity decisions.

McCaskey tackles the issue of uncertainty through the concept of mapping. He points out the organizing function and selective basis of maps, and highlights some of the reasons why people are reluctant to let go of familiar maps. He suggests that mapping is a useful tool for dealing with uncertainty and lists some steps that can help when maps are weak.

A growing body of evidence suggests that traditional hierarchies are not the most conducive structure for enhancing creativity and innovation at work. Indeed, it seems that many innovations happen because of the information and support offered by informal channels of communication within an organization. Networking is an umbrella term for this type of communication between individuals. Mueller likens networking to cultivating a wild garden: 'you permit and create an environment where they can come out and grow'. Networking can take place through many media: face to face, by phone or computer. Mueller believes this form of communication is appropriate for the information age and that the networks offer 'the art of linking human beings in constructive teams and catalysing their full creative growth'.

Agor attempts to outline how top executives use intuition in decision making, based on a survey he conducted into this area. He goes so far as to suggest that highly intuitive executives attributed faulty decision making to failure to attend to intuitive cues.

Vickers addresses the related skill of judgement. He distinguishes between reality judgements, action judgements and value judgements. He suggests good judgement requires detachment, commitment and discipline along with a sensitivity to form.

Imagery seems to be an important part of the creative process in many cases: dramatically so in the case of Kekule with his image of intertwined snakes revealing the structure of benzene, but perhaps also in a more commonplace way as a guide to what we believe is possible. Ainsworth-Land attempts to differentiate between four different levels of imaging, drawing on diverse sources, which include George Land's ideas of forming, norming, integrating and transforming.

10

Problem solving and creativity

Geir Kaufmann

A NEW DEAL FOR PROBLEM SOLVING

Human problem solving is now a major preoccupation in contemporary cognitive psychology (e.g. Anderson 1985). However, the field of creative thinking has not enjoyed the beneficial spin-offs one might have expected. It seems that creativity has received more acts of courtesy that acts of courtship by cognitive psychologists (e.g. Simon 1978). A possible reason for this state of affairs may lie in the intrinsic complexity and elusive nature of the phenomenon. Considerable basic knowledge obtained under well-defined and well-controlled conditions may be required before the more ill-defined area of creative thinking becomes available for manageable treatment. However, the fact that the field has been experimentally mapped in productive ways by psychologists of the previous generation makes one wonder if the issue of creative thinking may represent a deviant case for the computer-inspired paradigm currently dominating contemporary research.

WHAT IS A PROBLEM?

There is a considerable degree of consensus about what is meant by a 'problem'. In all definitions it is emphasized that the individual has a problem when he has a goal, but is uncertain as to what series of actions he should perform to reach it (e.g. Newell and Simon 1972).

In such a definition it is normally implied that a problem arises when the individual is confronted with a difficulty. This kind of definition is too narrow in limiting problems to the situation where the individual is set over against a presented difficulty. Particularly in the creativity domain it may often be the case that the difficulty is a result of comparing an existing situation with a future, imagined state of affairs that constitutes a desirable goal for problem solving. We argue (Kaufmann 1984a) that a satisfactory definition is to regard a problem as a discrepancy between an existing situation and a desired state

Adapted from 'Problem solving and creativity', in K. Gronhaug and G. Kaufmann, *Innovation: A Cross-Disciplinary Perspective* (Oslo: Norwegian University Press, 1988), pp. 87–139

of affairs. With this kind of definition at hand we are not limiting problem solving to tasks that present themselves with a 'gap'.

Aspects of difficulty

Problems are frequently described as varying on a continuum from 'well-structured' to 'ill-structured' (ISP), defined in terms of degree of definition in important respects (Simon 1973, p. 181). Mintzberg et al. (1976) define an ISP as a task calling for 'decision processes that have not been encountered in quite the same form and for which no predetermined and explicit set of ordered responses exists . . .' (p. 246). However, the concept of an ISP itself seems to be ill-structured and in need of being unpacked into its basic constituents. It is important to distinguish between different determinants of ill-structuredness which may be quite distinct. We may here distinguish between at least three conceptually distinct stimulus conditions responsible for turning a task into an ISP. These are *novelty*, *complexity* and *ambiguity*. The justification for nuancing between these stimulus conditions as distinct sources of an ISP may become more apparent when we consider the example of what makes a jig-saw puzzle difficult (unstructured). One source of difficulty may be located in the unfamiliarity of the goal structure that is to be attained (novelty). A quite different ISP-producing condition would be the number of pieces that are to be put together to make up the puzzle (complexity). A third condition of difficulty would surface if the task is indeterminate in the sense that quite different goal structures may be visualized and it is hard to see which is the correct one (ambiguity). It is easy to see that these dimensions can be varied systematically and *independently* of each other. The important point that needs to be underscored here is that novelty, complexity, and ambiguity may call for the use of quite different capacities and strategies on the part of the problem solver. In operating with an undifferentiated concept of an ISP, important differentiations in the problem-solving domain may be lost in the blur. Turning to the creativity aspect in particular, it is reasonable to argue that the novelty component of difficulty is of primary importance and should be a specific focus in creativity research.

Still another source of difficulty that is not entirely reducible to the above-mentioned task determinants, and that may be of special interest to map in the creativity domain, may materialize in what we will term 'deceptive problems'. In many tasks the problem may lie in 'apparent familiarity', when the presentation (or representation) of the task is such that a conventional, well-programmed line of attack is suggested which is, however, not adequately tailored to the solution, and a new twist is necessary to meet the goal specifications.

There is an important distinction to be made between handling a situation that is novel, and recognized as such, and a situation which looks familiar, but deceptively directs the problem solving to look for conventional solutions where a novel one is really required. In the former case, search for new information and creative use of past experience is required. In the latter case, successful problem solving requires the individual to shake off a misleading representation and to realize that solutions along conventional lines do not adequately meet the goal specifications.

Manoeuvring from an undifferentiated concept of ISP may, thus, entail the danger of glossing over important distinctions that must be made in the problem-solving domain. This confounded point of departure may also tempt researchers to make unwarranted generalizations from one kind of task domain to another with quite different properties, where conditions for success relate to a different set of processes and capacities. Scientific scrutiny of creative thinking therefore presupposes a clear conception of the properties that characterize that special class of problem solving.

THE ANATOMY OF CREATIVITY

Creativity is most intimately linked to problem solving that results in high-novelty solutions. However, novelty in thought product does not constitute a sufficient condition for defining creativity. The weird ideas of a psychotic person may rank high in originality and novelty, but we would hardly regard them as creative. To justify the use of the term 'creative thinking' a thought product also has to satisfy the criterion of having some *use* or *value*. This requirement may be fulfilled in the way of functional use, as in technical inventions, or in aesthetic value, as in artistic productions. In a lucid discussion of the concept of creative thinking, Newell, Shaw and Simon (1979) suggest some additional criteria which may provide an opportunity for a more precise delimiting of the concept.

These are:

* Creative thinking is unconventional by requiring the modification or rejection of previous accepted ideas.

  This defining characteristic is important to include since it legitimately brings into the line of creative thinking the kind of thinking required in what we have termed 'deceptive tasks'. Here the rejection of conventional lines of thinking is of primary importance for a successful solution to the problem.
* Creative thinking normally feeds on high motivation and persistence and takes place either over a relatively long period of time – continuously or intermittently – or at high-level intensity.

  The criterion suggested here seems well-motivated. It is interesting to note that creative thinking is now placed in the category of 'hot cognition' (e.g. Janis and Mann 1977). Including the dynamic dimension in the very definition of creativity may serve to raise questions that are normally absent in contemporary, computer-inspired research on problem solving (e.g. Kahney 1986).

* Finally, Newell, Shaw and Simon (1979) argue that a problem that requires creative thinking is normally vague and ill-defined, and that part of the task is to formulate the problem itself.

This point suggests that creative thinking is seen most clearly in the category of 'constructed problems', where the main share of creativity may lie in the formulation of the problem itself. The criterion of creativity also applies, of course, to the process of identifying a productive problem definition in a presented problem.

The defining characteristics presented above seem to place creative thinking in its proper kinship relation in the family of problem solving and to safeguard against too straightforward a generalization from the general body of problem-solving research to the special domain of creative thinking. In view of their careful consideration of the concept of creativity, it seems almost paradoxical when Newell, Shaw and Simon (1979) fall prey to exactly this line of hazardous reasoning when they extrapolate from research findings on problems where the difficulty is mainly that of complexity to the domain of creativity where task (and thought) *novelty* is the cardinal characteristic. Their main concern is with the issue of *reducing* complex problem spaces and what kind of heuristics are used for this purpose. As we shall see, however, the problem is often the exact opposite in the case of creative thinking, where good solutions are blocked by searching in too *narrow* a space. The implicit assumption underlying such dubious generalizations as those made by Newell, Shaw and Simon seems to be that ISPs constitute a unitary class of phenomena. While there may be important regularities pertaining to the general level of ISPs irrespective of differences in basic constituents, these are probably of a highly general nature and may not throw the kind of specific light on the sub-category of creative thinking that we are aiming at.

The prevailing general theory of human problem solving as presently worked out is not adequately developed to deal with the creativity aspects of problem solving.

THEORY OF PROBLEM SOLVING

The theory that dominates and directs research in the problem-solving field is worked out from an explicit information processing perspective, where the computer-metaphor is the cornerstone of the edifice (e.g. Simon 1978).

Of particular relevance for the creativity aspect is the distinction made with regard to the nature of problem spaces. We have distinguished between 'extent' and 'kind' of problem space. There is a striking tendency in contemporary problem-solving literature to hold forth the case of the *too large* problem space as the only interesting one. This aspect is of course, prominent when the difficulty of the task lies in its complexity. However, it is not as obvious when the problem is one of novelty or ambiguity, or in the case of the 'deceptive problem'. Quite the contrary, the difficulties observed in these tasks may often be aptly described as related to a *too narrow* problem space, where the problem solver has to enlarge the space and see new possibilities in order to succeed in solving the problem. There is a clear tendency for human problem solvers to stick too closely to established lines or procedures when the problem requires new lines of attack. With ambiguity, the problem is rather one of choosing between different *kinds* of problem spaces that are conflicting alternatives. In the case of the 'deceptive problem', an adequate description of the difficulties facing the problem solver is that the task directs the individual into the wrong problem space, where a solution cannot possibly be located. We feel that one reason why creative thinking has been so poorly treated by contemporary information processing oriented psychologists is the misguided over-emphasis on large problem spaces as the single most interesting case in problem solving. While complexity may certainly be involved in creative thinking problems, there is good reason to believe that this aspect is not the most interesting one, and that attempts to generalize to the creativity domain from evidence gathered on this kind of problem situation are not very illuminating, and may even be significantly misguided.

PHASES OF PROBLEM SOLVING

The central questions to be answered here are whether the process of problem solving can be divided into distinct phases which exist across a wide variety of different tasks, and whether they follow a simple and orderly sequence. The answer to the first question seems to be in the affirmative, while the answer to the second is essentially negative. It seems to be possible, then, to identify lawful regularities in the form of distinct phases in problem solving, but these phases do not seem to follow a simple and straightforward sequence.

There is striking agreement in the literature describing the phases of a problem-solving event. Normally, three major phases are identified. Johnson (1955) distinguishes between 'preparation' – understanding and identifying the problem; 'production' – development of different solution alternatives; and 'judgment' – which involves choice of the best solution. Johnson and his collaborators have provided evidence that suggests that these three phases are empirically distinguishable and independent of each other in important ways. An interesting implication is that there are important individual differences in profiles of problem-solving ability. High ability in one phase does not seem to imply success in other phases of problem solving. Simon (1977) has suggested a trichotomy that is essentially commensurate with the Johnson formulation. 'Intelligence' describes the phase of identifying the nature of the problem, 'design' involves 'inventing, developing and analyzing possible courses of action' (p. 41). The third phase deals with the 'selection' of a particular course of action from those available. (When dealing with problems in a practical management context, Simon argues that we may distinguish a fourth phase termed 'review', which involves evaluating past choices.) The finest and most extensive research on phases has probably been done by Mintzberg et al. (1976). On the basis of comprehensive studies of real-life problem solving, Mintzberg et al. were able to confirm the trichotomy theory of phases in problem solving. Mintzberg et al. distinguish the three major phases under the headings of 'identification', 'development', and 'selection', and go on to give a detailed picture of the microstructure of the problem-solving process by identifying seven recurring central 'routines' within the tripartite structure.

The three phases seem to be related logically to form a strict sequence with 'identification' first, followed by 'development', ending in 'selection'. However, the logic of the situation only requires that *some* identification has to be made before development, and a certain minimal level of development has to precede selection. The evidence presented by Mintzberg et al. seems to demonstrate very clearly that a simple, straightforward sequence is the rare case. Normally, the cycle of phases is a lot more complex, and a high degree of overlapping occurs with lots of commuting between the different phases.

Apart from the importance of having a detailed descriptive model of the phases of problem solving, research in this category also states the important question of where the most narrow bottlenecks in problem solving are located. The answer to these questions will probably vary a lot according to the particular aim of the problem solver (i.e. finding one workable solution vs. finding the best one possible vs. finding several good alternatives for an adequate solution, etc.). With the creativity aspect specifically in mind, the research that has been done in the context of these questions seems to point to some interesting answers of a more general nature.

According to Hayes (1978), what sets an ill-defined problem apart from a well-defined one is that 'ill-defined problems require problem solvers to contribute to the *problem definition*' (p. 212, our italics). Newell, Shaw, and Simon (1979) make the very same point when they claim that problems that require creative thinking are typically vague and ill-defined when initially posed and that an important part of the task is to formulate the problem itself. In a recent discussion of creative thinking, Perkins (1981) argues that the danger of 'premature closure' is a major obstacle to creativity. Premature closure means that the problem is encapsulated in too narrow a perspective which in turn prevents the consideration of alternative solution routes that may lead to high-quality, creative solutions to a problem. What these views have in common is the singling out of problem identification and definition as a particularly delicate phase in problem solving.

The view that choice of representation can make an important difference in our problem-solving performance has attracted quite a bit of research interest in contemporary experimental studies of thinking. To exemplify the point, we may consider the problem of the Mutilated Checkerboard, as illustrated in Figure 1.

The task consists of an ordinary checkerboard with 64 squares and a set of 32 rectangular dominoes. Each domino covers 2 checkerboard squares. Thus, the 32 dominoes can be arranged to cover the complete board. The

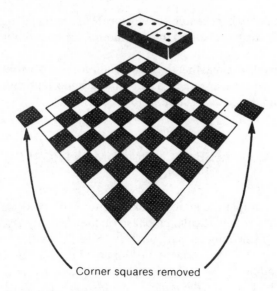

Corner squares removed

Figure 1 *The Mutilated Checkerboard problem*

problem is the following one: Suppose that two black squares are cut from opposite corners of the board, as shown in Figure 1, is it possible to cover the remaining 62 squares of the checkerboard by using exactly 31 dominoes?

Put this way, the problem is exceedingly difficult and very few can solve it (Hayes 1978). The correct answer is 'No', for the following reason: Since each domino covers 1 white square and 1 black square, 31 dominoes will cover 31 white squares and 31 black squares. But the two corners that have been removed are both black. The mutilated checkerboard therefore has 32 white squares and 30 black ones. Thus it cannot be covered by 31 dominoes. It is easily seen that a correct identification of the problem gives the correct solution immediately. Hayes contrasts the Mutilated Checkerboard problem with a so-called problem-isomorph, i.e. the same problem described in a different context: 'In a small but very proper Russian village, there were 32 bachelors and 32 unmarried women. Through timeless efforts, the village matchmaker succeeded in arranging 32 highly satisfactory marriages. The village was proud and happy. Then one Saturday night of drinking, two bachelors, in a test of strength, stuffed each other with pirogies and died. Can the matchmaker, through some quick arrangements, come up with 31 satisfactory marriages among the 62 survivors?'

This Matchmaker problem is an exact parallel to the Mutilated Checker-board problem and is trivially easy to solve. This example rather dramatically illustrates that the same problem can differ vastly in difficulty when presented in different ways, thus underscoring the importance of problem definition for success in subsequent problem solving.

Hayes and Simon (1977) have demonstrated that changes in problem representation may cause a large difference in performance (by a factor of 2). As Hayes (1978) points out, the effect is particularly prone to occur in 'discovery tasks', where search activity is often of minimal importance after the 'correct' (or productive) representation of the problem has been achieved.

It is reasonable to claim that the identification phase of problem solving is a particularly sensitive area and a potentially important bottleneck in the process of finding creative solutions to problems.

MAIN AREAS OF RESEARCH ON HUMAN PROBLEM
SOLVING

We will now consider the major areas of contemporary research on human problem solving with particular emphasis on the creativity aspect. Five areas of research will be singled out. First we will discuss the implications of research on *capacity* limitations in the human information processing system for understanding the way people approach problems. A major focus of research has here been on the *strategies* people use to cope with ill-structured problems. Research on the use of *symbolic tools* (e.g. verbal/imaginal) connects naturally with the strategy studies. More recently, a strong research emphasis has been placed on the knowledge base of problem solvers and the requirements for *expertise* in problem solving. Finally, we will provide a selective review of less system-oriented, empirical research on *antecedent and situational conditions* that either facilitate or inhibit the process of creative thinking in particular.

Capacity limitations and problem solving

A major source of direction for contemporary research on human problem solving is given in the theory of *bounded rationality* developed by Simon (1983). The theory has grown out of an attack on the classical Subjective Expected Utility (SEU) theory. The SEU theory assumes among other things that the individual will make decisions from an exhaustive set of alternative strategies, probability calculations of scenarios for the future associated with each strategy, and a policy of maximizing expected utility. Apart from the unrealistic assumptions of complete knowledge, Simon has also argued that the cognitive capacity assumptions implied in the SEU model are widely at odds with observed realities. As an alternative to the super-rationality assumed in SEU theory, he formulated the principle of bounded rationality: 'The capacity of the human mind for formulating and solving complex problems is very small compared with the size of the problems whose solution is required for objectively rational behaviour in the real world – or even for a reasonable approximation to such objective rationality' (1957, p. 198). Rather than maximizing, the individual will follow a strategy of *satisficing*, directed by a realistic aspiration level of what is 'good enough'. More precisely, the thinker is assumed to select the first alternative he encounters which meets some minimum standard of satisfaction. Substituting satisficing for maximizing greatly reduces the demands upon the computational capabilities of the thinker.

Research on capacity limitations in the human information processing system has clearly corroborated the basic thesis in Simon's theory. There are important bottlenecks in the cognitive system that easily impose cognitive strain on the individual confronted with a non-trivial task. Available evidence seems to show that only a small number of such limits exist, but these seem to be constant across a wide variety of tasks, and are of crucial importance for the processing capabilities involved in solving problems. Thus, insight into cognitive capacity limitations may have great implications for our understanding of basic features of problem-solving behaviour.

Schiffrin (1978) has argued that many of the computational limitations observed in cognitive tasks may be traced back to basic limitations in short-term memory (including working memory). 7 ± 2 units of information has been given as a 'magical number' (Miller 1956) of the storage capacity of short-term memory. Recent research by Simon (1979) suggests that this is an over-estimation, and that the true number is in the order of 5 units. Roughly, we may define a unit of information as the information contained in a unitary concept. The size of the unit may vary (letter, word, sentence) and it is interesting to note that the parameter seems to be constant across size of unit. To increase memory capacity the individual has to organize information in higher-order, unitary 'packages' called 'chunks of information'. The letters U, C, B represent three units of information. Drawn together they may mean University of California, Berkeley, which is one unit. Such capacity-increasing 'chunking' may be of great importance in tasks of memory and problem solving (e.g. Anderson 1985). Another bottleneck in the human cognitive system is given in the time it takes to transfer information from short- to long-term memory. Research reported by Simon (1979) indicates that it takes 8–10 seconds to transfer a new unit of information from short- to long-term memory. Again it is interesting to note that this parameter seems to be invariant across different types of information.

According to the information processing theory of problem solving, most non-trivial tasks contain an enormous number of paths to the goal. A basic difficulty in problem solving is thus that a problem solver with strongly limited computational capacities is confronted with a task that contains a vast number of possible solution paths. According to the theory of bounded rationality this makes it necessary for the individual to construct strongly simplified models of reality. The subjectively constructed model then serves as the basis for the individual's problem-solving activity (see also Johnson-Laird 1983). For most non-trivial problems, then, only a limited amount of search is possible within the realities of the problem solver's world.

The critical problem is therefore to identify promising sequences of operations. Here the so-called heuristic methods come into play. The basic aim of heuristics is to aid the problem solver to simplify the problem by serving to identify the most likely solution paths.

With this point of departure it is easy to understand why the major share of contemporary research on problem solving has been devoted to uncovering heuristic strategies used by problem solvers in their transactions with ill-structured task environments.

Strategies in problem solving

Newell (1969) has dealt with the issue of strategies in human problem solving from a particularly systematic point of view, and suggests a distinction between 'weak' and 'strong' methods be made. A strong method has high power in the sense of guaranteeing a solution to a problem. The generality of a strong method is low, however, and the need for information about the specific problem is high. Mathematical formulas for solving specific problems are good examples of this category of method. In an ill-structured problem, it is implied by definition that the information about the problem is low, and here the individual has to fall back on weak methods. A weak method makes very weak demands on the environment for information. The power of delivering a solution is low compared to strong methods, but it can be used across a wide variety of different tasks. Thus there seems to be an inverse relation between power and generality of problem-solving methods.

As Simon (1981) points out, a science of problem solving should deal with the process at a high level of generality and concentrate on invariant (or relatively invariant) features. In line with such a dictum, research on strategies is aimed at uncovering methods of high generality that are regularly used over a wide spectrum of tasks.

Inspired by the theory of bounded rationality, research has been heavily focused on the heuristics used for the purpose of simplifying problems and confining search activity to the most promising solution paths. Excellent reviews are found in Hayes (1978) and Winston (1977).

Heuristics of simplification

Hayes (1978) distinguishes between three varieties of search aimed at short-cutting the problem. These are: proximity methods, pattern matching, and planning.

Proximity methods

The hot and cold strategy.   Problem solvers often behave on the principle of the 'Hot and Cold' child's game, and look for 'hot' signals to move closer to, and 'cold' signs to move away from, a search route. An everyday example of use of this strategy would be the location of another person in a large house by manoeuvring on the basis of the loudness of the other person's voice.

Hill climbing.   The strategy derives its name from the analogy of climbing a hill under foggy conditions, where the climber chooses one step at a time that increases the altitude. A practical example of the hill-climbing strategy would be to improve the performance of a soccer team by taking one step at a time and evaluating its consequences. Altitude here corresponds to winning performance and standing in the league. We can take a single step at a time – for instance increase physical exercise – to improve the team by implementing the steps that help and rejecting those that do not. By a hill-climbing method we should arrive at good solutions to problems although we may not get the best possible solutions.

Means–end analysis.   Means–end analysis is a method with considerable problem-solving power and generality. It differs from those considered above by offering a choice among different *means* of approaching the goal. In means–end analysis, search is guided by attempts to *reduce the difference* between the initial state and the goal state, selecting from a set of available means.

Making a travel plan may exemplify the use of means–end analysis. If the goal is to go from Oslo to New York, the distance can be covered by using an aeroplane. But the precondition for this is having a ticket and getting to the airport. The problem of the ticket can be solved by using a travel agent, but then there is the problem of choosing the agent who will give the best deal. A new sub-problem then arises, and the process will continue until the solving of the subsidiary problems results in the solution of the overall problem.

This example also illustrates the important heuristic of the *sub-goal strategy*. Rather than attacking the problem head on, as a whole it is useful to follow the strategy of breaking it up into subsets of subsidiary sub-goals which are more well-structured than the total problem. The main purpose of the means–end analysis is to solve an ill-structured problem by reducing it to a series of smaller well-structured problems. Newell and Simon (1972) report that this is a procedure that is very frequently resorted to by their subjects presented with a variety of different problems.

Planning methods

Another class of heuristics that may be used to confine search in complex task environments is the planning methods. Hayes (1978) distinguishes between three types of planning strategies.

Planning by modelling.   To guide complex activities in a rational way, it is useful to construct a simplified model of the situation to avoid going in wrong directions and making errors. Before starting on the job of making a suit the tailor needs to draw a model of it.

Planning by analogy.   Plans may be formed by analogy where the solution of one problem is used as a platform for solving another problem. An example would be the problem of exploiting the energy in waves by way of the principle of a lens.

Planning by abstraction. Plans are formed by abstraction when the original problem is simplified to a related but easier one. The solution of the simpler problem can then be used as a plan for solving the original more complex problem.

Writing a book for the first time may be approached by building on the successful solution to the problem of writing a paper on a related topic.

Working backwards

The ordinary directional strategy in problem solving is to work forwards from initial state to goal state. However, when the goal is less connected than the givens, it may be more useful to work backwards from the goal to the givens. The reason is that fewer paths lead to the solution from the goal than from the givens. Such a situation is often present in mathematical problems involving formal proof.

The general problem-solving strategies considered so far all aim at simplifying problems. The research directed at identifying this bundle of heuristics is clearly driven from the theory of bounded rationality, which focuses on the issue of the too comprehensive problem space.

This is perhaps an example of how students of problem solving themselves may fall into the trap of illegitimately narrowing the problem space due to a certain problem representation. Heuristics of simplification are particularly relevant when the task is one of *complexity*. However, in creative thinking tasks, where *novelty* is the dominating determinant of difficulty, the problem is often that of operating within a too restricted problem space, or – as in 'deceptive problems' – in the wrong space. The scope for investigating strategy use thus clearly stands in need of expansion to cover these realities of problem solving. This kind of lacuna has intuitively been spotted by Anderson (1975). He considers a different class of strategies that he coins 'heuristics of stimulus variation'. This category contains exactly the kind of strategies that would be expected to be useful in typical creative thinking tasks.

Heuristics of variation

Anderson (1975) considers three kinds of strategies within this category:

Adding stimuli. New stimuli may be needed to expand a too narrow problem perspective, and to set up new patterns of activity in the representational system. One way of achieving this aim is to present the problem in *different terms*. An example given by Anderson (1975) is the problem of proving whether the hypotenuse of a right-angled triangle is longer or shorter than the sum of the two sides. If the problem were expressed in concrete terms, asking the student whether it would be shorter to take a path that cuts across a vacant lot or to take a sidewalk that goes around it, the answer would probably be much easier to see. In this connection it is interesting to note the observation that creative thinkers often shift between concrete and abstract ways of representing the problem (Kaufmann 1980).

Thinking in analogies is another way of adding stimuli. Gordon (1961) has reported numerous examples of using this strategy. In one case the problem was to construct a roof that would absorb heat under cold conditions and reflect heat under hot conditions. The analogy of a flounder than can change colour according to variations in light conditions was used. The problem was solved on the basis of this analogy by constructing a roof impregnated with white plastic balls that would contract under low temperatures, rendering the roof black, and expand under high temperatures, thus reflecting heat.

Removing stimuli. Particularly relevant to the case of the 'deceptive problem' is the presence of irrelevant or misleading stimuli that may lure the problem solver into the wrong space. Adamson and Taylor (1954) have shown that fixations in problem solving may decay over a period of some days. Theoretically, such an effect would be expected from the theory of selective forgetting (Anderson 1975, p. 284). Weaker items are forgotten more rapidly than stronger ones. It is reasonable to believe that in most cases incorrect items are weaker than stronger ones. When used deliberately as a strategy, the problem is of course to decide which stimuli are the irrelevant ones. Anderson (1975) suggests that the problem solver should ask himself exactly what the solution requires.

Rearranging stimuli. A final way of achieving the aim of restructuring a problem space by deliberate, strategical means is to rearrange stimuli. Temporal orderings may here play a significant role. Given the task of crossing out the word that does not fit into the sequence *skyscraper, female, cathedral, prayer*, a subject will normally choose *prayer*. When the list is presented in the reverse order, the word *skyscraper* is most likely to be crossed out (Anderson 1975, p. 285). Spatial arrangements are also important. The chessboard looks different from the opponent's viewpoint. A useful strategy in solving a chess problem could therefore be to imagine the chessboard from the opponent's perspective.

Heuristics of stimulus variation comprise a much more loosely defined category than heuristics of simplification. The reason is not that the former are less important. Rather, it seems they fall outside the scope of the prevailing paradigm, which is largely driven from the basic ideas derived from the concept of bounded rationality. Our main point here is that this theory tends to confine the area of search mainly to the aspect of difficulty defined by complexity. A more differentiated view of what constitutes an ISP may serve the fruitful purpose of widening the scope for research on human problem solving.

Symbolic activity in problem solving

Closely related to research on heuristics is the issue of the usefulness of different kinds of symbolic strategies in problem solving. Research in this category has concentrated on the basic question of the nature of the symbolic systems at disposal in cognition.

The spotlight of research has been cast specifically on the use of imagery as a symbolic medium. Reports pertaining to major inventions and scientific discoveries suggest that the inventors were visualizing complex situations when their revealing 'flash of insight' took place (Kaufmann 1980; Shepard 1978). Such informal evidence suggests that somehow imagery is of particular service to creative thought. Corroborating this hypothesis, reviews of the experimental literature suggest quite strongly that imagery gains increasing importance in direct proportion to the degree of ill-structuredness of the task. With high novelty, complexity or ambiguity the subject seems to switch from a linguistic–propositional code to an imagery-based representation (Kaufmann 1984b). Why is this so?

With reference to the general theory of strong and weak methods in problem solving, we have suggested that imagery is a back-up system that gives access to a set of simpler cognitive processes of a perceptual kind. Such simpler processes may be needed in an ISP where computational processes in the form of rule-governed inferences are difficult or impossible to perform (Kaufmann 1987).

Imagery is ambiguous, sluggish and less easily manipulated and only realizes simple cognitive operations of a perceptual kind, like anticipations and comparisons. This may be useful and even necessary in ill-structured task environments, where computational operations in the sense of rule-governed inferences are difficult or impossible to perform.

This theory offers an explanation of the evidence that links the usefulness of imagery to ill-structuredness in the task environment and to creative thinking specifically.

Expert performance

We have considered the use of very general strategies and capacities that may facilitate performance in ill-structured task environments. This picture needs to be supplemented with research evidence that relates to the significance of domain-specific knowledge for effective and creative problem solving.

In his seminal work on human intelligence, Spearman (1927) arrived at the conclusion that successful problem solving is determined by two factors: general intelligence and knowledge specifically bearing on the task in question. The factor of general intelligence has in recent years been unpacked by Sternberg (1985). He claims that the realities behind the term 'general intelligence' consist of the efficient use of highly general problem-solving strategies; of the kind we have described above. The positive correlations between most problem-solving tasks is, according to Sternberg, due to the fact that the same general strategies are used across a wide variety of different tasks.

In addition to efficient use of general problem-solving strategies, it seems that expertise in problem solving is highly dependent on the availability of extensive, well-organized domain-specific knowledge. Chase and Simon (1973a, b) conclude that the chess master's superior ability is due to the possession of a vast number of stored patterns in long-term memory which allow them to match perceived board positions with stored memory representations. Thus, the master can organize his information in a more efficient way. Chase and Simon estimated that a chess master has stored in memory 50,000–100,000 such 'chunks' of information. It is the advantage of possessing this extensive and well-organized knowledge that makes for superior problem-solving ability.

McKeithen et al. (1981) have corroborated these findings in a study with computer programmers. Where novices and experts in other domains like physics and architecture have been studied, the same results are found (Kahney 1986).

Differences in the strategies employed by experts and novices have also been studied. Bhaskar and Simon (1977) report that experts tend to work forwards when searching for a solution to a problem, while novices more typically use the 'weak' strategy of working backwards or resort to general means–end strategies. With specific reference to the question of problem representation, Chi et al. (1981) have shown that novices try to understand a problem by working from its surface features, paying attention to the kinds of objects mentioned in the problem statement, while experts focus on the deeper, underlying principles.

The results of the research on expertise, then, seem to show that the possession of extensive, well-organized domain-specific knowledge is a crucial factor in expert performance. The point here is not only the rather trivial one that experts outperform novices because they have more factual information about the task. Rather the important point is that a higher level of organized, domain-specific knowledge gives the expert access to more powerful problem-solving methods. Thus, high-level cognitive abilities should not be seen as existing apart from knowledge. Rather, powerful cognitive operations seem only to materialize in a system of well-organized, extensive knowledge. This is a new and important insight in cognitive psychology.

Creative problem solving may be seen as expert performance that produces new insights. We may now expect that high-level creativity is crucially dependent on a large amount of well-organized domain-specific knowledge. Before the fruits of real creativity can be reaped, then, we may expect that a long history of building up domain-specific knowledge and skills must precede.

Hayes (reported in Simon 1983) has examined this question by way of biographical evidence on famous chess masters, composers, painters, and mathematicians. Hayes concludes that, for top performance, ten years of work in the field seems to be a magic number. Almost none of the individuals studied had produced world-class performance without first having invested at least ten years of intensive learning and practice. It is interesting to note that the folklore surrounding child prodigies seems to be distorted. For instance, by the standard Hayes used (five appearances in the Swann catalogue), he found no world-class work of Mozart before the age of seventeen.

On the basis of Hayes' extensive and systematic observations, Simon concludes: 'A *sine qua non* for outstanding work is diligent attention to the field over a decade or more' (p. 28).

In general, expertise and high-level creativity seem to require an extensive base of well-organized domain-specific knowledge that takes a long time to acquire. The point is not, of course, that having extensive knowledge in itself guarantees creativity of high rank. Rather, it seems to be a *necessary condition* for high-level performance. Wallach (1988) seems to be entirely justified when he argues that there has been a narrow perspective in the field of creativity research that has focused mainly on very general capacities underlying creativity at the expense of the extensive domain-specific knowledge and skills that have to be present for high-level creativity to unfold. The results of recent cognitive research on expertise and highly talented work in a number of different fields here seem definitely to have balanced the scales in a proper way.

Antecedent and situational determinants of problem solving

This section identifies antecedent and situational conditions that affect problem-solving performance. We may group these into two categories: conditions that *facilitate* and those that *inhibit* productive problem solving.

Facilitating conditions

Exploring the problem situation

We presented evidence to the effect that the initial *problem identification* is a most sensitive part of the problem-solving process. Differences in *problem representation* may strongly affect the success of solving a problem. It is to be expected that this relationship holds true especially in the area of creative thinking. Here we are often dealing with 'discovery tasks', where formulation of the problem is of critical importance for success, as is seen in the problem of the Mutilated Checkerboard.

Raaheim (1964) performed an interesting experiment that addressed this issue directly. The subjects were given a typical 'insight problem' to solve. The experimental group was carefully instructed to find out exactly what was missing, and then to replace it with the object available before starting on solving the problem. The control group was given no such instructions. The results showed an impressive 50 per cent increase in correct solutions in the experimental group compared with the control group.

Again it seems that spending time working out a suitable problem representation may greatly facilitate insightful problem-solving performance.

Along similar lines, Maier (1963) has advocated the strategy of exploring the problem by *locating multiple obstacles*, and has presented evidence that this approach will increase productive problem solving. However, the evidence in question is largely based on informal observations, and more precise and controlled experimentation is necessary before we can assess the potential benefits of such a strategy.

Turning a choice situation into a problem situation

Maier and Hoffman (1970) have argued that 'there is a tendency to seek solutions before the problem is understood' (p. 369). When the aim is for creative solutions to a problem, it is therefore important that an attitude of 'problem-mindedness' replaces the attitude of 'solution-mindedness'. Maier and Hoffman submitted this hypothesis to experimental test by having the subjects obtain a second solution after a first one had been produced. The problem given was the so-called Change of Work Procedure, where the task is to find a productive solution to an assembly-line problem. The assembly operation was divided into three positions and workers adopted a system of hourly rotation among the three jobs. Each worker has a best position, and the issue was to find a new method that would increase productivity. The interesting feature of this problem is that there are several possible solutions that may be graded on a scale of creativity. The creative solutions are called integrative. Here individual differences in ability are exploited, while the unfavourable effects of monotony are avoided.

Maier and Hoffman obtained results that confirmed their hypothesis by showing that, whereas only 16 per cent of the subjects produced integrative solutions on the first try, 52 per cent of the second solutions were of this type.

Such findings underscore the importance of sufficient problem exploration for creative problem solving and fall nicely in line with the general body of results that point to the critical importance of a problem representation for finding high-quality solutions to a problem.

Separate idea generation and idea evaluation

Osborn (1963) has argued that a major block in creative thinking is the tendency to premature evaluation of ideas. Consequently, Osborn argues for a strategy of 'brainstorming' in problem solving where creativity is a major requirement. The basic idea of brainstorming is to separate idea generation from idea evaluation.

Much experimental research has gone into testing the soundness of this principle. The general design has been to determine the effects of brainstorming instructions on originality and productivity when used as a group problem-solving method. The results have been rather depressing for the brainstorming thesis. Brainstorming instructions often turn out to have a *detrimental* effect on the quality and productivity of problem solving, as compared to the effect of neutral instructions. However, Parnes (1963) has reminded us that the brainstorming technique is not inherently a group technique. Anxiety over negative evaluations from others when suggesting 'wild ideas' may, indeed, block the productivity of the individual performing in a group setting. Research on the deferment-of-judgement principle used in individual problem solving tends to show a positive effect on performance. Furthermore, encouraging the subjects to 'free-wheel' and not resist wild ideas is not a necessary feature of the principle. Maier (1963), on the basis of several experiments, reports that the principle of separating idea generation and idea evaluation in itself seems to be sound policy for promoting productive problem solving.

Rickards and Freedman (1978) presented interesting evidence to the effect that a greater *variance* in quality of ideas is obtained under the deferment-of-judgement principle. This means that a greater number of poor solutions *and* high-quality solutions are obtained. These findings suggest that there is a special place for the deferment-of-judgement principle in idea-deficient situations, where the requirements for creativity are particularly strong.

Conflictual thinking

In the literature on problem solving and creativity, the conditions of a *conflict* between opposing ideas are seen as a potentially powerful spur for productive thinking (e.g. Duncker 1945). The general idea is that such a conflict puts pressure on the problem solver which may be resolved by finding a new idea containing elements from the two opposing base ideas.

Hoffman (1961) has spelled out this theory and subjected it to an experimental test. According to Hoffman, four conditions must be fulfilled for a conflict to have a productive function in problem solving: (1) Opposing, but compatible, cognitions must be present at the same time. (2) At least two opposing cognitions must have a higher value than a certain minimum to be accepted as interesting. These should have approximately the same value of attractiveness. (3) Problem solving must take place in a situation where there is pressure towards finding the best possible solution. (4) The cognitive components that give rise to the value of each solution should be identified and clarified.

The theory was put to the test in a series of experiments where the Change of Work Problem was employed in order to get a measure of the creativity of solutions. Conditions were manipulated to create the right 'conflict atmosphere'. The result clearly supported the theory. More creative solutions were obtained under the conflict conditions. Thus, a cognitive conflict seems to have the potential to facilitate creative restructuring in problem solving.

More recently, Rothenberg (1976) has defined a process termed 'Janusian thinking' that is held to be characteristic of creative thought. Janusian or 'oppositional thinking' is 'the capacity to conceive and utilise two or more opposite or contrary ideas, concepts, or images simultaneously' (Rothenberg 1976, p. 313).

Rothenberg points out that highly creative works of art (paintings, compositions, poetry, etc.), often rest on a simultaneous conception of opposites. This feature is also found in great scientific discoveries (the 'double helix' springs out of the notion of identical chains running in opposite directions). Rothenberg has pursued the issue by gathering clinical and experimental evidence on the importance of thinking in conflictual opposites in creativity. In his clinical studies, highly acclaimed writers (winners of Pulitzer prizes, etc.), and novice writers of high creative potential (rated by literary critics and teachers) have been compared with 'non-creative' persons who try to write a work of fiction or poetry for financial reward. According to the results, Janusian thinking figures frequently in the works of the creative writers, but never in non-creative persons. Experimental evidence has been produced by studying word association responding to the Kent-Rosanoff (K-R) test. Rothenberg finds a high tendency to rapid opposite responding ('white' to 'black', 'health' to 'sickness', etc.) in creatively oriented groups of male college students. Special association tasks as well as the K-R test were also given to prominent and novice creative writers. The results show a high tendency to rapid oppositional associations in these groups as well.

Taken together, the evidence tends to support the general idea that thinking in a context of cognitive conflict will promote creativity in solving problems.

High motivation and persistence

An attitude of persistence is mentioned as a defining criterion of creativity in problem solving. There are several good reasons for accepting this 'hot element' in the otherwise consistently 'cold' descriptions of creative problem solving.

Simon (1966) has pointed out that high-level creativity is a rare event in scientific discovery, and a theory of creativity also needs to account for this rarity of occurrence. The idea that high-level creativity requires extraordinarily high persistence fits nicely into this observation. Creativity often involves 'going against the tides' and a lot of resistance to change has to be overcome.

Anderson (1980) also points to the possibility that high persistence may have to do with the openness that high-level creativity requires. He posits that highly creative individuals may be willing to continue working because they are less willing than others to accept the many conflicting facts that are present on the route to creativity.

Several findings suggest that high motivation and persistence are indeed vital ingredients in the creative process. Roe (1953) examined characteristics of a group of 64 American physicists, biologists, and social scientists selected for the importance of their contributions to their fields. The only trait that Roe found to be common to her subjects was the willingness to work extremely hard. MacKinnon (1962), in his studies of creative architects, reports that his highly creative subjects had developed a 'healthy obsession' with their problems.

Hyman (1964) made the interesting observation that when people were asked to continue working on a problem beyond the point where they thought they had come up with their best effort, they frequently were able to produce the ideas that were even more creative than their previous ones. More research in this category would be welcome.

Inhibiting conditions

According to the theory of bounded rationality, a basic motive governing the cognitive behaviour of the individual is the preserved cognitive economy. A strategy of satisficing is chosen to reduce the strain on the computational capabilities of the thinker. This is a rational strategy that makes for good adjustment given the cognitive limitations of the human information processor. It may be argued, however, that preserving cognitive economy means keeping variation and changes to a minimum. Thus, we may expect dysfunctional consequences of this orientation where restructuring and creative change is required. To relinquish established perspectives and standard operating procedures that are associated with safety and predictability may conflict with the individual's striving for cognitive economy and meet with resistance to change. Thus, a rational orientation to solving problems, guided by the motive of preserving cognitive economy, may entail a danger of rigidity and stereotype when faced with a situation where a restructuring of established conceptions and lines of procedure is required.

The psychological literature on human problem solving confirms this expectation through many examples of rigidity, stereotype and dysfunctional resistance to change. The Gestalt psychologists in particular have been active in producing many striking demonstrations of this 'other side of the coin' of human cognitive adjustment. A major orientation in the experimental psychology of creative thinking has, indeed, been to investigate the conditions that inhibit creativity in problem solving. We will describe some of the major phenomena in the category on fixations and resistance to change in problem solving.

The Einstellung effect

According to the theory of satisficing, the problem solver is assumed to select the first alternative he encounters which meets some minimum standard of satisfaction. Luchins (1942) has shown how such a strategy, under certain conditions, may produce fixation and stereotype in problem-solving behaviour. The so-called 'Einstellung' effect shows itself under conditions where the individual has discovered a strategy that initially functions well in solving certain tasks, but later on blocks the realization of new and simpler solutions to similar problems. Luchins has investigated this phenomenon in a series of experiments and shown it to be a reliable and robust one.

The general conclusion from the Luchins water jar experiments is that the fixation in problem solving is dramatically strong. While just about all of the subjects in the control group solve the test problems by way of the simplest formulas, as many as 80 per cent in the experimental group use the complicated standard procedure on later problems. About 60 per cent are not at all able to solve the problem where the formula breaks down.

The Einstellung phenomenon also shows up in other types of tasks, like anagrams (letter combinations), concept formation tasks, and geometry tasks. Thus, it seems to reflect a dysfunctional consequence of the normal, rational way of approaching problems that now may block the establishment of a new perspective and more appropriate lines of procedure in task environments that resemble those encountered before. It is interesting to note that Cyert and March (1963) have observed similar behaviour among managers in real-life contexts. Typical managerial search is seen as 'simple minded', and as over-emphasizing previous experience, by selectively searching in regions close to where previous solutions have been found.

Functional fixedness

Duncker (1945) has also investigated how past experience may block productive problem solving. Duncker coined the term 'functional fixedness' to refer to a block against using an object in a new way that is required to solve a problem. In the so-called Box Problem the task was to mount a candle vertically on a screen nearby to serve as a lamp. The experimental group was given a box containing matches, a second box holding candles, and a third one that contained tacks. The same supplies were given to the control group, but with the matches, tacks, and candles outside the boxes. The solution to the problem is to mount a candle on top of a box. This may be achieved by melting wax onto the box, sticking the candle to it, and then tacking the box to the screen. This was much harder for the experimental group. Similar effects were found in other tasks, where the same general set-up was used.

Duncker takes the results of his experiments as a demonstration of how previous experience may have dysfunctional consequences in problem solving by blocking new insights and necessary restructuring in the face of the requirements of the task.

Some interesting examples of how the factor of functional fixedness may operate in real-life contexts and seriously hamper the process of technical invention are given by Weizenbaum (1984). According to Weizenbaum the steam engine had been in use for a hundred years to pump water out of mines before Trevithick had the idea of using it as a source of locomotive power. Another example is the computer, that for a long time was seen just as a calculator before its potential as general symbol manipulator was conceived.

Hidden assumptions

A similar dysfunctional effect of a mental set is due to the 'hidden assumption'. Fixation in problem solving may be caused by certain assumptions of how a problem has to be solved which delimit the search for productive solutions.

An illustrative experimental demonstration is provided by Scheerer (1963) through the case of the so-called Nine Dot problem (see Figure 2). The Nine

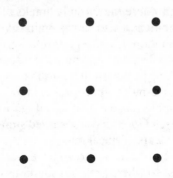

Figure 2   *The Nine Dot problem (B.F. Anderson 1980)*

Dot Problem presents the problem solver with a 3 × 3 grid of nine dots. The task is to draw four straight lines through all nine dots without lifting the pencil from the paper. The problem is difficult to solve, and the main reason for the difficulties seems to be the hidden assumption that one has to stay within the initial configuration of a square. Once this assumption is broken, several possible solutions are possible (see Figure 3). The difficulties involved in solving the Nine Dot Problem also illustrate the delicate nature of problem representation, and how it may affect success in problem solving.

Confirmation bias

Going back to our thesis about possible adverse consequences of the striving for cognitive economy, we may now posit that the individual will show resistance to relinquishing established hypotheses, and be generally reluctant to actively seek disconfirming evidence.

A number of experiments seem indeed to show that people have a natural propensity to seek confirming evidence and to avoid disconfirmation or discard disconfirming evidence when it is present.

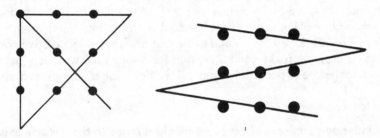

Figure 3   *Solutions to the Nine Dot problem (B.F. Anderson 1980)*

Wason (1968) observed a marked confirmation bias. The majority of subjects did not actively seek disconfirming evidence and tended to ignore it when it occurred. Einhorn and Hogarth (1978) observed that confidence in a hypothesis generally increases more following positive feedback than it decreases following negative feedback. Doherty et al. (1979) found that many people do not consult observations relevant to an alternative hypothesis, even when such observations are readily available.

Conservatism in hypothesis testing

Closely related to the experiments described above are a series of experiments purporting to demonstrate a marked bias in hypothesis-testing behaviour. Using normative prescriptions derived from Bayes theorem, people have been observed to manifest a *conservative bias* in hypothesis testing consisting of a reluctance to reduce their confidence in a decision following disconfirmation.

Phillips and Edwards (1966) investigated the effects on posterior probability estimates of (1) prior probabilities, amount of data, and diagnostic impact of data; (2) payoffs; and (3) response modes. In all the experiments the subjects typically behaved conservatively. This was manifested by the fact that the difference between their prior and posterior probability estimates was less than that prescribed by Bayes theorem.

Pitz, Downing and Rheinhold (1967) likewise observed striking departures from the predictions of Bayes theorem. Under conditions where revisions toward uncertainty should be identical to revisions toward certainty, the former was much less than the latter. Pitz (1969) has argued that commitment is an important cause of this 'inertia effect'. (See Pitz, 1975, for a review of experiments on conservatism in hypothesis testing.)

Taken together, the experiments on hypothesis-testing behaviour seem to suggest that there is a basic, natural tendency to resist change and restructuring in problem solving. Together with the experiments on Einstellung and fixations they point to dysfunctional cognitive tendencies that we may expect to block creativity in problem solving.

Are there 'creativity specials'?

In spite of our attempts to focus specifically on the case of creative thinking in our previous discussion, it may be argued that we have not been able to capture its unique flavour. According to such a view, the domain of creative thinking harbours special features of cognition that are not easily described or explained within the framework of a rational information processing model of the kind that has guided our treatment of the subject. Creative thinking, it will be argued, is driven largely by more irrational processes, and this is why the field is so badly understood within the context of a purely rational model of human cognition. The processes that are the dominant driving forces behind creative thinking are held to be largely unconscious, and stand in need of being described and explained within the framework of a totally different conceptual scheme. The processes referred to here are mainly those of 'intuition' and 'incubation' – both held to depend on the workings of the unconscious mind and to be driven by illogical, irrational processes. These phenomena are indeed often described as being intimately related to the process of high-level creativity in prominent scientists and artists (e.g. Patrick 1938), and present a challenge to the information processing approach.

Much of the discussion of these phenomena is of a rather popular and/or informal nature. We therefore need to address the question of how real these purportedly special features of the mind are. Only then can we say something meaningful about what *kind* of phenomena we are dealing with, with the special purpose of deciding whether they fall outside the scope of an information processing system as defined by current cognitive models.

Intuition – ESP or IPS?

In the popular writings, intuition is often described in rather occult terms as a kind of indefinable gift that only the highly creative person possesses to a full degree. In this view, intuition is not an ordinary, natural part of an infor- mation processing system (IPS). Rather, it is a kind of extra-rational, ESP- like ability that allows the individual who possesses it to point out the correct directions in problem solving without knowing why. It is like having a friendly homunculus in the back of the head that whispers sweet answers to the searching mind. Often such views are coupled with naive and oversimplified ideas about the human brain. According to the popular theory (e.g. Blakes- ley 1980), the left brain is the site of logic and language and is dry and editorial, while the right brain harbours all the goodies of intuition, imagina- tion and imagery, and is the engine of creativity. Such a picture of the division of labour in the human brain seems, however, to be totally misguided. In a recent review of the research available, Gazzaniga (1983) – a prominent researcher in the field – even argues that the right brain as an isolated system functions at the level of intelligence found in chimpanzees. Even if this assessment should turn out to be a bit overdrawn, we are not likely to find the magic sources of creativity exclusively in the right brain. Moreover, the issue of location in the brain is largely irrelevant to our inquiry. It would obviously not make much of a difference for the advance of the psychology of problem solving to know that creativity is to the left or to the right, or up or down in the brain for that matter. The psychological questions can only be answered by way of functional explanations at the 'software' and behavioural levels.

. With specific address to the case of intuition, Simon (1983) has thrown some cold water into the veins of the most ardent proponents of the extra- rational model. According to Simon, intuition is something that we all have, and it is not dependent on a mysterious, indescribable process. Intuition has to do with making a correct judgement without conscious awareness of the process behind it. Such a capacity is not the exclusive property of the chosen few. Rather it is a common ingredient in everyday, cognitive functioning. The skilled chess player will be able to make a move in a mid-game situation in just a few seconds without exactly knowing why, and often it turns out to be a correct move. The explanation of such good intuition is well known to cognitive psychologists. It depends on the availability of a large, well-organized knowledge base and a corresponding elaborate discrimination net that makes for quick and accurate judgements. According to Simon, it is no more mysterious than the ordinary ability to recognize immediately one of your friends in the street. The recognition ability here is likewise dependent on considerable experience with a large number of 'friends'. Thus, we have an elaborate, well-organized sorting net that allows us to perform the correct judgement very quickly.

We can now see that the phenomenon of intuition may depend on elaborate sorting nets derived from extensive experience. Since the knowledge is well organized in 'chunks', processing will occur at very high speed, largely outside the conscious awareness of the individual. Thus, it is not necessary to postulate fancy and elusive processes behind the power of human intuition. The phenomenon is real and available to every human information processor that possesses elaborate and well-organized discrimination nets derived from extensive experience. Thus, intuition can be seen as a natural IPS component rather than an occult ESP phenomenon.

Incubation – fact or fiction?

A closely related phenomenon that is held to be a 'creativity special' is the process of incubation. Incubation is said to occur when the individual sets the problem aside for a while and does something else that is unrelated to the problem. At a later occasion – often very suddenly – the correct solution springs to mind. Many dramatic examples of the phenomenon have been described in the literature (e.g. Ghiselin 1952; Patrick 1938). A good example has been provided by Amy Lowell, the poet (in Ghiselin 1952, p. 110):

> I registered the horses as a good subject for a poem: and having so registered them, I consciously thought no more about the matter. But what I had really done was to drop my subject into the subconscious, much as one drops a letter into a mail-box. Six months later, the words of the poem began to come into my head, the poem – to use my private language – was 'there'.

According to the popular theory, the incubation runs on active unconscious processes that go on in the interval. This is, however, not the only possible explanation. It may be due to the breaking of an unproductive set, stress reduction, reduction of fatigue, selective forgetting, and facilitating effects of incidental stimuli (Olton and Johnson 1976).

Informal descriptions are, of course, not sufficient to establish the reality of the phenomenon, or the possible mechanism behind it. Thus, several controlled experiments have been performed to study incubation at a more stringent level. Olton (1980) has provided a good review of the literature on experimental studies of incubation. In all the studies that deserve serious attention, incubation was examined by comparing the performance of an experimental group and a control group in solving problems that require creative insight. The experimental and the control groups worked for an equal amount of time on the actual problem, but the experimental groups spent an additional intermittent time working on unrelated tasks. In some studies, an incubation effect was present, but in others no difference was observed between the two groups. It is difficult to draw a definite conclusion from these experiments. Olton argues that a possible explanation for the difficulty in demonstrating the incubation effect could be the artificial and restricted nature of the laboratory situation. He then went on to examine the effect of an incubation period in a more ecologically valid situation. Here the subjects worked on an engaging mid-game chess problem. However, no incubation effect was observed in this study either.

The existence of the phenomenon thus seems difficult to prove in a controlled setting, even in situations closely resembling a real-life context. This does not, of course, prove that the phenomenon is a pure fiction. Some experiments have produced an incubation effect, and many suggestive informal descriptions of the phenomenon exist. We now turn to the next question: Given its existence, can we give a convincing explanation of the phenomenon in pure information processing terms, or do we have to admit the elusive explanation in terms of active unconscious processes?

According to Hayes (1978), selective forgetting is the most likely explanation for incubation effects. On the principle of selective forgetting it seems that incubation may be well understood as a natural ingredient of ordinary human information processing. Simon (1966) has given the following detailed explanation of the possible mechanisms behind incubation:

- In the early stages of problem solving, the individual forms a solution plan to guide his attempts at solving the problem. Solution plans are normally stored in working memory rather than in long-term memory.
- During attempts to execute the plan, the individual learns a great deal more about the problem (constraints, etc.). Thus, new information groups may be formed. Individual problem-solving steps may be formed into sub-routines. This sort of information may be stored in long-term memory.
- During a delay the initial plan is forgotten, or suffers more forgetting than the newly acquired information about the nature of the problem.
- When the problem is approached again after a delay, the old plan is forgotten, and a new one has to be formed. The new plan is based on better information about the nature of the problem than the old one and is likely to be a better plan. The break therefore should have the effects of increasing the probability of solution, and this is exactly what is supposed to happen during incubation.

The sudden realization of a solution may occur when we are dealing with discovery tasks, where the solution to the problem is largely dependent on a correct representation, as in the example of the Mutilated Checkerboard.

This account does not, of course, prove that this is what happens during incubation. It does prove, however, that a purely rational, information processing explanation can be expanded to cover also the phenomenon of incubation in a very satisfactory and convincing way.

It seems, then, that we do not have to borrow ingredients from extra-rational theories to account for the creativity domain of human problem solving. This is also the conclusion reached by Reitman (1965) and Simon and Sumner (1968) in a series of investigations of the processes involved in musical composition. In none of these investigations of creative problem solving was evidence obtained that made it necessary to posit processes that occur in creative acts only.

Is there, then, no limitation present in a computer-oriented information processing account of problem solving that is to include the processes involved in creativity?

We have already pointed to some potential lacunas above, particularly those that have to do with the nature of the problem space. It seems, however, that these difficulties can be remedied by expanding the conceptual scheme appropriately. More difficult is perhaps a potential limitation in the scope of problems that the IPS model is fit to deal with. We will wind up our discussion by raising some critical comments on this particular issue.

Three kinds of problems and IPS – from problem solving to problem finding

When Hayes (1978) claims that 'Problems are presented to us by the outside world' (p. 177), he voices well the spirit of the traditional conception of the nature of problems that has guided our discussion so far. Problems are thrust upon us, and this categorization of problems is exhaustive.

There is reason to believe, however, that this is an unduly myopic view of the world of problems that seems to reflect the traditional view of humans as basically reactive and responding to 'stimuli' or 'inputs'. To cover the full territory of problem solving, we may need a broader view. We will here suggest that there are three broad kinds of problems that a theory of human problem solving has to deal with in a satisfactory way.

First, there are *presented problems*. The individual is faced with a difficulty that has to be handled. Such a situation may be well-structured (initial conditions, goal conditions, and operators are clearly definable). At the other pole is the unstructured problem situation, where the number of unknowns is at a maximum. But these are not the only problems people deal with. There is also a class of problems that may be called *foreseen problems*; that is, the individual anticipates that a problem (serious pollution, a massive traffic jam, etc.) will result if present developmental trends continue. Evasive action may then be taken. Even more interesting in the context of the present discussion is the class of problems that may be called *constructed problems*. The initial condition may here be a consistently reinforcing, satisfactory state of affairs. Nevertheless, a problem may arise when an individual compares the existing situation to a future, hypothetical state of affairs that could represent an improvement over the present situation. An example would be the present TV technology which may be said to be quite satisfactory. Yet, an individual might see a problem here in that there is no TV set with an adjustable-sized monitor unit.

Wertheimer (1959) linked this aspect of problem solving explicitly to creativity when he claimed that 'The process starts, as in some creative processes in art and music, by envisaging some feature in an S2 that is to be created' (pp. 197–8).

Recently, Getzels and Csikszentmyhalyi (1976) argue a similar point and present evidence to the effect that problem finding is more intimately related to creativity than is problem solving in the traditional sense. However, Getzels and Csikszentmyhalyi consistently blur a subtle but important distinction between 'discovered' and 'constructed' problems. In the former case the problem finder is able to '. . . articulate out of vague tensions the significant problems' (p. 251). But this is a case of an 'indeterminate situation' (p. 172), where the more creative individual is able to discern a problem on weak signals. When Getzels and Csikszentmyhalyi speak of presented problems vs. discovered problems they often mean explicit vs. inexplicit problems. Conceptually, these situations both belong to the category of presented problems since the stimulus for problem solving is a 'tension' (clear or vague). In the case of constructed problems there is no 'tension' inherent in the situation. Rather, the first step in the problem-solving process is here to *create* a tension between an existing and a new, desirable future situation in order to propel the process of innovation. In the case of 'discovered problems' success is dependent on problem sensitivity, whereas with 'constructed problems' the driving force seems to be 'innovation-orientation' or 'opportunity seeking'.

It is interesting to note that this important aspect of problem solving has been clearly seen by researchers observing managerial problem solving in real-life contexts. Mintzberg et al. (1976) identify an important class of problems as 'opportunity decisions' which are 'initiated on a purely voluntary basis, to improve an already secure situation, such as the introduction of a new product to enlarge an already secure market share' (p. 251). These are to be contrasted with 'crisis decisions', where individuals and organizations 'respond to intense pressures' (p. 251).

The narrow, presented problem perspective is also found in keynote organizational theories of problem solving of the information processing type (e.g. Braybrooke and Lindblom 1963; Cyert and March 1963). In the traditional line of reasoning, Cyert and March (1963) argue that innovation occurs in the face of adversity. It is interesting to note that this is one of their major hypotheses that gains no support from the evidence obtained in their empirical studies of problem solving in organizations. Thus, Mintzberg et al. (1976) seem entirely justified when they blow the whistle on this perspective and claim that '. . . there is the need to reassess the increasingly popular point of view in the literature that organizations tend to react to problems and avoid uncertainty rather than seek risky opportunities' (p. 254).

Working in 'discovered' and 'constructed' problem environments, thus, seems to be intimately related to the creativity aspect of problem solving. It is possible that the popular computer-metaphor in this respect has put blinkers on students of problem solving. Computers, as we know them today, are *problem-solving systems* par excellence and work on given, explicit problem descriptions. As Simon et al. (1986) point out, development is under way in computer-aided design that may present new opportunities to provide human designers with computer-generated representations of their problems. However, these new features relate to problem representation in the narrow sense of clarifying different ways of interpreting a given problem. They do not capture the human processes involved in identification of problems on weak signals, and definitely not the creation of 'tensions' and discrepancies between existing and imagined situations. It would be foolish to forestall a development of these features in future computer technologies, but it is important to point out discrepancies between human and computer capabilities that may block perspectives and narrow our views on problem solving to those aspects that are assimilable to a computer-metaphor.

References

Adamson, R.E. (1952) 'Functional fixedness as related to problem solving: A repetition of three experiments', *Journal of Experimental Psychology, 44*, 228–91.

Adamson, R.W. and Taylor, D.W. (1954) 'Functional fixedness as related to elapsed time and to set', *Journal of Experimental Psychology, 47*, 122–6.

Anderson, B.F. (1975) *Cognitive psychology*. New York: Academic Press.

Anderson, B.F. (1980) *The complete thinker*. Englewood Cliffs, N.J.: Prentice Hall.

Anderson, F.R. (1985) *Cognitive psychology and its implications*. San Francisco: Freeman.

Bhaskar, R. and Simon, H.A. (1977) 'Problem solving in semantically rich domains: an example of engineering thermodynamics', *Cognitive Science, 1*, 193–215.

Birch, H.G. and Rabinowitz, H.S. (1951) 'The negative effect of previous experience on productive thinking', *Journal of Experimental Psychology, 41*, 121–5.

Blakesley, T.R. (1980) *The right brain*. New York: Doubleday & Company.

Boden, M.A. (1979) 'The computational metaphor in psychology'. In N. Bolton (Ed.), *Philosophical problems in psychology*. London: Methuen.

Braybrooke, D. and Lindblom, C.E. (1963) *A strategy of decision*. New York: Free Press.

Chase, W.G. and Simon, H.A. (1973a) 'Perception in chess', *Cognitive Psychology, 4*, 55–81.

Chase, W.G. and Simon, H.A. (1973b) 'The mind's eye in chess'. In W.G. Chase (Ed.), *Visual information processing*. New York: Academic Press.

Chi, M.T.H., Feltovich, P.J. and Glaser, R. (1981) 'Categorization and representation of physics problem by experts and novices', *Cognitive Science, 5*, 121–52.

Cyert, R.M. and March, J.G. (1963) *A behavioral theory of the firm*. Englewood Cliff, N.J.: Prentice Hall.

Dennett, D.C, (1981) *Brainstorms*. Brighton, Sussex: Harvester Press.

Dewey, J. (1910) *How we think*. Boston: D.C. Heath Company.

Doherty, M.E., Mynatt, C.R., Tweney, R.D. and Schiaro, M.D. (1979) 'Pseudo-diagnosticity', *Acta Psychologica*, *43*, 111–21.

Duncker, K. (1945) 'On problem solving', *Psychological Monographs*, *58*, No. 5 (Whole No. 270).

Einhorn, H.J. and Hogarth, R.M. (1978) 'Confidence in judgement: Persistence of the illusion of validity', *Psychological Review*, *85*, 395–416.

Gazzaniga, M.S. (1983) 'Right hemisphere language following brain bisection. A 20-year perspective', *American Psychologist*, May, 525–37.

Getzels, F. and Csikszentmyhalyi, M. (1976) *The creative vision: A longitudinal study of problem solving in art*. New York: Wiley.

Ghiselin, B. (1952) *The creative process*. Berkeley, CA: University of California Press.

Gordon, W.J. (1961) *Synectics*. New York: Harper & Row.

Greeno, J. and Simon, H.A. (1985) 'Problem solving and reasoning'. In R.C. Atkinson, R. Herrnstein, Q. Lindzey and R.D. Luce (Eds.), *Stevens handbook of experimental psychology*. New York: Wiley.

Hayes, J.R. (1978) *Cognitive psychology. Thinking and creating*. Homewood, Ill.: Dorsey Press.

Hayes, J.R. and Simon, H.A. (1974) 'Understanding written problem instructions'. In L.W. Gregg (Ed.), *Knowledge and cognition*. Potomac, Md.: Erlbaum.

Hayes, J.R. and Simon, H.A. (1977) 'Psychological differences among problem isomorphs'. In N.J. Castellan, D.B. Pisoni and G.R. Potts (Eds.), *Cognitive theory, Vol. 2*. Hillsdale, N.J.: Erlbaum.

Hoffmann, L.R. (1961) 'Conditions for creative problem solving', *Journal of Psychology*, *52*, 429–44.

Hyman, R. (1964) 'Creativity and the prepared mind: The role of information and induced attitudes'. In C.W. Taylor (Ed.), *Widening horizons in creativity*. New York: Wiley.

Janis, I.L. and Mann, L. (1977) *Decision making*. New York: The Free Press.

Johnson, D.M. (1955) *The psychology of thought*. New York: Harper & Row.

Johnson, D.M. and Jennings, J.W. (1963) 'Serial analysis of three problem solving processes', *Journal of Psychology*, *56*, 43–52.

Johnson-Laird, P.N. (1983) *Mental models*. Cambridge, Mass.: Harvard University Press.

Kahney, H. (1986) *Problem solving: A cognitive approach*. Milton Keynes: Open University Press.

Kaufmann, G. (1980) *Imagery, language and cognition*. Oslo/Bergen/Tromsø: Norwegian University Press.

Kaufmann, G. (1984a) 'Can Skinner define a problem?' *The Behavioral and Brain Sciences*, *7*, 599.

Kaufmann, G. (1984b) 'Mental imagery in problem solving', *International Review of Mental Imagery*, 23–55.

Kaufmann, G. (1986) 'The conceptual basis of cognitive imagery models: A critique and a theory'. In D. Marks (Ed.), *Theories of image formation*. New York: Brandon House.

Kaufmann, G. (1987) 'Mental imagery and problem solving'. In M. Denis (Ed.), *Imagery and cognitive processes*. Amsterdam: Martinus Nijhoff.

Kosslyn, S.M. (1980) *Image and mind*. Cambridge, Mass.: Harvard University Press.

Køhler, W. (1927) *The mentality of apes*. New York: Harcourt, Brace & World.

Luchins, A.A. (1942) 'Mechanization in problem solving: The effect of Einstellung', *Psychological Monographs*, *54*, (Whole No. 248).

MacKinnon, D.W. (1962) 'The nature and nurture of creative talent', *American Psychologist*, *17*, 484–95.

Maier, N.R.F. (1963) *Problem solving discussions and conferences*. New York: McGraw-Hill.

Maier, N.R.F. and Hoffman, L.R. (1970) 'Quality of first and second solutions in group problem solving'. In N.R.F. Maier (Ed.), *Problem solving and creativity*. Belmont, Ca.: Brooks/Cole.

Mayer, R.E. (1983) *Thinking, problem solving and cognition*. San Francisco: Freeman.

McKeithen, K.B., Raitman, J.S., Ruchter, H.H. and Hirtle, S.C. (1981) 'Knowledge organization and skill differences in computer-programmers', *Cognitive Psychology*, *13*, 307–25.

Miller, G.A. (1956) 'The magical number seven, plus or minus two: some limits on our capacity for processing information', *Psychological Review*, *63*, 81–97.

Mintzberg, H., Duru, R. and Theortet, A. (1976) 'The structure of unstructured decision processes', *Administrative Science Quarterly*, *21*, 246–75.

Mynatt, C.R., Doherty, M.E. and Tweney, R.D, (1977) 'Confirmation bias in a simulated research environment: An experimental study of scientific inference', *Quarterly Journal of Experimental Psychology*, *29*, 85–9.

Newell, A. (1969) 'Heuristic programming: Ill-structured problems'. In J. Aronsky (Ed.), *Progress in operations research. Vol. 3*. New York: Wiley.

Newell, A. and Simon, H.A. (1972) *Human problem solving*. Englewood Cliffs, N.J.: Prentice Hall.

Newell, A., Shaw, J.C. and Simon, H.A. (1958) 'Elements of a theory of human problem solving', *Psychological Review*, *65*, 151–66.

Newell, A., Shaw, J.C. and Simon, H.A. (1979) 'The processes of creative thinking'. In H.A. Simon (Ed.), *Models of thought*. New Haven: Yale University Press.

Olton, R.M. (1980) 'Experimental studies of incubation: Searching for the elusive', *Journal of Creative Behavior*, *13*, 9–22.

Olton, R.M. and Johnson, D.M. (1976) 'Mechanisms of incubation in problem solving', *American Journal of Psychology*, *89*, 617–30.

Osborn, A.F. (1963) *Applied Imagination*. New York: Scribners.

Paivio, A. (1971) *Imagery and verbal processes*. New York: Holt, Rinehart & Winston.

Paivio, A. (1986) *Mental representations*. Oxford: Oxford University Press.

Parnes, S.J. (1963) 'The deferment of judgment principle: A clarification of the literature', *Psychological Reports*, *52*, 117–22.

Patrick, C. (1938) 'Scientific thought', *Journal of Psychology*, *5*, 55–83.

Perkins, D.N. (1981) *The mind's best work*. Cambridge, Mass: Harvard University Press.

Phillips, L. and Edwards, W. (1966) 'Conservatism in a simple probability inference task', *Journal of Experimental Psychology*, *72*, 346–54.

Pitz, G.F. (1969) 'An inertia effect (resistance to change) in the revision of opinion', *Canadian Journal of Psychology*, *23*, 24–33.

Pitz, G.F. (1975) 'Bayes' Theorem: Can a theory of judgment and inference do without it?' In F.R. Restle, R.M. Schiffrin, N.J. Castellan, H.R. Lindman and D.B. Pisoni (Eds.), *Cognitive Theory. Vol. 1*. Hillsdale, N.J.: Erlbaum.

Pitz, G.F., Downing, L. and Rheinhold, H. (1967) 'Sequential effects in the revision of subjective probabilities', *Canadian Journal of Psychology*, *21*, 381–93.

Pounds, W. (1969) 'The process of problem finding', *Industrial and Management Review*, *11*, 1–19.

Raaheim, K. (1964) 'Analysis of the missing part in problem solving', *Scandinavian Journal of Psychology*, *5*, 149–52.

Raaheim, K. (1974) *Problem solving and intelligence*. Oslo/Bergen/Tromsø: Norwegian Universities Press.

Reitman, W.R. (1965) *Cognition and thought*. New York: Wiley.

Rickards, T. and Freedman, B.L. (1978) 'Procedures for management in idea-deficient situations: An examination of brainstorming approaches', *The Journal of Management Studies*, *15*, 43–55.

Roe, A. (1953) 'A psychological study of eminent psychologists, and a comparison with biological and physical scientists', *Psychological Monographs*, *67*, No. 2 (Whole No. 352).

Rothenberg, A. (1976) 'The process of Janusian thinking'. In A. Rothenberg (Ed.), *The creativity question*. Durham, N.C.: Duke University Press.

Sanford, A.J. (1985) *Cognition and cognitive psychology*. London: Weidenfeld & Nicolson.

Scheerer, M. (1963) 'Problem solving', *Scientific American*, *208*, 118–28.

Schriffrin, R.M. (1978) 'Capacity limitations in information processing, attention and memory'. In W.K. Estes (Ed.), *Handbook of learning and cognitive processes*. New York: Wiley.

Shepard, R.N. (1978) 'The mental image', *American Psychologist*, 125–37.

Simon, H.A. (1945) *Administrative behavior*. New York: Macmillan.

Simon, H.A. (1957) *Models of man*. New York: Wiley.

Simon, H.A. (1965) *The shape of automation*. New York: Harper and Row.

Simon, H.A. (1966) 'Scientific discovery and the psychology of problem solving'. In R.G. Colodny (Ed.), *Mind and cosmos: Essays in contemporary science and philosophy*. Pittsburgh: University of Pittsburgh Press.

Simon, H.A. (1969) *The sciences of the artificial*. Cambridge, Mass. M.I.T. Press.

Simon, H.A. (1973) 'The structure of ill structured problems', *Artificial Intelligence*, *4*, 181–201.

Simon, H.A. (1977) *The new science of management decision*. Englewood Cliffs, N.J.: Prentice-Hall.

Simon, H.A. (1978) 'Information processing theory of human problem solving'. In W.K. Estes (Ed.), *Handbook of learning and cognitive processes*. New York: Wiley.

Simon, H.A. (1979) *Models of thought*. New Haven: Yale University Press.

Simon, H.A. (1981) 'Cognitive science: The newest science of the artificial'. In D. Norman (Ed.), Perspectives on cognitive science. Hillsdale, N.J.: Erlbaum.

Simon, H.A. (1983) *Reasons in human affairs*. Oxford: Basil Blackwell.

Simon, H.A. and Sumner, R.K. (1968) 'Pattern in music'. In B. Kleinmuntz (Ed.), *Formal representation of human judgement*. New York: Wiley.

Simon, H.A. *et al*. (1986) 'Report of research briefing panel on decision making and problem solving', *Research Briefings 1986*. Washington D.C.: National Academy Press.

Spearman, C. (1904) 'General intelligence objectively determined and measured', *American Journal of Psychology*, *15*, 201–93.

Spearman, C. (1927) *The abilities of man*. New York: Macmillan.

Stein, M.I. (1975) *Stimulating creativity. Vol. 2. Group procedures*. New York: Academic Press.

Sternberg, R.J. (1979) 'The nature of mental abilities', *American Psychologist*, *34*, 214–30.

Sternberg, R.J. (1985) *Beyond IQ*. Cambridge: Cambridge University Press.

Wallach, M.A. (1988) 'Creativity and talent: A master symposium on the Applications of Psychology to the teaching and learning of music'. Music Educators National Conference.

Wason, P.C. (1960) 'On the failure to eliminate hypotheses in a conceptual task', *Journal of Experimental Psychology*, *12*, 129–40.

Wason, P.C. (1968) ' "On the failure to eliminate hypotheses . . ." – a second look'. In P.C. Wason and P. Johnson-Laird (Eds.), *Thinking and reasoning*. Baltimore: Penguin.

Weisberg, R.W. and Suls, J. (1973) 'An information processing model of Duncher's candle problem', *Cognitive Psychology*, *4*, 255–76.

Weizenbaum, J. (1984) *Computer power and human reason*. Harmondsworth: Penguin.

Wertheimer, M.I. (1959) *Productive thinking*. New York: Harper & Row.

Wickelgren, W.A. (1974) *How to solve problems: Elements of a theory of problems and problem solving*. San Francisco: Freeman.

Winston, P.H. (1977) *Artificial Intelligence*. Reading, Mass: Addison-Wesley.

11

Mapping: creating, maintaining, and relinquishing conceptual frameworks

Michael B. McCaskey

In 1973 William Crozier, a senior vice president of Baystate, a large Massachusetts bank holding company, faced the type of ambiguous, ill-defined problem we are studying. Twelve member banks had tried to centralize computer operations, but a tradition of local autonomy had eventually led to the development of five separate data processing centers. The larger banks vied for dominance. The banks did not cooperate in jointly purchasing or programming systems. Consequently, the systems were inefficient and largely incompatible. Over the years many similar group efforts had fallen apart or produced confusing and frustrating results.

Drawing on his ten years' experience at the bank holding company, Crozier analyzed the problem in a white paper addressed to the board of directors. The current president of the holding company was nearing retirement, and the report amounted to a statement of what Crozier would do if named CEO. He argued that a direct frontal assault on the problem was unwise; that instead one should begin by discussing business strategy and the changing nature of competition in the bank industry. Essentially the report maintained that instead of facing local competition, Baystate banks would have to compete on a regional and perhaps even a statewide basis. Thus, it would become important to coordinate the banks' marketing of financial services and to integrate banking operations, such as data processing. More unified marketing would require greater standardization of services and procedures. The report concluded by recommending that a task force be appointed to work on developing corporate unity and identity among the member banks.

Notice that in this situation the holding company does not face one simple problem. According to Crozier's analysis, computer operations are connected to marketing which in turn is linked to issues of common identity which is tied in to the banks' history and tradition. This nested and interconnected quality is typical of the problems we are studying. Also characteristic is the lack of solid, quantitative data on key questions.

Reprinted from *The Executive Challenge: Managing Change and Ambiguity* (Boston, Mass. and London: Pitman, 1982), pp. 14–33

Crozier was elected CEO in June 1974. In implementing a new direction for the banks, he and his staff began to investigate forms of electronic banking that might serve as a common product for all the banks to market. At this point, electronic banking was a largely untried new technology for banks in New England. Surveys indicated that customers might resist using machines, no hard data on costs or usage were available, and even a modest pilot program would cost over one million dollars. For a new president, in a year in which the banking industry was suffering, the electronic technology represented a sizable step. The personal stakes were high and information on key issues was incomplete. Crozier later described the period as 'extremely tense . . . punctuated by moments of sheer ecstasy.'

Briefly, Crozier won acceptance for his new concept of the bank holding company's role as follows. He curtailed member banks' efforts to innovate electronically and brought several of the brightest and most capable member bank officers into the corporate staff. He hired an outside consulting firm to supply ideas and help carry out staff analysis for a more highly visible and coordinated marketing effort. He appointed those who seemed to have the most to lose – namely the presidents of the largest banks – to a series of holding company task forces to explore the possibility of developing a common product. Crozier was determined that he and his staff should always behave in a cheerful and gentlemanly way toward member banks. One of his staff and an outside consulting firm ran contests among employees to find a new name and generate excitement about the newly defined banking system. Baystate became BayBanks and successfully introduced a network of automated teller machines (ATMs).

These steps all contributed to a successful transformation carried out over a three-year period. But the necessary starting point, and of Crozier's most significant contributions, was to create a new way of thinking about the bank's problems. Crozier developed a new perspective that turned the problems of infighting and computer inefficiencies into an opportunity for marketing the holding company's extensive network of locations. The terrain was mapped anew, new connections were drawn, and new possibilities opened up.

Not everyone agreed with this new map. Several bank presidents, especially those in the larger, wealthier banks, already had maps that seemed to work well for them. They said, 'We are doing well. Competition among us keeps us healthy. Why should we change?'

The new map or vision of the banks as a more fully coordinated system focused attention upon the need for a product common to all the banks. In spite of previous disappointments, Crozier felt that some form of electronic banking might supply that product. He and several staff members and project teams began to explore this terrain to obtain what solid information they could.

Their efforts convinced them that the potential of ATMs would justify the initial investment costs. With some adroit maneuvering, some coaxing, and some pushing, they were able to get enough agreement from officers of the member banks to proceed. They acted on the new map, and it proved to be a viable picture of what new services bank customers would like to have.

Before Crozier's white paper, the 'reality' was that the banks had a problem with lack of coordination and duplication of computer services. Crozier and his staff saw the problem from a more powerful perspective and developed a fuller picture of what was real, and most likely to be important, to the banks and their customers. They therefore changed what they and others saw when looking at their banking landscape.

Crozier's reframing of the problem, what we will call mapping, was a critical step. One of the manager's greatest leverage points in facing ambiguity and change is how he or she *thinks* about the situation.

The metaphor of mapping

We live in conceptual worlds composed of our ideas, images, memories, plans, and knowledge, which inform the way we talk and think about the physical world. Our conceptualizations, or representations, of the parts of reality we have learned to see as meaningful, interesting, and important guide our actions and our work with others. Many researchers have found the idea of a 'conceptual map' a helpful metaphor for these conceptual systems that are usually taken for granted and assumed to *be* reality.

At any moment we have only a limited, tangible physical reality around us – the office, the hallway, and the elevator, for example. We see chairs, walls, lights, colour, and other people. We have names for, and knowledge about, all of these familiar objects. Most of this knowledge lies in the background of our attention, to be called to the foreground as needed. Our sense of reality, however, is not limited to the world immediately before us. We can visualize buildings, spaces, people, and events beyond our eyes. We can picture current and historical events around the world and use tools to extend our senses. These images, our names, our knowledge of how things fit together and what causes what to happen, constitute our 'map.' *A map is an interconnected set of understandings, formed by frequently implicit views of what one's interests and concerns are, what is important, and what demands action and what does not. It is a cognitive representation of the world and ourselves in it.*

Each of us has unique maps that have grown out of our experiences and needs. Of course, we also share some maps more or less closely with family, office colleagues, neighbors, members of a political party, and with other groups of which we feel a part.

A complete description of the process of conceptualizing reality would be extremely complex and lies outside the scope of this book. As we consider how managers cope with ambiguity, however, mapping represents a useful *tool* for understanding and exploring our mental representations and their connection to action. Maps come in many sizes, shapes, and degrees of accuracy. Think of a car's glove compartment, filled with road maps of

different areas and of the same area drawn to different scales. Another kind
of map can be as simple as the sketch a friend draws to show us the way to his
house. Maps of the New World drawn during the age of discovery show large
unknown areas and coastlines that gradually became more accurate. Maps
can also include pictorial representations that uncover new relationships by
depicting the known in an unfamiliar way. Like many of these physical
maps, mental maps are guides that are not always correct and are subject to
revision.

The metaphor of mapping embraces both product and process. Since we
are talking about managers operating in poorly mapped terrain, we will
emphasize the process of creating new knowledge and extending old knowledge through exploration, study, and action. Horace Freeland Judson,
examining the role of physical maps in the history of ideas, likens maps to
models. The maps of early explorers reduced the complexity of the world to
a model that people could conveniently study. Figure 1 shows the new world
as mapped by a French priest in 1546. By that time detailed knowledge of the
coastline was available, but little was reliably known about the American
interior. Maps as models, Judson says, 'are ships in which explorers journey
into the unknown. They embody what we know and carry us toward what we
don't know.'[1]

The manager who realizes he is following a conceptual map has taken an
important first step toward being able to manage ambiguity. Our maps can
be priceless guides, but they can also limit our perceptions, sometimes
becoming rigid and confining. Understanding a map as a revisable model
generally induces a healthy skepticism as to its infallibility, and engenders
more flexible thinking. Mapping and remapping is a fundamental process
that a manager facing ambiguity and change must master.

How are maps created and maintained?

Ordinarily people think of reality as objective, factual, and as undeniable as
the physical world within our reach. What we experience as real are the
events that we notice and can make sense of, those that have some significance for our lives and well-being. Reality is what we have become familiar
with, and have learned to attend to, through our experience. Yet the
recognized and named 'world' is complex and ever-changing, and so we
need to organize what is important and what is trivial, what is safe and what
is dangerous, what is associated with what, and what causes what. The
mental process and the product of this *organizing of reality*, this creating and
maintaining a frame of reference, is what we call 'conceptual mapping.'

Imagine, for example, that you are coming out of a building in a foreign
country and find the street unexpectedly jammed with people. What is going
on? This is *real*, but it doesn't make any sense yet. You haven't related it to
anything else. The event needs to be interpreted. Is it a disaster or a
celebration? Are people panicky or cheerful? If the crowds are gathering on

either side of the street, that usually means a parade and not a riot. If you recall mention of a festival, you have a plausible *reason* for a parade. You begin to map the reality of the crowd in the street. You search your experience and try to find a name for what is happening which will tell you how to act.

People have maps for different domains and for different purposes. Perhaps it helps to think of your head as a chart room full of maps – maps for your personal life, history, work, particular problem areas, routine procedures, and so on. Maps are pulled out according to occasion and purpose, and differ in degree of clarity, reliability, and completeness.

Because our information processing abilities are limited, mapping is selective. On the basis of our values and past experience, we perceive some events as noteworthy, while most features of the world around us are relegated to the background. Otherwise we would be overwhelmed by complexity and change. Out of what is noticed, people build a picture that makes sense to themselves and provides a common base of understanding with others. Although necessary, the selectivity of mapping has its dangers, as illustrated by the experience of US automakers, who ignored or downplayed the early signals that their business was undergoing fundamental change, since those signals conflicted with the main tenets of their map. While we can never grasp all of reality, what we defend against knowing can hurt us.

Mapping is a dialectic between events and our ideas about those events. Our conceptual maps determine what elements in the turbulence of daily events we focus on and how we interpret them; our experience of events in turn can refine and enlarge our maps. This means that ambiguity resides in the situation, in the mind of the manager, and in the interaction of the two. Like the paradox of Escher's two hands drawing each other, it is both the situation that is perplexing and the manager who is perplexed.

A map becomes increasingly 'objective' as more people come to share its view of reality. While one person holds a unique map it is a fragile construction. The map is strengthened as it is transmitted and accepted by more people.[2] Because the coherence of a social group depends upon developing a common map, mapping is heavily influenced by the social setting in which it occurs.

Mapping by a social group is not always a straightforward nor an easy process. Recall the bank presidents. They were concerned with maintaining their traditional autonomy within the holding company. Crozier and the central staff, on the other hand, were eager to realize the potential of closer coordination. Two sociologists who have studied the process of clashing views point out that, 'He who has the bigger stick has the better chance of imposing his definitions of reality.'[3] So it was in the banking case. Crozier had the backing of the majority stockholders and imposed his map on the sometimes reluctant presidents.

In a managerial group the social process of constructing reality this way involves the interaction, perhaps the collision, of several subjective readings

Figure 1   *Descelier's Map of the Coastline of the New World, 1546.*
(Reproduced courtesy of Map Division, The New York Public Library,
Astor, Lenox and Tilden Foundations)

(or personal maps) of the surrounding world. The work of a group in its early
stages includes forming a publicly held map that is generally agreed to by all
members. Once formed, this version of reality is treated as real; it *is real* for
group members and is slow to change. The map guides a member's daily
decisions about what to notice, what to do, and how to interact with others.

  When a map is more completely drawn and begins to make the surround-

'Descelier's map was 9 feet by 3 feet, so large that it was designed to be laid out on a table and read from both top and bottom, which is why the lettering in this detail is upside down. Most of the land mass of North America is a blur of speculation inhabited by confident aborigines and nervous Europeans.'[4]

ing landscape of events intelligible, group members often pressure each other to conform to using the group's map. The group has a range of punishments and inducements which few can withstand and still remain a group member in good standing. During a recent strike by Chicago firefighters, for example, most men refused a federal court order to return to work. A television news report captured the dynamics of the situation by focusing on one fireman who had been working, but then decided to rejoin his fellows amidst much cheering and backslapping. The firefighters' map of what was fair and what was legal obviously differed from the maps held by the mayor and the courts, and the firefighters were able to enforce the norms implied by their map on most of their fellows.

Groups and individuals use maps in such a way that the existing maps tend to be reconfirmed. Argyris and Schön have called this the 'self-stealing' quality of some systems or models.[5] Since a map points out what is to be noticed and valued among the plethora of events in each day, those events that do not jibe with the map tend to be ignored, or called aberrations, and thus forgotten. Discrepant events can create anxiety or, more rarely, wonder. If the discrepancy is too great, the map holder is likely to defend against seeing or appreciating the event. If the discrepancy is not too great, and individuals vary widely on this, the event provides an opportunity to redefine one's understanding of reality.

The same territory can be mapped in different ways. The map of the Roman empire presented in Figure 2, for example, reflects the needs, strengths, and worries of its inhabitants. The land masses where Roman armies operated are given proportionately more space than are the seas on which the enemy, Carthage, operated her superior navy. And just as the territory can be depicted politically, topographically, or geographically, organizations or groups will map their worlds in distinctive ways. The more maps of groups diverge, the more problematic communication becomes.

Finally, mapping is so natural a dimension of our everyday lives that large parts of our own maps are created outside our awareness. Mapping organizes what is put in the foreground and is often itself unnoticed. Frequently, a map and its embedded assumptions only becomes visible when they fail to provide a suitable basis for action. Only after its demise in 1969 were the top managers of the old *Saturday Evening Post* able to see that they had been wrong in expecting increased circulation to improve profitability.[6] Managers must search for ways to make maps visible before they break down. Some specific suggestions on what to do when maps are weak are presented later in this chapter.

Maps and ambiguity: imposing order on chaos

One way of defining an ambiguous situation is to say it is one in which none of your maps works well. Events are puzzling, confusing, and don't fit with what you know. The world seems baffling when events outpace ideas. Remember how frightening the initial outbreak of Legionnaire's Disease was? Many of those attending a Philadelphia convention mysteriously fell ill, no one knew why, and several died. People were deeply shaken by an occurrence that seemed to expose the limits of modern medicine.

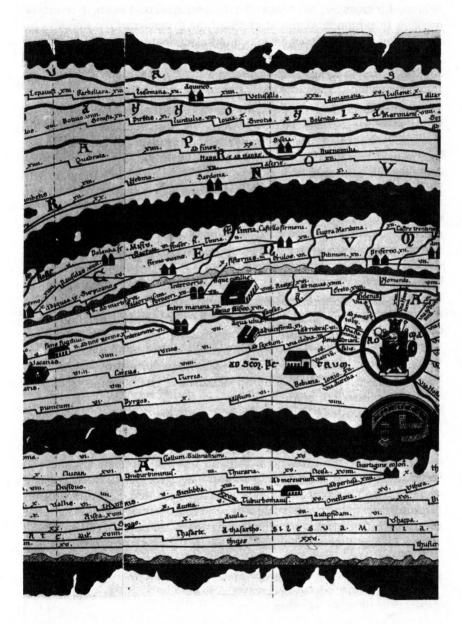

Figure 2 *Map of Ancient Rome and Italy* (Reproduced courtesy of Map Division, The New York Public Library, Astor, Lenox and Tilden Foundations)

'Roman road maps distorted sea and land masses in order to fit the imperial road system into a confined space ... The center strip is Italy; the Adriatic and Mediterranean are attenuated into mere rivers. Across from Rome and her harbor lies Carthage.'[7]

Crisis situations like this expose the transient quality of any map. A messy problem disrupts the map's ability to explain the everyday activities of members of a group. Members may have differing ways of stating what the problem is, but no one way appears adequate to solve the problem or compels widespread agreement. Since the ambiguous problem cannot be adequately defined, people do not respond to it in predictable, dependable ways. Because familiar routines and patterns are disrupted, group members feel increased stress. As the consensus about what is real breaks down, individuals are thrown upon more subjective and idiosyncratic interpretations and tend to want to withdraw from the situation. Without an adequate and commonly shared way to define the problem, communication and coordination become problematic.

Half a century ago John Dewey clearly pointed out how ill at ease we tend to be when nature is indeterminate. We greatly dislike confusion, disorder, obscurity, and indeterminateness, but 'nature is characterized by a constant mixture of the precarious and stable.'[8] Our reaction sometimes is to think and take intelligent action, but more often we settle for a feeling or an illusion of order. People want 'to do something at once; there is impatience with suspense, and lust for immediate action.'[9] We invent theories, rituals, or superstitions to make what was uncertain and confused into something clear and stable.

Dewey's observations on human nature are strongly supported by a review of work in cognitive psychology during the last several decades. Steinbruner found that, while researchers might disagree at the frontiers of knowledge about how the mind works, there was general agreement on five basic principles.[10] Researchers found:

1 The mind is an inference machine that actively imposes order on highly ambiguous situations.
2 The mind works to keep internal core beliefs consistent and unchallenged. (The stress literature also shows that the mind will deny, distort, or ignore signals that contradict core beliefs.)
3 The mind prefers simplicity.
4 The mind is constrained by reality (here the objective side of reality) in important ways.
5 The mind prefers stable and enduring relationships among its core beliefs.

The five principles are all of interest to managers facing ambiguity but the first is perhaps the most important; the others can all be gathered into it. *The mind is an inference machine that strives mightily to bring order, simplicity, consistency, and stability to the world it encounters. In other words, where nature is ambiguous, people develop strong beliefs and act upon them.* People tend to simplify complexity and make the inconsistent seem consistent. These tendencies are heightened when we perceive a threat to our identity, safety, security, or status. Generally speaking, we dislike disorder especially in areas where we are invested.

Mapping is affected by the mind's very active, interpretive quality. Our cognitive faculties operate ahead of conscious awareness, sorting through a wealth of potential information. Our mental processes make rapid estimates of what is valuable to notice and what can be treated as background. The mind takes fragments and makes something that fits existing organizing schemes. In the felicitous apothegm of Norwood Russell Hanson, 'There is more to seeing than meets the eyeball.'[11] Everywhere we look, we see with theory-laden vision.

Holding on to maps and 'little dying'

Perhaps because maps are so hard-won and so necessary for orderly interaction with others, people are very reluctant to change them. In fact, people fight to retain their maps. They want to hold onto that order, and suffer a little death if they have to relinquish it. 'Little dying' is Keleman's term for the painful letting-go of any of the major anchors of our life: separation from a loved one, moving from the home town. Leaving a successful position in a company. 'Big dying' is biological death.[12]

Little deaths compel the acknowledgement of our finiteness; we see that we cannot do or be everything we value, and that forces exist outside of us that have their own power. Acknowledgement of such hard facts is difficult and often avoided. Little dying involves giving up something central and important in our map.

In a thought-provoking paper that is the basis for this section of the chapter, Robert Tannenbaum has urged that more attention be paid to the process of little dying and holding on in organizational change.[13] Organization development specialists and managers often underestimate the need for people in a system to maintain continuity and to hold onto what they know has worked in the past. Tannenbaum argues for a balance in attending to the *yin* of stability and the *yang* of change. An organizational unit may have to die in order to clear the ground for something new to grow or for the unit, phoenix-like, to be reborn into new vitality. Each person undergoing such change faces the prospect of a little death and can be expected to try to maintain the existing map.

Other researchers have seen parallels to something like little dying on the organizational level. Fink, Beak, and Taddeo have identified four phases in an organization's response to a crisis:

1 *Shock* – organizational members become aware of a threat to existing structure
2 *Defensive retreat* – holding onto the old map
3 *Acknowledgement* – giving up the old map

Modes representing ~~~~ structure and a sense of Progression of the emotion when facing a threatening disruption.

The process resembles that seen by psychiatrist Elisabeth Kubler-Ross in her studies of the terminally ill. She finds that patients pass through the following stages in coming to terms with their own deaths:

1 *Denial and isolation* – the patient is shocked and disbelieves, puts off, or forgets
2 *Anger* – also rage, resentment, and envy – 'Why me?'
3 *Bargaining* – an extension of time is sought to complete unfinished business
4 *Depression and grief* – two phases: mourning what has already been lost and then mourning losses that lie in the future
5 *Acceptance* – accompanied by an inner and outer peace.[15]

Leaving one safe spot becomes easier when the next is in sight.

[...] f an organization and an
i[...] isruption is perceived to
b[...] feel shocked, deny the
d[...] d maps. This phase gives
way to feelings of anger and resentment and eventually to a period of mourning that looks backward and then toward the future. Only after grieving can the past be relinquished. Leaving one safe spot becomes easier when the next is in sight. Individuals create new meanings and definitions – a new or revised map – for what is happening. We have seen that our perceived reality is at least partly a social construct, and the transition to the acceptance phase of the sequence can be greatly facilitated by the help of friends and others who have undergone the pain of mourning and renewal.

Maintaining order by dynamic conservatism

How powerful the need is to hold onto familiar ways of knowing can be seen in Elting Morison's history of the adoption of continuous-aim firing in the United States Navy.[16] First devised by an English officer in 1898, this system allowed a ship's gun to be continuously aimed and readjusted as it was being fired. (Technically, this was achieved by altering the gear ratio in a battery's elevating gear so that the gun could adjust to the inertial roll of the ship and mounting a telescopic sight away from the recoil of the gun barrel.) A US Navy lieutenant stationed in China, William Sims, learned about the system from its originator, Percy Scott of the British Royal Navy. With Scott's assistance, Sims had the system installed on an American ship and trained a crew to use it. After a few months, the American crew showed the same remarkable improvement in accuracy as British crews had. Sims wrote 13 official reports, complete with great masses of data, to naval officers in Washington arguing the merits of the new system.

At first Washington officials made no response. According to their conceptual maps of naval gunnery, Sims's claims simply were not credible. As Sims became deliberately challenging and shocking in his reports, officials began to rebut the claims. They argued that existing American equipment was as good as British equipment and that any deficiencies must lie in the training of the men. They also conducted gunnery practice *on dry land* where, deprived of the benefits of the inertial movement, their results *proved* that the new system could not work as Sims claimed. They called Sims a 'crack-brain egoist' and accused him of deliberately falsifying evidence.

Not to be denied, Sims, who had the combative personality of a bantam rooster, circulated news of the new gunnery system among his fellow officers in the fleet. Finally in 1902, he took the bold step of writing directly to President Theodore Roosevelt. Roosevelt brought Sims back from China and forced change upon the Navy by installing Sims as Inspector of Target Practice.

In his analysis of the events, Morison points out that the Navy had its own reasons for resisting the technological innovation. The officers in Washington identified strongly with the existing equipment and their instinctive desire was to protect the established pecking order of the Navy. Intuitively they realized that the Navy's social system was organized around its major weapons systems and that a change would significantly disrupt the existing hierarchy of status. Indeed, the chaos of subsequent events proved this fear justified. In the terms of our discussion, the Washington officers sought to protect their map and the culture in which it was embedded. They held onto the map as long as possible and only let go when forced to do so by greater, outside authority.

Commenting on the same case, Donald Schön uses the term 'dynamic conservatism' to describe the tendency to fight to remain the same. He goes on to depict a social system as a set of concentric rings.[17] Change is more readily accommodated in the outer rings – that is, in the more superficially held elements of the system. But toward the center are core values and ideas whose change would necessarily induce a large-scale restructuring of the whole system. Here human systems fight hardest to conserve their sense of identity and reality. Maintaining a map becomes a fight to protect what is familiar and known – and to maintain identity, status, income, and standing.

Comparison with scientific communities

The same conserving tendency can be observed in the social systems of scientific communities. To be sure, groups in the scientific community also show some significant differences from military or business groups in how they operate. Both the differences and the similarities are instructive.

Thomas Kuhn, a historian and philosopher of science, has characterized the scientific enterprise as consisting of long periods of steady development, infrequently broken by revolutionary periods. The steady development of 'normal science' is made possible by a culture of shared values and norms, and by the existence of exemplary 'paradigms.'[18]

Paradigms in this sense are models for solving important problems in a given scientific field; these models embody what scientists know, but cannot verbalize. The tacit knowledge of these paradigms directs scientists to seek out and devote themselves to solving puzzles that contribute to the steady advancement of the field. According to Kuhn, a scientist working on a puzzle can be assured that, if he or she is clever enough, the puzzle can be solved. Because of the guidance and knowledge that paradigms offer, a group of scientists is very reluctant to give them up. Mitroff's study of 'moon scientists' showed that those whose theories of the moon's geology were contradicted by the first examination of moon rocks were more willing to dismiss the rocks than change their theories.[19] The rare revolutionary breaks in the steady development of normal science come when a scientist becomes dissatisfied with a paradigm's ability to suggest simple and accurate explanations for what is observed in nature. Kuhn cites Darwin, Copernicus, and Newton as examples of the extraordinary scientific work that involves shifting to a new paradigm.

In business and government, managers and administrators have maps that are based on some knowledge, but are much less complete than the exemplary paradigms of scientists. So managers more often face situations in which their maps are vague or may need to be reconstituted. In comparison to scientific problems, the situations faced by managers are also less general. In the example that began this chapter, the president of the bank holding company was not trying to solve everyone's electronic banking problem. He was trying to solve *his* electronic banking problem, as it existed in 1974.

Scientists doing normal science are puzzle-solvers; managers facing ambiguity are problem-attackers. Kuhn notes that large pressing problems, such as finding a design for world peace, are characteristically perceived as having no solution. Consequently, not much scientific work, and none of what he calls normal science, is directed toward solving such problems. Managers and administrators, on the other hand, often do not have the option of avoiding seemingly unsolvable problems. External circumstances commonly force them to try to do something to attack the problem, even though prospects for solving it are dim.

What to do when maps are weak

When the terrain is poorly mapped, what can managers do? Researchers of business and public administration have made several suggestions. In such situations managers often shift from optimizing to 'satisficing.'[20] Instead of trying to perform a complete analysis that will identify the *best* course of action, they settle for taking the first *satisfactory* alternative that comes along. This represents an important shift in outlook and captures an attitude of mind more likely to be effective in moving through uncharted territory. However, it is not, and is not meant to be, a detailed method for dealing with a particular problem.

Lindblom comes closer to describing a method. Government administrators, he observes, regularly muddle through poorly mapped problems.[21] They make limited comparisons with the recent past and take circumscribed steps into the future that conform to past trends. Administrators, he says, should accept their limited ability to foresee or plan for the long term and should advance by small, often uncoordinated steps. There is no room for revolutions here, and thus such an approach will not work well in a crisis that demands a complete shift in paradigm.

Christenson argues that when the terrain is poorly mapped managers should turn to 'negative thinking.'[22] Negative thinking proceeds more by refuting errors than by positively and conclusively proving a case. According to this view, managers confronting a poorly defined problem should not seek conclusive evidence and argument. They should instead treat contradictions as opportunities and aspire only to reasoning in terms of sufficient rather than necessary causes. Learning to recognize errors and avoid an associated course of action is the more important logical operation for advancing into unknown territory.

Barnard would, I think, agree with Christenson. As decision materials become more speculative, Barnard argues, the balance of a manager's mental operations should move toward nonlogical processes, thoughts that cannot be expressed in words, and which derive from judgment, intuition, and the grasp of an overall pattern.[23] Barnard is uncertain, however, about how to enhance these qualities in managers, or how to judge them except after the fact, on the basis of performance.

In an earlier work, I also advocated more explicit use of metaphorical and intuitive processes.[24] I suggest an alternative to goal setting, one that employs a more holistic sensing of the situation. When goals cannot be specified with confidence, as when the terrain is poorly mapped, you can shift your focus away from goals and toward influencing the domain in which you are working and the direction in which you are heading. March has also argued that managers should not always wait to act until goals are clear; rather, in some situations they should act in order to discover what their goals are.[25] Among other provocative recommendations, he urges that we treat memory as an enemy that preserves too many past answers that no longer work, and that we view a plan more as a summary of past decisions than as a program for future use.

Mason and Mitroff describe how to attack ill-structured organizational problems through a dialectical process.[26] Central to this method, the assumptions made in framing the problem must be brought to the surface. Two groups are put to work, one using the original assumptions, the other using directly opposite assumptions. Both groups go through a cycle of searching out relevant data and building a strategy. Since what one sees depends on one's theory, the second group should uncover new facts unnoticed by the first group. Under conditions designed to prevent premature compromise, the two groups meet and argue their positions. Out of this dialectic a new pool of assumptions is created from which a strategy is drawn.

These various suggestions for dealing with weak maps each have some value. They can best be tested by using them to explore the specifics of a case.

In closing let us look at one final example, Figure 3, of how a different way of mapping can reveal new features in what might seem familiar.

Notes

1 Horace Freedland Judson. *The Search for Solutions*. New York: Holt, Rinehart and Winston, 1980, p. 109.
2 Peter L. Berger and Thomas Luckmann. *The Social Construction of Reality*. Garden City, NY: Doubleday & Company, 1966.
3 Ibid., p. 109.
4 Judson, *The Search for Solutions*, p. 109.
5 Chris Argyris and Donald A. Schön. *Theory in Practice: Increasing Professional Effectiveness*. San Francisco: Jossey-Bass, 1974.
6 Roger I. Hall. 'A System Pathology of an Organization: The Rise and Fall of the Old Saturday Evening Post,' *Administrative Science Quarterly*, June 1976, 21(2): 185–211.
7 R.V. Tooley. *Landmarks of Mapmaking*. Text written by Charles Bricker, New York: Thomas E. Crowell, 1976.
8 John Dewey. *The Quest for Certainty*. New York: G.P. Putnam's Sons, 1929, p. 243.
9 Ibid., p. 223.
10 John D. Steinbruner. *The Cybernetic Theory of Decision*. Princeton: Princeton University Press, 1974.
11 Norwood Russell Hanson. *Patterns of Discovery*. Cambridge, England: Cambridge University Press, 1965.
12 Stanley Keleman. *Living Your Dying*. New York: Random House, Inc., 1974.
13 Robert Tannenbaum. 'Some Matters of Life and Death,' Human Systems Study Center, Working Paper 76–2. Graduate School of Management UCLA, April 1976.
14 Stephen L. Fink, Joel Beak, and Kenneth Taddeo. 'Organizational Crisis and Change,' *The Journal of Applied Behavioral Science*, 1971, 7(1): 15–41.
15 Elisabeth Kubler-Ross. *On Death and Dying*. New York: Macmillan Publishing Co., Inc., 1969.
16 Elting E. Morison. 'A Case Study of Innovation,' *Engineering and Science Monthly*. April 1950.
17 Donald A. Schön. *Beyond the Stable State*. New York: Random House, Inc., 1971.
18 Thomas S. Kuhn. *The Essential Tension – Selected Studies in Scientific Tradition and Change*. Chicago: University of Chicago Press, 1977; Thomas S. Kuhn. *The Structure of Scientific Revolutions*. Chicago: The University of Chicago Press. 2nd edition, 1970.
19 Ian I. Mitroff. *The Subjective Side of Science*. Amsterdam: Elsevier Scientific Publishing Company, 1974.
20 James G. March and Herbert A. Simon. *Organizations*. New York: John Wiley, 1958.
21 Charles E. Lindblom. 'Still Muddling, Not Yet Through.' *Public Administration Review*, Nov/Dec 1979: 517–26.
22 Charles Christenson. 'The Power of Negative Thinking.' Working Paper, HBS 72–41.

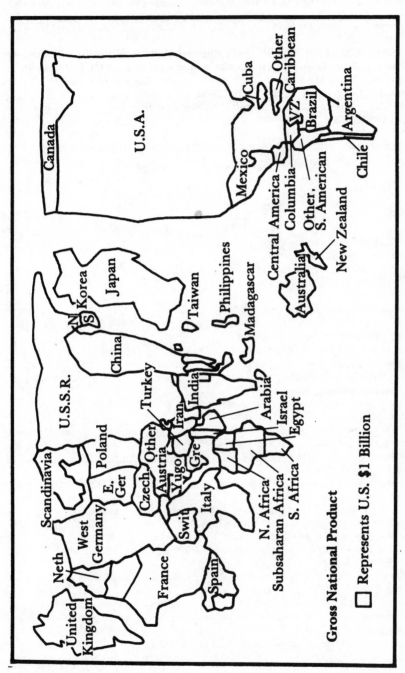

Figure 3 *A map of the world constructed under new rules, with countries sized in proportion to their gross national product. This particular way of representing the territory highlights relationships that perhaps not everyone has recognized before.*

Boston: Graduate School of Business Administration, Harvard University, December 1972.
23 Chester I. Barnard. *The Functions of the Executive*. Cambridge, Mass.: Harvard University Press, 1938.
24 Michael B. McCaskey. 'A Contingency Approach to Planning; Planning with Goals and Planning without Goals.' *Academy of Management Journal*. June 1974, 17(2): 281–91.
25 James G. March and Johan P. Olsen. *Ambiguity and Choice in Organizations*. Bergen, Norway: Universitetsforlaget, 1976, pp. 69–81.
26 Richard O. Mason and Ian D. Mitroff. *Challenging Strategic Planning Assumptions*. New York: John Wiley, 1981.

12

Corporate networking: how to tap unconventional wisdom

Robert K. Mueller

Organization as we know it is obsolete in the information society in which we now exist. Those of us in management who weave human networks have confounded both ourselves and our establishments. These human networks are thriving while the organizations around them struggle to be effective – or even to survive. There seems to be an intuitive notion that somehow, someway, networking may be basic to organizing and managing people in the future.

The challenge is to create a proper dynamic balance in the management and control of our organizational system. This balancing requires the fostering of the human, innovative side of business systems management, which is where networks and networking play a key role.

In dealing with such a challenge, we are presented with a choice between the management of human systems and human systems management. The management of human systems is the science and technology of managing productivity and efficiency. Institutionalization, hierarchical structures, orderly process, and bureaucracy abound. Human systems management is the art of linking human beings in constructive teams and catalyzing their full creative growth through leadership. Innovation, entrepreneurship, risk taking, networking, motivation, communications, recognition, individualism, self-fulfillment, strong peer relationships, and professional dedication are key attributes of this type of management.

This chapter argues that the concept of human networks and the process of social networking are prime components for a properly balanced organizational system in these turbulent and exciting times. Formal recognition and use of human networks is limited and somewhat unacceptable in the traditional hierarchical and structured makeup of most of our institutions. However, the good news is that networks and networking can cohabit with hierarchy and bureaucracy. Effectiveness and action-timing can often be enhanced with proper empowerment of the human networks which already

Edited with permission of The Free Press, a Division of Macmillan Inc. from *Corporate Networking: Building Channels for Information and Influence* (New York: Free Press, 1986). Copyright © 1986 by Robert Kirk Mueller

exist in the organizations. One way to get things done quicker and better, given the barriers and complexities in our political, economic, educational, social, and technological institutions, is to 'think networks,' i.e., identify and encourage them where appropriate.

This proposed networking mind-set is alien to most executives and managers. They got where they are by climbing the ladder of traditional, hierarchical, organizational pyramids. The Orwellian mentality, which is so often the result of this process, needs to be blended with a Renaissance mentality to enable managers to recognize the value of new strains of organizations such as human networks. Classical institutional structures, process, and concepts have failed to keep up with the demands for survival, interdependence, growth, and improved effectiveness of many of our organizations. Networks and networking warrant special attention from leaders and managers for the future.

The heart of networking: blest be weak ties that bind

Networking is like trying to cultivate wild-flowers. You don't plant and hover over them. You permit or create an environment where they can come out and grow.

Many large corporate organizations are experiencing a disruption of traditional structures and management information processes. Their efforts to keep up with people needs, value shifts, and exploding networks have been in vain. Networks and networking, like wild-flowers, spring up in such an atmosphere of transformation in big institutions.

Networks are needs-driven and deliberate. Some of them are even sanctioned. For example, Tandem Computers Inc. is a computer hardware manufacturer with a $624 million turnover and a reputation for its enlightened management culture. Tandem's president and chief executive, Jim Treybig, provides each employee with a personal computer and after an employee has worked at Tandem for six months the computer becomes his or her personal property.

The company functions effectively and routinely with most everyone hooked up electronically to one another to carry out the conventional administrative and engineering tasks. Cathode ray tube (CRT) dialoguing is encouraged and practiced in conducting daily business affairs. One goes direct, via his or her computer hookup, to the person who can get something done. The normal hierarchy and bureaucracy are by-passed.

However, Treybig also emphasizes human networking beyond the computer. Politicians call it 'pressing the flesh.' The term refers to one-to-one relationships. Treybig believes in communication between all levels of his workforce worldwide. Tandem supplements its electronic networking with a free beer and pretzel party at each plant every Friday night. All employees are invited to gather at the end of the computer-dominated week of work to engage in human networking and chat about the business. The management doesn't label these informal happenings as human network-shops. But that is precisely what they are. These are vital ceremonies or rituals that serve four major functions. The provide an opportunity to socialize, allay anxieties, reduce ambiguities and convey the message that the company cares and values its employees.

The nature of networks and networking

Networks are informal systems where dissonance is encouraged and consensus a common goal. The nature of networks is that they are short-lived, self-camouflaging, and adisciplinary. They are invisible, uncountable, unpollable, and may be active or inactive. In practical terms, networks nurture spontaneous feedback via telephone, mail, meetings, computers, or a shout across the room. Network *structures* have one or more of five characteristics according to Lipnack and Stamps (1982):

1. 'Wholeparts' – self-reliant and autonomous participants, i.e., independent 'wholes' and interdependent 'parts'
2. Levels – the result of networks interconnecting on an ever-expanding scale
3. Distributed powers and responsibility along horizontal or wavy lines (*not* the rigid, vertical lines found in bureaucracies)
4. Fly-eyed perception – having one apparent eye or focus that embodies a plethora of other eyes
5. Hydra-headed direction – having many 'leaders' (polycephalous) yet few rings of power

Network *processes* have one or more of five characteristics:

1. Relationships – abstract and qualitative as well as concrete and quantitative
2. Fuzziness – having few inner divisions and indistinct borderlines
3. Nodes and links – serving as entry points or connectors for conveying information
4. 'Me' and 'we' relationships – according equal importance to the individual and the group
5. Values – self-reliance, self-interest, interdependence, and collective interest

We tend to forget the value of social networking, the informal gossip channels, and verbal and written grapevines that persist in all organizations like crabgrass in a well-trimmed lawn. Stamping out these informal channels is not possible, nor should it be a goal. Actually, grapevines can provide a check and balance on poorly conceived plans, the rise of favoritism, and emotional situations and decisions. Grapevines provide management with uncontrolled feedback about climate, morale, and social health of the firm, and about what is really happening in the organization.

The employee grapevine should be harvested continually and particularly during periods of excitement, change, and insecurity. Grapevines flourish whenever a firm's communication policy and practice are not in good shape, when there is little company news, and formal communications channels are too rigid or adhered to too narrowly. Wise managers know which individuals serve as grapevine links and can assist them in influencing the direction of informal communncations which supplement the formal channels. It's like side communication in a boardroom. If you whisper something to your neighbor, the message gets undue attention.

Managing innovative networks

The temper of innovation is that of positive networking rather than revolutionary or rebellious. If it antagonizes and is unacceptable, by definition an innovation lapses. If, through interpersonal linkages, an innovation satisfies a want or nullifies an annoyance, it gathers a following and is accepted. Human networks play a key role in such acceptance.

Networking is vital to the introduction of novel products and processes, and to the acceptance of culture, attitude, and mind-set changes of an organization. Unfortunately, most managers are unskilled and often unaware of the interpersonal process of networking and its potential for effecting influence and wielding power.

Managing innovation, with or without networking, is not a crisply defined process. There must be elbow room for serendipitous happenings. No real guide-lines can be set for such events, other than the principle that the corporate attitude should be favorable to nonconformists and divergent thinking. Consider the baker in a small Florida town who was a volunteer fireman. Twenty minutes after he had placed rolls in the oven, the fire alarm sounded. Rather than let the rolls burn, he took them out, thinking they were ruined. On his return three hours later, he rebaked them instead of throwing them out. Thus he discovered brown-and-serve rolls, for which General Mills paid him $400,000. The phrase 'half-baked' doesn't have a bad connotation any more.

The major barrier to important entrepreneurial innovations within the modern corporate framework is the organizational hierarchy itself. The structure and mind-set hierarchical hang-up is manifested by the inertia of the managers in power, whose tendency is often to neglect, sequester, or smother the entrepreneur or the networker. The management challenge is to open up the system to networking and unconventional thinking while still maintaining adequate control. This is a management balancing act and no rigid guide-lines exist for the process.

However, large organizations have long been experimenting with this management balance. One of the most evident experimental trials has been in the new venture realm. Companies such as AT&T, Dow, Westinghouse, Monsanto, Dupont, E.G, & G., 3M, and many others, have good and bad experiences to observe in this more open system approach to innovation via the venture organization route.

The 3M Company is renowned for its innovations. It is less known for its dedication to the process of networking. 3M looks for 'uninhabited markets' and 'entrepreneurs from within.' According to Robert M. Adams, director and R&D chieftain, 'start little and build.'

The bedrock principle of free communication within 3M is recognized in the motto: 'If you need help, go find it anywhere.' Two corollary principles are required: (1) know where to look for the information you need and (2) have it be made available when you ask. Many observers have put their fingers on these company rules as 3M's key strengths over the years. The emphasis is on internal communications (networks) as illustrated by the well-known 3M Technical Forum, which the company established to encourage professional people to mix and exchange ideas. The Forum is an internal society network run by professionals which holds seminars on all sorts of technical topics drawn from the work going on in various company laboratories. In more recent years, it has been broadened to include management and behavioral science subjects. The essence is networking at any time or place, i.e., formal or informal communication and action.

Networking provides tremendous power to get ideas accepted or new actions underway and can empower an organization to alter its course or accept change.

Innovation is one of the most important attributes distinguishing the leading companies within different industry segments. In addition, a company's ability to successfully manage innovation correlates with its value as a long-term investment. Innovative companies are continually alert to change and they take specific actions. They create a proper climate, stimulate the search for new ideas and opportunities, energize idea development, and motivate, reward and sustain innovators. In all four of these initiatives, organization structure networking practices is one key to success (ADL 1985).

* Increased attention to innovation is caused by several factors, the first of which is accelerated dissemination of new ideas. The acceleration is helped by information technologies and direct person-to-person communication in large organizations. It is also occurring intraorganizationally through professional society, trade association, and other industry and governmental communication channels.

* Japanese quality and productivity circles are well known. The notion of employee discussion groups is spreading worldwide. The TRW company in the United States uses a 'one-in-five' system for discussion groups. Each year 20 percent of the employees are selected to participate. One out of five persons from various organizational units create a mix across the company

departments and functions. The networking groups meet frequently with the CEO or senior managers. The personnel director moderates. Networks and networking are thereby endorsed and empowered

* Club Méditerranée provides a striking example of induced networking with its staff rotation scheme which breaks down hierarchical barriers. The managers call the practice 'nomadism.' The staff of each vacation village is moved every six months. In addition, managers swap jobs every two to four years. Everyone agrees that this cross-fertilization, continual formation and reformation of close human network linkages between staff members enhances direct communication, action, and innovation. Networks and networking can be a powerful factor in management effectiveness.

* Medtronic, the world's largest manufacturer of implantable cardiac pacemakers, achieves lateral thinking through encouragement of direct networking between staff members. Medtronic's business and technology centre is laid out like a shopping mall; each new business venture is a separate 'store,' but the staff have ready, direct access to all the other 'stores' and their personnel at all times without formal approval policies or procedures.

* Bromont uses an Idea Exchange Committee on Technology to review all ideas and help employees define them. The communication linkage is direct networking with those concerned, regardless of the organizational hierarchy.

* ASEA (Allmänna Svenska Elektriska Aktiebolaget), AB, in Sweden features an ideal sponsorship program. Top management empowers five well-known senior managers to advocate and promote new ideas. These five stimulating 'nodes' form a network designed to foster the bottom-up generation of new ideas.

How to design and set up a network

Networkers are already motivated or they wouldn't be in the network the biggest problem networks have is how to pay the phone bills.
Byron Kennard

Designing and setting up a network can serve a variety of purposes. Usually networks are established for the purpose of finding alternative pathways for personal or group action. Networks may be for (1) enhancing our intellectual, social, and leisure activities, (2) keeping in touch with certain people who share common interests or concerns, (3) exploring the value and potential of a more formally organized endeavor, (4) keeping informed and trading information with others, (5) influencing, politically or otherwise, and learning from others who elect to network with you, (6) linking individuals with individuals, organizations with organizations, or individuals with organizations, (7) affecting change in complex organizations or situations by offering alternative methods of increasing awareness, unfreezing attitudes, and refreezing them in changed directions, and finally, (8) expanding, without undue risk but with lower acquisition costs and improved stability, awareness of what we personally have to offer others. Given one or more purposes it is easy to design and create a network.

A logical approach to designing your network can consist of the following eight steps:

1: Purpose and objectives

Clarify the purpose(s) of the proposed network.

2: Resource inventory

Inventory your personal network. Take stock of your personal and material resources, such as your knowledge, skills, experiences, contacts, intuitive interests, values, beliefs, aspirations, expectations, and natural talents.

3: Resource gap

Estimate or identify resources which you find missing in step two and which are needed to accomplish the purpose(s) of your network.

4: Structural nature

Decide on the kind of network which intuitively seems most appropriate to serve the purpose(s).

5: Actor assessment

Assess the proposed networkers as to their probable role in the communications function of the network.

6: Networking process

Consider the process of networking to be used. If your primary experience has been limited to highly structured organizations, such as a large business corporation, government, or religious hierarchy, you will find networking processes differ considerably and can be much more fun. As Tim Heald (1983) puts it, 'Networking, like sex, is one of the few activities at which a gifted and enthusiastic amateur has built-in advantage over the purely professional.'

The process which you may find most effective in your own networking is one that encourages relationships with those with whom you have or can establish a collegial connection. Conversely, you skip or discourage connections where one person is dominant and nonegalitarian. Ideally, there is no dominate–subordinate equation in a network. The relationship or connection made in a network is a thing in itself separate from either participant. If

160   *Robert K. Mueller*

you don't want or can't establish a relationship separate from the actors involved, your network process may become influenced by the control of the relationship and run the risk of introducing a personal bias of those serving as stars, weavers, linkers, gatekeepers, or isolates.

The connection which has a life of its own is one of trust. Trust develops over a period of time where exchanges take place. Competition has no role in network relationships, contrary to the essential nature of dominant–subordinate relationship in hierarchical structures. The collegial nature of the networking process works on the freedom to explore associations and information exchange.

Management by objectives does not work well in networking. Rather Parker and Hedin (1983) specify five 'positions' which take place sequentially, with some by-passing and recycling as innovative ideas or problems to be solved move from their origin to fruition or solution.

Briefly, Position I is where isolated innovators and problem solvers become willing to share the idea or problem with others. Position II is called an unintentional informal network of dispersed people who know others and make contacts on a nonprearranged basis. If this exchange and interaction creates a strong common concern, the process moves to Position III, intentional informal network. Meetings, newsletters, and more formal communications begin. Funds are sought, if needed. If this step proceeds, Position IV, the formal network, is reached. The Position IV effort establishes identity and purpose, participants are listed, meetings or exchanges are planned. At this point the network may have achieved its goal and is often disbanded.

Alternatively, Position V may be sought and reached. This is the institutionalized network creature. Centralization takes place with a facilitating centre in a nonprofit corporation, or a wing of an established institution. Funding, formal organization, and structure are introduced. If everyone is not careful a bureaucracy will grow and destroy the nature of the network by introducing competition and hierarchy. If a competitive culture develops, the comparative analysis with others may limit the freedom of participants, elitism creeps in, and the withholding of network information gathered from others becomes a practice to preserve the institution. Position V, when routinized, can be shifted to established professional societies, associations, or consortium of organizations. The human network features then have to exist in conflict with institutionalized goals and norms. The essence of collegial networking may be jeopardized.

7: Informational data base

Start a repository for your information and ideas. There may be more than one data base. This can be a computer log, a library, a card file, or any other means that is comfortable and accessible for you to use as you nurture and empower your network.

Key associates in various locations can be linked by a computer network service, through their 'electronic mailbox' personal computers. Messaging goes on at all hours, at any place, without face-to-face meetings, which are difficult to achieve. The individuals check their electronic mailboxes, when convenient, for the stored messages.

8: Action

Remember that the core of the network concept is to exchange information, expedite the process, recognize patterns of information processing, and learn. To get going, make a trial run as an initial stage. The following are some of the considerations on where and how to start.

1. The skills of networking require the ability to combine appreciation of problem structure, 'opportunity space', human behavior, and symbolism. Appreciation of these four items must be accompanied by some knowledge of where the interested parties may be, e.g. industry sectors, educational domains, government information sources, communities, organizations, and friends operating in the field of interest or exploration.

2. Recognize that when a little help from your friends – your network – becomes an outright imposition it's time to observe some networking proto-col and a few courtesies, such as timing your requests, watching for expenses incurred, avoiding excessive requests, respecting your contact's sense of timing, being specific about the inquiry, being appreciative, and providing feedback. Don't abuse your network. Some of the most common abuses are in job-hunting situations, the ensnaring of friends for charity advisory roles, and in seeking information for investment purposes.

3. Obey the conventional, common sense 'rules' of the networking process. Smith and Wagner (1983) suggest four rules are useful: 'Don't be too boring, listen, ask questions, and don't make assumptions.'

4. Keep three indices in mind to track the effectiveness of your networking. Sociologists have worked this system out for measuring interchange of information in a network. *Centrality* is the tendency of one person, or of a unit's members, to be cited (referred to in the networking process) by others in the network, or by others outside the unit. *Integration* is the tendency of a networker to cite other networkers. *Dependence* is the tendency of an individual networker, or a member of some unit, to cite networkers or others outside the unit or network. By keeping tabs on these three indices you can get some measure of the effectiveness and activity of your network *if*, for some reason, you have need to assess the vitality and effectiveness of the network.

5. Start-ups should have a focus rather than a specific goal. If we knew specific goals it wouldn't be networking. For example, if the purpose of the

network is to raise consciousness about the protection of quality of an inland lake, articulate that general focus in clear terms, not specific goals. Specific goals can come later and their pursuit be handled by processes other than networking, i.e., task forces, projects, or organizational programs.

6. Have a 'mother' or 'father' figure, a leader who is the initiator, arranger, and central communicator, and one who needs or knows what's up and keeps track. This can be an executive secretary, a staff expert on a paid or volunteer basis.

7. Create a modest, regular newsletter as a regular communications vehicle. Use computers if the network 'messages' by electronic means, or the mail. The newsletter should be quick to produce and easy to read – not a professional reference or research journal. Don't make a chore out of it.

8. Publish a list of members with a sentence or two about what each member is up to and their affiliations. Anyone interested in networking with another can go directly to him or her.

9. Identify a group you know for initial contact, rather than a committee of networkers, to start your inquiry and information exchange. Don't institutionalize or structure the networking. It's not the organization structure or network chart that counts. It's the people.

10. Set some target event to exchange fruits of the networking. If the project warrants feedback to the contributors, set a tentative target date to share your findings, thinking, solution, or perplexity. Those who volunteer to network with you will probably want some feedback.

Networkers are already motivated or they wouldn't be in the network. Operating a network is a subtle behavioral process of creating information exchange and of learning. Properly empowered through networking, 'our self interests can be transformed into a personally and intellectually satisfying mutuality.'

References

ADL (1985) *From vision to reality: Successfully managing innovation.* Arthur D. Little: Cambridge, Mass.

Heald, T. (1983) *Networks: Who we know and how we use them.* Hodder and Stoughton: London, p. 178.

Lipnack, J. and Stamps, J. (1982) *Networking: The first report and directory.* Doubleday: New York.

Parker, A. and Hedin, M. (1983) 'Networks in education', *Forum*, March, p. 30–32.

Smith, L. and Wagner, P. (1983) *The networking game.* Network resources: Denver, Colorado.

13

The logic of intuition: how top executives make important decisions

Weston H. Agor

The decade of the 1980s may well have become known as that benchmark period in management history when intuition finally gained acceptance as a powerful tool guiding executive decision making. The first half of the decade has witnessed a crescendo of interest in the topic of both top executives and students of management: certainly, managers are far more comfortable today than they were ten years ago to admit that they often actually use intuition to help make their most important decisions.

For example, Thomas Peters and Robert Waterman, Jr. report in their best-selling book, *In Search of Excellence*, that the ten best-run companies in America now encourage the use of intuitive skills and nurture its development in their management cultures. Similarly, John Naisbitt pointed out in his new book, *Reinventing the Corporation*, that the use of intuition in corporate decision making has gained new respectability. Such well-known scientists and inventors as Jonas Salk and the late Buckminster Fuller recently published books extolling intuition for its role in their most important discoveries.

Why is so much interest in this brain skill being generated right now? A number of reasons can easily be identified. One significant factor is that top managers often find that left-brain analytical techniques (for example, management by objectives, PERT and forecasting) are not always as useful as they once were for guiding decisions. This is so because top executives now have to make major decisions in a climate characterized by rapid change and at times also laden with crisis events. In addition, emerging new trends often make linear models based on past trends either inaccurate or misleading.

Intuition as a managerial skill

What is intuition? Frances E. Vaughan, psychologist and author of *Awakening Intuition*, defines it as a 'way of knowing ... [a way of] recognizing the possibilities in any situation.' Webster's defines intuition as 'the power of knowing . . . a quick or ready apprehension.' Intuitive decisions come from a capacity to integrate and make use of *both* the left and the right sides of the brain. Intuition is a product of *both* factual and feeling cues – unclouded by deep personal ego involvement in the issue at hand.

Laurence R. Sprecher, senior associate with Public Management Associates in Oregon, posits that intuition is really a *subspecies of logical thinking* – one in which the steps of the process are hidden in the subconscious portion of the brain. He argues:

> If we accepted that intuition is an extension of the logical, wouldn't we be more comfortable using it? By treating intuition as something mysterious or, worse, feminine, do we make it more difficult for most managers, who tend to be biologically masculine and theoretically logical, to use intuition?

Carl Jung, the famous psychologist, found in his research, which has more recently been corroborated by others, that those skilled in the use of intuition tend to have particular decision-making skills not normally possessed by others. Thus managers with good intuition can see new possibilities in any given situation. They have a sense or vision of the future and thus are better equipped to move their organization in response to it. These managers are particularly adept at generating new ideas and providing ingenious new solutions to old problems; usually, they function best in rapidly changing environments or crisis settings.

Field studies on the use of intuition among managers

If the future management climate becomes anything like that painted in recent best-selling books, then intuitive decision-making skills will become increasingly valuable in decision making in the decade ahead. I began a series of studies concerning executives' *ability to use* intuition – and their actual use of it – to make management decisions.

The findings were dramatic; one of the most important was that intuitive ability varied by managerial level. Managers at the top in every organization studied scored higher than middle- or lower-level managers on their ability to use intuition to guide their key decisions.

During 1984, I completed a major follow-up study to answer the question: How do executives who score highly intuitive *actually use* their skill to guide their decisions – particularly their most important ones? Top executives who scored in the top 10% on the intuition scale were included in the follow-up.

The questionnaire let me probe more deeply into how managers actually use their intuitive ability. It was my hope that the answers to these questions would give me a more complete picture of the total intuitive process in a managerial context. Topics covered were whether these top executives *believed they used their intuition* to guide their most important decisions; *how they actually used their intuition* to guide their most important decisions;

specific examples of key decisions; which particular technique(s) they used (if any) to help draw on their intuitive ability more effectively and *develop it further*; and *whether they kept it a secret that they used intuition* to make key decisions or shared this information with their colleagues.

Responses were received from top executives in such major organizations as General Motors, Chrysler Corporation, Burroughs, the Ford Foundation, the National Security Agency, and the Department of the Army. The excellent response rate suggests that top executives value intuition as a tool for managing organizations.

The study findings

All but one executive acknowledged that they actually used their intuitive ability to guide their most important decisions. One experienced executive volunteered, 'I do believe in using my intuitive powers on most of my decisions, large or small.' Another respondent described the process this way: 'I don't think intuition is some magical thing. I think it is a subconscious drawing from innumerable experiences that are stored. You draw from this reserve without conscious thought.'

These descriptions of how the intuitive process works are much like those of Frances E. Vaughan, psychologist and author of *Awakening Intuition*. She states:

> At any given moment one is conscious of only a small portion of what one knows. Intuition allows one to draw on that vast storehouse of unconscious knowledge that includes not only everything that one has experienced or learned, either consciously or subliminally, but also the infinite reservoir of the collective or universal unconscious, in which individual separateness and ego boundaries are transcended.

The executives were quick to point out that they considered intuition to be *only one* tool of many to use in guiding their decisions. They did not advocate relying exclusively on intuition or abandoning traditional 'left-brain' management practices. On the other hand, respondents emphasized that intuition is also a key management resource that should be used to help guide strategic decisions. Many top executives stressed that good intuitive decisions were, in part, based on input from facts and experience gained over the years, combined and integrated with a well-honed sensitivity or openness to other, more unconscious processes. William G. McGinnis, city manager of Crescent City, California, offered this humorous but wise operating definition of an intuitive decision in a recent article:

> I believe that good intuitive decisions are directly proportional to one's years of challenging experience, plus the number of related and worthwhile years of training and education, all divided by lack of confidence or the fear of being replaced.

Management situations and important decisions in which intuition was most useful

As a group, respondents were clearly able to identify management situations and important decisions in which they have learned from experience to rely on their intuitive ability most for guidance in how to act. When executives were asked if intuition was most useful in particular circumstances or if they used it freely to help guide all major decisions, they identified the following conditions as those under which intuitive ability seems to function best:

- When a high level of uncertainty exists.
- When little previous precedent exists.
- When variables are less scientifically predictable.
- When 'facts' are limited.
- When facts don't clearly point the way to go.
- When analytical data are of little use.
- When several plausible alternative solutions exist to choose from, with good arguments for each.
- When time is limited and there is pressure to come up with the right decision.

Respondents were asked to name examples of very important decisions in which they followed their intuition and the decisions proved to be right. Here are some of the more representative examples given:

- Recommended not to invest in a $500 million capital project that was supported by our scientific staff, and that we were technically capable of implementing. I questioned its economic value.
- Refused to pull a drug off the market as recommended by the FDA on the basis of adverse animal reactions to tests.
- Decided on a multimillion-dollar production expansion at one of our major plants with a strong quality performance record over another plant with lower production costs but a poorer quality performance record.
- Supported the regional decentralization of the mental health department statewide over strong internal objections.

These decisions were indeed of strategic magnitude – they involved millions of dollars, impacted the public welfare, and/or were likely to set a course for the organization in question for years to come. When viewed as a whole, these decisions also appeared to be in the context of those circumstances that executives described as most conducive to intuitive decision making: The decisions involved a high degree of risk; required a choice among several plausible options, none of which was clearly favored by the data available; or involved situations in which data might be inadequate or the chosen course was even contrary to the direction suggested by the data at hand.

Let's look at how these executives recall some of their most important intuitive decisions – first the highly placed respondent who recommended that his company not invest in a half-billion-dollar capital project. His 'feel for the future' proved to be right, and his company has had to take a substantial loss as a result of not taking his advice. He said, 'My own recommendation was a judgment call requiring an intuitive feel for future events.' At times, following intuition in the face of 'facts' that point in another direction can mean putting one's own career on the line. The executive who decided not to pull a drug off the market in accordance with the recommendation of the Food and Drug Administration said, 'I nearly killed myself in the organization on that one.'

If we accept the executives' assertions that the intuition-guided decisions named were in fact successful, this question remains: How did the respondents know which course to take when faced with the choices in front of them? These intuitive executives commonly described the feelings they experienced at the point of decision: 'A sense of excitement – almost euphoric'; 'growing excitement in the pit of my stomach'; 'a total sense of commitment'; 'a feeling of total harmony'; and 'a bolt of lightning or sudden flash that this is the solution.'

Alternatively these executives also seemed to share a common set of feelings when they sensed an impending decision might be wrong, that a particular option was inappropriate, or that they needed to take more time to adequately process the cues they were receiving to arrive at the best decision possible. At these times, managers speak of 'a sense of anxiety,' 'mixed signals' being received, 'discomfort,' 'sleepless nights,' or an upset stomach.

The situations and types of decisions in which respondents found their intuition to be most useful, and the specific cues they received to guide their actions, are consistent with the experiences described by many other successful executives and artists. For example, Marilee Zdenek interviewed across a wide spectrum of fields for her recent book, *The Right-Brain Experience*. She found that these people were clearly aware that they used intuition to guide their most important decisions, and received cues similar to those described here.

Factors that impede the use of intuition

Intuitive executives received clear signals that served as guideposts telling them when they had chosen a workable option, when they had not, and when they needed to take more time before reaching a final decision. But if this was so, why weren't these executives always right? The survey also asked executives if they could name important decisions in which they followed their intuition and it proved to be wrong and, if so, if they could pinpoint specific factors in themselves or their surroundings that were present at that time.

Their responses suggested that they indeed made errors, but these errors did not appear to be caused by following their intuition. Rather, faulty decisions often seemed to result from failing to follow intuition. That is, judgment errors made by top executives appeared to result, at least in part, from a violation of one or more of the basic principles identified by psychologists working in this field as most effective for using intuition to guide major decisions. Table 1 summarizes these principles.

Table 1   *Guidelines for developing intuition for decision making*

Principles	Definitions
Intention	Value intuition and have the intention to develop it.
Time	Devote time to intuition and create a special space for developing it.
Relaxation	Let go of physical and emotional tension.
Silence	Learn to quiet the mind through such techniques as meditation.
Honesty	Face self-deception and be honest with yourself and others.
Receptivity	Learn to be quiet and receptive.
Sensitivity	Tune in to both inner and outer processes.
Nonverbal play	Produce nonverbal expressions, such as drawings or music, without a specific goal in mind.
Trust	Trust yourself and your experience.
Openness	Be open to all outer and inner experiences.
Courage	Be willing to experience and confront your fears.
Acceptance	Have a nonjudgmental attitude toward things as they are.
Love	Practice love and compassion.
Non-attachment	Be willing to accept things as they are.
Daily practice	Practice paying daily attention to intuition.
Journal keeping	Keep a record of intuitive insights.
Support group	Find friends with whom you can share your intuitive experiences and who do not judge you.
Enjoyment	Find intrinsic satisfaction from expanded consciousness.

Source: Adapted from Frances E. Vaughan's *Awakening Intuition* (Anchor Books, 1979)

Common errors that executives made included a failure to be honest (facing self-deception and pretense) and to remain non-attached (accepting the way things are rather than trying to make them the way we would like them to be) in reference to themselves and/or the decision they were about to make. Put another way, they engaged in what psychologists commonly refer to as projection, the process by which we distort reality – in this case, intuitive cues. Hence we project our own conscious or unconscious process onto a situation and thus transform reality so that it fits with what we would like to be true (or what we fear is true).

For example, a particular executive can become personally involved with someone connected with a management decision and thus fail to see the person objectively, or may not be open to intuitive cues because he or she fears that the resulting accurate picture will not fit well with a preconceived notion or preference.

Individual examples of executives' responses are revealing in this regard. One top manager stated:

I can't recall any wrong decisions where intuition was the final step in the process. I have had situations in which I failed to follow up on a feeling that 'things weren't right' and made a decision that really screwed things up. At other times, I ignored the 'hard nosed' rational assessment phase and allowed 'wishful thinking' to control the decision.

Another highly placed executive vice-president of one of the largest corporations in America spoke of how the president of that same organization sometimes let his own ego involvement cloud his normal ability to make sound decisions: 'Sometimes he just gets too ego involved. He wants 100% on an issue when he could get 95% with a lot less grief. I've often had conflicts with him about his tendency to be this way.'

Responding executives admitted that effective use of their intuitive ability was impeded when they also made other errors – for example, making critical decisions under time pressures, when they were not relaxed, or when they were not confident (see Table 2). Typical statements were: 'I've made

Table 2 *Factors that impede the use of intuition*

Projection mechanisms	*Stress factors*
Attachment.	Physical/emotional tension.
Dishonesty.	Fatigue, illness.
Time constraints	*Lack of confidence/anxiety*
Rushed to make decision.	Fear.
Failed to get necessary background facts.	Confusion.
Failed to do homework required.	Feeling of unbalance.
Acted impulsively.	Accommodation of too many desires/feelings/ arguments of others, despite one's own feelings.

mistakes when fatigue, boredom, or anger were present'; 'My wrong decisions come when physical or emotional stress are present'; 'Most things go wrong when I don't listen to myself'; and 'When time pressure exists, I make the wrong decision. Supervisors or subordinates often just sit there expecting a decision right now.'

Using intuition in the decision-making process

We have seen thus far that the top executives tested definitely felt they consciously use their intuition to guide their most important decisions. They identified a specific body of cues or indicators employed as guideposts for action, and this process has resulted by their own admission in very successful major decisions. At the same time, they stated that their mistakes resulted primarily from the fact that they failed to use their intuition effectively to guide their decisions. They allowed themselves to get 'off course' by letting such factors as ego involvement block the signals normally picked up by their intuitive radar. What we have identified, then, according to interview data, is a decision-making skill that top executives *believe in and use* to guide their most important decisions. If this is the case, do all executives use their intuitive ability in the same way and at the same stage in their decision-making process, or does the use of this tool vary from executive to executive? The survey asked the executives how they go about using intuition to make their most important decisions.

Each was conscious of a methodology or system that worked best for them. Many executives shared and used the same or similar systems: They activated intuition in a similar manner and employed it at the same stage in their decision-making process. Nevertheless, several executives in the sample used distinctly different techniques, which varied from executive to executive. In this group, each decision maker had fashioned his or her own particular system (custom-designed to work for them), and each used intuition at different stages in the decision-making process.

Many executives in the sample indicated that they used intuitive ability like *an explorer*. When making decisions about the organization's future, they tried to use intuition *to foresee* the correct path to follow. Under these circumstances, this group of executives was particularly careful to give intuition 'free rein,' since they were trying to generate unusual possibilities and new options that might not normally emerge from an analysis of past data or traditional ways of doing things. The most effective method for achieving this goal, they found, was *not to adopt* a rigid system or step-by-step method of decision making. What worked was allowing the mind 'to flow' where it wanted to go – whether it was sifting past experience or simply playing with concepts and ideas. One executive described the process this way: 'The idea of a technique suggests to me a rigidity that chokes off intuition. My own intuition requires freedom that can chew on all sorts of ideas and methods for nourishment.'

Another top decision maker explained the intuitive method in this way: 'I strive to be independent, nonconformist, and nontraditional in the "best" sense of these terms. ... This leads me to consider the possibilities of the unusual – in people and ideas.'

On the other hand, a large number of respondents used their intuitive ability quite differently. They had a more structured decision-making system that they routinely employed; it involved specific steps that were regularly followed – often including as the first step the gathering and analyzing of all the relevant data available concerning the problem at hand. For these executives, intuition was used at the back end, not the front end, of the process – not so much as an explorer, but rather as a *synthesizer and integrator*. These executives often insisted on having an adequate amount of time for incubation, or the process of digesting and sifting through the information they have consumed, before they would make a final decision. One person described a typical example of this particular approach:

> I establish a clear, concise objective. I gather whatever information is available, digest it and, if time is available, allow a day or two for my intuition to work on it. An acceptable answer, if not 'the' answer has always evolved.

The third group of executives (those who had developed their own individual technique or system) might be termed *eclectic*. As mentioned before, the use of intuition to guide decisions varied from individual to individual. For example, one respondent said he used intuition to make early judgments on issues before him *long before* actual decisions were required. But he did not cut off the flow of data he received during the time between his initial assessments and actual decisions. Instead, he consciously cross-checked his initial 'intuitive feel' against the data until the actual decision was finally required. He stated, 'My initial intuitive decision turns out to be right more than 75% of the time.' Another executive in this group used his intuition as a basis for delaying a final decision. He described his process this way:

> When the available options set off an internal signal that cries 'wrong,' I accept the need to give the decision more time. I start asking logical questions and test my feelings of comfort/discomfort with the answers given.

Techniques used to activate/facilitate intuition for decision making

Whether the respondents used their intuitive ability for exploration or integration, or in an eclectic fashion, as a total group they had in common several specific techniques for activating or facilitating intuition whenever they wished to use it in decision making. When asked how they did this, executives volunteered a long list of techniques they found helpful. (See Table 3.) I have summarized these techniques under the headings of relaxation techniques, mental exercises and analytical exercises. What is worthy of note here is that this list corroborates many of the techniques recommended by experts in the field of intuitional development. For example, Philip Goldberg, author of *The Intuitive Edge*, recommends 'adopting a certain playfulness and an appreciation of whimsy.' This is very similar to the top executives' practice of 'playing freely with ideas without a specific goal in mind.' Goldberg also says that intuition will work more effectively if the problem to be solved is precisely defined. Goldberg explains one technique as writing out one's thoughts and another as 'brainstorming with yourself – or allowing intuition to generate alternatives.' Again, these are similar to the techniques that top executives actually used in decision-making processes when they practiced the mental and analytical exercises that are listed in Table 3.

Keeping intuitive ability a secret

Expert psychologists working in this field generally agreed that one important way to strengthen intuitive ability is to develop a support group – friends and colleagues with whom you can share the experience of intuition. However, executives are in large measure reluctant to engage in such practices. This is so at least in part because management training in recent years has heavily emphasized the use of analytical skills, logic, and other techniques

Table 3 *Techniques and exercises used by executives to activate intuition for decision making*

Relaxation techniques	*Mental exercises*
Clear mind mentally.	Play freely with ideas without a specific goal
Seek quiet times.	in mind.
Seek solitude.	Practice guided imagery.
Listen to classical music.	Practice tolerating ambiguity and accepting
Sleep on problem.	lack of control.
Fast.	Practice flexibility and openness to
Meditate.	unknowns as they appear.
Pray.	Practice concentration.
Drop problem and return to it later.	Try to think of unique solutions.
Exercise.	Be willing to follow up on points that have
Joke.	no factual justification.

Analytical exercises

Discuss problem with many colleagues who have different perspectives as well as with respected friends.

Concentrate on listening not only to what but also to how one expresses oneself.

Immerse self totally in the issue at hand.

Identify pros and cons; then assess feeling about each option.

Consider problem only when most alert.

Tune into internal reactions to outside stimuli.

Analyze dreams.

Insist on creative pause before reaching decision.

Ask, 'What do I want to do, and what is "right" to do?'

associated with the left brain almost to the total exclusion of other potentially useful skills and methods. Moreover, our organizations and the larger Western culture reinforce this tendency.

It was not surprising, then, to find that nearly half of the respondents, when asked if they tended to keep their use of intuition a secret or felt comfortable sharing this information with others, indicated that they kept it a secret! One top female executive explained that revealing this fact would tend to undermine her effectiveness:

> At work, I work with men, men who tend to regard the use of intuition as suspect, female, and unscientific. . . . If I revealed my 'secret,' I'd have an even harder time persuading them to accept my suggestions. They wouldn't regard my ideas or decisions as being properly rational. Yet they can justify the worst kind of screw-ups with a chart and a computer printout.

Many intuitive executives – whether male or female – would probably agree that this woman described the kind of organizational environment they often have to endure. As one male manager explained:

> I have tried explanations without success. Also, superiors seem to believe some sort of witchcraft or other dark art is being employed. Better to use it to advantage than go through the hassle of explanation. I've even gotten to the point of telling others I'm just a good guesser.

Because intuitive executives often felt that their colleagues did not or would not understand that intuition can be a reliable basis on which to make important decisions, they often played elaborate games to legitimize the direction they proposed taking. While the decision was actually made on the basis of intuition, the justification used was quite different. One top executive at one of the largest and most successful corporations in America quipped, sometimes one must dress up a gut decision in 'data clothes' to make it acceptable or palatable, but this fine tuning is usually after the fact of the decision.

Another typical response is both illuminating and also instructive in that it points out the need for more theory and research on the use of intuition in decision making.

> I share this fact easily with other friendly intuitives, but try to disguise it as careful planning, research, or an intellectual effort around others. This is not a matter of adopting a cunning strategy; those without the willingness/ability to use their own intuition are often frightened by intuitive demonstrations or reject any evidence not fitting their current paradigm. It's hard, however, for anyone to talk about intuition – we lack theory that also fits our rational body of knowledge.

Practicing techniques to strengthen intuitive ability

Numerous experts recommend daily practice of a variety of specific techniques to develop intuitive ability further. But, for all the reasons already mentioned, such practice as a rule is not normally encouraged in organizations today. Even if an executive is aware that he or she has special skills in this area, the person is seldom encouraged to develop the talent further.

It is not surprising then to find even in this sample of highly intuitive executives a certain reluctance to actively embark on a program to further develop this talent. When asked if they regularly practice any technique to this end, only one-third indicated they did. Table 4 summarizes these

Table 4   *Techniques top executives regularly practice to expand intuitive ability*

Relaxation techniques	*Mental analytical techniques*
Meditating.	Work with I Ching.
Using guided imagery.	Work with mind mapping.
Listening to inner self when relaxed.	Read and attend psychic-related events.
Writing journal.	Expose oneself to new ideas and situations outside specialty.
Keeping in good physical shape.	Stay open and flexible.
Praying; reading Scripture.	Read philosophy and philosophy of science.
Fasting once a month.	Read science fiction.
	Look for patterns where none appear to exist.
	Keep note pad nearby for recording ideas/insights before they are forgotten and to use for further development.

techniques. Once again, this list corroborates the recommendations of experts in the field.

Of course, further empirical research is needed to demonstrate that practicing such techniques actually strengthens intuitive ability. Several intuitive executives appeared to believe that practice itself might somehow undercut or hinder their present ability. One manager openly asked, 'If I practiced such techniques, would I still be intuitive?' Several executives also admitted that they had never even thought about practicing any expansive techniques. One respondent said, 'I do not know how to develop my intuitive ability further,' and another exclaimed, 'I would probably benefit from a process that would let me build my effectiveness based on my intuitive sense.' It is quite probable that if they were made more aware of some of these techniques in a supportive setting, they could well make great strides in expanding their present capabilities.

Conclusions

The sample of top executives studied strongly believed that intuition was one of the skills they used to guide their most important decisions. They were able to clearly recall examples of such major decisions, their character and type, and the circumstances under which they were made. It also appears that these intuitive executives shared a common body of cues that they use to help make, delay, or not make critical decisions. Many (but not a majority) of executives in the sample regularly practiced a variety of techniques to expand their intuitive skills – exercises that are similar to those recommended as effective by psychologists working in the field for several years now.

Much more research is required on the process of intuitive decision making among top executives before definite conclusions can be reached. Right now, our research suggests that the effective use of intuition could well be a significant factor in increasing managerial productivity in the decade ahead, for several reasons. First, research on how the human brain functions is growing rapidly. Increasingly, processes such as intuition are better understood, as are methods for enhancing them. As the mystery and magic of how intuition works is dispelled through hard science research, executives will more likely understand, accept, and use this skill that we all possess to some degree.

Second, the research findings presented here suggest that even among highly intuitive executives, considerable opportunity exists for honing and developing their skills. Executives admitted to frequently making a variety of errors in their decision-making processes which interfered with the natural flow and effectiveness of their intuitive ability. Further training to help eliminate these errors is likely to increase present productivity. Less than half of the top executives in the sample were willing to share with colleagues the fact that they used intuition to guide their most important decisions. Instead, they spent time and resources 'covering up' how they actually made decisions.

No doubt organizational productivity and job satisfaction could be increased if top executives would instead focus their energy in a new and more innovative direction. Specifically, they could adopt a more positive

attitude about their own intuitive ability and take an active role in establishing support groups within their organizations in which such skills and
techniques could be shared and experimented with. They could also
implement research programs whereby intuitive decision-making processes
could be quantified objectively and success records could be established.
Sharing these findings could help all of us better understand how intuition
may best be developed and applied in organizational settings likely to
emerge in the decades ahead.

Note

I would like to thank the Alden B. Dow Creativity Center in Midland, Michigan, which
provided financial and staff support for conducting this study as well as a 1984 Summer
Residence Fellowship to complete this research.

Selected bibliography

It is unlikely that the study reported on here could have been conducted ten years ago. For a
book that discusses how difficult it was in 1974 to get executives to openly discuss such subjects
as intuition and ESP, see Douglas Dean et al.'s *Executive ESP* (Prentice-Hall, Inc., 1974). The
results of the first field study on intuition discussed in this article may be found in *Intuitive
Management: Integrating Left and Right Brain Management Skills*, by Weston H. Agor (Prentice-Hall, Inc., 1984). The statistical test, One-Way Anova, was used to measure the significance of the high scores top managers received on intuitive ability. The standard of 0.05 or
better was established for rejecting the null hypothesis. For a discussion of how this procedure is
conducted, see Lyman Ott and David K. Hildebrand's *Statistical Thinking for Managers*
(Duxbury Press, 1983).

Thomas J. Peters and Robert H. Waterman, Jr. report on new attitudes toward intuitive skill
in *In Search of Excellence: Lessons From America's Best-Run Companies* (Warner Books,
1984). John Naisbitt discusses the new respectability for intuitive skill in management in
Reinventing the Corporation (by Naisbitt and Patricia Aburdene, Warner Books, 1985).

Jonas Salk and Buckminster Fuller discuss intuition in *Anatomy of Reality: Merging of
Intuition and Reason* (Columbia University Press, 1983), and *Intuition* (Impact Publishers,
1983), respectively.

One article that discusses the limitations of traditional linear models in predicting outcomes is
'Forecasters Overhaul Models of Economy in Wake of 1982 Errors,' by Laurie McGinley (*Wall
Street Journal*, February 1983).

Nearly every year, the Whole Brain Corporation holds a conference in Key West, Florida
where participants discuss some of the latest findings in brain research. Norman Cousins
discusses in an article one example of recent research by Richard Bergland at Harvard
University who has developed the concept of the brain as a gland that controls the secretion of
several hundred chemicals that affect our thinking skills. See 'An Adventure of Ideas' (*New
Realities*, January–February 1985).

Frances E. Vaughan's *Awakening Intuition* (Anchor Books, 1979) is one of the best books on
intuition available. Other valuable books that discuss this subject include *The Mind's Best
Work*, by D.N. Perkins (Harvard University Press, 1981); *The Right-Brain Experience: An
Intimate Program to Free the Powers of Your Imagination* by Marilee Zdenek (McGraw-Hill,
1983); *Intuition: How We Think and Act*, by Tony Bostick (John Wiley & Sons, 1982); and *The
Intuitive Edge: Understanding and Developing Intuition*, by Phillip Goldberg (Jeremy P.
Tarcher Inc., 1983). Two books that recommend techniques for developing intuitive skills are
The Possible Human: A Course in Enhancing Your Physical, Mental, and Creative Abilities, by

Jean Houston (Jeremy Tarcher, 1982) and *Beyond Ego: Transpersonal Dimensions in Psychology* (Jeremy Tarcher, 1980).

Lawrence Sprecher's definition of intuition appears in 'Intuition Anyone?' (*Public Management*, February 1983); William McGinnis' definition appears in 'Decision-Making Process' (*Public Management*, February 1983). A discussion of the usefulness of intuition as a managerial tool may be found in 'Tomorrow's Intuitive Leaders,' by Weston H. Agor (*The Futurist*, August 1983).

Carl Jung's definition of types appears in *Introduction to Type* by Isabel Briggs Myers (Consulting Psychologists Press, Inc., 1980). For more recent findings, see Gordon Lawrence's *People Types and Tiger Stripes: A Practical Guide to Learning Styles* (Center for Applications of Psychological Type, Inc., 1982).

For a detailed description of the entire Type Indicator Test, see Isabel Briggs Myers' *The Myers–Briggs Type Indicator: Manual 1962* (Consulting Psychologists Press, 1962).

For an instrument that measures underlying intuitive ability and how one uses this skill to make decisions, see Agor's *Test Your Intuitive Powers: AIM Survey* (Organization Design and Development, Inc., 1985).

14

Judgment

Geoffrey Vickers

Judgment is an important quality in a manager; perhaps more eagerly sought and more highly paid than any. It is also an elusive quality, easier to recognize than to define, easier to define than to teach. To some it has an aura of mystery, suggesting unidentified, intuitive powers behind the inexplicably accurate hunch. Others believe that its deepest secrets are already familiar to those who programme computers. Our language and our thought on the subject are alike imprecise.

We use the word judgment in many contexts. Applying it to business executives, we have in mind, I think, the power of reaching 'right' decisions (whatever that may mean) when the apparent criteria are so complex, inadequate, doubtful or conflicting as to defeat the ordinary man. Even in this sense judgment is, of course, not confined to business executives for it is required equally by statesmen, generals and princes of the Church; and even in this sense we may be unsure where it begins and ends. When our Government in 1940 shipped tanks to Egypt, through precarious seas, away from a country still in danger, to take part in operations still unplanned, Sir Winston Churchill took responsibility for a decision, apparently rash, which was justified by results. Shall we call this 'good judgment'? What of the decision of Bolivar, when, in the swampy delta of the Orinoco, he announced to a few ragged followers that he had that day founded the Republic of Gran Columbia and had fixed its capital at Bogota, a thousand miles away across the Andes? He too was justified by results. Are these exercises of the same faculty which led Mr Henry Ford to create Model T40?

Judges of the Supreme Court exercise judgment; yet politicians and civil servants, who take what they call administrative decisions, have generally maintained, in a controversy now thirty years old, that the rightness of their judgments is not a matter which courts of law can competently review. The opposite view is now gaining ground. What is the difference between the judgment of judges and the judgment of administrators?

What of the scientists? Vesalius rejected the view, accepted in his day,

Adapted from Open Systems Group (eds), *The Vickers Papers* (1984), pp. 230–45. Its origin was the 6th Elbourne Memorial Lecture given at the British Institute of Management in November 1960. Reprinted by permission of Paul Chapman Publishing Ltd and Jeanne Vickers

that the dividing wall of the heart is pierced by invisible passages. He proved to be right, and he is rightly remembered as a hero of scientific scepticism. Harvey assumed the existence of invisible passages connecting the arteries with the veins, an assumption then new and commended only by the fact that it was required by his theory of the circulation of the blood. He proved to be right too; and he is rightly remembered as a hero of – scientific intuition. Did these two men show 'good judgment' in the same sense?

What of the doctor making a diagnosis? What of the artist painting out a tone or a form which, in his judgment, disturbs the balance of his picture? What of the connoisseur who chooses that artist's work from among a hundred others, because he judges it to be of higher and more enduring merit? What of the man in a moral dilemma who judges one personal claim on him to be more weighty than another; and of his neighbours, who judge his decision as right or wrong? All these are exercising judgment; and though their fields are remote from that of the business executive, their activities are not. For the business executive also has occasion to act judicially, to make diagnoses, to weigh moral issues, to judge as connoisseur, even, perhaps, to compose in his own medium as an artist. It seems that we shall have to decide whether the word 'judgment' in all these contexts stands for one mental activity or many.

Three types of judgment

I shall distinguish three broad types of judgment. Harvey and Vesalius made judgments about the state of affairs 'out there'. They revised the currently accepted view of external reality. I will call such judgments 'reality judgments'.

Churchill, Bolivar and Ford also made reality judgments; but they went further. They made judgments of what to do about it; and they committed themselves to action on the basis of these judgments. I will call such judgments 'action judgments'. In my examples, what strikes us most about their action judgment is that it 'came off'. In each case it achieved the desired result.

There is, however, a third element in these judgments – the judgment of what result was most to be desired. This I will call a value judgment. Churchill, Bolivar and Ford would not be remembered in these contexts unless they had been convinced of the value of victory in the Middle East, of creating independent republics of the Spanish American colonies, of building a popular car; and these were not the only judgments of value which underlay their decisions.

In each case the value judgment is separate from the action judgment: it can be separately criticized. That the action succeeded does not prove that it was well conceived. Some strategists criticized the British emphasis on the Middle Eastern theatre of war. San Martin thought that the new states of South America should have been set up as constitutional monarchies. Even

Henry Ford's 'Tin Lizzie' was criticized – on aesthetic grounds. Hindsight often leads us to wish that our well-laid plans had failed.

I shall consider the part played by these three kinds of judgment – value judgment, reality judgment, action judgment – in the making of business decisions. First, I want to inquire how we recognize these judgments as good. The answer is curious and somewhat disturbing.

The credentials of judgment

The capillaries which were invisible to Harvey can now be demonstrated by improved microscopy. His judgment has been confirmed by observation. Yet even the so-called facts of observation need judgment to give them meaning, a judgment often difficult and hazardous. Moreover, few reality judgments can be confirmed by observation, even after the event; for many relevant facts of a situation – the state of someone's mind for example – are not observable and change constantly and unpredictably, not least through the effects of judgments made about them. In the ultimate analysis, all reality judgments are matters of inference and can be confirmed or challenged only by new judgments, based on further inferences.

With action judgments we feel on firmer ground; we can check them against their results. Yet this is at best a rough and ready test, especially at the level of my examples. Who can say whether the courses which were not tried would not have worked out better than the one which was chosen? Moreover, every choice involves weighing probabilities. The course rightly chosen as of least risk may none the less prove lethal; the course of most risk may still come off. Results no doubt confirm judgments with some assurance when similar choices are repeated in controlled conditions often enough for the laws of probability to speak with authority; but it is hard to see how such an objective test can be applied to the judgments of the statesman or the top executive. It would seem that the validation of action judgments also is a matter of judgment.

When we consider value judgments we find the same situation in a much more extreme form. The validation of a value judgment is necessarily a value judgment. Churchill, Bolivar and Ford told themselves what they meant by success. Those who disagreed with them could do so only by appealing to different standards, representing value judgments of their own. There would seem to be no means whereby the adjudicating mind can escape responsibility for the standards of value to which it commits itself.

I have distinguished three kinds of judgment, often present together – value judgment, reality judgment and action judgment – and I have reached the conclusion that the higher the level of judgment involved, the less possible it is to find an objective test by which to prove that the judgment is good. The appraisal of judgment is itself an act of judgment. In particular, value judgments are logically incapable of being validated by any objective test. They cannot be proved true or false. They can only be approved as right or condemned as wrong by the exercise of another value judgment.

Does this condemn us to pure subjectivism? In my view definitely not. The status of judgments which are neither objective nor subjective has been analysed on a grand scale, with special regard to scientific judgments, by Professor Michael Polanyi,[1] himself an outstanding physical scientist. The concept of responsible choice – that is, of decision which is personal yet made with a sense of obligation to discover the 'rules of rightness'[2] applicable to the particular situation – is a familiar concept in business, which we trust and use many times a day, even though neither philosophers nor psychologists can explain it.

Judgment and decision

We sometimes use the word 'judgment' as if it meant the same as 'decision', but this is too narrow an interpretation. A good judge of men, for example, *reveals* his good judgment by the appointments and changes he makes, but the judgment which guides those decisions is something which he exercises continually as he observes and appraises the people around him. I will ask you to consider an example of this sort in some detail.

One morning, Mr Redletter, the managing director of the Weathercock Company (all the characters in my illustrations are imaginary) reached the conclusion that the company's chief supplies officer, Mr A, was not up to his job; that somehow he must be removed from his post and replaced by Mr B. What precipitated this decision I will inquire later. For the moment I ask you to accept it as a fact and to follow it backwards and forwards in time.

To reach this conclusion Mr Redletter must have had in his head an idea of where the Weathercock Company was going and of where he wanted it to go; of the part which the supplies department was playing in the company's effectiveness and the part which it should be playing; of Mr A's performance as its head and of what its head's performance should be; and of the probable performance of Mr B. All these ideas were the cumulative result of several years' experience of the company and its staff. They were not mere observations, they were judgments. These judgments go in pairs; a judgment of the situation as it is, is compared with a judgment of the situation as it might be. It is the disparity between the two which has moved Mr Redletter to his decision. These are the two types of judgment which I have already distinguished as reality judgment and value judgment. They are closely connected.

Mr Redletter's idea of Mr A is not a mere catalogue of Mr A's past performances. It is an hypothesis sufficiently comprehensive to explain all he knows about Mr A, and from which he can assess Mr A's probable performance in various roles: his potentialities and power of learning: his current trend of development or deterioration: his probable response to promotion or transfer. Even so, it is not complete. It is selective and the selection reflects the nature of his interest in Mr A, which is that of a manager in a functional subordinate. Mr A's doctor or wife or colleague on the local borough council would each have a different picture of Mr A – different not merely because of their differing gifts and opportunities for forming a judgment, but also because of their differing interests in Mr A. Someone who had no interest at all in Mr A could have no picture of him.

Thus the nature of Mr Redletter's interest in Mr A defines what aspects of Mr A he shall select for attention and valuation. The same is true of his interest in the supplies department. So when Mr Redletter asked himself, 'Can we wear Mr A any longer as Chief Supplies Officer?', he found the materials for an answer already in his head. Nor were these merely 'raw' materials. They were an accumulation of judgments, leading to ever more complete hypotheses about Mr A and the supplies department. On the other hand, what he found in his head was not *the* answer. This question redefined his interest and called for a revaluation of the problem, leaving his ideas of Mr A and the supplies department however slightly changed.

The result we know. For the first time, on this particular morning, Mr Redletter, comparing his value judgment with his reality judgment, reached the answer 'no'.

Let us now follow that silent decision forwards. What is to be done? This I have called the action judgment. It takes the form of a dialogue between Mr Redletter, the man of judgment, and an invaluable but irritating boffin in his head who makes uncritical but sometimes brilliant suggestions.

'Move him to another job?'
'He'd be worse elsewhere.'

'Retire him early under the pension scheme?'
'We can't – he's below the minimum age.'

'Give him his notice and let him go?'
'We couldn't do that with old A in all the circumstances, it wouldn't be fair.'

'Make him an ex gratia *allowance?'*
'Anything big enough to mitigate hardship would be a most awkward precedent.'

'Must you really do it now?'
'Yes.'

Silence: then –

'Well, you could divide the department, leave A in charge of the bit he knows, put B in charge of the rest, let them both report to C for the time being; then, in two years when C retires . . .'
'M'yes. We *might . . .*'

You will notice that all these tentative action judgments except the last one are rejected because they are either impracticable or inconsistent with Mr Redletter's idea of the sort of employer the company wished to be: in other words, by a reality judgment or a value judgment.

I have now squeezed all I want from this example. I summarize the results.

1. Judgment is a fundamental, continuous process, integral with our thinking.
2. It has three aspects – for simplicity, three kinds of judgment – value judgment, reality judgment, action judgment. The first two are the more fundamental and important. Action judgment is only called for by the interaction of value judgment and reality judgment, and is only selected by further use of the same criteria.
3. The aspects of the situation which are appreciated (reality judgment) and evaluated (value judgment) are determined by the interest of the judging mind.

All these forms of judgment are mental skills. It remains to ask in what they consist; and how they may be trained. Before I turn to these questions I will take up one which I have left unanswered. Why did Mr Redletter reach his conclusions just then? This inquiry will lead me to explore the meaning of initiative and the relation between initiative and judgment.

Judgment and initiative

What precipitated Mr Redletter's action judgment? Had Mr A just dropped an enormous 'clanger', costing the company most of a year's profit? Or had Mr Redletter so radically revised his ideas of what a supplies department should be that Mr A's interpretation of his role, though unchanged and accepted for many years, suddenly became intolerable?

These are remote points on a continuous scale. The disparity between reality judgment and value judgment may widen, because of a change either in the situation as we see it (our reality judgment) or in the standards of value which we apply to it (our value judgment). This scale is important and I will illustrate it by two other episodes in the earlier history of the Weathercock Company. The decision involved in both is collective. What I have said applies equally, as I believe, to collective and to individual decisions. In collective decisions, however, varying views on reality, value and action are expressed by different voices and are more easily distinguished than when their clashes and accommodations take place within a single head.

The first episode presents the directors of the Weathercock Company in an emergency meeting one Thursday. The bank has refused to extend the overdraft sufficiently to provide the pay packets on the following day except upon unwelcome and onerous terms. After long debate, the directors accept the bank's terms, telling each other that they have no choice. Strictly speaking they had a choice; they might have said 'no' or failed to say 'yes', which would have been the same thing. To choose this alternative, however, would be to choose the immediate and irreversible dissolution of the undertaking and of their own authority, and that in the most untidy fashion. The bank's terms raised no objections which could make such a course preferable.

I will now introduce you to the board of the Weathercock Company some years later. The situation has been transformed. Output is maximal, orders and cash are alike embarrassing in their abundance. The only troubles are troubles of growth, and the worst of these is that the company has no longer any physical room to grow.

They are agreed that something must be done but embarrassed by the variety of possible courses and divided on the merits of the few which are seriously considered. Mr Redletter wants to build a new factory and a new site in a new town 20 miles away; and in it he wants an impressive slice of space to develop a new business in moulded plastics, which, with the reluctant consent of his board, he had set up in some precious floor space of the present works a year or two before.

None of his colleagues supports the managing director; the arguments against his plan are impressive. The firm will lose most of its present employees and face others with hard choices. It will break its connections with its home town and its home site. The economies claimed for the move are offset by an x representing the unknown variables which will be set loose by so radical a change. And why moulded plastics, when the traditional business is doing so well?

The final decision was in no one's mind when the debate began but was unanimously adopted in the end and pleased everyone. The undertaking would stay where it was, make better use of existing space, and would swallow the coveted area begrudged to plastics. It would also buy a large site in the place favoured by Mr Redletter and build there a small factory – for the moulded plastic business only. Mr Redletter was well content; his pet venture could expand all the better in this relative isolation; the rest could still move out, maybe, one day later on. The others were content also. They got what they wanted, escaped all threats – and kept the managing director happy. You will note that the managing director, though in a minority of one, got his way in what most mattered to him, because all his colleagues felt it was essential to any settlement that they should keep him, and keep him happy. These two situations illustrate what I will call the gradient of initiative.

The gradient of initiative

The first is an extreme case. The company is on the verge of insolvency. An instability – the imbalance between money in and money out – which has been progressively affecting its performance for some time, is about to cross a critical threshold, beyond which its effects will overflow in all directions and bring the system to disorganization and dissolution.

The effect of instability on a system is usually of this form. The most clear-cut example is physical death. A living organism is an organization, maintained by the delicately balanced intake and outflow of air, food and water, and equipped with admirable devices for keeping these balances – and many others – within critical limits. The maintenance of this system is a necessary, though not of course a sufficient, condition for the highest achievement of human intellect and feeling; and among the humble but necessary skills of living we recognize the skill of keeping alive and healthy – normally as a condition of all we want to do with life, occasionally, as when we are escaping from a fire or a furious bull, as an end in itself.

Similarly, for businesses, solvency is not an end, but it is a pre-condition of successful existence and when threatened it may become an end in itself.

Political organizations such as nation states are similarly liable to changes of this step–function form. There is, however, a difference in the degree of irreversible change illustrated by these examples. The dead organism dissolves; all its constituents rearrange themselves in new and less improbable configurations. The bankrupt business, after liquidation, may reappear more or less changed. Someone will probably carry on much the same business in the same building with some of the old plant. Some of the former employees may be re-engaged. Only the accounts will show a complete break. Alternatively, if technical liquidation is avoided the only continuity may be the old losses, carefully preserved for the benefit of the newcomer's future income tax.

I wish to distinguish first between the conditions which establish a given measure of freedom and the reasons which explain how that freedom is actually used. In my case-history, the establishment of the company's liquidity was one of the conditions which enabled it to grow and ultimately to go in for moulding plastics; but it throws no light at all on why the company chose to go in for moulding plastics. For this we must explore the past history of the managing director.

This may seem obvious; but it is often by no means easy to be sure whether a given explanation explains why something happened or merely explains how its happening was possible. The theory of evolution has been supposed for the last century to explain why life on this planet has developed as it has; but serious and respected thinkers today contend that the theory merely explains how that development, among others, became possible.[3]

Arising out of this distinction, I wish to establish the idea that an organization, like an organism, can conveniently be regarded as a hierarchy of systems, each dependent on, but not explained by, those below. The variables which determine the solvency of a business could be described and discussed without any reference to the nature of the undertaking's product, the interests of its staff, the ambitions of its directors or a host of other things which fill the agenda at its meetings. In the first situation, solvency was in such peril that the field of choice was minimal. As with the man escaping from the bull, the preservation of basic conditions had become itself a dominating goal of policy. In the second situation, the basic conditions of existence were sufficiently secure to enable the directors to realize a variety of possible values, even some which they had not contemplated before. The future depended not on the adroitness of their actions but on the quality of their dreams. The gradient of initiative leads from the familiar track, where events are in control, to the uncharted spaces where dreams, whether 'right' dreams or 'wrong' dreams, can and must take charge and where that man is lost who cannot dream at all.

Thus skill in value judgment is increasingly demanded as human initiative widens. It is to be expected that some leaders who show the greatest resource in conditions of extreme difficulty will be less successful when they must seek guidance, not from without, but from within themselves.

The action judgment

What are the mental processes underlying the three aspects of judgment?

The judgment which has been most carefully studied is what I have called the 'pure' action judgment. This is typified in Köhler's classic learning experiments with apes. The motivation (value judgment) is standardized; the animal wants a bunch of bananas which is out of reach. The situation is standardized; the materials for a solution are all in sight. Only one solution is possible, so no choice between solutions is involved. The means to be used – a hooked stick, a few boxes – are not, as far as can be avoided, charged with an affective meaning of their own. The issue is simply whether the creature can see how to use these neutral objects as means to an end.

The process by which one ape does, while another ape does not, succeed – suddenly, but after prolonged incubation – in 'seeing' the boxes as a potential increase in height, the stick as a potential increase in reach, remains a fascinating psychological puzzle.

Now consider a human example. When I was a very inexperienced subaltern in the old war, my company commander once said to me, 'Vickers, the company will bathe this afternoon. Arrange.' In the Flemish hamlet where we were billeted the only bath of any kind was in the local nunnery. The nuns were charity itself but I could not ask them to bathe a hundred men. I reviewed other fluid-containing objects – cattle drinking troughs, empty beer barrels – and found practical or ethical objections to them all; and at that point I had the misfortune to meet my company commander again and was forced to admit that I had not yet found the answer. He was annoyed. 'Whatever have you been doing all this time?' he said, and then, turning his own mind to the problem, as it seemed for the first time, he added, 'Take the company limbers off their wheels, put the tilts inside, four baths each four feet square, four men to a bath, do the job in an hour, why don't you use your brains?'

Simple indeed; but his solution involved two steps which my mind had not taken – the apprehension that a vehicle is a collection of bits and pieces, of which, for some purposes, the wheels may be irrelevant; and the apprehension that a tilt tailored to cover a protruding load and keep rainwater out, would fit and serve equally well, pushed into the empty waggon, to keep bathwater in.

My company commander – unlike myself – showed a mental ability like that of Köhler's more successful apes, though higher in degree; a facility for uncoupling the elements of a familiar idea and recombining them in a new way – for seeing a limber as two potential baths on irrelevant wheels, without forgetting that it is primarily and must again become a vehicle. This is a faculty useful in the research and development department and equally in the board room. Let us call it ingenuity.

The meaning of ingenuity

Yet it must involve more than we usually associate with ingenuity. The mere multiplication of alternative means to an end might only make the choice harder, unless it were accompanied by some gift which guides the problem-solver in the general direction of the still undiscovered solution. The literature of problem solving, no less than common experience, attests our capacity for searching with a lively sense of 'warm ... warmer ... *warmer* ...', when we do not know what we are looking for.

It would seem then that even the pure action judgment involves mental faculties which are still highly obscure. Yet the pure action judgment is too simple a process to be seen outside the laboratory. Even my efforts to improvise bathing facilities were hedged about with reality judgments and value judgments of great complexity; reality judgments about what our Flemish hosts would stand with equanimity from their British billetees, and value judgments defining the kind of solution which would be acceptable to me, having regard to its impact on the troops, the inhabitants, my company commander and myself.

The action judgment is involved in answering any question of the form, 'What shall I do about it?' when 'it' has been defined by judgments of reality and value. In implementing a decision, this question may have to be asked several times. 'What shall we do about the supplies department?' 'We will change the head.' 'What shall we do about changing the head?' 'We will divide the department and ...' 'What shall we do about this decision to divide ...?' 'First we will tell A and then B and then ...'

Thus each decision sets a more precise problem for the next exercise of action judgment; and at each stage there is assumed a set of criteria for determining between different solutions. These criteria are supplied by further judgments of reality and value. 'That would not be legal.' 'That would not be fair.' 'That would not be possible.' And so on.

This process has many interesting aspects which I have no time to pursue. I will refer to two only.

First, what solutions are considered and in what order? Professor Simon[4] has pointed out that the solutions which are weighed are usually far fewer than the totality of possible solutions which exist. Often the totality is too large to be reviewed, however briefly, in the time available. Random selection seldom if ever occurs. Some mental process narrows the field rapidly to a short list of alternatives, which alone are carefully compared.

Some elements of this selective process are apparent. A man seeking a solution to a problem will usually review first the solutions which are approved by custom or his own experience for dealing with problems which seem similar; or he may try first the responses which are most accessible to him or which he most enjoys. Occasionally, however, explanations fail us and we have to credit the problem-solver with an intuitive feeling for the approach which is likely to prove fruitful, though we can see no clue by which it is recognized. This is the heuristic element in ingenuity, to which I have already referred.

Professor Simon assumes that the fully rational course is to examine every possible solution and to choose the 'best'. It seems clear to me that this is not the way the brain works. The criterion, I suggest, is not the best but the 'good enough'. The human brain scans possible solutions in an order which is itself determined by the complex and obscure factors to which I have referred; and it stops as soon as a solution is not rejected by criteria of reality or value.

If all solutions are rejected and no new ones can be devised, the standard of the acceptable has to be lowered and the process is then repeated. The unsuccessful series of rehearsals is not wasted, for it prepares the mind for the change of standard.

The reality judgment

I turn now to the reality judgment. This, too, involves analysis and synthesis, often repeated. It requires the ready handling, dissociating, reassociating of the elements in our thought which I have called ideas or concepts. It, too, has scope for ingenuity. Yet it seems to me to require somewhat different qualities of mind.

The problem-solver has his problem to guide him. The reality judgment, on the other hand, leads us as far afield as we let it; for the aspect of the situation with which it is concerned is as wide as our interest, and we can follow it in time until imagination fails us. One of the gifts needed by those who make reality judgments is to know where to stop: to sense the point beyond which the best estimate of trends is not worth making.

The maker of reality judgments is for the time being an observer; not, like the maker of action judgments, an agent. He needs detachment, objectivity, balance, a clear head to follow the complex permutations of the possible and the practicable; a stout heart, to give as much reality to the unwelcome as to the welcome. Where the maker of action judgments must above all be ingenious, persistent and bold, the maker of reality judgments must be honest, clear-sighted and brave. Above all, perhaps, he needs a ready sense for those aspects of the situation which are most relevant. And here, too, the man of outstanding judgment shows such an unerring sense for those facts which will be found to matter most that it is safer to give his unexplained facility a special name and call it also an heuristic gift.

The value judgment

The value judgment raises problems far more obscure. Clearly it is fundamental; if we were not concerned with values which we wanted to realize and preserve we should have no interest in the situation and no incentive to action. The basic difficulty in all complex decisions is to reconcile the conflicting values involved – in my first example, the supply needs of the undertaking, the deserts of Mr A, the board's reputation as an employer, the preservation of tacit rules governing promotion and discharge and so on.

All these values are standards of what the undertaking should seek and expect of itself and others. I will call them norms. They are not settled in abstract terms but they are implicit in every major decision. Executives absorb them from these decisions and still more from the experience of participating in the making of decisions, and by the same process they contribute to the setting of these standards and to their constant revision. Thus the maker of value judgments is not an observer but an agent. He needs not so much detachment as commitment, for his judgment commits him to implications far wider than he can know.

In approaching their decisions, executives usually find the appropriate standards of value ready to hand. They cannot depart abruptly either from their own past standard or from those current in their industry. In deciding how to treat Mr A, for example, the possible range of decision was closely limited. Thus executives, in making value judgments, are seldom conscious of doing more than apply a rule.

Yet, viewed over time, it is obvious that these standards are constantly changed by the very process of applying them, just as the common law is developed and even changed by accumulating precedents. The ghost of the economic man should not persuade us to ignore the fact that business undertakings today are governed by most complex value systems. Those who direct them must somehow provide themselves with standards of what the undertaking expects of itself – standards sufficiently coherent to be usable, yet sufficiently comprehensive to define its divergent responsibilities to employees, shareholders, consumers, suppliers, locality, industry, government and community. In every one of these fields the standards of industry today are markedly different from what they were a few decades ago; and the standards of individual undertakings differ from one to another and also change with time.

Thus in every value judgment there is latent a creative process; a resetting of the norms which are being applied.

We can as yet give no satisfactory account of the process by which we resolve problems of conflicting value. We only beg the question when we talk of maximizing satisfactions, for the satisfactions we maximize are set by ourselves; and there is no evidence that we reduce those disparate imponderables to a common measure, so that they can be added and weighed. There is indeed much evidence that we do not.

I have already expressed the belief that in the ultimate analysis, the validity of our norm-setting cannot be validated or falsified by results. It can be approved or condemned only by reference to a sense of rightness for which the adjudicating mind must take responsibility. This is obviously true of the artist and the connoisseur of art and conduct. That it is equally true of the scientist is the theme of Professor Polanyi's book. I believe it to be equally true of the business executive.

This survey of the processes involved in judgment may well leave us in doubt how far the mechanical and mathematical models of decision-making – now so popular – as distinct from mechanical and mathematical aids to decision-making are of any relevance. On this important and controversial question I have time for only one comment. In so far as these models are concerned only with what I have called pure action judgment they would seem to have no bearing on any of the main issues which I have raised; for the pure action judgment is unknown in real life. In so far as they assert or suggest that the pure action judgment is the typical decision-making situation, they do a vast disservice both to the inquiry and to the undoubtedly great contribution which, with a more modest approach, they could make to it.

Innate capacities for judgment

The extent to which we can develop judgment in ourselves and others is limited by our, and their, inherent capacity for the many mental activities involved. In these it seems clear that human beings differ widely. Minds differ greatly in their capacity for handling, arranging and combining the symbols with which we think. They differ in their ability to recognize causal and other relationships within actual or imagined sequences of events. We can say with confidence of some problems that they are too difficult for A to solve: of some situations that they are too complex for B to comprehend.

It may be that men differ in the faculties they use. Dr Grey Walter[5] has suggested that those who are unusually gifted with visual imagination reach some decisions in ways quite different from the ways used by others, not less intelligent, who are unusually devoid of this gift. He claims further that the electro-encephalogram distinguishes the two types, each of which contains, he suggests, about a tenth of the population.

Men differ further in the moral qualities involved in judgment. C could comprehend the situation, he could solve the problem: but has he the guts to go on trying until he succeeds? Will the mere stress of having to try impair his capacity for success? (Examinations rightly test this moral quality, no less than the intellectual ones which they are designed to explore.) This difference is so important that we rate executives for decisiveness, as well as for good judgment, reserving the highest rewards for those who excel in both, but recognizing that the ability to decide at all is a prior requisite, and in some cases a major one. Lord Wavell, in some famous lectures on generalship, said that stupidity in generals should never excite surprise. For generals are chosen from that small, pre-selected class of men who are tough enough to be generals at all. From such heavy-duty animals, refinements of intellect and sensibility should not be expected.

Lord Wavell's dictum, to which he was so notable an exception, is of general application. No one can exercise good judgment unless he can support both the stress of the office in which the judgment is to be exercised, and the stress of the judgment itself. Not all high offices are in themselves as stressful as that of a general in the field; but the stress inherent in judgment itself is inescapable. Between value judgment and reality judgment there is tension, characteristic of all human life. It may lead to the kind of breakdown which psychiatrists meet in patients who have lost touch with reality, or who torment themselves with an impossible level of aspiration. Distortions of judgment due to the same cause are common enough in board rooms, as for instance, when a board is faced with a problem of redundancy too large to be handled within the rules of what it has come to regard as fair. The opposite error of those who protect themselves by failing to aspire enough is more common, and much more wasteful, but more easily overlooked.

Again, the sheer difficulty of keeping the judgment of value and reality from running away into irresolvable complexity is itself a source of stress, and accounts for the familiar distinction between men of action and men of thought. The simplicity which characterizes the thought processes of men of action has often seemed to me excessive; but it is nevertheless essential to individual good judgment that a man's capacity for judgments of value and reality shall be related to his own capacity for action judgment. One of the merits of business organization is that these different human capacities can be combined.

Finally, clear judgment of value and reality only makes more frustrating the common human state of helplessness, when no effective action can be taken; and this is as common in business life as in life at large.

Courage and endurance are not the only moral qualities associated with good judgment. D has guts in plenty but he is conceited, full of personal prejudice, takes offence easily; in brief, is not sufficiently selfless or sufficiently disciplined to achieve that combination of detachment and commitment which good judgment demands.

Finally, apart from these moral qualities, I have expressed the belief that judgment needs that sensitivity to form, which, in various guises, distinguishes the connoisseur of art or conduct, the scientist and the judge, and which is equally required in the business executive.

The training of management

Have I given the impression that good judgment is to be expected only from those who combine the qualities of philosopher, hero and saint to a degree rarely found even among top people? I hope not. In so far as it involves peculiarly human qualities of intellect, sensibility, character and will, it does indeed give scope for every kind of excellence, yet equally, just because it is so human a quality, it is not likely to be lacking in anyone we recognize as fully human.

It is indeed ubiquitous; for it is involved in some degree in every exercise of discretion. Among the debts of gratitude which business people owe to Dr Elliott Jaques, I give a high place to his finding[6] that, among all the jobs, from highest to lowest, in the undertaking which he has studied so carefully, not one fails to involve some element of discretion, some duty, essential to its performance, which is not and cannot be specified in the instructions given to the holder. We are not paid, says Dr Elliott Jaques, for doing what we are told to do, but for doing rightly that part of our job which is left to our discretion; and we rate our own and our fellows' jobs on our estimate of the weight of the discretionary element.

If Dr Jaques is right, judgment is the most universal requirement not only of managerial work but of all work. The distribution of roles on an organization chart may thus be seen, not merely as an allocation of duties but as an allocation of discretions, increasing up the hierarchy in the quality of the judgment they demand.

This picture helps us to answer the questions, 'How is judgment developed?' The whole structure of industry is or should be a school of judgment, in the course of which individuals may develop, by practice and example, both the general qualities of mind, heart and will which all judgment demands, and their own particular aptitudes which determine the kind of judgment in which they can become most proficient.

In such a school everyone is both learner and teacher. The teaching function is both positive and negative. It is positive in that it requires every member of the organization, in his daily work, to set an example in the exercise of judgment, and to supervise its exercise by those for whom he is responsible. It is negative in that it requires everyone to respect the field of discretion of his subordinates, as he expects his superiors to respect his own – especially when he himself is more expert than they in the very same field.

Conclusion

Apart from displaying what I believe to be the main dimensions of the problem and setting question marks in the appropriate places, I have tried to do no more than to couple the higher executive – in the exercise of this, his most precious and highly-paid endowment – on the one hand with those excellent minds in other fields, whose function he must so often copy unawares; on the other hand, to link him with the humblest servants in his own undertaking, on whose judgment he must rely, as they on his, and from among whom it should be his delight, as it is his duty, to develop minds capable of better judgment than his own.

Notes

1 Michael Polanyi, *Personal Knowledge*, London, Routledge & Kegan Paul, 1958.
2 The expression is Polanyi's, op. cit.
3 See, for example, M. Grene, *British Journal for Philosophy of Science*, 1958, IX, 34 and 35.
4 H.A. Simon, *Administrative Behaviour* (2nd edn), New York, Macmillan, 1959.
5 Dr Grey Walter, *The Living Brain*, London, Duckworth, 1953, p. 152.
6 Elliott Jaques, *Measures of Responsibility*, London, Tavistock Publications, 1956.

15
Imaging and creativity: an integrating perspective

Vaune Ainsworth-Land

Introduction

The literature abounds with reports from artists and scientists on the presence and importance of images in creative breakthroughs. Current psychological studies have shown definite relationships between specific aspects of creativity and imagery.

The model presented in this chapter attempts to account for a variety of definitions and manifestations of the process of creativity and imaging by viewing their interrelationship *in a developmental framework*. This perspective aims to facilitate the conscious employment of appropriate techniques and approaches for achieving higher levels of creativity.

Background

Creativity is sometimes loosely equated with imagination. Osborn (1953) described creativity as 'imagination combined with intent and effort.' Arieti (1976) stressed the importance of imagination as a precursor of creativity. Parnes (1977) related the function of imagination to the functions of knowledge and judgment as they form together the essence of the creative process. Imagination was seen as a vital human capacity by Assagioli (1965):

> The imagination, in the precise sense of the function of evoking and creating images, is one of the most important and spontaneous active functions of the human psyche, both in its conscious and unconscious levels.

Gruber (1978) distinguishes between simple or 'narrow' images and complex, 'wide scope' images. The former, he found, could be produced at a rate of six hundred per hour, whereas only a few wide scope images may be produced in a lifetime. The latter were charged with intense emotion. Gruber relates these directly to scientific thought and discovery. Bucke (1901) attempted to relate intellectual functioning and the imagination while at the same time recognizing the varying complexity of images.

Adapted from *Journal of Creative Behavior*, 16, 1 (1982), pp. 5–29

> The human intellect is made up principally of concepts, just as a forest is made up of trees or a city of houses: these concepts are mental images of things, acts or relations. The registration of these we call memory; the comparison of them with one another reasoning: for the building of these up into more complex images (as bricks are built into a house) we have in English no good expression: we sometimes call this act imagination.

Langer's reference to 'situational' images, Gruber's 'wide scope images,' Bucke's images of 'acts or relations' all suggest a deficiency in the language used to describe imagery.

Imaging allows one to classify and abstract, to relate past and present in facilitating personal adaptational learning, and acts as the raw material of man's capacity to imagine and symbolize (Gordon, 1972). Psychologists have recognized its function in producing behavioral changes. Indeed, in the past decade, imaging has been applied to sex therapy, weight loss, enhanced performance in sports, memory improvement, setting life goals and solving complex problems. Imaging has been used to break through, to control, to run from, to manipulate, to cure, to create, to censor, to build ego, to tear it down, to expand consciousness. Images have been classified according to modality, function, vividness, method of evocation, content, action, clarity and more. Creativity has been subjected to the same widespread application and classification. Just as there is no one creative process, there is no one imaging process or function.

An integrating framework

Yuille and Catchpole (1977) have suggested that imaging reflects the cognitive complexity or stage that a person has achieved. Each progressive stage is not an isolate but reorganizes, reintegrates and builds upon the preceding stage. Bartlett (1927), in suggesting various levels or divisions of images, stated this well.

> Life is an evolution and to talk of levels is to use a device for separating things and reactions which in fact run into one another. In particular, when we pass from one stage to another, we take with us the acquirements of the earlier and use most of them, transforming them to meet our enlarged problems.

Table 1 outlines four orders of imaging as related to three aspects of the creative process: self-involvement, product and processes. Table 2 outlines developmental theories of five individuals as they support and enhance the framework set forth. Blake (as cited in Barron, 1963) wrote about a 'four fold' vision as in artistic production. Land proposed four stages or levels of creativity, specifically highlighting personal involvement in products at each level (Land and Kenneally, 1977). Werner (1957) proposed three levels of personal development. Bucke (1901) actually outlined four levels of consciousness, the first being a registration of sense impressions preceding simple consciousness. Liberty has been taken in re-presenting these levels

Table 1   *Developmental integration of creativity and imaging*

Imaging	Creativity		
Orders	Self-involvement	Product	Processes
1st order Spontaneous, sense-based, concrete; direct representation, realistic	Non-awareness of 'self,' creating out of need, survival motivation, 'self-creating'	Realistic, concrete representation, discovery learning, memory building, invention	Perceiving, exploring, spontaneous acting
2nd order Comfortable, predictable; awareness of ability to manipulate and control, analogical, comparative	Belonging, self-extension, goal directing, ego building and verifying, self-consciousness	Improvements and modifications, impressions, strengthening and enhancing, analogical	Categorizing, conjuring, analyzing, evaluating
3rd order Abstract, symbolic, superimposing, metaphorical, controlled and spontaneous	Sharing differences, 'selves' realization and reintegration; giving up rigid control, opening to 'flow'	Innovation, integrated synthesis of old and new abstractions, symbols	Abstracting, synthesizing, combining, metaphorical thinking, intuiting
4th order Renunciation of control, chaotic, psychodelic, illuminating, receptivity to unconscious material	Self as part of larger reality, 'meta-consciousness,' disintegration of barriers: conscious–unconscious	Invention of new order, new paradigm, philosophical shifts, new pattern formation, 'inspired' creations	Disintegrating, surrendering, accepting, opening, building new perceptual order

and in leaving a gap where a stage was perceived to have been deleted. Bennett (1966) discusses human functioning divided into three groups of abilities: intellectual, affective and sensory motor. These have been combined into one group, as they relate to the four levels of human energies defined by Bennett.

Many studies of the creative personality list qualities and characteristics attributed to these people. However, many individuals are capable of exhibiting high levels of creativity in relation to a single problem situation. One can move through higher stages of creativity without manifesting all of these personal characteristics in other aspects of living and dealing with challenges. The key to this stepped-up processing is the *high* degree of intense personal involvement with and commitment to the problem. These motivate one to go beyond one's 'normal' capabilities or 'usual' behaviors.

First order

Imaging and creativity of the first order are based on creation out of necessity. This occurs when an adult adopts some behavior in response to an immediate need.

First order imaging is not an analytical or introspective process. Images as

Table 2   *Comparison of developmental frameworks*

Orders/ Stages	*Blake*	*Land*	*Werner*	*Bucke*	*Bennett*
1st	*Single vision* What ordinary eyesight perceives	*Formative* Pattern forming	*Undifferentiated state of being* Separateness – self/others, inner/ outer	*Simple consciousness* Receptive mind	*Automatic* Learning by rote, conditioned reflexes, habits, automatic affective reactions
2nd	*Two-fold vision* Limited imagination, simile and analogy	*Normative* Extending and verifying	*Differentiated state of being* Separateness – divisions within self	*Self-consciousness* Conceptual mind	*Sensitive* Analytical skill, social sense, loyalty, ability to drive oneself
3rd	*Three-fold vision* 'Thing' as symbol	*Integrative* Sharing destructuring/ restructuring	*Hierarchic integration* Unified integration of polarities		*Conscious* Synthetic power, combine theory and practice, emotional stability, imagination, critical judgment
4th	*Four-fold vision* Mystic, seer, prophet, intense feeling	*Transformative* Loss of identity, search for new pattern		*Cosmic consciousness* Intuitive mind	*Creative* Genius, inspirational leadership, mystical, creative invention

pictures or other sensory based encodings are of this type. A person perceives and creates a mental warehouse of imprints without being consciously aware of what is happening. Images are a part of, rather than apart from, a person's reality. While a person may not be 'undifferentiated' (Werner, 1957) in the majority of activities engaged in, any particular problem of urgent safety or survival could force one into this order of functioning in relation to that problem. A need for invention or discovery would be required.

This is a spontaneous and 'un-self-conscious' mode of imaging and creating. Creating is also 'self-creating.' Bucke describes this as an order of 'simple consciousness,' Land as a 'formative' stage where one is exploring and building a pattern. Bennett (1966) refers to an automatic state where one adopts conditioned reflexes and habits, displays automatic affective reactions and learns by rote.

Second order

Creativity and imaging of the second order are most accurately characterized as seeking improvement or modification of an existing idea, object, pattern or behavior. Imaging can be consciously employed in the conception and enactment of this modification. Analysis, evaluation and goal direction are descriptive of the second order imaging process. Whether it be to improve self-concept, stop smoking, 'cure' cancer or change the design of a table, all have a specific goal, and conscious manipulation of images can be employed.

An individual's involvement with this order of creativity is usually closely bound to the ego. It is the intent – improving, strengthening, extending, modifying – that is more significant than imaginal content. Second order is an enhancing and modifying process – of self, tangible objects, ideas, behaviors, concepts. The initial pattern is still obvious but one leaves a personal mark on the new 'product.' A great deal of conscious control is exercised.

In second order one realizes the self as a separate being. One acquires a social sense and the ability to act as a self-motivator (Bennett, 1966). The product becomes a reflection of its creator. There is great pride in one's creation. One feels good, said Land and Kenneally (1977), at having influenced something else.

Third order

Third order creating and its activating and accompanying imaging becomes necessary when one has used up improvements, modifications and alterations.

Combination and synthesis characterize third order creating and imaging. This is the order of innovation. This results in the creation of a new product, theory or the like that is an integral combination of two or more ideas or products or functions. The resulting product is novel and contains at least as much 'new' as 'old.' One must be willing to give up images of what exists 'out there' and be willing to encounter a new way of thinking and imaging in discovering what can be. Fixed images can become prisons, preventing change in perception and action. Breaking through these is vital.

Bry (1978) described three types of imaging based on evocation. One is spontaneous imaging that can be attributed to first order processes. She called this receptive or 'open screen' imaging. The next type is programmed or guided imagery that belongs to the goal-directed process of the second order. The third type is a combination imaging that is appropriate to the third order. One must be able to create a mood of receptive spontaneity, to be open and have access to more unconscious material, yet to direct and manipulate imaging to fit with a purpose or goal. This involves abstracting, synthesizing and superimposing images.

Much suppressed material emerges. Old ideas and fixed perceptions must disintegrate in order to be reintegrated at a higher order. There is certain pain that accompanies breaking old connections, said Land and Kenneally (1977), but good feelings about forming new connections. A person subsumes the characteristics of preceding stages of the creative process. Werner (1957) related this idea:

> ... the more creative the person, the wider his range of operations in terms of developmental level, or in other words, the greater his capacity to utilize primitive as well as advanced operations.

This is the order in which one surrenders the very strong security of the second order and goes from self-realization to *selves realization*. Hillman (1975) gave a good account of this painful and rewarding process. Following the Jungian tradition, he emphasized the multiple internal personalities lurking within. One was unable to recognize these in second order development of self. Strange ideas and intruding personalities were suppressed or repressed, so that one could verify and strengthen one's ego. It is only when the ego is built up sufficiently that one can tear it down to create an expanded perception through reintegration.

Maslow (1968) recognized that in self-actualization internal dichotomies were resolved into unities. One need not be either/or but could encompass both/and. This is the order of personality synthesis. He made the following observation of highly creative persons.

> My subjects were unselfish in one sense and very selfish in another sense. And the two fused together, not like uncompatibles, but rather in a sensible, dynamic unity or synthesis.

Torrance and Hall (1980) reaffirm this notion of highly creative people by pointing out that they 'successfully integrate polar opposites into their personality and their thinking and they seem to have an unexplained ability to solve problems which appear to defy logical, rational solutions.'

In tackling these problems and in the process of interrelating two seemingly disparate ideas or concepts, one is bound to encounter conflict, paradox, ambiguity. Heisenberg (1974) realized the necessity of integrating polarities in one's thinking.

> ... physics has forced us to think in different areas of connection which stand to each other in a relation that Bohr has described by means of the notion of 'complementarity.' The areas in question may exclude each other, so that only through the interplay between them does the full unity become apparent.

He encouraged one to 'expose oneself' in one way or another to these intensified oppositions and their conflicts. The intensity of the encounter determines the degree of novelty of the outcome.

Gruber (1978) also called for an interplay of these opposites within science. He characterized two aesthetic moods in science: the aesthetics of objectivity, simplicity, harmony and order and the aesthetic mood of the erotic, of wildness, of passionate involvement, of pleasure in complexity and of unpredictability. This is reflective of the interplay between convergence and divergence, sense and 'non-sense,' the conscious and unconscious minds, inner and outer experience. Gruber stated the internal dichotomy of all things: 'The perfection of the rose and the tangle of the rose bush are both part of reality.'

Whether achieving new approaches to art through re-visioning, abstracting, symbolizing or bringing together ideas in a 'complementarity,' one is engaging in the same fundamental process. In both areas, said Gordon (1961):

> ... To achieve radical new approaches to old problems it is essential to take

'psychological chances,' to abandon familiar ways of looking at things, even to transcend one's image of oneself.

For this to be possible, Gordon continues, 'we must risk at least temporary ambiguity and disorder.' One can only lend oneself to this intense encounter and take the risks that it demands if there is a sense of purpose and commitment to the problem, and to life. Parnes (1977) stated that the 'creative person usually doesn't know what he/she is going to do next, but most probably knows why.' As we progress through the orders of creating and imaging, our relation to the world becomes more dynamic, more giving, more extracting, more meaning-filled. We become more open to ourselves and therefore to our world.

Fourth order

There is a *renunciation of imaging control* in fourth order. This imaging most closely resembles the spontaneous process of first order.

The magnitude of disintegration is immense in this order. One is losing a former perception of reality and creating a new paradigm. Commitment and faith are essential here in order to progress. Faith propels one into this new perceptual order. Renouncing conscious control and becoming receptive is part of this transcending process. One's whole being comes into play with the conscious and unconscious minds, reason and intuition, inner and outer, subsumed into a kind of meta-consciousness. Said Koestler (1964), the creative person is 'multi-level headed' as opposed to level headed. It is only after a person has become self-actualized that he/she can be homonomous, or 'merge himself as a part in a larger whole than himself' (Maslow, 1962).

Imaging of the fourth order may have the sense of illuminating or experiencing mystic vision. There may be no conscious awareness or focusing on the stream of inner imaging. Most likely, the imaging will be conceptual, highly emotive and fast paced. One is entering a transformed first order and is faced with creating a framework for new perceptions. One is receptive to spontaneous imaging without being highly analytical or introspective.

Art of this order manifests itself as inspired productions. One feels somehow directed or guided by a greater force. One becomes an agent through whom a larger idea can be expressed. Blake called this 'four fold vision,' the vision of the mystic, the seer, the prophet. It is a vision infused with intense feeling: horror, ecstasy, desolation (Barron, 1963). This represents the epitome of breaking through the limits of conscious perception. Einstein (1935) experienced this in scientific investigation: 'The mystical is the source of all true science.'

It is important to note that one can experience glimpses of 'cosmic consciousness' or 'transcendence' without shifting one's whole life perspective. Also, a particular area of expression or focus can be affected by a transformation without one's entire self and relation to the world following the same course.

When a person enters into full cosmic consciousness, said Bucke, he knows without learning that the universe is a living process with a tendency toward that which is good. He also believes that individual existence continues beyond death. At the same time, said Bucke, he takes on an enormously greater capacity for learning and living.

Practical applications

> We cannot *will* to have insights. We cannot will creativity. But we can will to give ourselves to the encounter with intensity of dedication and commitment. The deeper aspects of awareness are activated to the extent that the person is committed to the encounter. (May, 1975)

Taoism views one's life as an art and believes the most creative process is in the living. Imaging studied apart from its function and purpose loses meaning and potential significance. It needs to be viewed in the context of living and creating.

To begin working with the imaginal mind, one must believe that there is value in gaining conscious awareness of the imaging process. One needs also to set aside judgment. Said Hillman (1975):

> The first step in recovering the imaginative perspective is to set aside all moral points of view toward the images of fantasy, dream, and pathology. Images are to be left free of judgments: good or bad, positive or negative.

Hillman goes on to say that it is less a matter of program than of attitude. It means bringing the imaginal perspective to all that we see. Thus everything is transformed into images of significance, and with that change, we view ourselves differently.

Perceptual awareness training may offer a key to discovering more about the imaging process, especially as it relates to the earlier orders described above. Shepard (as quoted in Gowan, 1979) made this conclusion:

> ... as we probe still further into either the process of perception or the process of imagery, we are likely to gain a deeper understanding of both – and just possibly, some significant insights into the sources of creative thought.

Milner (1957) viewed perceptual awareness itself as a creative process.

> ... awareness of the external world is itself a creative process, an immensely complex creative interchange between what comes from inside and what comes from outside, a complex alternation of fusing and separating.

Beginning awareness and focus on inner imaging is necessarily intentional. One can experiment with sensory based imagery by calling to mind memory images. One can attempt to manipulate, to guide, or to use 'open screen' and receptive techniques (Bry, 1978; Wenger, 1979). Awareness of imaging becomes less and less deliberate as one practices.

Frankl (1959) stated that the true meaning of life is found in the world rather than in one's psyche. Again, this is a two way process with inner and outer 'two sides of the same fabric' (Vaughan, 1979). As one becomes more effective in changing one's environment, internal changes result. If one effects internal change and develops awareness, the world appears changed as well.

Appropriateness of imagery techniques will be examined in relation to each order.

First order techniques

First order is not an introspective process. This is the order of the one to one correspondence of images. What we see, hear, taste, smell, feel is encoded and stored as sensory based images. Studies have examined various modalities of imagery in relationship to a person's perceptual type.

First order techniques have been applied to learning a new language and to psychotherapy through suggestology (Lozanov, 1978). Its learning technique, suggestopedia, removes blocks to learning and prepares a receptive state of mind. A nonthreatening atmosphere is created through the process of suggestion and desuggestion. The instructor inspires confidence and raises levels of expectation. Classical music, rhythmic breathing, role playing, intonation and relaxation are essential components of this fast paced memory learning. Limits are removed and a new perceptual order is created.

It is difficult to create artificial situations for first order imaging and creating. An individual must perceive a need before being motivated to learn or create. Any situation requiring new learning or invention must clearly communicate this need.

Second order techniques

There is a plethora of material on second order creating and imaging. Second order is goal-directed. Whether it involves solving a particular problem, improving one's health or self-concept, rehearsing for athletic or musical performances, there are special techniques for each. Second order involves building on or changing an existing pattern, design, concept, and requires intentional action.

Technical books for intentional imaging contain relaxation and breathing exercises, guided fantasies, scripts answering various purposes. Imaging is usually limited to the development of visual imaging, though other modalities receive some attention. Second order techniques use the power of the conscious mind to control, manipulate and modify situations.

The Simontons (1978) have used mental imagery as a tool for self-discovery. The idea they have expressed is 'picture what you want and it will happen' – the self-fulfilling prophecy. They have successfully combined imagery and medication in cancer treatment. With this very intense goal of 'curing' or arresting cancer, they have found the following in sincere patients: a decrease in fear, attitudinal changes, physical changes, altered beliefs, decreased stress, and communication with the unconscious mind in its revelations about the illness. As one becomes more aware of the power within, he or she can make improvements in health and well being.

The ancient Huna (Glover, 1972) religion of Hawaii, with roots dating back over 7000 years, is the precursor of all positive thinking programs. It offers a practical philosophy for achieving what one desires in life. Huna believes in three 'selves' – low self, middle self, and High Self. These can be equated with the unconscious, conscious and superconscious. It is worth while stating the steps of Huna prayer for the ancient wisdoms they contain. The process utilizes relaxation and breathing, is goal-directed, utilizes verbalizing and visualizing and is founded upon *belief* and *commitment*.

1. Decide what it is you really want and desire it fervently.
2. Think about, clarify, and solidify your desire.
3. Relax the low self through suggestion (mind and body).
4. Breathe hard – either through exercise or deep breathing – to accumulate energy (mana).
5. Speak the suggestion to the low self – verbalizing.
6. Visualize the suggestion in detail, using imagery of all sensory modalities. See yourself in the desired state. Picture ends, not means.
7. Tell the lower self to stop relaxing.
8. Expect the low self to react and send the message to the High Self. Believe the suggestion will come about.

Perceptual training of the second order would develop the ability to perceive detail, to see things in relation to one another – comparing and contrasting. One would develop interpretations and impressions. Similes are appropriate second order calls for specific problem definition before ideation. Quantity or fluency of ideas is sought in seeking ways to improve. Brainstorming is a particularly useful tool for generating ideas to modify something. A fresh approach may emerge, but novelty usually is not produced. Osborn's (1953) idea-spurring questions are very appropriate to this order of creating. These questions encourage one to manipulate images to produce conceptions of change.

Third order techniques

Third order creativity and imaging require a change of perception. One needs to look through and into ideas, objects, functions, in order to break up one's perceptual set. This allows for new connections to be made by combining seemingly unrelated 'things.' An innovation must be called for in the solution of a problem of this order. A simple improvement would not be adequate.

Third order demands that one push against the limits of normal perception, creating dynamic tension, internal paradox, a dialectic. There are ways to prepare oneself for this type of thinking. Metaphorical thinking encouraged in synectics (Gordon, 1961) and Janusian thinking (Rothenberg, 1976) are examples of appropriate techniques. Synectics encourages play with words, with laws or basic scientific concepts, with paradoxical metaphor. Janusian thinking is 'the capacity to conceive and utilize two or more contradictory ideas, concepts, or images simultaneously.'

Another means of creating internal paradox is through Zen koans. Said Royce (1964):

> Koans are of great variety in terms of paradox, ambiguity, and specific purpose. In toto, they are concerned with keeping the psyche open, not just in intellect, but more importantly, the senses, feelings, and intuitions as well. It is a technique designed to force an individual out of his well-worn ruts into new ways of seeing, into broader awareness.

Third order has an intent and need to find a solution. There is, however, no preconceived concept of the form or shape this solution will take. One needs to take the problem seriously, said Bennett (1964), and have the confidence that something can be done, that there is a way out. The creative and imaging processes of third order are a paradoxical metaphor in themselves. One tries to cultivate deliberate spontaneity, consciously opening oneself to the flow of ideas. This is accomplished by first creating an internal conflict or tension within the problem situation.

Stanislavsky (1961) outlines dramatic techniques that accomplish the purpose for actors. He claimed that one must 'break the bonds' of experience before being ready to open the heart to all the perceptions of life. For creative work, said Stanislavsky, one needs internal and external attention, goodwill and fearlessness.

In third order, there is an expansion of self-definition as one realizes internal 'selves.' There is an interplay of opposites – self and nonself, conscious and unconscious, subject and object, known and unknown. One cannot consciously strive to bring these together in dynamic unity. Unity 'is achieved by immediate, spontaneous interaction' (Chung-Yuan, 1963).

Self-actualization cannot be an end in itself. Said Frankl (1959): 'Only to the extent to which man commits himself to the fulfillment of his life's meaning, to this extent he also actualizes himself.' Music, movement, spontaneous writing, play, painting, giving oneself over to some automatic activity – these will induce a state of receptivity. They facilitate the move from a focus on the problem to an openness to emerging solutions. One cannot be completely ego-directed, but must allow for unconscious work and play to interact with conscious efforts. Developing techniques to catalyze this process could make the incubation process less mysterious and more intentional. The stage could be set for unusual combinations to surface. Once the conscious mind starts the stream of ideas flowing, it can step out and *allow* the unconscious flow to continue, to meander without obstacles. The two can together realize a solution.

Fourth order techniques

One cannot prepare oneself with techniques for bringing about fourth order creativity. One can only cultivate a receptive attitude for the phenomena that occur. A sense of purpose and search for life's meaning, not the pursuit of a goal, are the motivating factors that lead one to an order that is beyond 'normal' perceptions.

There is an abandonment of conscious striving in the fourth order. It is necessary to 'let go,' to disintegrate, to open oneself up to the spontaneous flow of arising thoughts and images. Limits and boundaries between consciousness and unconsciousness explode. One becomes a cosmic receiver, perceiving self as part of a larger reality. This reality is experienced often as 'imageless' awareness, 'metaconsciousness.'

Kardinsky (1913) looked forward to the day when we not only studied the 'outer' workings but the inner world of all things. 'Then,' he said, 'the atmosphere will be created that will enable men as a whole to feel the spirit of things, to experience this spirit, if even unconsciously.'

In 'peak experiences' or Satori, many individuals glimpse another reality which transcends what is now defined and measured as creativity. Torrance and Hall (1980) describe these experiences as part of a suprarational view of creativity which demands commitment, persistence and intense absorption. The door is opening to a more thorough study of these experiences and abilities.

Conclusion

The framework presented here is intended to further understanding of the varieties of creative experience and its accompanying imaging. It opens the door for structuring additional techniques to facilitate the practical attainment of higher orders of creative functioning. Techniques can enable individuals to experience their creative capacities more fully and thereby motivate or precipitate further commitment.

Techniques, however, are not ends in themselves. While they may spark commitment, they certainly cannot replace it. Research reveals that personal purpose and commitment are the key motivational factors, behind creative achievement. Each order, as described in the above framework, carries its own purpose. This purpose overrides technique.

> When the right man (white magician) makes use of the wrong means, the wrong means work in the right way. If the wrong man uses the right means, the right means work in the wrong way.   (from the Chinese Books of Ethics)

This study has clearly pointed out the need for developing means and measures for understanding the motivation behind creative activity. Purpose and commitment cannot be artificially instilled through a carefully planned program of progressive techniques. Yet, these factors are most significant to creative living. 'Without this intense cosmological commitment no amount of mental activity of the sort measured by IQ tests will suffice to produce a genuinely creative act' (Barron, 1963). The challenge becomes one of developing purposeful connection in any creative activity.

Imaging and creativity have been inextricably linked in the developmental framework presented. They have been examined as part of intentional activity. To examine content without intent is to miss the forest for the trees. This framework has presented the reader with a lens through which to view imaging and creativity, superimposed, in a new perspective.

References

Arieti, S. (1976) *Creativity: the magic synthesis*. NYC: Basic Books.

Arnheim, R. (1969) *Visual thinking*. Los Angeles: University of California Press.

Assagioli, R. (1965) *Psychosynthesis*. NYC: Penguin Books.

Barron, F. (1963) *Creativity and psychological health*. NYC: Van Nostrand.

Bartlett, F.C. (1927) The relevance of visual imagery to the process of thinking. *British Journal of Psychology 18*. 23–29.

Bennett, J.G. (1964) *Creative thinking*. Sherborne, England: Coombe Springs Press.

Bennett, J.G. (1966) The specification and assessment of human beings. *Systematics, 4*. 281–303.

Bry, A. (1978) *Directing the movies of your mind*. NYC: Harper & Row.

Bucke, R.M. (1901) *Cosmic consciousness*. NYC: Dutton (18th ed., 1956).

Chung-Yuan, C. (1963) *Creativity and Taoism*, NYC: Harper & Row.

Dellas, M. & Gaier, E.M. (1970) Identification of creativity. *Psychological Bulletin, 73*. 55–73.

Duradell, A.J. & Wetherick, N.E. (1976) The relation of reported imagery to cognitive performance. *British Journal of Psychology, 67*, 501–506.

Durio, H.F. (1975) Mental image and creativity. *Journal of Creative Behavior, 9(4)*, 233–244.

Einstein, A. (1935) *The world as I see it*. London.

Forisha, B. (1978) Mental imagery and creativity: review and speculations. *Journal of Mental Imagery, 2*, 209–238.

Frankl, V.E. (1959) *Man's search for meaning: an introduction to logotherapy*. NYC: Washington Square Press.

Glover, W.R. (1972) *Huna: the ancient religion of positive thinking*. Sunset Beach, CA: Author.

Gordon, R. (1972) A very private world. In Sheehan, P.W. (ed.), *The function and nature of imagery*. Academic Press, 63–80.

Gordon, W.J.J. (1961) *Synectics*. NYC: Harper.

Gowan, J.C. (1975) *Trance, art, and creativity*. Northridge, CA: Author.

Gowan, J.C. (1978) Creativity and the gifted child movement. *Journal of Creative Behavior, 12(1)*, 1–13.

Gowan, J.C. (1979) The production of creativity through right hemisphere imagery. *Journal of Creative Behavior, 13(1)*, 39–51.

Gruber, H.E. (1978) Darwin's 'tree of nature' and other images of wide scope. In Wechsler, J. (ed.). *On aesthetics in science*. Cambridge, MA: The MIT Press.

Heisenberg, W. (1974) *Across the frontiers*. NYC: Harper & Row.

Hicks, G.D. (1924) On the nature of images. *British Journal of Psychology, 15*, 121–148.

Hillman, J. (1975) *Revisioning psychology*. NYC: Harper & Row.

Holt, R.R. (1953) Imagery: the return of the ostracized. *American Psychologist, 19*, 254–264.

Jung, C.G. (1923) from Psychological types. In DeLaszo, V.S. (ed.), *The basic writings of C.G. Jung*. NYC: The Modern Library (1959), 183–285.

Jung, C.G. (1954) from On the nature of the psyche. In DeLaszo, V.S. (ed.), *The basic writings of C.G. Jung*. NYC: The Modern Library (1959), 37–104.

Jung, C.G. (1957) God, the devil and the human soul. *The Atlantic Monthly*, 57–63.

Jung, C.G. (1963) *Memories, dreams, reflections*. NYC: Vintage Books.

Kardinsky, W. (1913) Reminiscences. In Herbert, R.L. (ed.), *Modern artists on art*. Englewood Cliffs, NJ: Prentice-Hall, (1964).

Khatena, J. (1978) Identification and stimulation of creative imagination imagery. *Journal of Creative Behavior, 12(1)*, 30–38.

Koestler, A. (1964) *The act of creation*. NYC: Macmillan.

Land, G.T. & Kenneally, C. (1977) Creativity, reality, and general systems: a personal viewpoint. *Journal of Creative Behavior, 11(1)*, 12–35.

Langer, S.K. (1967) *Mind: an essay on human feeling* (vol. 1). Baltimore, MD: The Johns Hopkins Press.

Lozanov, G. (1978) *Suggestology and outlines of suggestopedy*. Hall-Pozharlieva, M. & Pahmakova, K. (trans.). NYC: Gordon and Breach.

Maslow, A.H. (1962) Some basic propositions for a growth and self-actualization psychology. *Perceiving, behaving, becoming: a new focus for education*. Yearbook of the Association for Supervision and Curriculum Development, Washington, DC: 307–315.

Maslow, A.H. (1968) *Toward a psychology of being*. NYC: Van Nostrand Reinhold.

May, R. (1975) *The courage to create*. NYC: Norton.

Milner, M. (1957) *On not being able to paint*. NYC: International Universities Press.

Monod, J. (1971) *Chance and necessity*. NYC: Alfred A. Knopf.

Neisser, U. (1972) Changing conceptions of imagery. In Sheehan, P.W. (ed.). *The function and nature of imagery*. NYC: Academic Press, 233–251.

Osborn, A.F. (1953) *Applied imagination*. NYC: Charles Scribners.

Parnes, S.J. (1977) CPSI: the general system. *Journal of Creative Behavior, 11(1)*, 1–11.

Parnes, S.J., Noller, R.B. & Biondi, A.M. (1977) *Guide to creative action*. NYC: Charles Scribners.

Richardson, A. (1969) *Mental Imagery*. NYC: Springer.

Roe, A. (1963) Psychological approaches to creativity in science. In Coler, M. (ed.), *Essays on creativity in the sciences*. NYC: New York University Press, 153–182.

Rothenberg, A. (1976) The process of Janusian thinking in creativity. In Rothenberg, A. & Hausman, C. (eds.), *The creativity question*. Durham, NC: Duke University Press.

Royce, J. (1964) *The encapsulated man*. Princeton, NJ: Van Nostrand.

Short, P.L. (1953) The objective study of mental imagery. *British Journal of Psychology, 44*, 38–51.

Simonton, O.C., Matthews-Simonton, S. & Creighton, J. (1978) *Getting well again*. Los Angeles: J.P. Tarcher.

Singer, J.L. (1966) *The inner world of daydreaming*. NYC: Harper & Row.

Stanislavsky, (1961) *Stanislavsky on the art of the stage*. NYC: Hill & Wang.

Swartz, B.A. (1976) *Amotfa: a magazine of the fine arts, 2(15)*, 34–41.

Torrance, E.P. & Hall, L.K. (1980) Assessing the further reaches of creative potential. *Journal of Creative Behavior, 14(1)*, 1–19.

Treffinger, D.J. & Poggio, J. (1976) Needed research on the measurement of creativity. In Biondi, A.M. & Parnes, S.J. (eds). *Assessing creative growth: measuring changes* (book 2). Great Neck, NY: Creative Synergetic Associates, 207–224.

Vaughan, F.E. (1979) *Awakening intuition*. Garden City, NY: Anchor Press.

Wallas, G. (1926) *The art of thought*. London: Watts.

Watkins, M.M. (1976) *Waking dreams*. NYC: Harper & Row.

Wenger, W. (1979) *Beyond o.k. – some psychogenic tools relating to health of body and mind: a self-instructing course*. Gaithersburg, MD: Psychogenics Press.

Werner, H. (1957) The concept of development from a comparative and organismic point of view. In Harris, D.B. (ed.) *The concept of development*. Minneapolis, MN: University of Minnesota Press.

Yuille, J.C. & Catchpole, M.G. (1977) The role of imagery in models of organization. *Journal of Mental Imagery, 1*, 171–180.

SECTION 4
CREATIVE DEVELOPMENT

Section 4, on creative development, highlights some of the ways in which learning and thinking style can affect the type of information attended to, and lead to different strategy preferences and ways of tackling problems. It draws out the implications of these styles for the possibility of creative action in individuals, teams and organizations.

Kirton outlines his Adaption–Innovation theory, and shows how differences in thinking style can affect the manager's response to problem solving, creativity and relationships. The Kirton Adaptor–Innovator Inventory is a well-tested British scale now widely used as measure of creative style here and abroad.

Kolb et al. stress the importance of integrative skills such as visioning, generative leadership and integrity to strategic management. They argue that integrative learning or wisdom is increasingly important in the management of ever more complex and changeable environments. Using experiential learning theory they show how distinct perceptual, affective, symbolic and behavioural competencies manifest at different levels of management.

Hurst's model of creative management highlights the part played by cognitive style. He uses the Jungian typology of Intuition, Sensing, Feeling and Thinking to argue the benefits of a mixed management team. He points out the different time orientation and strategy preference associated with each type and their implications for the prospects of creative renewal in organizations.

The chapter by Lessem takes a rather different tack, concentrating not so much on differences between individuals, but within the same individual over time. He discusses Levinson's idea of life phases and relates the transitions associated with each to a creative process of anticipation, separation and incubation, expansion and incorporation, which he suggests affords the basis for creating your own life.

16

Adaptors and innovators – why new initiatives get blocked

Michael J. Kirton

Background

The Adaption–Innovation theory defines and measures two styles of decision-making,[1-3] clarifying earlier literature on problem-solving and creativity which concentrates more on defining and assessing *level* rather than *style*. This shift of emphasis has advantages in the practical world of business, commerce and administration.

According to the Adaption–Innovation theory, everyone can be located on a continuum ranging from highly adaptive to highly innovative according to their score on the Kirton Adaption–Innovation Inventory. The range of responses is relatively fixed and stable,[a] and in the general population approaches the normal curve distribution. For the purpose of clarity the following descriptions characterize those individuals at the extreme ends of the continuum.

Adaptors characteristically produce a sufficiency of ideas,[b] based closely on, but stretching, existing agreed definitions of the problem and likely solutions. They look at these in detail and proceed within the established mores (theories, policies, practices) of their organizations. Much of their effort in change is in improving and 'doing better' (which tends to dominate management, e.g. Drucker).[4]

Innovators, by contrast, are more likely in the pursuit of change to reconstruct the problem, separating it from its enveloping accepted thought, paradigms and customary viewpoints, and emerge with much less expected, and probably less acceptable solutions (see Fig. 1). They are less concerned with 'doing things better' than with 'doing things differently'.

The development of the A–I theory began with observations made and conclusions reached as a result of a study of management initiative.[5] The aim of this study was to investigate the ways in which ideas which had led to radical changes in the companies studied were developed and implemented.

Reprinted with permission from *Long Range Planning*, 17, 2 (1984), pp. 137–43. Copyright 1984 Pergamon Press PLC

Adaptor	Innovator
Characterized by Precision, Reliability, Efficiency, Methodicalness, Prudence, Discipline, Conformity	Seen as Undisciplined, Thinking Tangentially, Approaching Tasks from Unsuspected Angles
Concerned with Resolving Problems Rather Than Finding Them	Could be Said to Discover Problems and Discover Avenues of Solution
Seeks Solutions to Problems in Tried and Understood Ways	Queries Problems' Concomitant Assumptions; Manipulates Problems
Reduces Problems by Improvement and Greater Efficiency, with Maximum of Continuity and Stability	Is Catalyst to Settled Groups, Irreverent of their Consensual Views; Seen as Abrasive, Creating Dissonance
Seen as Sound, Conforming, Safe, Dependable	Seen as Unsound, Impractical; Often Shocks his Opposite
Liable to Make Goals of Means	In Pursuit of Goals Treats Accepted Means with Little Regard
Seems Impervious to Boredom, Seems Able to Maintain High Accuracy in Long Spells of Detailed Work	Capable of Detailed Routine (System Maintenance) Work for Only Short Bursts; Quick to Delegate Routine Tasks
Is an Authority Within Given Structures	Tends to Take Control in Unstructured Situations
Challenges Rules Rarely, Cautiously, When Assured of Strong Support	Often Challenges Rules, Has Little Respect for Past Custom
Tends to High Self-doubt. Reacts to Criticism by Closer Outward Conformity. Vulnerable to Social Pressures and Authority; Compliant	Appears to Have Low Self-doubt When Generating Ideas, Not Needing Consensus to Maintain Certitude in Face of Opposition
Is Essential to the Functioning of the Institution All the Time, but Occasionally Needs to be 'Dug Out' of His Systems	In the Institution is Ideal in Unscheduled Crises, or Better Still to Help to Avoid them, if he Can be Controlled
When collaborating with innovators: Supplies Stability, Order and Continuity to the Partnership	*When collaborating with adaptors*: Supplies the Task Orientations, the Break with the Past and Accepted Theory
Sensitive to People, Maintains Group Cohesion and Co-operation	Appears Insensitive to People, Often Threatens Group Cohesion and Co-operation
Provides a Safe Base for the Innovator's Riskier Operations	Provides the Dynamics to Bring About Periodic Radical Change, Without which Institutions Tend to Ossify

Originally published in the *Journal of Applied Psychology* (reference 1)

Figure 1   *Behaviour descriptions of adaptors and innovators*

In each of the examples of initiative studied the resulting changes had required the co-operation of many managers and others in more than one department.

Numerous examples of successful 'corporate' initiative, such as the introduction of a new product or new accounting procedures, were examined, and this analysis highlighted the stages through which such initiative passed on the way to becoming part of the accepted routine of the company, i.e. perception of the problem, analysis of the problem, analysis of the solution, agreement to change, acceptance of change, delegation and finally implementation. The study also looked at what went wrong at these various stages, and how the development of a particular initiative was thus affected. From this, a number of anomalies were thrown up that at the time remained unexplained.

(1) Delays in introducing change

Despite the assertion of managers that they were collectively both sensitive to the need for changes and willing to embark on them, the time lag between the first public airing of most of the ideas studied, and the date on which an idea was clearly accepted as a possible course of action, was a matter of years – usually two or three. Conversely, a few were accepted almost immediately, with the bare minimum of in-depth analysis. (The size of proposed changes did not much affect this time scale, although all the changes studied were large.)

(2) Objections to new ideas

All too often, the new idea had been formally blocked by a series of well-argued and reasoned objections which were upheld until some critical event – a 'precipitating event' – occurred, so that none of these quondam cogent contrary arguments (lack of need, lack of resource, etc.) was ever heard again. Indeed, it appeared at times as if management had been hit by almost total collective amnesia concerning past objections.

(3) Rejection of individuals

There was a marked tendency for the majority of ideas which encountered opposition and delays to have been put forward by managers who were themselves unacceptable to an 'establishment' group, not just before, but also after the ideas they advocated had not only become accepted, but even been rated highly successful. At the same time, other managers putting forward the more palatable ideas not only were themselves initially acceptable, but remained so, even if these ideas were later rejected or failed.

The A–I theory now offers a rational, measured explanation of these findings.

Adaptors and innovators – two different styles of thinking

Adaptive solutions are those that depend directly and obviously on generally agreed paradigms, are more easily grasped intellectually, and therefore more readily accepted by most – by adaptors as well as the many innovators not so directly involved in the resolution of the problem under scrutiny. The familiar assumptions on which the solution depends are not under attack, and help 'butter' the solution advanced, making it more palatable. Such derived ideas, being more readily acceptable, favourably affect the status of their authors, often even when they fail – and the authors of such ideas are much more likely to be themselves adaptors, characterized as being personally more acceptable to the 'establishment' with whom they share those underlying familiar assumptions.[1] Indeed, almost irrespective of their rank, they are likely to be part of that establishment, which in the past has led innovators to claim somewhat crudely that adaptors owe their success to agreeing with their bosses. However, Kirton[9] conducted a study in which KAI scores were compared with superior/subordinate identification in a sample of 93 middle managers. No connection was found between KAI scores and tendency to agree with one's boss. Instead a more subtle relationship is suggested, i.e. that those in the upper hierarchy are more likely to accept the same paradigms as their adaptor juniors, and that there is, therefore, a greater chance of agreement between them on broad issues and on approved courses of action. Where they disagree on detail within the accepted paradigm, innovators may be inclined to attach less significance to this and view the broad agreements reached as simple conformity.

It can thus be seen how failure of ideas is less damaging to the adaptor than to the innovator, since any erroneous assumptions upon which the ideas were based were also shared with colleagues and other influential people. The consequence is that such failure is more likely to be written off as 'bad luck' or due to 'unforeseeable events', thereby directing the blame away from the individuals concerned.

In stark contrast to this, innovative ideas, not being as closely related to the group's prevailing, relevant paradigms, and even opposing such consensus views, are more strongly resisted, and their originators are liable to be treated with suspicion and even derision. This rejection of individuals tends to persist even after their ideas are adopted and acknowledged as successful. (It should be noted that both these and the further descriptions to come are put in a rather extreme form (as a heuristic device) and usually therefore occur in a somewhat less dramatic form.)

Differences in behaviour

Evidence is now accumulating from a number of studies[1,2,10] that *personality* is implicated in these characteristic differences between adaptors and innovators. Indeed it must be so, since the way in which one thinks affects the way in which one behaves, and is seen to behave, in much the same way as there are differences in personality characteristics between those who are left brain dominated and those who are right brain dominated – the former being described as tending towards methodical, planned thinking and the latter towards more intuitive thinking[11] (there is a significant correlation between left–right brain preference scores and adaptation–innovation). The personality characteristics of adaptors and innovators that are part of their cognitive style are here described.

Innovators are generally seen by adaptors as being abrasive and insensitive, despite the former's denial of these traits. This misunderstanding usually occurs because the innovator attacks the adaptor's theories and assumptions, both explicitly when he feels that the adaptor needs a push to hurry him in the right direction or to get him out of his rut, and implicitly by showing a disregard for the rules, conventions, standards of behaviour, etc. What is even more upsetting for the adaptor is the fact that the innovator does not even seem to be aware of the havoc he is causing. Innovators may also appear abrasive to each other, since neither will show much respect for the other's theories, unless of course their two points of view happen temporarily to coincide. Adaptors can also be viewed pejoratively by innovators, suggesting that the more extreme types are far more likely to disagree than collaborate. Innovators tend to see adaptors as stuffy and unenterprising, wedded to systems, rules and norms which, however useful, are too restricting for their (the innovators') liking. Innovators seem to overlook how much of the smooth running of all around them depends on good adaptiveness[7,8] but are acutely aware of the less acceptable face of efficient bureaucracy. Disregard of convention when in pursuit of their own ideas has the effect of isolating innovators in a similar way to Rogers' creative loner.[6]

While innovators find it difficult to combine with others, adaptors find it easier. The latter will more rapidly establish common agreed ground, assumptions, guidelines and accepted practices on which to ground their collaboration. Innovators also have to do these things in order to fit at all into a company but they are less good at doing so, less concerned with finding out the anomalies within a system, and less likely to stick to the patterns they help form. This is at once the innovators' weakness and a source of potential advantage.

Where are the innovators and the adaptors?

Much of Kirton's earlier research was devoted to the description and classification of these two cognitive styles. More recently, attention has been focused on the issue of how they are distributed and whether any distinctive patterns emerge. It has been found from a large number of studies that KAI scores are by no means haphazardly distributed. Individuals' scores are derived from a 32-item inventory, giving a theoretical range of 32–160, and mean of 96. The observed range is slightly more restricted, 46–146, based on over 1000 subjects; the observed mean is near to 95 and the distribution conforms almost exactly to a normal curve. The studies have also shown that variations by identifiable subsets are predictable, their means shifting from the population mean in accordance with the theory. However, the groups' range of scores is rarely restricted – even smallish groups showing ranges of approximately 70–120 – a finding with important implications for change, against the background of differences found at cultural level, at organizational level, between jobs, between departments and between individuals within departments. This is a somewhat arbitrary grouping since norms of cognitive style can be detected wherever a group of people define themselves as differing or distinct from others, by whatever criteria they choose, be it type of work, religion, philosophy, etc. However, while allowing for a certain amount of overlap, the majority of research studies can be classified according to these groupings.

Innovators and adaptors in different cultures

A considerable amount of research information has been accumulating regarding the extent to which mean scores of different samples shift from culture to culture. For example, published normative samples collected from Britain,[1,2,12,13] USA,[14] Canada[12] and New Zealand[15] have all produced remarkably similar means. When the KAI was validated on a sample of Eastern managers from Singapore and Malaysia[16] their mean scores of 95 were compatible with those of their Western counterparts (e.g. UK managerial sample had a mean of 97; compared to general UK samples which together yielded a mean of 95.3).

However, samples of Indian and Iranian managers[17-19] yielded lower means than similar samples in UK, USA, Canada and Singapore (91). More adaptive norms were also found in work still in progress in a sample of black South African business students.[1A] These differences may not simply be a split between Western and Chinese Western groups vs others, since tentative results from a sample of Flemish-speaking job applicants for professional posts in a leading Belgian pharmaceutical company[2A] have yielded an even more adaptive mean^c (85.6) than that of the South African sample. Clearly there may be cultural differences of adaptor–innovator norms.

There is also a further speculation put forward by Kirton[20] that people who are most willing to cross boundaries of any sort are likely to be more innovative, and the more boundaries there are and the more rigidly they are held, the higher the innovative score should be of those who cross. In the Thomson study managers in Western-owned companies in Singapore scored higher in innovativeness then either those working for a private local company or those in the Civil Service, and those in this last category had the most adaptive scores of the triad. Further evidence for cultural differences emerges in work on Indian and Iranian managers.[17-19] Here, it was found that, as expected, entrepreneurs scored higher on the KAI than non-entrepreneurs (97.9 and 90.5 as opposed to 77.2 for Government Officers), but Indian women entrepreneurial managers were found to be even more innovative than their male counterparts. They had had to cross two boundaries: they broke with tradition by becoming a manager in the first place, and they had succeeded in becoming a manager in a risky entrepreneurial business.

Innovators and adaptors in different organizations

Organizations in general[7,21,22] and especially organizations which are large in size and budget[23,24] have a tendency to encourage bureaucracy and adaptation in order to minimize risk. It has been said by Weber,[7] Merton[8] and Parsons[25] that the aims of a bureaucratic structure are precision, reliability and efficiency, and that the bureaucratic structure exerts constant pressure on officials to be methodical, prudent and disciplined, and to attain an unusual degree of conformity. These are the qualities that the adaptor–innovator theory attributes to the 'adaptor' personality. For the marked adaptor, the longer an institutional practice has existed, the more he feels it can be taken for granted. So when confronted by a problem, he does not see it as a stimulus to question or change the structure in which the problem is embedded, but seeks a solution within that structure, in ways already tried and understood – ways which are safe, sure, predictable. He can be relied upon to carry out a thorough, disciplined search for ways to eliminate problems by 'doing things better' with a minimum of risk and a maximum of continuity and stability. This behaviour contrasts strongly with that of the marked innovator. The latter's solution, because it is less understood, and its assumption untested, appears more risky, less sound, involves more 'ripple-effect' changes in areas less obviously needing to be affected; in short, it brings about changes with outcomes that cannot be envisaged so precisely. This diminution of predictive certainty is unsettling and not to be undertaken lightly, if at all, by most people – but particularly by adaptors, who feel not only more loyal to consensus policy but less willing to jeopardize the integrity of the system (or even the institution). The innovator, in contrast to the adaptor, is liable to be less respectful of the views of others, more abrasive in the presentation of his solution, more at home in a turbulent environment, seen initially as less relevant in his thinking towards company needs (since his perceptions may differ as to what is needed), less concerned with people in the pursuit of his goals than adaptors readily tolerate. Tolerance of the innovator is thinnest when adaptors feel under pressure from the need for imminent radical change. Yet the innovators' very disadvantages to institutions make them as necessary as the adaptors' virtues in turn make them.

Every organization has its own particular 'climate', and at any given time most of its key individuals reflect the general outlook. They gradually communicate this to others in the organization, and in time due to recruitment, turn-over and such processes the cognitive style will reflect the general organizational ethos. However, the range seems to remain unaffected, and this is critical when one wishes to consider who might be the potential agents for a change in the mode of the whole group.

Sufficient evidence has been collected to enable predictions to be made about not only the direction of, but the extent to which these shifts in KAI mean will occur from organization to organization. For example, Kirton[2, 12] hypothesized that the mean scores of managers who work in a particularly stable environment will incline more towards adaption, while the mean scores of those whose environment could be described as turbulent will tend towards innovation. This hypothesis was supported by Thomson,[16] whose study showed that a Singapore sample of middle-ranking Civil Servants were markedly adaptor-inclined (mean = 89) whereas the means of a sample of managers in multi-national companies were just as markedly innovator-inclined (mean = 107).

A dissertation by Holland[26] suggests that bank employees are inclined to be adaptors; so are local government employees.[27] Employees of R & D oriented companies, however, show the opposite inclination.[28] Two of these studies support and refine the hypothesis that, given time, the mean KAI score of a group will reflect its ethos. Both Holland and Hayward and Everett found that groups of new recruits had means away from those of the established groups they were joining. However, within 3 (Holland) or at most 5 (Hayward and Everett) years, as a result of staff changes, the gaps between the means of the new groups and the established groups narrowed sharply.

If there are predictable variations between companies wherever selection has been allowed to operate for a sufficient length of time, then variations may be expected within a company as adaptors and innovators are placed in the parts of the organization which suit them best. It is unlikely (as well as undesirable), that any organization is so monolithic in its structure and in the 'demands' on its personnel that it produces a total conformity of personality profiles. This hypothesis was tested and supported by Kirton[12] when adaptors were found to be more at home in departments of a company that must concentrate on solving problems which mainly emanate from within their departmental system (e.g. production) and innovators tend to be more numerous in departments that acts as interfaces (e.g. sales, progress chasing). Studies by Keller and Holland[14, 28, 29] in American R & D departments found that adaptors and innovators had different roles in internal company communications: adaptors being more valued for communications on the workings of the company and innovators being more valued for communications on advanced technological information.[28] Kirton[3, 12] also found that managers who tend to select themselves to go on courses (i.e. selected) will have significantly different mean KAI scores from the managers on courses who were just sent as part of the general scheme (i.e. personally unselected), the former being innovator-inclined. Members of three groups of courses were tested: one British 'unselected', one British 'selected' and one Canadian 'selected'. The results[12] showed that the unselected managers scored significantly more adaptively than the selected groups. Among the Canadian sample of managers, there was sufficient information on their job titles to be able to divide them into two groups of occupations: those liable to be found in adaptor-oriented departments (e.g. line manager) and those liable to be found in innovator-oriented departments (e.g. personnel consultant). The latter group were found to be significantly more innovative than the former, having a mean of 116.4 for non-line managers as opposed to a mean of 100.14 for line managers.[d] These findings later led to a full-scale study[13] in which data on 2375 subjects collected in 15 independent studies were cross-tabulated with reference to different occupational types and varying degrees of self-selection to courses. Engineering instructors and apprentices were studied as examples of occupations involving a narrow

range of paradigms, thorough rigid training and a closely structured environment, while research and development personnel were examined as examples of occupations involving a number of flexible paradigms and a relatively
unstructured environment. The differences were large, significant and in the
expected direction.

These variations which exist between companies and between occupational groups are also found within the relatively narrow boundaries of the
job itself. For example, work in progress suggests that within a job there may
be clear subsets whose tasks differ and whose cognitive styles differ, e.g. an
examination of the job of quality control workers for a local government
body revealed that the job contained two major aspects. One was the vital
task of monitoring, and one was the task of solving anomalies which were
thrown up in the system from time to time. The first of these tasks was
carried out by an adaptive inclined group, and the second by an innovative
one.

Such knowledge about jobs and who is inclined to do them could eventually lead to better integration of adaptors and innovators within a
company.

Who are the change agents?

It has already been noted that the mean adaptor–innovator score of a group
may shift quite considerably depending on the population in question, whilst
the range remains relatively stable. This suggests that many a person is part
of a group whose mean adaptor–innovator score is markedly different from
his[c] own. There are three possible reasons why these individuals should be
caught up in this potentially stressful situation:

(a) they are in transit, for example, under training schemes;
(b) they are trapped and unhappy and may soon leave;[26, 27]
(c) they have found a niche which suits them and have developed a
     particular role identity.

(These three categories should be regarded as fluid, since given a change in
the individual's peer group, boss, department or even organizational outlook, he may well find himself shifting from one category to another.)

It is the identification of the third category which will most repay further
investigation since it contains refinements of the A–I theory which have
considerable practical implications, though these are as yet speculations and
work is currently being undertaken to explore their ramifications more fully.

The individual who can successfully accept and be accepted into an
environment alien to his own cognitive style must have particular survival
characteristics, and it is those characteristics which make him a potential
agent for change within that particular group. In order to effect a change an
individual must first have job 'know-how' which is also an important quality

keeping him functioning as a valuable group member when major changes are not needed. He must also be able to gain the respect of his colleagues and superiors, and with this comes commensurate status, which is essential if he wants his ideas to be recognized. Lastly, if a person is embarked on a course of action for change, he will of course require the general capacity, e.g. leadership, management qualities, to carry out such a task. His different cognitive style gives him a powerful advantage over his colleagues in being able to anticipate events which others may not see (since due to their cognitive styles, they may not think to look in that direction).

Therefore, the agent for change can be seen as a competent individual who has enough skill to be successful in a particular environment (which he may in fact have made easier by selecting or being selected for tasks within the unit less alien to his cognitive style). At this point he plays a supportive role to the main thrust of the group with its contrasting cognitive style. Given a 'precipitating event' however (particularly if he has anticipated and prepared for it), the individual becomes at once a potential leader in a new situation. In order to be able to take advantage of this position, he must have personal qualities to bring to bear, management must have the insight to recognize the position, and management development must have also played its part. However, this may need to be reinforced by individual and group counselling which makes use of an understanding of Adaption–Innovation theory.[3A, 4A]

It should be emphasized here that the change agent can be either an adaptor or an innovator, and this is solely determined by the group composition, so that if it is an innovator group, the change agent will be an adaptor, and vice versa. This discovery challenges traditional assumptions that heralding and initiating change is the innovator's prerogative because a precipitating event could demand either an adaptive or innovative solution, depending on the original orientation of the group and the work. An example in which an adaptor is the change agent in a team of innovators might be where the precipitating event takes the form of a bank's refusal to give further financial support to a new business enterprise. At this stage the change agent (who may have been anticipating this event for months) is at hand with the facts, figures and a cost cutting contingency plan all neatly worked out. It is now that the personal qualities of know-how, respect, status and ability will be crucial for success. All this assumes that many groups will have means away from the centre. It seems likely that the more the mean is displaced in either direction, the harder it will be, the bigger the precipitating event needed, to pull the group back to the middle, which may be unfortunate both for the group and the change agent. However, an 'unbalanced' team is what may be required at any particular time. To hold such a position and yet to be capable of flexibility is a key task of management to which this theory may make a contribution.

In a wider context, it is hoped that the Adaption–Innovation theory will offer an insight into the interactions between the individual, the organization and change. By using the theory as an additional informational resource when forward planning, it may also be possible to anticipate, and retain control in the face of changes brought about by extraneous factors. This hopefully will enable such changes to take place amid less inbalance and confusion, thereby rendering them more effective.

Notes

Thanks are due to Miss Yvonne Deighan for her help in the preparation of this paper.

[a] Test–retest coefficients of 0.82 for 6th formers ($N = 412$) on one New Zealand study[15] after 8 months; South African study (unpublished)[1A] after 5 months on $N = 143$, means: 91.18, S.D. 9.31; and 91.10, S.D. 8.52.

[b] Factor analyses show that total adaptor–innovator scores are composed of three traits: sufficiency versus proliferation of originality; degree of (personal) efficiency and degree of group-rule conformity. They are closely related respectively to Rogers'[6] creative loner, and Weber's[7] and Merton's[8] typical bureaucrat and bureaucratic behaviour.

[c] Caution: based on a Dutch version of KAI which is still being tested.

[d] Because of the nature of this course and selection system, both groups' means were displaced towards innovativeness; however, they retain their distance *vis-à-vis* each other.

[e] Throughout for he, him, his read also she, her, hers.

References

(1) M.J. Kirton, Adaptors and innovators: a description and measure, *Journal of Applied Psychology, 61*, 622–629 (1976).

(2) M.J. Kirton, *Manual of the Kirton Adaption–Innovation Inventory*, National Foundation for Educational Research, London (1977).

(3) M.J. Kirton, Adaptors and innovators: the way people approach problems, *Planned Innovation, 3*, 51–54 (1980).

(4) P.F. Drucker, Managements' new role, *Harvard Business Review, 47*, 49–54 (1969).

(5) M.J. Kirton, *Management Initiative*, Acton Society Trust, London (1961).

(6) C.R. Rogers, Towards a theory of creativity, in H.H. Anderson (Ed.), *Creativity And Its Cultivation*. Harper, New York (1959).

(7) M. Weber, In H.H. Gerth and C.W. Mills (Eds. and trans.), *From Max Weber: Essays in Sociology*, Routledge & Kegan Paul, London (1970).

(8) R.K. Merton (Ed.), Bureaucratic structure and personality, in *Social Theory and Social Structure*. Free Press of Glencoe, New York (1957).

(9) M.J. Kirton, Adaptors and innovators and superior–subordinate identification, *Psychological Reports, 41*, 289–290 (1977).

(10) J.C. Carne and M.J. Kirton, Styles of creativity: test score correlations between the Kirton Adaption–Innovation Inventory and the Myers-Briggs Type Indicator, *Psychological Reports, 50*, 31–36 (1982).

(11) E.P. Torrance, Hemisphericity and creative functioning, *Journal of Research & Development in Education, 15*, 29–37 (1982).

(12) M.J. Kirton, Adaptors and innovators in organizations, *Human Relations, 3*, 213–224 (1980).

(13) M.J. Kirton and S.R. Pender, The adaption–innovation continuum: occupational type and course selection, *Psychological Reports, 51*, 883–886 (1982).

(14) R.T. Keller and W.E. Holland, A cross-validation study of the Kirton Adaption–Innovation Inventory in three research and development organizations, *Applied Psychological Measurement, 2*, 563–570 (1978).

(15) M.J. Kirton, Have adaptors and innovators equal levels of creativity? *Psychological Reports, 42*, 695–698 (1978).

(16) D. Thomson, Adaptors and innovators: a replication study on managers in Singapore and Malaysia, *Psychological Reports*, *47*, 383–387 (1980).

(17) S. Dewan, Personality characteristics of entrepreneurs, Ph.D. Thesis, Institute of Technology, Delhi (1982).

(18) H.R. Hossaini, Leadership effectiveness and cognitive style among Iranian and Indian middle managers, Ph.D. Thesis, Institute of Technology, Delhi (1981).

(19) D.K. Khaneja, Relationship of the adaption–innovation continuum to achievement orientation in entrepreneurs and non-entrepreneurs, Ph.D. Thesis, Institute of Technology, Delhi (1982).

(20) M.J. Kirton, Adaptors and innovators in culture clash, *Current Anthropology*, *19*, 611–612 (1978).

(21) E.W. Bakke, Concept of the social organisation, in M. Haire (Ed.), *Modern Organization Theory*, Wiley, New York (1965).

(22) M.S, Mulkay, *The Social Process of Innovation*, Macmillan, London (1972).

(23) G.M. Swatez, The social organization of a university laboratory, Minerva, *A Review of Science Learning & Policy*, *VIII*, 36–58 (1970).

(24) T. Veblen, *The Theory of the Leisure Class*, Vanguard Press, New York (1928).

(25) T. Parsons, *The Social System*, Free Press of Glencoe, New York (1951).

(26) P.A. Holland, Creative thinking: an asset or liability in employment, M.Ed. Dissertation, University of Manchester (1982).

(27) G. Hayward and C. Everett, Adaptors and innovators: data from the Kirton Adaption–Innovation Inventory in a local authority setting, *Journal of Occupational Psychology*, *56*, 339–342 (1983).

(28) R.T. Keller and W.E. Holland, Individual characteristics of innovativeness and communication in research and development organizations. *Journal of Applied Psychology*, *63*, 759–762 (1978).

(29) R.T. Keller and W. E. Holland, Towards a selection battery for research and development professional employees, *IEEE Transactions on Engineering Management*, *EM-26* (4), November (1979).

Thanks are due for the use of their unpublished data to:
(1A) C. D. Pottas, University of Pretoria, South Africa.
(2A) L. Peeters, Janssen Pharmaceutical, Belgium.
(3A) P. Lindsay (in Press), Cambridge Management Centre, UK.
(4A) G. B. Davies (in preparation), Cambridge Management Centre, U.K.

17

Strategic management development: experiential learning and managerial competencies

David Kolb, Stuart Lublin, Juliann Spoth and Richard Baker

This chapter is addressed to an educational agenda that is of critical import-ance for the effective functioning of modern organizations: the development of the specialized competencies and integrative knowledge (sometimes referred to as wisdom) necessary to prepare managers for the complex dynamic leadership roles they occupy. Management of change and uncer-tainty requires that increasingly sophisticated and highly differentiated *specialized* knowledge be brought to bear on organizational problems and that these specialized viewpoints be *integrated* into effective solutions to these problems.

H.G. Wells predicted many years ago [in *The Outline of History*] that 'human history becomes more and more a race between education and catastrophe'. Managerial leadership in large corporations and public insti-tutions is at the forefront of this race, facing complex issues that require not only decisiveness but creativity; not only managerial control but visionary leadership; not only the technical skills necessary to achieve the organiza-tion's mission but the integrity to resolve the value conflicts inherent in shaping that mission.

Our perspective will be training for management development. There is a recognition of the need for learning to cope with change and complexity, a relative openness to innovation, and the availability of resources to develop educational technologies that respond to the organization's learning/know-ledge needs. It is in organizations that the race between learning and survival is most heated. From the perspective of management development we see increasingly that the organization's ability to survive and thrive in a complex dynamic environment is constrained by the capabilities of managers who must learn to manage both this greater environmental complexity and the complex organizational forms developed to cope with the environment. Any review of recent industrial history in the US and the UK shows how close we

Adapted from *Journal of Management Development*, 3, 5 (1986), pp. 13–24 have come to H.G. Wells' catastrophe. With the clarity of hindsight we see how the complacency, limited vision, 'Me-too' business strategies, and short-term perspective of top management have nearly destroyed companies in the automotive, aircraft, steel and other major industries. What is most disturbing is that these failures to revitalize and innovate are not the result of isolated cases of mismanagement. Rather there is a general pattern of limited vision and lack of knowledge that is a result of a systematic failure to provide managers with opportunities to learn and prepare for the complex realities they face. Where does the steel executive, hardened in the realities of wage and benefit focused labour negotiations, steeped in the tangible certainties of the production process, immersed in the isolationism of middle American culture, and comforted in the company of like-minded colleagues, acquire the knowledge and judgement required to predict the threat of foreign competition, the payoff of 'mini-mills' and high cost/high tech production processes, the political popularity of a clean environment or the power of participative management? The answer – from experience. But experience, as someone once noted, is a severe teacher – it gives the test first and the lesson afterwards.

Towards a strategic view of management development

Should not education have a role to play in helping managers at all levels to prepare in advance to cope with these challenges? Historically this has not been the case as training and development functions have focused primarily on lower management level, high certainty, specific skill training. But as organizations have become more complex in their attempts to master dynamic, uncertain environments, this new educational agenda is catching the attention of those concerned with management development. A major stimulus for this attention is the fact that the complex organizational structures and management systems required to deal effectively with environmental complexity and change are not working; primarily because managers are not prepared to use them effectively. Matrix management, for example, is currently out of favour because of the confusion and conflict it has caused in many organizations. This is in spite of the increasing need for such integrative mechanisms. In the words of the Australian marketing manager for a large multinational corporation:

> We have gone way beyond matrix. We have it now in about five dimensions – by function, by product, by market, by technology, by country. There are so many lines of reporting that in some ways it's like having none. As a manager there is a lot of uncertainty that you have to take responsibility for. You have to negotiate for the authority to act, or sometimes you act first and hope to work it out later.

Much more is required of managers in these circumstances than was the case in the classical organization structure with a limited span of control, non-overlapping job definitions, a single chain of command, and formal authority that matched responsibility. Greater *behavioural* competence in taking initiative and responsibility under conditions of risk and uncertainty, greater *perceptual* competence in gathering and organizing information and taking the perspective of different organizational sub-units, greater *affective* competence in empathizing with others and in resolving conflicts among managers with different viewpoints and greater *symbolic* competence in one's ability to conceptualize the organization as a system are all required to make modern organizational forms works effectively. The same is true of modern management processes such as participative management or sophisticated operations management systems such as the just-in-time inventory system.

A strategic approach to management development recognizes these critical linkages among complex environmental circumstances, the sophisticated organizational structure and processes necessary to cope with these circumstances, and the ability of managers to make the organization work effectively. Such a perspective suggests an expanded role for the human resource development function by linking management development programmes to the strategic mission of the organization. This perspective anticipates emerging management development requirements by analysing strategic projections for the organization's future environment, and develops educational programmes to help managers prepare in advance for these more complex responsibilities. It suggests the development of systematic long-range career development programmes designed to grow the skilled human resources necessary to manage the organization's future challenges.

Assessing managerial learning needs

The focal point of strategic management development is a learning needs assessment process that identifies the managerial competencies required to effectively manage complex organizations in complex environments. Such a system needs to identify not only highly specialized, specific knowledge requirements, but also the more integrative learning and problem-solving competencies needed to cope with uncertainty and complexity.

Experiential learning theory [1] provides one such approach for mapping the terrain of managerial competence based on what is called the 'competency circle'. This two dimensional map arranges the specialized adaptive competencies of managerial knowledge around the experiential learning cycle based on their association with the four basic modes of the experiential learning process – affective competencies (e.g. being sensitive to people's feelings) are related to the concrete experience mode; perceptual competencies (e.g. gathering information) are related to the reflective observation mode; symbolic competencies (e.g. building conceptual models) are related to the abstract conceptualizaton mode; and behavioural competencies (e.g. making decisions) are related to the active experimentation learning mode.

The focus on adaptive (learning) competence accomplishes two things. First, since adaptation and learning are the central characteristics of all person/situation transactions, the competency circle technique is holistic, making it possible to compare and contrast the essential learning needs in different jobs, in different organizations, career paths and professions. Secondly, the focus on competence emphasizes the importance of congruence or 'fit' between managerial knowledge and job demands. Competence is not a judgement about an individual alone, but about the effective match between individual knowledge and skill and work environment demands. The competency circle approach defines individual knowledge and job demands in commensurate terms such that this effective match can be determined. Mismatches between current and future job demands and current managerial knowledge identify the educational objectives for management development programmes.

The competency circle technique has proven successful in identifying and differentiating job demands in different job roles within and between professions, in different jobs along organizational career paths, and at relating mismatches between managerial knowledge and job demand to individual performance and satisfaction [2]. For example, Figure 1 shows the difference in competency circle profiles among the major job roles in the engineering profession – 'bench' engineer, technical manager, and general manager. These data were collected in a cross-sectional study of engineering alumni from a major engineering school and represent individuals at different career stages from many different organizations. Generally these results show that managerial jobs require more affective (e.g. dealing with people) and behavioural competence (e.g. making decisions and setting goals), while direct engineering work requires greater symbolic (e.g. testing theories and ideas) and perceptual competence (e.g. gathering information). Among other things, these results suggest specific management development implications for professional engineers who are making transitions into management roles.

While this two dimensional map of managerial competence has proven useful in identifying specialized managerial competencies, it became clear as we began using the technique in organizational settings that a third dimension needed to be added to describe the increasing complexity of managerial jobs as one moves up the organizational hierarchy and as organizations seek to relate to more complex environments. Elliott Jaques' [3] work on the time span of discretion, for example, shows that the work environments that managers must adapt to and master increase in their extension in time and space as one moves to higher levels of management. The first line supervisor works within a time span of days or weeks in a single location with highly certain information, whereas at the highest levels of the organization, managers operate within time spans of decades in a worldwide environment, characterized by high uncertainty and rapid change. Managerial competencies differ, therefore, not only in their specialized focus but also in the degree of sophistication and flexibility of application – in integrative complexity.

As a result the competency circle has been extended into a hierarchical

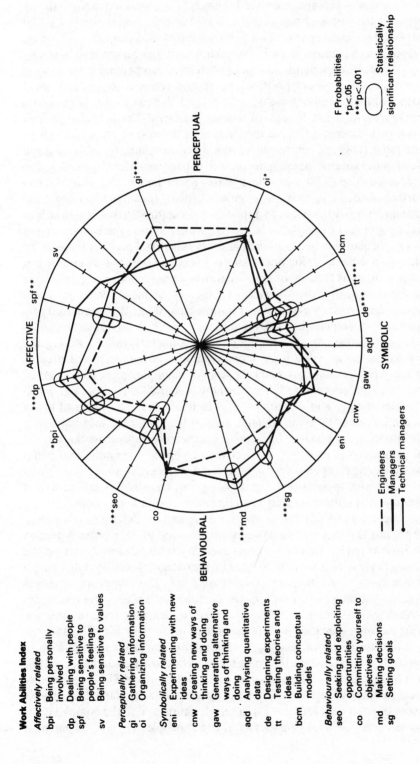

Work Abilities Index

Affectively related
bpi   Being personally involved
dp   Dealing with people
spf   Being sensitive to people's feelings
sv   Being sensitive to values

Perceptually related
gi   Gathering information
oi   Organizing information

Symbolically related
eni   Experimenting with new ideas
cnw   Creating new ways of thinking and doing
gaw   Generating alternative ways of thinking and doing
aqd   Analysing quantitative data
de   Designing experiments
tt   Testing theories and ideas
bcm   Building conceptual models

Behaviourally related
seo   Seeking and exploiting opportunities
co   Committing yourself to objectives
md   Making decisions
sg   Setting goals

Figure 1   *Competency circle profiles of job demands for three job roles in the engineering profession*

map of managerial competence (see Figure 2). The competency circle shown in Figure 1 has been refined and elaborated into a competence clock that defines twelve generic performance competencies whose hourly position on the clock is determined by their association with the higher level learning competencies of experiential learning. Affective competencies are located at the 11, 12, and 1 o'clock positions, perceptual competencies at 2, 3, and 4 o'clock, symbolic competencies at 5, 6, and 7 o'clock and behavioural competencies at the 8, 9, and 10 o'clock positions. These twelve generic performance competencies are then extended downward one or two levels to analyse managerial competencies in a specific organizational setting and to identify the specific learning needs and management development activities required. The 12:00 competence dealing with people, for example, can be further divided into 'working in groups', 'being sensitive to feelings' and 'communicating with others'. In a specific work setting further specifications of working in groups might be made to identify learning needs associated with a particular type of group such as cross-functional product teams.

This specialized learning needs analysis is complemented by an integrative needs analysis focused on the integrative competence required to cope with the complexity and uncertainty inherent in higher level jobs and complex organization/environment relationships. While the specialized performance competencies become increasingly simple, behavioural, and content focused as one moves down the hierarchy, the integrative learning and development competencies are more complex, internalized and process focused. Affective learning competence, for example, represents a set of higher level, process centred 'learning how to learn' skills – valuing, 'intuitive' experiencing, and empathy – that facilitate the acquisition of lower level specialized skills in the affective area and direct the flexible and timely applications of these skills. Integrative competence represents the highest level of development wherein affective, perceptual, symbolic and behavioural learning competencies are integrated into a highly sophisticated and flexible adaptive process that can organize and focus highly differentiated knowledge and skills on rapidly changing environmental demands.

One measure of these integrative learning and development competencies that has shown great promise in our research to date is the Adaptive Style Inventory [1]. This self-report inventory is an advanced form of the Learning Style Inventory that assesses an individual's learning style in eight different specific situations in that person's life. The inventory measures integrative learning by determining the person's level of adaptive flexibility, i.e. the degree to which one changes his or her learning style to meet the varying learning demands of different situations in their life. The assumption is that flexibility of response in learning orientations reflects a more integrated and sophisticated learning style. So far, research data support this idea. Overall, adaptive flexibility as measured by the ASI is significantly related to level of ego development as measured by Jane Loevinger's measure of adult development [4] to self-direction and to the complexity of the constructs one uses to understand other people. Ego development is

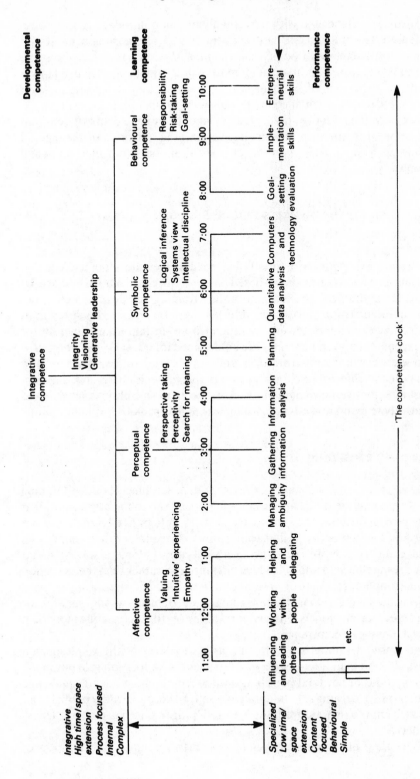

Figure 2 *A hierarchical map of managerial competence*

most strongly associated with perceptual and symbolic adaptive flexibility. Increased self-direction and control over one's life are more associated with behavioural adaptive flexibility and richness in one's constructs about the interpersonal world is associated most strongly with affective adaptive flexibility. These results are promising because they offer measures of integrative developmental competence and more specialized learning competencies in the affective, perceptual, symbolic, and behavioural areas that can be used to identify the integrative learning demands of managerial positions with differing levels of organizational and environmental complexity.

Education for the management of complexity and change

One result of our work with the strategic management development concept and learning needs assessments based on the hierarchical map of managerial competence has been the recognition that training and development functions in organizations focus their efforts largely on training for specialized competencies. This is and will continue to be an important function for management development. But the unmet need for education in integrative competence will continue to grow and must somehow be addressed. By taking leadership in meeting this need, corporate training and development functions can contribute to their organization's ability to actively and creatively respond to the strategic challenges they face.

Integrative learning

How is this to be accomplished? Integrative learning requires learning conditions that are different, at times in opposition, to the approaches that have proven effective for specialized learning. Integrative learning is more concerned with process, with learning how to learn rather than simple skill acquisition. It is more concerned with executive problem solving about which competence to apply in which circumstance rather than the execution of the competence. As such, it is more internalized and specifically tailored to each unique individual. There are no simple 'right' or 'wrong' answers, or more specifically, there is only *one* correct answer for each unique individual in each unique circumstance.

Integrative learning is holistic and as such addresses the whole person physically and mentally; not only in a specialized skill or job role but in the context of his or her total life situation. Indeed, the fundamental challenge of integrative learning is to integrate oneself, to become whole publicly and privately and to operate from the 'centred' judgement that such wholeness produces.

From the holistic perspective, disagreement, conflict, and differences among people are the fuel that energizes the integrative learning process. The constructive use of differences to explore the parts of the whole and the contribution each makes defines a co-operative approach to differences and disagreements that stands in contrast to the competitive view underlying analytic approaches to learning. Integrative learning programmes, therefore, need to focus on learning from differences in content, point of view, and learning style by creating a climate where these differences can be examined constructively. Argyris and Schön [5], for example, have found that the learning climate in most organizations discourages learning from differences by norms that reinforce winning over understanding and suppression of conflict by unilateral protection of self and others. They have identified the elements of organization learning climate that stimulate what they call double-loop learning – norms supporting valid information, free and informed choice and internal commitment. Sims found that individuals from organizations with an organization climate that fostered learning and growth had a better match between their competency circle ability profile and their job demands than individuals from organizations with a poor growth climate [2].

Experiential learning theory and the associated methods of experiential education provide a framework for the conduct of integrative education. The use of experiential exercises, games, and simulations in training programmes actively engages learners in situations where they must act and observe the consequences of their actions. Since everyone shares the same experiences, learning occurs through dialogue among participants who share observations, feelings, and thoughts and arrive together at conclusions about what has been learned. The facilitator or manager of this learning process is an expert with his or her own ideas but so are the other participants who bring their own expertise and point of view for understanding the experiences. Most importantly, participants are not only learning specialized content, but are at the same time learning how to learn the specialized material that is under study. Our experiential learning curriculum for Organizational Psychology [6], for example, develops specialized understanding of behavioural science concepts such as motivation, decision making and group dynamics. Participants over the years, however, consistently report that their major learning from the course was learning how to learn by using the experiential learning cycle to better understand their relationships with other people.

Integrative learning occurs best when the learning process is integrated with work in real time. While off-site sessions and training programmes have some role to play in developing integrative competence, a greater payoff lies in the creation of organization climates that allow learning from experience during work itself. Other approaches to experiential learning emphasize these 'real-life', on-the-job learning experiences such as Revans' action learning programmes [7] and systematic career development processes that use careful assignment and rotation of job functions to develop the integrative general management perspective.

Summary

Integrative learning requires a re-examination of our role as teachers or trainers. Rather than being dispensers of knowledge and wisdom, our role in integrative learning is to manage the process of learning; to facilitate adult learners in the process of learning from their own experiences in life. In all its forms, experiential learning emphasizes the integration of the abstract concepts of social knowledge with the concrete, subjective experiences of personal knowledge. One means to this integration is dialogue – a special form of communication where both abstract ideas and personal feelings about them are shared in a spirit of provisionalism, mutuality, and co-inquiry. Adult learners learn best in situations where they are acknowledged as experts and equals. As adults they have a need to teach as well as learn. Paulo Freire describes this learning relationship as follows:

> Through dialogue, the teacher of the students and students-of-the-teacher cease to exist and a new term emerges: teacher-student with students-teachers. The teacher is no longer merely the one who teaches, but one who is himself taught in dialogue with the students who in turn, while being taught also teach. They become jointly responsible for a process in which all grow. In this process, agreements based on 'authority' are no longer valid . . . no one teaches another, nor is anyone self-taught [8].

Finally, integrative learning suggests an open system, networking approach to the management of knowledge and learning resource acquisition. A key function of strategic management development at the integrative level is to provide managers with access to knowledge and relationship networks that can help them become life-long learners and cope with the issues on their continually changing agendas. Of particular value here is the establishment of alliances between business and higher education that promise to increase the effectiveness of both. Much corporate education is intellectually shallow because it lacks substantive relationships with the knowledge base of academia. Much academic education, on the other hand, is irrelevant and out of date for lack of connection to the problems and practicalities of the real world. The development of relationships in the spirit of dialogue identified above would allow managers and academics to teach and learn from one another. The creation of these real time feedback loops between ideas and action would do much to give substance to the concept of life-long learning, reducing the job shock experienced by younger workers entering organizations from academia, and the obsolescence of older workers who have been cut off from ideas at the leading edge of academic inquiry.

References

1 Kolb, D.A., *Experiential Learning: Experience as the Source of Learning and Development*, Prentice-Hall, Englewood Cliffs, N.J., 1984

2 Kolb, D.A. and Wolfe, D.M. with collaborators, 'Professional Education and Career Development: A Cross-Sectional Study of Adaptive Competencies in Experiential Learning', Final Report, NIE Grant No. NIE-G-77-0053, 1981, ERIC No. ED 209 493 CE 030519.
3 Jaques, E., 'Taking Time Seriously in Evaluating Jobs', *Harvard Business Review*, September–October 1979, pp. 124–33.
4 Loevinger, J., *Ego Development*, Jossey Bass, San Francisco, 1976.
5 Argyris, C. and Schön, D., *Organizational Learning: A Theory of Action Perspective*, Addison-Wesley, Reading, Mass., 1978.
6 Kolb, D., Rubin, I. and McIntyre, J., *Organizational Psychology: An Experiential Approach to Organizational Behavior*, Prentice-Hall, Englewood Cliffs, N.J., 1984 (4th Edition).
7 Revans, R.W., 'Action Learning and Development of Self' in Boydell, T. and Pedler, M. (Eds.) *Management Self-Development*, Gower Press, 1981.
8 Freire, P., *Pedagogy of the Oppressed*, Seabury Press, New York, 1974.

18

Top management teams and organizational renewal

David K. Hurst, James C. Rush and Roderick E. White

The strategic management (SM) framework which has evolved over the past 40 years and has come to dominate thinking about the principal functions of senior managers has been the subject of a good deal of criticism, both from practitioners (Peters and Waterman, 1983) and theoreticians (Weick, 1979; Pascale, 1984). It seems that while the conventional SM process allows managers to maintain, direct and improve existing activities, it is less able to promote and accommodate the radical ideas and innovative behaviors needed to renew established businesses. Indeed it may be counter-productive in this regard.

With its emphasis on problem-solving, the SM framework implicitly stresses the role of the senior, synoptic, singular executive: one individual, or group, with an established understanding of how the business functions. Within this group there exists a shared 'cause map' (Weick, 1979) or a 'dominant logic' (Prahalad and Bettis, 1986): a structure of knowledge about their business which for them defines 'rationality'. Facts which can be plotted onto this map of the business are accepted; data which cannot be assigned coordinates are not perceived, are ignored if they are perceived or are treated as an aberration.

For the top management group, behaviors consistent with rational thought are implied. Individuals predisposed to plan, act and evaluate would fit; others, with different behavioral predispositions, would not. Intuition, insight and feelings are suppressed because they do not fit within the accepted SM process. Individuals openly exhibiting these types of behaviors cannot be accommodated within the conventional SM framework and are often excluded from the process, even though their contributions may be valuable. SM fits the people within its rational-analytic procedures, rather than expanding the process to fit the people, and their different abilities, predispositions and preferences.

For these reasons dissatisfaction with the SM framework has increased,

Adapted from *Strategic Management Journal*, 10 (1989), pp. 87–105. © 1989 by John Wiley & Sons, Ltd. Reproduced by permission of John Wiley & Sons, Ltd.

resulting in a renewed focus on the top management group, the dominant coalition (Cyert and March, 1963), as it impacts firm strategy and organizational performance. As Hambrick (1987: 88) explains, 'This view contends that performance of an organization is ultimately a reflection of its top managers.' Implicitly this view holds that when it comes to understanding strategy and performance, the people are equally as important, and perhaps more important, than the process. But neither is this view entirely satisfactory, for it ignores the processes needed by any large organization to make decisions and take concerted action. Even more importantly, it lacks a sense for the role and function of the executive group.

The composition, or form, of the top management group needs to be related to its function. Barnard (1938: 215) contends 'Executive work is not that *of* the organization, but the specialized work of *maintaining* the organization in operation.' When narrowly interpreted, this view can be construed as supporting the limited plan–act–evaluate functions for the executive implicit in the SM model. However, in any changing, competitive environment, long-term maintenance/existence of the business requires the ongoing (re)creation of the business and the logic by which it is managed. This renewal, too, is a critical executive function.

Large organizations require a process for taking concerted actions. The broad-based adoption of SM technology suggests it has fulfilled a need in this regard. We must be careful not to discard, out of hand, even a partially useful process. The SM model is powerful because it prescribes a process, as well as a function (or functions) for the top management group within that process. However, the process and prescribed functions are limited and do not take advantage of the full range of human cognitive abilities. The SM framework is not so much incorrect as it is incomplete. A broader perspective on the top management process, an enhanced model, taking more complete advantage of the human potential, could help bridge the gap between the appropriate function of the executive and the makeup of the top management group.

Beyond strategic management

Stepping back and viewing the question from a philosophical perspective, the SM framework's principal shortcoming is its base in a naive realism. It tacitly assumes that reality is a given which exists 'out there' and is accessible through our senses. These sensations, these supposed objective perceptions or facts, can then be subjected to rational thought. Although the need for action is recognized, it is regarded largely as the servant of thought. Facts evaluated by a rational analytic thinking process are regarded as more important than insight, feelings and even empirical experience! The classic SM framework emphasizes the use of conscious, analytic thought processes to the exclusion of any other; even though non-rational or, to use Barnard's word, 'non-logical' processes and their importance have long been recognized (Barnard, 1938; McKenney and Keen, 1974; Mintzberg, 1976).

In a recent article, Hurst (1986) suggested that the emphasis of the SM framework on logic and rationality precludes it from being helpful in the innovative, creative processes which allow organizations to enact fundamental change, to renew themselves. Logic and rationality depend upon normative structures based in the past, and methodologies such as SM which appeal to norms of rationality – measurability, efficiency, consistency – perpetuate the past. In short, because SM is based on a logic developed from past experiences, it is an appropriate methodology for defending an established business, but is less able to prospect. It cannot deal well with novelty and ambiguity; it cannot bring into being those new activities which lie outside the structure of the managers' current understanding of their existing business, but which may well be required as part of tomorrow's business.

A classic example of a flawed logic based upon past experiences is illustrated by the actions of Sewell Avery, CEO of Montgomery Ward following World War II. Avery convinced himself, based upon a study of economic history and his own experiences after World War I, that economic depressions followed wars. Based on this logic, Montgomery Ward, in the years following 1945, did not expand, and even deferred basic maintenance expenditures in order to preserve cash for the anticipated depression. Meanwhile Robert Wood at Sears correctly perceived the 'tremendous foundation of purchasing power that had been held back by the war.' Sears expanded aggressively to become the dominant US department store chain. Avery was forced to depart Wards in 1955 (Worthy, 1984: 219).

The Avery story provides a simple, yet dramatic, example of a flawed logic retrospectively derived from past experiences. The complex of logics and their relationships underlying a sophisticated SM approach in any large organization are many, subtle and difficult to surface. However, business redefinition requires a shift in the logic that is imbedded in any well-developed SM process. Conventional SM incorporates no means to unlearn what has been learnt, although there have been developments in this direction (De Geus, 1988). To deal conceptually with this shortcoming, Hurst (1986) has extended the SM framework to encompass what he calls the creative management model.

The creative management model

The creative management (CM) model is built on the philosophical assumption that the real world which surrounds the organization is a dynamic construct enacted by the members of the organization over time. This view is shared by Weick (1979: 228), as he explains, 'the environment is viewed as an output rather than an input. On the basis of enactments and interpretations people construct a belated picture of some environment that could have produced these actions.' Organizational realities, like personal realities, consist of complex interactions of the objective, tangible ('out there') and the subjective cognitive ('in here') elements.

Implicit in the CM model is the assertion that organizations capable of creating tomorrow's businesses while maintaining today's will require a diverse group of senior managers, able to perceive the world differently, yet able to participate in a process that transcends these different views to enact a complex organizational reality. In the CM framework the emphasis is on top management teams which can envision, or recognize and frame, new opportunities, as well as solve or exploit them (Bower, 1982). By embracing recognition, opportunity-framing and problem-solving, the CM model subsumes strategic management and provides additional insights into the composition, leadership and processes of top management teams.

As illustrated in Figure 1, the CM process is conceived of as passing

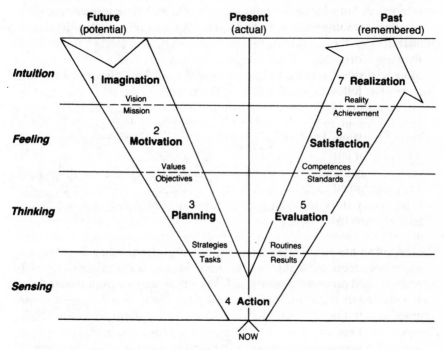

Figure 1   *The creative management model*

through four levels or modes of cognition. When (subjective) time is considered, the model incorporates seven recursive and not necessarily completely sequential stages whereby an original idea is transformed from an intuitive insight, a vision, into action – eventually to become a remembered 'reality.' Tracking the progress of an idea from its original conception to its final realization helps to explain the model. The classic SM model deals explicitly with only Stages 3 through 5, the 'plan–act–evaluate' stages. Because it does not consider the cognitive levels of intuition and feeling, the SM framework is unable to supply insight into the nature of recognition by organizations. How do organizations come to fundamentally new approaches to the way they go about their business? How do they learn? By ignoring the other stages in the process and overemphasizing the linear, in what is in fact a recursive process, the SM paradigm misses key aspects of the creative learning process.

The CM model makes it clear that strategic thinking (Stage 3) does not take place without antecedents. It is based heavily upon earlier expectations and past experiences (Stages 4 through 7), modified by what happens in Stages 1 and 2. In addition, rationality depends on logic structures developed after action. People, and especially organizations, truly understand (Stage 5) only after they act (Stage 4), not before. Anything else is speculation. The model makes it clear that radical innovation (Stage 1) represents a break with the thought structures, the logic of the past. Initially, an innovation will not be based on rationality and logic because the supporting conceptual structures are not yet in place. Conversely, highly structured thought, as well as tradition, can interfere with, and inhibit, insight and innovation.

Thus, in the CM model a strategy is initially a *post-hoc* rationalization of a successful activity. As Weick (1979: 188) explains:

> The only thing that can be selected and preserved is something that is already there. This simple reality keeps getting lost amidst the preoccupation of people in organizations with planning, forecasting, anticipating and predicting. . . . Organizations formulate strategy *after* they implement it, not before. . . . The more common (and misleading) way to look at this sequence in organizations is to say that first comes strategy and then comes implementation. That commonplace recipe ignores the fact that meaning is always imposed after elapsed actions are available for review.

As the activity becomes standardized, feedback from Stage 5 to Stage 3 occurs. Successful behaviors are interpreted into a causal model which drives the organization's routines and corrects deviations from course.

By making explicit the dimension of time the CM model allows the renewal function to be seen as a learning process. The time dimension in Figure 1 is not the objective time of physics but subjective time, views of the future and memories of the past as seen from the perpetual 'now' in which all human cognitive systems function (Jaques, 1982). With subjective time the creative process can be seen to be a learning process whereby successful innovations within an organization, new logics for doing business, are institutionalized and made routine. Not all organizations, and more particularly not all top management groups, are necessarily equally adept at, and receptive to, the development of new logics. These biases may be reflected in the organization's pattern of actions, its strategy.

There is more to the CM model than the capacity for prospective or retrospective thought. The model, as shown in Figure 1, contends that different modes of cognition are dominant at different levels in the process. These different modes are believed to have an underlying relationship with subjective time orientation; sensing may be associated more with the present, intuition more with the future (Mann, Siegler and Osmond, 1971) and one might also suspect with the remembered past (in contrast to the experience of the present). But, more fundamentally, these different modes are believed to represent distinct cognitive preferences.

Cognitive modes

The different levels in the CM model are related to and emphasize different modes of cognition corresponding to the four fundamental psychological functions outlined by Jung (1960). These processes are arranged by CM level and function in Table 1. Jung contends that while all individuals have

Table 1   *Level in the CM model and cognitive model*

CM level	Function	
	Information gathering	Information evaluation
I	INTUITION	
II		FEELING
III		THINKING
IV	SENSATION	

the capacity for, and make use of, all four modes, each has a dominant function. The Myers–Briggs Type Indicators (MBTI) (Myers, 1982) has been used extensively as a measure of an individual's preference on each of these four functions.

The two information gathering modes are *Sensation* (S) and *Intuition* (N). *Sensation* mediates the perception of physical stimuli via the five senses. Through *Sensation* an individual becomes conscious that something exists physically. *Intuition*, on the other hand, mediates perception via what is thought to be an unconscious patterning process – the individual goes beyond the differentiations yielded by the *Sensation* process to see whole relationships and patterns, either in the world of physical phenomena (Extrovert preference), or in the world of ideas (Introvert preference).[1] By allowing the detection of gaps between perceived parts this mode gives individuals the ability to see unrealized potential within the stream of events which surround them. *Sensation* and *Intuition* then are opposite but complementary mental processes used to gather information about the world.

The two information evaluation modes are *Thinking* (T) and *Feeling* (F). Each mode appeals to a different type of evaluative process. *Thinking* links ideas impersonally using logic and notions of cause and effect. *Feeling*, on the other hand, bases evaluation on personal and group values. As Jung makes clear, *Thinking* and *Feeling* are complementary functions for the *evaluation* of information, just as *Sensing* and *Intuition* are complementary processes used in the *gathering* of information. Each process within a pair is in tension with the other, but it can be a creative tension. Subjective time is the dimension which mediates the tension. It is these functions or layers which creative management must transcend.

The levels in the CM process are layered to reflect the renewal function of the executive as it relates to Jung's cognitive functions. Sensing deals with physical stimuli, action and reaction, in the here and now. Behaviors based simply on sensation can be thought of as reflexive; a stimulus evokes an instinctive or reflex response. Actions, other than reflex responses, have input from the higher levels. For example, the thinking–planning level will, based upon accepted logics, delineate tasks to guide action. The results of actions taken also feed back into the thinking/evaluation activity. Sensing and thinking are adjacent layers in the model because, prescriptively, prospective thinking precedes, and retrospective analysis, or sensemaking, follows action.

At the intuitive level a vision or insight into a new way of doing business does not by itself result in action. Because it is outside the established logic of the business, it cannot be evaluated by the thinking process. Therefore its worth, whether positive or negative, cannot be logically derived and must be based upon personal or group values. A positive feeling must be created for the idea if it is to overcome the established logic, result in action and thus change the understanding of the business. Accordingly, the feeling mode is positioned between the intuition and thinking layers in the model.

The layering in the CM model is based upon Jung's conception of the 'psychological functions' for several reasons. This conception may be related to basic human physiology. As Taggart and Robey (1981: 189) point out, 'Jung's theory of personality identifies two dimensions of human information processing that seem directly related to right and left brain activity.' Typically, *Sensing* and *Thinking* are left hemisphere related and *Intuition* and *Feeling* right hemisphere related. This duality and Jung's conception may have deep and perhaps related roots in human information processing, psychology and philosophy. Although there are other cognitive typologies (Hampden-Turner, 1981; Gardener, 1985) on which a model of creative management could be built, in our estimation none has as strong a conceptual and philosophical base for this application. However, in the last analysis this model will be judged by its utility: the meaningful implications it has for the practice of management.

Top managers' behaviors and cognitive preference

The conceptual linkages between the creative management process, cognitive mode and behaviors are sketched in Table 2. Each type has been associated with a particular cluster of behaviors and positioned within the layers of the CM model. The implication is that to effectively handle a creative process a management group needs these different behaviors, and accordingly should be composed of individuals with the different cognitive preferences. Although individuals may be able to exhibit a variety of behaviors it is unlikely they will be equally able at each set of behaviors, or indifferent amongst them. They will have a preference.

Of course, cognitive preference is not the only factor to consider in

Table 2   *Relationship between cognitive preference and behaviors*

Level in CM process	Cognitive preference	Concerned with	Handles these with	Tends to be	Examples of behaviors
I	Intuition	Possibilities and patterns, ideas	Metaphors and symbols	Ingenious and integrative	Sees what others do not. Espouses new ways of working at things. Proposes new ideas. Disregards practical details. Describes with metaphors and symbols. Creates organizational stories and myths.
II	Feeling	People and values	Force of personality	Enthusiastic and insightful	Inspires peers and subordinates. Responds to a challenge. Sponsors new ideas. Shares information, power and resources. Brings people together. Rewards with recognition and praise. Promulgates organizational stories and myths.
III	Thinking	Cause and effect things	Regulations and language	Reliable and orderly	Matches goals to resources to results (i.e. plans). Organizes people; coordinates. Balances novel with routine. Rewards when outcome exceeds plan.
IV	Sensation	Activities, events	Spontaneity and action	Adaptable and practical	Matches skills to tasks. Attention to practical details. Makes things work. Describes what has occurred in concrete terms. Results are their own reward.

Source: Adapted from Myers (1982) and Keirsey and Bates (1978).

forming a top management team. Much of the information available to a top management group will be directly related to the personal background and experience of team members. Simon (1988: 16) contends that 'expertness is the prerequisite to creativity.' He suggests that experts have 50,000 'chunks' of knowledge in their area of expertise which it takes at least 10 years of experience to acquire. But not every expert (with 50,000 chunks of knowledge in a given area) can necessarily use that knowledge creatively.

Indeed, as Koestler (1976) reports, often the insight occurs after the idea generators have disassociated themselves from the specifics of the puzzle they are attempting to solve. James Watson, whose insight uncovered the double-helix structure of DNA, recounts his need to remove himself from data derived from months of chemical and X-ray experiments, while Francis Crick, his co-researcher, felt a need to remain immersed in the data. (Sensation–Thinking preference versus Intuition–Thinking preference?)

The next few days saw Francis becoming increasingly agitated by my failure to stick close to the molecular models. .... Almost every afternoon, knowing that I was on the tennis court, he would fretfully twist his head away from his work to see the polynucleotide backbone unattended. ... Francis' grumbles did not disturb me, however, because further refining of our latest backbone without a solution to the bases would not represent a real step forward (Watson, 1969: 114).

None of this is to diminish the importance of expertise acquired through diligence and hard work, but rather to suggest other factors are also at work. We would argue that individual cognitive preference merits consideration.

Creative management: a need for integration

With differentiation in cognitive orientations comes a need for integration (Lawrence and Lorsch, 1969) – a way of allowing for, or facilitating, the exchanges necessary to bring about coherent action. The most efficient means of achieving the required integration depends on the type of interdependence (Thompson, 1967; Galbraith, 1973). As illustrated in Table 3, the CM process presents different types of interdependence between its different levels.

Table 3 *Integrating cognitive types and levels within the creative management process*

Level	Cognitive type	Concern	Integrative mechanism	Type of interdependence
I	Intuitive	Patterns and◄ ············ possibilities, ideas	Individual's perceptive abilities	Independent
		◄ ·····················	Informal, face-to-face	Reciprocal
II	Feeler	People		
		◄ ·····················	Task forces	Reciprocal/sequential
III	Thinker	Cause and effect, plans		
		◄ ·····················	Policies, procedures, rules, hierarchy	Sequential
IV	Sensor	Activities, events		

In explaining the interdependences it is helpful to make the simplifying assumption of a different individual at each level. Even though radically new ideas may be stimulated by certain antecedent conditions, they seem to be the independent creation of a single mind (with intuitive preferences and abilities) (Koestler, 1976). Generating new insights is not thought to be a group activity. Once discerned the exchange between the intuitive, idea generator, and the feeler would appear to be reciprocal. If the feeler is to inspire and energize the organization, the feeler and idea generator must talk face-to-face. (They can, of course, be one and the same person.) The feeler must appreciate the idea sufficiently well to move it forward. This requires the feeler to listen to, and question, the idea generator. Also it is likely that articulating the idea causes the idea generator to better define his 'vision.'

Because the idea cannot be evaluated logically the feeler must not only communicate it to the thinker, but also create a sense of energy and excitement about the idea. The thinker can then prepare for implementation. This relationship is also a reciprocal type of interdependence, but may tend towards the sequential as the link between idea generator and feeler may need to be richer interpersonally than the link between feeler and thinker. Given the nature of the task, and their concern for people, feelers are likely to use task forces to accomplish the necessary integration.

The link between thinkers and sensors can be more sequential. Once the thinker has 'planned' for implementation the sensor's role (doing) can be communicated by policy, procedures, rules and specification of tasks (hierarchy). However, to the extent the new idea requires new tasks which are in conflict with established and accepted routines it will be important for the sensor to also have enthusiasm for the initiative.

Such sequencing of interdependent activities may represent a normative ideal; it is not necessarily descriptive of practice. For example, feelers may bypass thinkers, interacting directly with sensors, 'bootlegging' the initial implementation of the creative idea. At the thinking level plans may be developed only after early implementation, not before. Of course, this is more likely to happen when the thinkers in the top management group are wedded to their established plans based upon existing logics and are unwilling to experiment with novel approaches.

This sequence also recognizes that the dominant coalition may not be a group in the social-psychological sense, where all members have frequent face-to-face interactions. Rather, it may be a series of interchanges over (objective) time between individuals, each with a predisposition for certain behaviors. Belbin's (1981) work suggests that effective groups had members (Belbin called them Chairman and Teamworker) concerned with transcending individual differences and facilitating the process. In our framework such individuals would be oriented towards integrating the levels of the CM process amongst people and organizational units, and over time.

Power and influence in the creative management process

The CM model has significant implications for the study and practice of the processes through which power and influence are exercised within organizations. In the SM model the communication channels and relationships considered important in the exercise of power are those of the formal organization hierarchy. This is consonant with the framework's underlying philosophy – if reality exists objectively and is accessible to rational instruments, then where else can the many partial views be integrated except in the synoptic mind of the CEO/strategist? For only he or she has the panoramic view of reality by virtue of a superior position at the apex of the organization. Information flows up, directives down. In contrast the CM model stresses rich and fluid communication channels and relationships making up the 'neural' network, a cognitive framework within which the organization will scan, describe and develop its version of 'reality.'

How then should an organization in search of renewal proceed? The interaction patterns required for renewal assume a broad distribution of influence within the management team, and that all cognitive types are represented. No single cognitive mode dominates the ongoing negotiation process. In support of this view Friedlander (1983: 200) states that sustained 'power imbalances diminish [the benefits of] heterogeneity and contact and thereby diminish system learning.'

This does not necessarily mean power should, or will, be uniformly and statically distributed. Rather, power must shift according to the 'authority of the situation' (Follett, 1941). At the outset, when the issue is highly ambiguous, the intuitive mode is required and those individuals with significant capacity in this area should assume more influence, regardless of their hierarchical level within the formal organization. As the renewal process moves to the feeling dimension the motivation of the team becomes critical. Individuals capable of evoking and expressing shared values should now have more influence. The intuitives, while still involved, would exhibit less influence. Subsequently as the task shifts to planning and action, the process requires that thinkers and sensors become predominant. Thus, in an ideal process, each cognitive type assumes influence as determined by the needs of the evolving renewal process. The relationships between the individuals in the (temporarily) dominant role and the rest of the team have been described by Greenleaf (1977) as *primus inter pares*, first amongst equals. Like strands in a tapestry, now in the front, now in the back, individuals on the team together weave a cognitive fabric, the pattern of which will express their version of a renewed organizational reality.

What happens when a cognitive type is not available on the team? Theoretically, a cognitive (and therefore behavioral) void exists. There is no-one with the cognitive preference needed to influence the renewal process in the desired way at a particular stage. If, however, there exists within the group an awareness of the need for different types of cognition and behavior, as well as some capacity to perform the role, then it is possible that one or more members of the team may spontaneously assume the 'vacant' role. In this process of self-organization the renewal process proceeds by evoking the needed but less preferred cognitive processes from members of the management team. Organizational adaptation and individual learning are combined.

Implications for top management groups

The CM model generates a number of insights into the composition of, and processes within, top management teams. From a *prescriptive* point of view, the CM model suggests that an 'ideal' top management group would be made up of individuals capable of functioning in each of the four cognitive modes. Since individuals seem to have stable cognitive preferences (Myers and McCaulley, 1985), an 'ideal' team needs several different 'types' of individuals to assume the variety of roles required. The general implication is that in addition to the *Sensing* and *Thinking* modes implied by the SM model, *Intuition* and *Feeling* modes are required by the CM model. All four modes need to be represented within the effective top management group and utilized in the management process.

From a *descriptive* point of view, cognitive composition might be expected to evolve as an organization matures. One would expect founders of organizations to be predominantly intuitive in their gathering of information, and to evaluate information using the feeling mode. As organizations mature, intuition and feeling would be expected to give way to sensation and thinking. Although it need not necessarily be the case, the latter style can easily drive out the former. This occurs most dramatically when founders leave (or are forced out) and replaced by 'professional managers,' those trained in the SM methodology. More generally, differences in composition within the top management group can be expected to change as an organization develops, and these differences are expected to yield different patterns of behavior. However, the actions of an organization are not directly impacted by the cognitive preferences of its top managers. It is the behaviors of this group and the integration of these behaviors into a pattern of organizational actions which impacts strategy and performance.

Business strategy and the creative management model

The CM model is basically an adaptive process and, as such, relates best to strategy concepts, which share this perspective. Miles and Snow (1978: 14) identified four patterns of behavior which they reduced to four strategic archetypes, 'representing alternative ways of moving through the adaptive cycle.' These are defender, prospector, analyzer and reactor.

In our view, truly *prospecting* organizations have dominant coalitions which search for new ways of doing business and continually use visions of possible futures, ideas about new and different ways of doing business, to feed forward into present behavior and actions. By contrast, in *preserving* organizations past norms and traditions feed back to dominate present behavior. As shown in Figure 2, when viewed in this way, the CM model can be used to distinguish between organizations with a preference for either prospecting or preserving strategies.

The management groups in both prospecting and preserving organizations are oriented towards the intuition and feeling levels of the CM model. Preserving managements are able, with their intuitive ability, to perceive patterns in past decisions, actions and events; and by way of their feeling level they extract and express meaning from their firm's past. They have a strong sense of history and tradition: 'what we have been.' Their orientation is towards the past. Prospective managements use the same cognitive abilities (intuition and feeling) but focus them on the future: 'what we might become.' Although both types of organization must function in the perpetual 'now,' they do so with different (subjective) time orientations: the

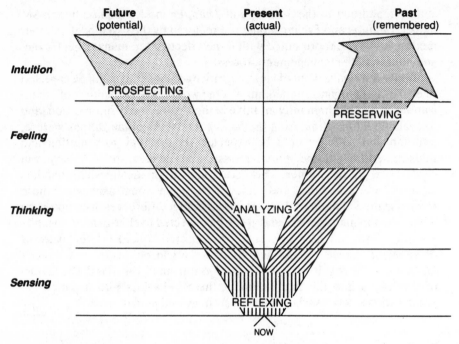

Figure 2   *Strategy and the creative management model*

managements of prospecting organizations are oriented towards the potential of what might be the future; in preserving organizations the orientation
is towards the remembrance of what has been, the realized vision, the past.

Prospecting organizations can be expected to be radical innovators, willing to experiment with new ideas that do not fit within the accepted logic for
the business. In preserving organizations realized vision and tradition guide
action, resulting in an adherence to past strategies; even incremental adjustments may be difficult because intentions and results are evaluated against
values (at the feeling level) not standards derived from a logic (at the
thinking level). Both of these strategies, because vision and values drive
behaviors, often lack the coherence to their actions provided by the thinking–planning level. Furthermore, these organizations are not highly responsive to direct environmental stimuli.

Within the context of the CM model, the dominant coalition of an
analyzing organization can be seen as more oriented towards the present
than either its preserving or prospecting counterparts. It also functions more
at the thinking and sensing levels, less so at the intuition and feeling levels.
As a consequence the management of an analyzing organization is less
accepting of radical, unproven ideas than the pure prospecting organization,
but also less bound by tradition than the preserving organization. Accordingly, the analyzing organization is less likely to be first with a radical
innovation, although it may follow an initiative of a prospecting firm once it

can be rationalized. It is not just the (subjective) time orientation of the management of an analyzing organization that prevents it from pursuing radical innovations. This inability is also bound up in the interrelated issue of its preferred or dominant cognitive functions, thinking and sensing. The management of an analyzing organization functions more at the thinking and sensing levels, and therefore needs to develop a plausible logic before action. However, the actions it does take are well planned and coherent extensions of the established logic.

The remaining strategy orientation outlined in Figure 2 is the reflexing organization. Reflexing organizations (and their managers) exist only in here and now. They have no view of their firm's future, nor sense for its past. Their behaviors are guided by instinctive or reflex responses to given stimuli. They do not attempt to understand their behaviors and actions, either before or after these actions occur. They function solely at the sensation level. Such organizations are highly responsive to a given set of environmental stimuli, but should the environment and the appropriate response pattern change these organizations are unable to adapt, to learn new behaviors.

Given the strategy types identified within the CM model – prospecting, analyzing, reflexing and preserving – what are the corresponding organizational attributes? Consistent with Miles and Snow's original observation about the importance of the dominant coalition's perceptions, the CM model links perception and cognitive preferences suggesting that the composition of the top management teams and their mix of cognitive and time orientations is key to understanding this conception of organization strategy.

Prescriptively it would appear organizations able to renew themselves need some of the attributes of each strategy orientation. The ideal management team needs both prospecting and preserving abilities; these combine a basis in its past with the ability to create its future. This is the problem of renewal: preserving the core of the business while allowing for the ongoing redefinition of that core. Like Janus, the Roman god of the threshold, truly adaptive organizations and their management teams simultaneously look forward, and create their future; and back, and appreciate their past. However, they also strive to understand their actions, and anticipate outcomes while being responsive to environmental stimuli. Even though a balance amongst all strategy orientations might be desirable, it seems likely that most organizations, like most individuals, will have a distinct preference.

Strategy and the composition of top management

The composition and interactions of the top management group affect behaviors which are ultimately reflected in the decisions and actions of the organization. Therefore, differences in composition of the management group should be manifested in patterns of action, that is in strategies (Mintzberg, 1978). The behaviors of the dominant coalition derived from the CM model can be related to the different cognitive types. Accordingly, relationships between the makeup of a top management group and the strategic types of Preserving, Analyzing, Reflexing and Prospecting can be hypothesized (see Table 4). The assertions made are largely descriptive. Prescriptive statements require a link to behaviors, patterns of action and performance.

Table 4 *Hypothesized relationship between cognitive composition of the dominant coalition and business strategy*

Dominant coalition's		
Cognitive composition	Time orientation	Strategy orientation
Mostly Intuitives with some Feelers	Future	Prospecting
Mostly Thinkers with some Sensors	Near term future and past	Analyzing
Mostly Sensors	Now	Reflecting
Mostly Feelers with some Intuitives	Past	Preserving
Mix of Intuitives, Feelers, Thinkers and Sensors	Future←→Past	Renewing

On causality

To this point the discussion has been largely conceptual, linking cognitive styles, behaviors, team composition and decisions and actions. However, it is recognized that other factors, like personal background and skills, influence managerial behaviors; as do organizational context factors, such as hierarchy, norms, rules, and decision-making style.

Empirical evidence

A complete review of the empirical work related to the CM model and top management team composition is beyond the scope of this paper. However, this section will examine some of the existing work, much of which indirectly supports aspects of the CM framework.

Team composition → decisions/actions/performance

Miles and Snow (1978) observed patterns in action, strategies, consistent with the CM process. Moreover, their strategy typology has been found to be reasonably descriptive of observed strategic attributes (Hambrick, 1983a). However, their observations about the composition of the dominant coalition are limited to functional backgrounds. For Defenders they note that the dominant coalition was typically composed of the general manager, the controller, and the heads of production and sales. They go on to state, 'the Prospector's dominant coalition centers around the marketing and research and development functions. Moreover, the Prospector's dominant coalition is also larger, more diverse and more transitory than the

Defender's.' Their rationale is based upon the fit between managerial skills and the technical task requirements of the strategy.

Belbin (1981) administered a battery of psychological tests to executives taking part in a management training course. During the course, managers participated in business simulations. Team composition was varied and performance was measured. Evidence from this research suggests that:

1. The effectiveness of a team will be promoted by the extent to which members correctly recognize and adjust themselves to the relative strengths within the team, both in expertise and ability to engage in specific team-roles.
2. Personal qualities fit members for some team-roles while limiting the likelihood that they will succeed in others (Belbin, 1981: 132-3).

Belbin's work, although illuminating and highly descriptive, was not done in managerial settings. Neither was it a test, nor development of a theory of management team effectiveness.

The assertion that heterogeneous groups are more effective than homogeneous groups is not new. Filley, House and Kerr (1976) surveyed the literature on group dynamics and concluded that novel problems are best handled by a heterogeneous group and routine problems most efficiently dealt with by a homogeneous group. Ziller (1972) suggested that short-term groups ought to have homogeneous membership while long-standing groups have heterogeneous membership. He concluded that heterogeneity on a wide variety of variables, including race, age, ability and personality and training in group dynamics, improved productivity.

The outstanding question pertains not so much to the situational conditions favoring heterogeneity but rather to the appropriate dimensions for the heterogeneity. The perspective of the CM model links the executive function of business renewal to cognitive preferences to managerial behaviors and organizational action.

Cognitive modes → behaviors

The empirical link between the group composition based upon differences or similarities in cognitive preferences and outcomes from group activity is sparse. Evidence associating individual behaviors and cognitive preference is more prevalent.

Several studies have indicated a link between MBTI (Myers–Briggs Type Indicator) and behavioral patterns. Mitroff and Kilmann (1975), Mitroff, Barabba and Kilmann (1977), and Hellriegel and Slocum (1980) have researched how different types view ideal organizations and their heroes. Most of these support the relationships posited by Myers (1982). They found that Sensing–Thinking managers concentrated on specific, factual details, preferring situations in which there is certainty, specificity and control. Their heroes used others to get things done; they were problem-solvers. Intuitive–Thinking managers focused on broad, global issues, general con-

cepts and ill-defined macro-level goals. Their heroes were broad conceptua-
lizers and problem-framers. Sensing–Feeling managers were more concerned with specific people issues, not tasks. Their heroes created personal,
warm climates and made organizations like 'home.' Finally Intuitive–
Feeling managers focused on broad global themes serving mankind. Their
heroes were able to envision new goals and create organizations with a
personal sense.

Reporting on the validity of MBTI, Carlyn (1977) states that Intuitives are
more likely to participate in imagined events and engage in possibilities
while Sensors prefer a command of reality. Although validity studies have
been done relating MBTI scores to other personality measures, very little
evidence is available linking MBTI directly to managerial behaviors. To the
extent that profession and position correlate to behaviors, the data presented in Table 5 tend to inferentially support the relationships posited in
Table 3.

Table 5   *Cognitive style by profession and managerial position*

	Information gathering		Information evaluation		
	Intuition	Sensing	Thinking	Feeling	*n*
Managerial					
Management consultants	58%	42%	92%	8%	71
High-level executives	43%	57%	90%	10%	136
Supervisors and managers	42%	58%	64%	36%	3678
Accountants	38%	62%	59%	41%	427
Small-business managers	14%	86%	81%	19%	150
Other professions					
Artists	91%	9%	30%	70%	114
Architects	82%	18%	56%	44%	124
Steelworkers	14%	86%	74%	26%	105
Teachers (grades 1–12)	26%	74%	31%	69%	281

Source: Adapted from Macdaid, McCaulley and Kainz (1986).

As a group, management consultants and high-level executives have a
predominant thinking preference for evaluating information; as one would
expect, consultants prefer to gather their information more broadly and
look for whole relationships (intuition preference). Practicing managers, be
they high-level executives, supervisors, accountants or small-business
managers, have a stronger preference for grounding their information
gathering in the immediate representations of the world with which they
must deal (sensation preference). Moreover, the proportions of cognitive
types do appear to differ by level in the hierarchy. Roach (1986) distinguishes between supervisors–managers–executives and reports that
'over half the executives were Intuition–Thinking' while for supervisors
Sensation–Thinking was the largest category. Sensation–Feeling declined
dramatically in relation to increasing organizational level.

While intuitive preference appears to increase modestly with level in hierarchy, it varies more dramatically among professions. As shown in Table 5, professions requiring a high degree of creativity (artists and architects) have a strong intuition preference. Architects, however, deal with a technical subject and tend towards the thinking preference for evaluating the content of their intuitive insights. Artists, unconstrained by many technical requirements, evaluate their insights based upon feelings. Teachers and steelworkers, by way of further example, whose professions require them to deal with and respond to direct stimuli, have a stronger sensation preference. Dealing with children, most teachers (grades 1 through 12) evaluate stimuli using feeling; while steelworkers working with a process technology prefer thinking.

While these data are provocative, they do not directly address the question of whether or not cognitive preferences are associated with the behaviors expected at the different levels of the CM model. These questions need to be addressed by empirical research.

Towards practice

The ideas of teamwork at the top, cognitive style and innovation are not new to practicing managers (Rowan, 1979; Sherman, 1984; Moore, 1987). Furthermore, Jungian concepts and MBTI types are to a limited extent already being used to help managers better understand their organizations (Mitroff and Kilmann, 1975; Mason and Mitroff, 1981; Moore, 1987). The CM model synthesizes many of these ideas as they relate to the executive function of business renewal. It infers roles, behaviors and differences in cognitive type for the top management group.

The conceptual insights can still be of use to practitioners even though as yet unsupported by detailed direct evidence. The CM model provides managers with an understanding that can make them more aware of their own behaviors and tolerant of others, especially when they appreciate the individual differences in cognitive preference which underlie those behaviors, and that such behaviors may play an important role in the CM process.

If those responsible for the overall direction of the enterprise were aware of the behavioral requirements of its members as posited by the CM model they could use that understanding in several ways. First, an examination of the members of the top management team (TMT) may reveal that they are inclined to exhibit the required behaviors, but feel, because of organizational factors, they cannot do so. A further examination of the cultural norms, power relationships and the reward systems might reveal that those behaviors were discouraged or even punished. It might be a relatively easy step to legitimize those previously suppressed behaviors.

Often a change of context can help. The 'outward-bound' experience for managers, by providing a dramatic shift in context and in some respects tasks, presents an opportunity for latent preferences, suppressed in the normal organization context, to surface. It is well accepted that children learn through play. However, playful experiences for managers need not always occur outside the normal organizational context. It is now being suggested that certain organizational activities be conducted in a playful manner in order to facilitate institutional learning (Rutenburg, 1986; De Geus, 1988).

A second, and possibly a more controversial, use would be to employ the CM model for selection to, and development of, the TMT. With an understanding of the model those responsible for these activities might attend to, document and evaluate the behaviors of potential or current members of the TMT in terms of cognitive type. These behaviors, framed within the CM model, could be assessed and used as one criterion for selection. Development activities might also be suggested for some members who could most likely exhibit certain required behaviors. As a cautionary note we do not believe that use of the MBTI as a cognitive indicator is warranted at this time. The test was not developed, nor has sufficient evidence of reliability and predictive validity been shown, for use in selection or promotion decisions. However, we do feel that Jung's conception of cognitive types does provide a useful way for managers to appreciate observable, individual behaviors and their contribution to the process of organizational renewal.

Summary/conclusions

This chapter attempts to build a model of the behavioral requirements for the top management team from two perspectives. First, from the perspective of the individual, it is posited that the behaviors relevant to the renewal function of the executive which need to be exhibited by top managers are at least partly a function of their cognitive preferences. It is argued that the Jungian/Myers–Briggs typology is consistent with the model of renewal based upon the creative management (CM) model and an established framework for understanding and predicting these behaviors. Second, it has been asserted that organizations will evolve a pattern of actions, a strategy reflecting the cognitive composition of the top management team. As the cognitive preferences of the top management group vary so too will strategy.

This chapter makes a case for a management process that utilizes the full range of human potential. The need for a CM model to replace the conventional strategic management framework has been argued on the basis of the latter's inability to utilize the full range of cognitive functions and accordingly its failure to promote new and innovative strategies. The CM model, however, has implications for the dominant coalition. Since theory and evidence suggest individuals have superior or dominant functions a mixture of cognitive types is implied. The CM process suggests that top management groups not only include the *Thinkers* and *Sensors* needed by the SM process but also embrace the *Intuitives* and *Feelers* needed to generate and infuse unconventional insights and new ideas. But difference without synthesis is anarchy. The organization and its members must also have the ability to achieve unity from diversity, the ability to transcend.

Notes

We would like to acknowledge the support of the Plan for Excellence, School of Business Administration, The University of Western Ontario and the assistance of Yasminka Kresic and Ramon Baltazar and three anonymous *Strategic Management Journal* reviewers in the preparation of this paper.
1 Jung described Extroversion and Introversion as orientations in attitudes of personality. This distinction can be helpful in a detailed understanding of the CMM and management teams, but will not be developed in this paper.

References

Barnard, C.I. (1938), *The Functions of the Executive*, Harvard University Press, Cambridge, MA.

Belbin, R.M. (1981), *Management Teams: Why They Succeed or Fail*, Heinemann, London.

Blaylock, B.K. (1983), 'Teamwork in a simulated production environment', *Research in Psychological Type*, 6, pp. 58–67.

Bower, J.L. (1982), 'Solving the problems of business planning', *Journal of Business Strategy*, 2(3), Winter, pp. 32–44.

Carlson, R.O. (1972), *School Superintendents: Careers and Performance*. Merrill, Columbia, OH.

Carlyn, M. (1977), 'An assessment of the Myers–Briggs type indicator', *Journal of Personality Assessment*, 41, pp. 461–473.

Child, J. (1974), 'Managerial and organizational factors associated with company performance', *Journal of Management Studies*, 11, pp. 13–27.

Cyert, R.M. and J.G. March (1963), *A Behavioral Theory of the Firm*, Prentice-Hall, Englewood Cliffs, NJ.

De Geus, A.P. (1988), 'Planning as learning', *Harvard Business Review*, March–April, pp. 62–69.

Filley, A.C., R.J. House and S. Kerr (1976), *Managerial Process and Organizational Behavior*, Scott Foresman, Glenview, IL.

Follett, M.P. (1941), *Dynamic Administration: the collected papers of Mary Parker Follett*, edited by Metcalf, H. and L. Urwick, Harper & Bros, New York.

Friedlander, F. (1983), 'Patterns of individual and organizational learning'. In Srivesta, S. and Associates, *The Executive Mind*, Jossey-Bass, San Francisco, CA.

Galbraith, J. (1973), *Designing Complex Organizations*, Addison-Wesley Publishing Co., Reading, MA.

Gardener, H. (1985), *The Mind's New Science: A History of the Cognitive Revolution*, Basic Books, New York.

Greenleaf, R.K. (1977), *Servant Leadership*, Paulish Press, New York.

Hambrick, D.C. (1983a), 'High profit strategies in mature capital goods industries: a contingency approach', *Academy of Management Journal*, 26(4), pp. 687–707.

Hambrick, D.C. (1983b), 'Some tests of the effectiveness and functional attributes of Miles and Snow's strategic types', *Academy of Management Journal*, 26(1), pp. 5–26.

Hambrick, D.C. (1987), 'The top management team: key to strategic success', *California Management Review*, Fall, pp. 88–108.

Hambrick, D.C. and P.A. Mason. (1984), 'Upper echelons: the organization as a reflection of its top managers', *Academy of Management Review*, 9(2), pp. 193–206.

Hampden-Turner, C. (1981), *Maps of the Mind*, Macmillan, New York.

Hellriegel, D. and J.W. Slocum (1980), 'Preferred organizational designs and problem solving styles: interesting companions', *Human Systems Management*, No. 1, pp. 151–158.

Hurst, D.K. (1986), 'Why strategic management is bankrupt', *Organizational Dynamics*, Autumn, pp. 5–27.

Jaques, E. (1982), *The Form of Time*, Crane Russak, New York.

Jung, C.G. (1960), 'The structure and dynamics of the psyche'. In *Collected Works*, vol. 8, Princeton University Press, Princeton, NJ.

Keirsey, D.W. and M. Bates (1978), *Please Understand Me*. Prometheus Nemesis Books, Del Mar, CA.

Kimberly, J.R. and M.J. Evanisko (1981), 'Organizational innovation: the influence of individual, organizational and contextual factors on hospital adoption of technological and administrative innovations', *Academy of Management Journal*, 24, pp. 689–713.

Koestler, A. (1976), *The Act of Creation*, Hutchinson, London.

Lawrence, P.R. and J.W. Lorsch (1969), *Organization and Environment*, R. D. Irwin. Homewood, IL.

Macdaid, G.P., M.H. McCaulley and R.I. Kainz (1986), *Atlas of Type Tables*, Center for Applications of Psychological Types, Gainesville, FL.

Mann, H., M. Siegler and H. Osmond (1971), 'The psychotypology of time'. In Yaker, H., H., Osmond and F. Cheek (eds), The Future of Time: Man's Temporal Environment, Doubleday, Garden City, NY, pp. 142–178.

Mason, R.O. and I.I. Mitroff (1981), *Challenging Strategic Planning Assumptions*, John Wiley & Sons. New York.

McKenny, J.L. and P.G.W. Keen (1974), 'How managers' minds work'. *Harvard Business Review*, May–June, pp. 79–90.

Miles, R.E. and C.C. Snow (1978), *Organizational Strategy, Structure and Process*. McGraw-Hill, New York.

Mintzberg, H. (1976), 'Planning on the left side and managing on the right', *Harvard Business Review*, July–August, pp. 49–58 [also reprinted in this volume].

Mintzberg, H. (1978), 'Patterns in strategy formation', *Management Science*, 24, pp. 934–948.

Mitroff, I.I. and R. H. Kilmann (1975), 'Stories managers tell: a new tool for organizational problem solving', *Management Review*, 64(7), pp. 18–28.

Mitroff, I., V. Barabba and R. Kilmann (1977), 'The application of behavioral and philosophical technologies to strategic planning: a case study of a large federal agency', *Management Science*, 24, pp. 44–58.

Moore, T. (1987), 'Personality tests are back', *Fortune*, 30 March, pp. 74–82.

Myers, I.B. (1982), *Introduction to Type*, Consulting Psychologists Press, Palo Alto, CA.

Myers, I.B. and M.H. McCaulley (1985) *Manual: A Guide to the Development and Use of the Myers–Briggs Type Indicator*, Consulting Psychologists Press, Palo Alto, CA.

Pascale, R.T. (1984), 'Perspectives on strategy: the real story behind Honda's success', *California Management Review*, Spring, pp. 47–72.

Peters, T.J. and R.H. Waterman, (1983), 'Beyond the rational model', *The McKinsey Quarterly*, Spring, pp. 19–30.

Prahalad, C.K. and R.A. Bettis (1986), 'The dominant logic: a new linkage between diversity and performance', *Strategic Management Journal*, 7, pp. 485–501.

Roach, B. (1986), 'Organizational decision-makers: different types for different levels', *Journal of Psychological Type*, 12, pp. 16–24.

Rowan, R. (1979), 'Those business hunches are more than blind faith', *Fortune*, 23 April, pp. 110–114.

Rutenberg, D. (1986), 'Playful Plans'. Working paper, Queens University.

Sherman, S.P. (1984), 'Eight big masters of innovation', *Fortune*, 15 October, pp. 66–78.

Simon, H.A. (1988), 'Understanding creativity and creative management'. In Kuhn, R.L. (ed.), *Handbook for Creative and Innovative Managers*, McGraw-Hill, New York.

Taggart, W. and D. Robey. (1981), 'Minds and managers: on the dual nature of human information processing and management', *Academy of Management Review*, 6(2), pp. 187–195.

Thompson, J.D. (1967), *Organizations in Action*. McGraw-Hill, New York.

Watson, J.D. (1969), *The Double Helix*, Mentor Books, New York.

Weick, K.E. (1979), *The Social Psychology of Organizing*, Addison-Wesley Publishing Co., Reading, MA.

Worthy, J.C. (1984), *Shaping An American Institution: Robert E. Wood and Sears, Roebuck*, University of Illinois Press, Chicago, IL.

Ziller, R.C. (1972), 'Homogeneity and heterogeneity of group membership'. In McClintoch, C.G. (ed.), *Experimental Social Psychology*, Holt, Rinehart and Winston, New York.

19

Developing in phases

Ronnie Lessem

In the course of becoming an intrapreneur, of one kind or another, you will develop in phases. Bernard Lievegoed,[1] the Dutch organizational psychologist, says that we pass through three major stages in our lives: a time to learn, up till the age of twenty; a time to expand, between twenty and forty; and a time to grow wise, from forty onwards. I want to focus on such phases of intrapreneurial development.

As the American biologist George Land[2] has said, we grow, qualitatively speaking, or we die, psychologically speaking. So you only realize your full intrapreneurial potential, whether as an animateur or an innovator, as an entrepreneur or an adventurer, if you successfully undergo life's transitions.

Your development path

The person who has most comprehensively charted our adult development is the American researcher, Daniel Levinson, who wrote *The Seasons of Man's Life*.[3] Although his particular focus was on men in the course of their adult development, most of his findings would seem to apply equally to women.

Your development path, over the course of a lifetime, includes four phases, interspersed with transitions. These phases and transitions together comprise what Levinson calls your 'life structure'. In this chapter I want, firstly, to uncover this developmental life structure for a business individual, and, secondly, to reveal the general preconditions for healthy development.

Your underlying life structure

Your life structure is not a random set of events, like pebbles washed up on the shore. Rather, like threads in a tapestry, the events are woven into an encompassing design. Recurring themes help to unify the overall pattern of the tapestry. However, your lives differ widely in the nature and patterning of their specific elements.

Adapted from *Intrapreneurship* (Aldershot: Gower, 1987), pp. 193–210

Your life structure, then, evolves through a relatively orderly sequence during your adult years. It consists of alternating stable, structure building and transitional, structure changing periods.

To construct anything, something else must be destructured and restructured. In human reproduction, an ovum and a sperm are joined to create a new being, but many others are left to die. The balance of nature is a mixture of destruction and creation. Both are essential to the harmony and evolution of individuals, organizations and societies.

In fact, at each phase of your development, a new balance has to be created between the forces not only of creativity and destruction, but also of youth and age, of masculinity and femininity and of separation and attachment.

The primary task of every stable period, then, is to build a life structure that reconciles those four sets of opposing forces in a new and appropriate way. You must make certain key choices, form a structure around them, and pursue your values and goals within that structure. A transitional period terminates the existing life structure and creates the possibility for a new one.

Your decision to 'stay put' within a stable period is not always based on commitment. It may stem from resignation, inertia, passive acceptance or controlled despair – a self restriction in the context of severe external constraints. This kind of surface stability marks the beginning of long term decline unless new factors intervene (perhaps in the next transitional period) and enable you to form a more satisfactory life structure.

The primary tasks of every transitional period are to question and to reappraise the existing structure, to explore various possibilities for change in yourself and in your world, and to move towards commitment to the crucial choices that form the basis for your new life structure in the ensuing stable period.

Your task in a developmental transition, therefore, is to terminate a time in your life; to accept the losses that termination entails; to review and evaluate the past; to decide which aspects of the past to keep and which to reject; and to consider your wishes and possibilities for the future. You are suspended between past and future, struggling to overcome the gap that separates them. Much from the past must be given up, separated from, cut out of your life; and there is much that can be used as a basis for the future.

In every transitional period, throughout the cycle of your life, the internal figures of Young and Old are modified and placed in a new balance. The end of the preceding period stimulates Old thoughts and feelings about being in a rut, rotting, coming to the brink of death. The start of a new period stimulates New thoughts and feelings about being reborn, making a fresh start, discovering fresh possibilities in oneself and new vistas in one's world.

The task in every transition is to create a new Young/Old integration appropriate to that time of life. With the change of eras there is normally an increase in the Old qualities of maturity, judgement, self awareness, magnanimity, integrated structure, breadth of perspective. But these qualities are of value only if they continue to be vitalized by the Young's energy, imagination, capacity for foolishness and fancy.

In summary, the most fundamental tasks of a stable period are to make firm choices, rebuild one's life structure and enhance one's life within it. Those of a transitional period are to question and reappraise the existing period, to search for new possibilities in oneself and in the world, and to modify the present structure enough for a new one to be formed.

So much for your life structure. What about your life's phases?

The phases and transitions you need to undergo

Levinson divides the course of your life into four transitional periods, and four stable life structures, as can be seen in Table 1.

Table 1 *Life phases*

Age	Transitional period	Stable structure
17–22	Early adult transition	
22–28		Novice phase
28–33	Age thirty transition	
33–40		Settling down phase
40–45	Midlife transition	
45–52		Phase of renewal
52–57	Age fifty transition	
58–		The legacy phase

Early adult transition (17–22)

The first task, in your early adult transition, is to terminate your adolescent life structure, thereby leaving the pre-adult world behind you. This involves modifying existing relationships with important persons and institutions, as well as the self you formed in adolescence. Separations from family and schoolfriends are required as well as the loss of a certain degree of dependence.

The second task is to take a preliminary step into the adult world: to explore its possibilities, to imagine oneself as a participant in it, to make and test some tentative choices, before entering it.

The first task involves a process of termination, the second a process of initiation. Both are essential in a transitional period. Out of this opening transition emerges the young adult life structure, that is 'the novice phase'.

The novice phase (22–28)

Three major tasks, in your twenties, are crucial to your vocational and management development. These comprise the formation of your 'dream', of a suitable mentor relationship, and of an appropriate occupation. I shall start with the most important of these tasks, the uncovering of 'the dream'.

Forming a dream and giving it a place in the
life structure

Your 'dream', like Conran's dream of self sufficiency, lends prolonged
excitement and vitality to the novice's life. It is associated with the 'I am'
feeling.

Your 'dream' may be modest ('there is no happiness like shared happiness') or heroic ('I'm going to change the world'). It is usually vaguely
defined, at first, and only very occasionally crystal clear; it may be a burning
passion or a quiet guiding force, a source of inspiration or of gentle comfort.
In dramatic terms, your 'dream' is your personal myth, an imagined drama
in which you are the central character, a would-be hero or heroine engaged
in a noble quest.

Forming a dream

The vicissitudes and fate of the Dream have fundamental qualities for adult
development. In its primordial form, the Dream is a vague sense of self-in-adult-
world. It has the quality of a vision, an imagined possibility that generates
excitement and vitality.

At the start it is usually poorly articulated and only tenuously connected to
reality, although it may contain concrete images such as winning the Nobel prize
or making the national football team.

It may take dramatic form as in the myth of the hero: the great artist, business
tycoon, athletic or intellectual superstar peforming magnificent feats and receiving special honours. It may, alternatively, take the mundane forms that are not
yet inspiring and sustaining: the excellent craftsman, the husband–father in a
certain kind of family, the highly respected man of one's community.

Daniel Levinson, *The Seasons of Man's Life*[4]

Whatever its nature, as a young person you have the developmental task
of giving the dream greater definition and finding ways of living it out. It
makes a great difference in your growth whether your novice phase is in tune
with, and infused by, the 'dream', or opposed to it. If the 'dream' remains
unconnected to your life it may simply die, and with it your sense of aliveness
and purpose.

Many of you, in fact, develop a conflict between your life direction
expressing the 'dream' and another that is quite different. In your youth you
may be pushed away from your 'dream' by your parents, by various external
constraints, such as lack of money or opportunity, and by various aspects of
your personality, such as guilt, passivity, competitiveness and special
talents. You may thus succeed in an occupation that holds no interest for
you.

Alternatively, if you do fulfil your 'dream' you will inevitably find,
particularly as you approach midlife, that the hero of the 'dream' is only one
of many figures in your life. To the extent that this figure plays a predomi-

nant part in the evolution of the novice phase, other parts of yourself tend to be neglected. For example, if you fulfil your 'dream' by becoming a millionaire you may neglect to develop the artistic side of your nature.

Inevitably, therefore, whether or not you work on and through your 'dream' in early adulthood, it will have to be reworked in later life. Mentor relationships are likely to help in that process. In fact the second task of your novice phase lies therein.

Forming mentor relationships

In your early twenties, in particular, you stand to gain from an 'apprenticeship' with an appropriately more advanced, expert and authoritative 'mentor'. As the relationship evolves, you gain a fuller sense of your own authority and of your capability for autonomous, responsible action.

More specifically the mentor involved may act, firstly, as a teacher, serving to enhance your skills and intellectual development. Secondly, he may serve as a sponsor, using his influence to facilitate your advancement. Thirdly, he may act as a host and guide, welcoming you into a new occupational role and social world, and acquainting you with its customs, values, resources and cast of characters. Fourthly, the mentor may serve as an exemplar that you can admire and seek to emulate.

The mentor has a fifth and final function, and this is developmentally the most crucial one: to support and facilitate the realization of your dream. He fosters your development by believing in you, sharing the youthful 'dream' and giving it his blessing, helping to define your newly discovered self in its freshly discovered world, and creating space in which you can work on a life structure that contains the 'dream'.

Forming an occupation

In every period of your life, though, the developmental tasks are contrasting, even antithetical. Just as the 'Early adult transition' requires you both to terminate one era and to initiate the next, 'Entering the adult world' requires you both to explore freely and to make firm choices.

The exploratory stage requires you to 'hang loose', keeping your options open and avoiding strong commitments. To varying degrees, the outside world provides multiple possibilities. Also your own youthful vitality generates a sense of adventure and wonder, a wish to seek out all the treasures of the new world you are entering.

At the same time, in your early to mid twenties, you must take on adult responsibilities and begin to make something of your life. Externally there are pressures to 'grow up', get married, enter an occupation, and lead a more organized life. Internally there are desires for stability and order, for roots, lasting ties, and for the fulfilment of core values.

Certain circumstances are more conducive to what Levinson terms 'forming' an occupation (as opposed to choosing one once and for all) over the course of the novice phase, than others. Supportive conditions, on the one hand, involve the granting of room to manoeuvre, and the freedom to make mistakes, together with the setting of clear limits and expectations. Challenging conditions, on the other hand, involve the setting of appropriate problems and opportunities for the individual to resolve.

No particular set of circumstances, though, is ideal. Forming an occupation, as has been indicated, is inherently paradoxical. If you make a strong occupational commitment in your early twenties, without sufficient exploration of external options and inner preferences, you often come to regret it later. On the other hand, if you don't make a commitment until your thirties, or never make one, you are deprived of the satisfaction of engaging in enduring work that is suitable for yourself and for society. So there is always a need to redress an occupational imbalance in later life.

Age 30 transition (28–32)

Levinson maintains that, at about 28, the provisional qualities of the twenties begin to end and life becomes more serious, more for real. A voice within you says: 'If I am to change my life – if there are things in it I want to modify or exclude, or things missing I want to add – I must now make a start, for soon it will be too late.'

The 'age 30 transition', in fact, provides an opportunity to work on the flaws in your life structure formed during the previous period, and to create the basis for a more enduring future. For some people, according to Levinson, the transition proceeds smoothly. A person's life and work become modified and enriched.

However, for most, the transition takes on a more stressful form, just like the fraught transition from a 'Pioneering' to a 'Managed' organization. You often fear that you can move neither forward or back. The integrity of your 'enterprise' is in serious doubt.

As this age 30 transition extends itself, you move towards new choices or recommit yourself to existing ones. A great deal hinges on these choices. If they are well made – from the point of view of your 'dream', values, talents, possibilities – they provide the basis for a relatively satisfactory second, adult life structure. If the preparatory work has been poorly done and the new structure is flawed, life in 'settling down' will become increasingly painful.

The settling down phase (32–40)

In the 'settling down' phase you have two important tasks. Firstly, you must try to establish a niche in society, to anchor your life and work more firmly, to develop competence in a chosen field, and to become a valued member of a world you in turn value. Secondly, you have the task of striving to 'make it', to advance, to progress according to some inner or outward looking timetable.

Establishing a niche involves digging in, forming an occupation and pursuing your interests within a prescribed pattern. This is the initial step in 'settling down'. You need a relatively ordered, stable life, in order to become established in your life and work.

Working at advancement involves striving to succeed, moving onward and upward, progressing according to a pre-ordained schedule. Whereas the first task – establishing a niche – contributes to the stability and order of a defined structure, the second – 'making it' – involves a progression within the structure.

The 'settling down' life structure, then, gives certain of your aspirations and relationships a prominent place, while requiring that others be made secondary or put aside altogether. It may, depending on the case in point, permit expression of many or few aspects of yourself.

A relatively integrated structure has a few central elements which serve as focal points for the structure as a whole, while other peripheral elements enrich and expand the structure.

Second life structure

The underlying task is to 'settle for' a few key choices, to create a broader structure around them, to invest oneself fully in the various components of the structure – such as work, family, community – and to pursue long range goals and plans within it. An individual has a stronger sense of urgency to 'get serious', to be responsible, to decide what is truly important and to shape his life accordingly.

Daniel Levinson, *The Seasons of Man's Life*[5]

To the extent, however, that you want order and stability you must be ready to moderate your upward striving which may rock your personal and familial boat. Conversely, an individual who wants desperately to make a mark, to attain great heights of power, virtue or achievement, cannot afford to place great value on stability.

The imagery of the ladder, finally, is central to the settling down phase. It reflects the interest in advancement and affirmation so central to this period. By 'ladder', Levinson refers to all dimensions of advancement – increases in social rank, income, power, fame. The ladder has both objective and subjective aspects. It reflects the realities of the external world, but it is also defined by you in terms of your own meanings and strivings – be they physically, socially, technologically, economically, aesthetically, or culturally circumscribed.

The midlife transition (40–45)

At around 40, when you reach the top rung of your early adult ladder, you have to reappraise the ladder itself. It is not just a matter of evaluating how well you have done within the current definitions of success and failure. You have to question the basic meanings of success and failure, including the value of the ladder.

In reworking your 'dream', then, you need to modify the meaning of the ladder, to evaluate your success or failure in more complex terms, and to give more emphasis to the quality of experience, to the intrinsic value of this work and productivity, and their meaning to yourself and to others.

For the great majority, according to Levinson's research into people from all walks of life, midlife transition spans a period of struggle. The individuals he investigated began to question nearly every aspect of their lives, feeling they could not continue as before. Past and future coexist in the present, but the individual suffers from corrosive doubt as to whether they can be joined.

During the period from 40 to 45, then, you need to reduce your heavy investment in the external world. To do the work of reappraisal you must turn inward. You have to discover what your turmoil is about, and where it hurts. Having been overly engaged with worldly struggles, you need to be more engaged with yourself. Hence the recent wave of interest, amongst the maturer business enterprises, in 'corporate culture', that inner manifestation of a corporation's other being.

Inner mapping

The 'geographical study' is a mapping expedition in a territory often experienced as a desert, with long stretches of sand enlivened by occasional oases. The traveller discovers that some of the perceived water holes are mirages, others real, and that the territory contains far more resources than he has been able to see. Slowly he learns how to look below the surface and to make use of the treasures he finds there . . .

Daniel Levinson, *The Seasons of Man's Life*[6]

The midlife phase of renewal (45–52)

Every transition presents you with the opportunity of moving towards an integration of each of the four sets of polarities – young/old; destruction/creation; masculine/feminine; attachment/separateness.

At midlife, however, the demand for integration is particularly strong. The energy and vigour of youthful aspiration needs to be tempered by the durability and perspective of seasoned wisdom. The 'destructive' features of cut and thrust need to be counterbalanced by the 'creative' features of development and renewal.

The power of 'masculine' analysis and competitiveness needs to be tempered by 'feminine' intuition and co-operation. Attachment to self centred, material goals needs to be re-balanced, through a growing separation from tangible aspirations, towards a more spiritually oriented search for self actualization.

Every life structure, Levinson maintains, gives high priority to certain aspects of yourself and neglects others. In midlife these neglected aspects seek particularly urgent expression. Internal voices that have been silent for years now clamour to be heard. You hear the voice of an identity prematurely rejected, of a goal lost sight of or not pursued, of a valued connection given up in acquiescence to authority, of an internal figure who wants to be an academic or an entrepreneur. You must learn to listen to these voices and decide consciously what part you will give them in your life.

In fact, the great developmental task of this era – for an organization, perhaps, as well as for an individual – is not to retire early from worldly responsibilities but to seek a new balance between power and love. It is critically important, both to society and to yourself in middle adulthood, that you accept the burdens and the pleasure of responsibility, that you learn to exercise authority with more wisdom and compassion, and that you tolerate the guilt and pain that are the price of the self conscious use of power.

In midlife, then, you should consciously set out to re-balance the needs of self and society. You can develop greater wisdom if you are less focused on the acquisition of specific skills, knowledge and rewards, and more focused on the intrinsic pleasure of work and of having more individualized, loving relationships. While you might still enjoy the tangible rewards of power and influence, in some shape or form, you gain even greater satisfaction from empowering others.

Age 50 transition into maturity, and the legacy phase (52–)

The imagery of the 'legacy' begins to emerge in your midlife transition. Your legacy, according to Levinson, is what you pass on to future generations. It includes material possessions, creative products, business enterprises, influences on others. People, he says, differ enormously in their views about what constitutes a legacy. Although the real value of any such legacy is impossible to measure, in his mind it defines, to a large degree, the ultimate value of your life.

In every era, in fact, you have the need and the capability to generate a legacy. But it is in the final phase of life that the task of building one acquires its greatest developmental significance. It can also become your ultimate vision, or source of profound creativity.

The creative impulse is not merely to make something. It is to bring something into being, to give birth, to generate life.

Negotiating your life's course

There is no guarantee that you will successfully negotiate your life's course, thereby developing as an individual, and as an intrapreneur. For whatever intrapreneurial path you are following or forging – be it a path of adventure, happiness, change, enterprise, leadership, development or creativity – you will need certain attributes.

Your pathfinding attributes

There are five particular attributes that you need to possess. Without them you will fail to negotiate life's transitions. In other words you will remain stuck in a particular phase, and fail to develop your full intrapreneurial potential. These specific attributes are:

- Capacity for insight
- Possession of foresight
- Tolerance of uncertainty
- Willingness of risk
- Courage to change

As a developing intrapreneur, firstly, you need sufficient insight into yourself, at a particular stage of your life, to realize that you are undergoing a phase of development. This kind of insight requires a certain sensitivity to needs emerging from within. It also often means discarding roles and behaviours expected from without.

Secondly, as an intrapreneur successfully engaged in your own self development, you need sufficient foresight to avoid going down blind alleys. You can somehow tell which path of development offers the greatest potential for personal and business growth.

Thirdly, you are able to tolerate uncertainty in that you allow your life to move in fits and starts. Development, as we have already seen, is not a smooth and continuous process. Thrusts of energy are often followed by periods of uncertainty and retrenchment. Progress is usually slow, and seldom steady. Pathfinders know and can accept this, even though it makes their lives uncomfortable.

You are prepared, fourthly, to take 'psychological' risks whereby you are willing to give up personally restrictive practices. A secondment to a new venture, or to a community project, is a typical case in point.

Fifthly, if you are engaged in intrapreneurial self development, you have the courage to change your closely held beliefs, in the light of new information and experience, and also dare to include others in your pathfinding, whose values are fundamentally different from your own. Finally, you have the inclination to set out on your own, despite personal or family misgivings, in order to pursue your 'dream'.

Creating your own life

If these are the general attributes of successful intrapreneurs, what are the particular, and creative, steps that you have to take in negotiating a life transition? In other words, what is the creative process in which si ccessfully developing business individuals engage? What emerges from your capacity for insight and foresight, from your tolerance of uncertainty, willingness to take personal risks, and from your courageous accommodation of change?

How do you manage the personal transition from an immature intrapreneurial state, like that of a trainee manager or salesman, to that of a business executive or entrepreneur? The general rules for each and every developmental point are set out in Table 2.

Table 2 *Managing personal transition*

The creative process	The process of transition
PREPARATION	ANTICIPATION
Gathering impressions and images	Imagining oneself into the next phase of life and work
INCUBATION	INCUBATION/SEPARATION
Letting go of certainties	Letting go of an outlived identity
ILLUMINATION	EXPANSION
Leaping into the unknown	Being swept along in a fast current
REVISION	INCORPORATION
Conscious restructuring, and editing of creative material	Reflection on, and integration of, new aspects of one's life and work

Whether you are negotiating the 'early adult', 'age thirty', 'midlife', or 'age fifty' transition, the following common and creative process applies:

ANTICIPATION, firstly, like the gathering of impressions and images, involves preparing to meet a prospective transition rather than becoming lost in everyday detail, or in vague procrastination. Intrapreneurs who are particularly well prepared have:

• collected the skills they are likely to require
• developed a picture, an image of how things will be
• couched such a picture in positive terms, and enthusiastically pursued it

Secondly, SEPARATION AND INCUBATION: as you painfully let go of old certainties, you give up increasingly destructive aspects of your old self to form space for newly creative aspects. So an expanded identity replaces the previous and restricted one. Outgrown social roles and 'shoulds', along with old fears and handicapping defences, are re-examined in the light of new possibilities for integrating your personality in the stage to come.

Thirdly, as you leap into the physical, economic or psychological unknown, you plunge into new territory of one kind or another, often experiencing heightened sensations through this process of EXPANSION. Your senses are thereby enlivened, your insights quicken, and their focus often becomes selective. However, having dared to get your feet wet in a new stream, you may well be swept along in such a fast current of events that they become temporarily out of control.

Finally, after the hurly burly of expansion, there is a dormant period in which you are able consciously to restructure yourself and your world. Through this process of INCORPORATION, you reflect on what has changed, and integrate the meaning of these changes into your philosophy of life and work. It is important to allow time for the whole of yourself to absorb and clear, and to allow for your batteries to be recharged.

Summary

There is a series of four life phases – structure forming – and four life transitions – structure changing – that underpin your intrapreneurial development. In each of these phases, duly interspersed with transitions, the polarities of creation and destruction, youth and age, masculinity and femininity, separation and attachment, need to be newly and appropriately balanced.

If you are to develop intrapreneurially you will pass through four stages (combinations of phases and transitions): exploration, consolidation, renewal, and individuation. Each of them needs to contain different resolutions of the above mentioned polarities.

In order to negotiate these stages successfully you need to anticipate the future, separate from the past, expand outwards without overdue self control, and incorporate yourself into the evolving situation.

References

1 Lievegoed, B., *Phases*, Rudolf Steiner Press, 1979.
2 Land, G., *To Grow or to Die*, Wiley, 1986.
3 Levinson, D., *The Seasons of Man's Life*, Knopf, 1978.
4 Levinson, D., op.cit.
5 Levinson, D., op.cit.
6 Levinson, D., op.cit.

SECTION 5

CREATIVE FUTURE

A creative perspective is future-orientated; it looks for possibilities and new ways of seeing and doing. Many commentators argue that the capacity to take a creative viewpoint is particularly important now, because of the fundamental changes in economic, social, technological, and political balance we now face. This crossroads involves an all-pervasive shift in world view: from analysis and control to perception and creativity. Naisbitt and Aburdene (1990: 286) see this as an 'era where humankind earns their daily bread through the creativity of the individual'. Toffler (1980: 456) argues that it is the destiny of our age to create new forms. To do this he tells us to embrace paradox, imagination and daring synthesis.

> Most people are culturally more skilled as analysts than synthesists. This is one reason why our images of the future (and of ourselves in that future) are so fragmentary, haphazard and wrong. Our job here is to think like generalists, not specialists. (Toffler 1980: 245–6)

This section presents some ideas about the future and the creative perception and thinking needed to meet its challenge. It examines some implications for individuals, organizations, global action and technology.

Handy believes the changes we now face will have a radical effect on the kind of world we live in. He envisages a future with multi-skilled, self-motivating people working for various destructured organizations. He highlights the far-reaching effects of apparently small changes, and the impact of technology on social custom. He presents a personal view of the role of creativity in change and describes the kind of upside-down thinking he believes necessary to meet the discontinuities we now face.

Morgan argues that 'it is not enough to look at what excellent organizations are already doing. It is also necessary to be proactive in relation to the future: to anticipate some of the changes that are likely to occur and ... to address these effectively.' He discusses the organizational skills that managers will need to meet the challenge of the emerging world economy. The key competencies he focuses on include a proactive mindset, visionary leadership, promoting creativity, learning and innovation, remote management skills and the ability to reframe problems into new solutions.

In *Megatrends*, Naisbitt (1984) described ten fundamental shifts including the move to a high tech information society, self-help, participative democracy and networking. Naisbitt and Aburdene's predictions for the nineties include the already present free-market socialism, but more surprisingly a decade of women in leadership and the triumph of the individual, claiming that the most exciting breakthroughs of the 21st century will occur not because of technology but because of an expanding concept of what it means to be human. Focusing more on 'what to do today in contemplation of tomorrow', Drucker addresses the rising concern with environmental issues, an area that does not sit happily with traditional economic thinking. He argues for transnational action to abate this great threat.

Everyone is aware of the change wrought by information technology (IT) in its various guises. Rockart and Short argue that IT provides the tools for organizations to manage the interdependence so many futurists predict.

References

Naisbitt J. (1984) *Megatrends*. New York: Warner.
Naisbitt J. and Aburdene P. (1990) *Megatrends 2000*. London: Sidgwick and Jackson.
Toffler A. (1980) *The third wave*. London: William Collins.

20

The age of unreason

Charles Handy

The scene was the General Synod of the Church of England in the 1980s. The topic being debated was the controversial proposition that women be admitted to the priesthood. A speaker from the floor of the Chamber spoke with passion, 'In this matter,' he cried, 'as in so much else in our great country, why cannot the status quo be the way forward?'

It was the heartfelt plea not only of the traditionalists in that Church but of those in power, anywhere, throughout the ages. If change there has to be let it be more of the same, continuous change. That way, the cynic might observe, nothing changes very much.

Continuous change is comfortable change. The past is then the guide to the future. An American friend, visiting Britain and Europe for the first time wondered, 'Why is it that over here whenever I ask the reason for anything, any institution or ceremony or set of rules, they always give me an historical answer – because . . ., whereas in my country we always want a functional answer – in order to . . .?' Europeans, I suggested, look backwards to the best of their history and change as little as they can; Americans look forward and want to change as much as they may.

Circumstances do, however, combine occasionally to discomfort the advocates of the status quo. Wars, of course, are the great discomforters, but so is technology, when it takes one of its leaps forward as it did in the Industrial Revolution, so is demography, when it throws up baby booms or busts, so is a changing set of values, like that which occurred during the student unrest of 1968, and so are economics.

Circumstances are now once again, I believe, combining in curious ways. Change is not what it used to be. The status quo will no longer be the best way forward. That way will be less comfortable and less easy but, no doubt, more interesting – a word the English use to signal an uncertain mix of danger and opportunity. If we wish to enjoy more of the opportunity and less of the risk we need to understand the changes better. Those who know why changes come waste less effort in protecting themselves or in fighting the inevitable. Those who realize where changes are heading are better able to

Adapted and reprinted by permission of Random Century Ltd from *The Age of Unreason* (London: Business Books, 1989), pp. 3–23

use those changes to their own advantage. The society which welcomes change can use that change instead of just reacting to it.

George Bernard Shaw once observed that all progress depends on the unreasonable man. His argument was that the reasonable man adapts himself to the world while the unreasonable persists in trying to adapt the world to himself, therefore for any change of consequence we must look to the unreasonable man, or, I must add, to the unreasonable woman.

In that sense we are entering an Age of Unreason, when the future, in so many areas, is there to be shaped, by us and for us; a time when the only prediction that will hold true is that no predictions will hold true; a time, therefore, for bold imaginings in private life as well as public, for thinking the unlikely and doing the unreasonable.

That, then, is the purpose of this book – to understand better the changes which are already about us in order that we may, as individuals and as a society, suffer less and profit more. Change, after all, is only another word for growth, another synonym for learning. We can all do it, and enjoy it, if we want to.

The story or argument of this chapter rests on three assumptions:

- that the changes are different this time: they are discontinuous and not part of a pattern; that such discontinuity happens from time to time in history, although it is confusing and disturbing, particularly to those in power;
- that it is the little changes which can in fact make the biggest differences to our lives, even if these go unnoticed at the time, and that it is the change in the way our *work* is organized which will make the biggest differences to the way we all will *live*;
- that discontinuous change requires discontinuous upside-down thinking to deal with it, even if both thinkers and thoughts appear absurd at first sight.

Change is not what it used to be

Thirty years ago I started work in a world-famous multinational company. By way of encouragement they produced an outline of my future career – 'This will be your life,' they said, 'with titles of likely jobs.' The line ended, I remember, with myself as chief executive of a particular company in a particular far-off country. I was, at the time, suitably flattered. I left them long before I reached the heights they planned for me, but already I knew that not only did the job they had picked out no longer exist, neither did the company I would have directed nor even the country in which I was to have operated.

Thirty years ago I thought that life would be one long continuous line, sloping upwards with luck. Today I know better. Thirty years ago that company saw the future as largely predictable, to be planned for and managed. Today they are less certain. Thirty years ago most people thought that change would mean more of the same, only better. That was incremental change and to be welcomed. Today we know that in many areas of life we cannot guarantee more of the same, be it work or money, peace or freedom, health or happiness, and cannot even predict with confidence what will be happening in our own lives. Change is now more chancy, but also more exciting if we want to see it that way.

Change has, of course, always been what we choose to make it, good or bad, trivial or crucial. Take, for instance, the one word 'change' and consider how we use it. Can any other word be asked to do so many things?

'Change is part of life' (a noun universal)
'There is a change in the arrangements' (a noun particular)
'Please count your change' (a noun metaphorical)
'Please change this wheel' (a verb transitive)
'I will not change' (a verb intransitive)
'Where do I change trains?' (a verb metaphorical)
'She is a clever change agent' (an adjective)

Where the same word is used to describe the trivial (a change of clothes) and the profound (a change of life), how can we easily distinguish whether it is heralding something important or not? When the same word can mean 'progress' and 'inconsistency', how should we know which is which? We might well ask whether the English language was devised to confuse the foreigner, or ourselves?

More of the same only better, and, if possible, for more people. It was a comfortable view of change, one which, in Britain, inspired the socialism of Gaitskell and Crosland and allowed so many to marry idealism to their personal prosperity. It allowed the big to grow bigger, the powerful to look forward to more power, and even the dispossessed to hope for some share of the action one day. It was a view of change that upset no one. The only trouble was that it did not work, it never has worked anywhere for very long, and even those societies in which it has seemed to be working, Japan, Germany and, perhaps, the USA are about to see that it does not work for ever. In each of those societies it is now increasingly relevant to ask 'what is the next trick?' because the current one shows every sign of ending.

It is not just because the pace of change has speeded up, which it has done, of course. We must all, some time, have seen one of those graphs comparing, say, the speed of travel in 500 BC and every 100 years thereafter, with the line suddenly zooming upwards ever steeper in the last inch or two of the chart as we approached modern times, when horses are superseded by cars, then by planes and then by rockets. Faster change on its own sits quite comfortably with the 'more only better' school. It is only when the graph goes off the chart that we need to start to worry, because then things get less predictable and less manageable. Incremental change suddenly becomes discontinuous change. Catastrophe theory, they call it in mathematics, interestingly and symbolically, the study of discontinuous curves in observed phenomena, graphs that loop back on themselves or go into precipitous falls or unsuspected plateaux. Trends, after all, cannot accelerate forever on a graph paper without looping the loop.

I believe that discontinuity is not catastrophe, and that it certainly *need* not be catastrophe. Indeed, I will argue that discontinuous change is the only way forward for a tramlined society, one that has got used to its ruts and its blinkers and prefers its own ways, however dreary, to untrodden paths and new ways of looking at things. I like the story of the Peruvian Indians who, seeing the sails of their Spanish invaders on the horizon, put it down to a freak of the weather and went on about their business, having no concept of sailing ships in their limited experience. Assuming continuity, they screened out what did not fit and let disaster in. I like less the story that a frog if put in cold water will not bestir itself if that water is heated up slowly and gradually and will in the end let itself be boiled alive, too comfortable with continuity to realize that continuous change at some point becomes discontinuous and demands a change in behaviour. If we want to avoid the fate of the Peruvian Indians or the boiling frog we must learn to look for and embrace discontinuous change.

That is more revolutionary than it sounds. Discontinuous, after all, is hardly a word to stir the multitudes; yet to embrace discontinuous change means, for instance, completely re-thinking the way in which we learn things. In a world of incremental change it is sensible to ape your elders in order to take over where they leave off, in both knowledge and responsibility. But under conditions of discontinuity it is no longer obvious that their ways should continue to be your ways; we may all need new rules for new ball games and will have to discover them for ourselves. Learning then becomes the voyage of exploration, of questing and experimenting, that scientists and tiny children know it to be but which we are soon reminded, by parents, teachers and supervisors, can be time-wasting when others already know what we need to learn. It is a way of learning which can even be seen as disrespectful if not downright rebellious. Assume discontinuity in our affairs, in other words, and you threaten the authority of the holders of knowledge, of those in charge or those in power.

For those in charge continuity is comfort, and predictability ensures that they can continue in control. Instinctively, therefore, they prefer to believe that things will go on as they have before. It requires, as Marcus Olsen has argued, revolutions to unblock societies and shocks to galvanize organizations. Perhaps that is why Britain, untouched by revolution for over 300 years, seems to prefer that the status quo should be the way forward and why organizations too often learn too late.

Major change in organizations seems to follow a predictable and sad sequence:

FRIGHT   –   the possibility of bankruptcy, takeover or
                                   collapse

NEW FACES	–	new people are brought in at the top
NEW QUESTIONS	–	questions, study groups, investigations into old ways and new options
NEW STRUCTURES	–	the existing pattern is broken up and re-arranged to give new talent scope and break up old clubs
NEW GOALS & STANDARDS	–	the new organization sets itself new aims and targets.

Do we always need a painful jolt to start re-thinking? Did it need the *Titanic* to sink before it became compulsory for ships to carry enough lifeboats for all the passengers? Did the *Challenger* shuttle have to explode before NASA reorganized its decision-making systems and priorities?

How many have to die before we make cars safer and less powerful?

Discontinuous change is all around us. We would be foolish to block our eyes to its signs as those Peruvian Indians did to their invaders' sails. We need not leave it too late, like the frog in boiling water, nor wait for a revolution. There are opportunities as well as problems in discontinuous change. If we change our attitudes, our habits and the ways of some of our institutions it can be an age of new discovery, new enlightenment and new freedoms, an age of true learning.

Ask people as I have often done, to recall two or three of the most important learning experiences in their lives and they will never tell you of courses taken or degrees obtained, but of brushes with death, of crises encountered, of new and unexpected challenges or confrontations. They will tell you, in other words, of times when continuity ran out on them, when they had no past experience to fall back on, no rules or handbook. They survived, however, and came to count it as learning, as a growth experience. Discontinuous change, therefore, when properly handled is the way we grow up.

The beginnings are small

We live life on two levels. A teenager in the USA was asked to produce a list of the kinds of critical events which she saw looming in the future. It went like this:

A US/USSR alliance
Cancer cure
Test-tube babies
An accidental nuclear explosion
Spread of anarchy throughout the world
Robots holding political office in the USA

We could each provide our own such lists of triumphs and disasters. When she was asked, however, to list the critical events looming in her personal life she wrote down:

Moving into my own apartment
Interior design school
Driver's licence
Getting a dog
Marriage
Having children
Death

This chapter is about changes, but it is about the changes which will accept the *second* list more than the first. Not that a cancer cure or a nuclear war would not have an effect on the way we live our daily lives, but it is often the little things in life which change things most and last the longest.

The chimney, for instance, may have caused more social change than any war. Without a chimney everyone had to huddle together in one central place around a fire with a hole in the roof above. The chimney, with its separate flues, made it possible for one dwelling to heat a variety of rooms. Small units could huddle together independently. The cohesion of the tribe in winter slipped away.

Central heating – meaning in reality *de*centralized heating – carried it even further, doing away with fireplaces altogether, making it possible to pile dwelling units on top of dwelling units into the sky and for so many people to live alone, often far above the ground, but warm.

No one would want to disinvent the chimney or central heating, but their inventors (whose names are long lost if they were ever known) could not have guessed at the changes which they would make to our social architecture. The telephone line has been and will be the modern day equivalent of the chimney, unintentionally changing the way we work and live.

I saw a man sitting in his car in the parking place I coveted. 'Are you about to move?' I asked.'Not for a couple of hours yet,' he replied. It was then I saw the portable computer on the seat beside him and the fax connected to his car telephone line. He was using his car as a mobile office.

Rather like central heating, the telephone and its attachments make it possible today for people to work together without being together in one place. The scattered organization is now a reality. The implications, as we shall see, are considerable. It is not an unmixed blessing, for being together has always been part of the fun. As Pascal once said, all the world's ills stem from the fact that a man cannot sit in a room alone. Increasingly, he, and she, may have to.

Chimneys and telephones are technology – always a potential trigger of discontinuity. Economic reality is another. Governments can stave it off for a while but not forever. In the end countries live or die according to their comparative advantage. Comparative advantage means that there is something for which others will pay a price, be it oil and minerals, cheap labour, golden sun or brains. For Britain and the rest of the industrialized world it has, increasingly, to be brains. Clever people, making clever things or providing clever services add value, sometimes lots of value, to minimal amounts of raw material. Their sales allow the import of all the things we cannot grow and cannot afford to make. That way prosperity advances. It sounds straightforward and simple enough, but its consequences ramble everywhere. Many more clever people are now needed, for one thing, with fewer places for the less clever. Organizations making or doing clever things spend much of their time handling information in all sorts of forms. Facts, figures, words, pictures, ideas, arguments, meetings, committees, papers, conferences all proliferate. Information goes down telephone lines, so technology and economics begin to blend together to create a massive discontinuity in the shape, and skills and purposes of many of our organizations. Clever organizations do not, it seems, work the way organizations used to work, they have different shapes, different working habits, different age profiles, different traditions of authority.

Barry Jones, now an Australian Cabinet Minister, has listed the typical activities of the information sector.

teaching	creative arts and architecture
research	design
office work	music
public service	data processing
communications	computer software
the media	selling
films	accountancy
theatre	law
photography	psychiatry and psychology
post and telecommunications	social work
book publishing	management
printing	advertising
banking	church
real estate	science
administration	trade unions
museums and television	parliament

One could add to it: stockbroking, consultancy, journalism, conference organizing, secretarial work, medicine, politics and local government.

It is unlikely that anyone reading this chapter will not find his or her work included in this list.

Technology and economics is a potent blend. It is the premise of this chapter that from that blend all sorts of changes ensue. Social customs can be transformed. An information society makes it easier for more women to do satisfying jobs. Technology has turned child-bearing into an act of positive decision for most. Marriage then becomes, increasingly, a public commitment to starting a family. Relationships that do not involve the start of a family no longer need the stamp of public commitment. Women can support themselves and can in theory support a family on their own, and many will prefer to do just that. What was in former times technologically and economically impossible, and therefore socially unacceptable, becomes both possible and acceptable. Discontinuity abroad creeps unnoticed into the family.

Words are the bugles of social change. When our language changes, behaviour will not be far behind. House-husbands, single-parent families, 'dinkies' and 'telecommuters', these and many other words were unknown ten years ago. They were not needed. Organizations used to invite men to bring their wives to functions, then it became 'spouses' in recognition of the growing number of female employees, then 'partners' as an acceptance that marriage is not the only stable relationship, and now in California it is the 'significant other' to take care of any conceivable situation.

Just think of it!

It is the combination of a changing technology and economics, in particular of information technology and biotechnology and the economics associated with them, which causes this discontinuity. Between them they will make the world a different place.

Information technology links the processing power of the computer with the microwaves, the satellites, and the fibre optic cables of telecommunications. It is a technology which is leaping rather than creeping into the future. It is said that if the automobile industry had developed as rapidly as the processing capacity of the computer we would now be able to buy a 400 mile-per-gallon Rolls-Royce for £1.

Biotechnology is the completely new industry that has grown out of the interpretation of DNA, the genetic code at the heart of life. It is only one generation old as a science and as an industry, and is only now becoming evident in everyday life with new types of crops, genetic fingerprinting and all the possibilities, good and bad, of what is called bio-engineering.

These two technologies are developing so fast that their outputs are unpredictable, but some of the more likely developments in the next ten to twenty years could change parts of our lives, and other peoples' lives, in a dramatic fashion. A group of young executives who were asked by their companies to contemplate AD 2000 came up with the following possibilities and probabilities.

Cordless telephones Mark 2

The next generation of cordless telephones (already being tested in Britain) may give everyone their own portable personal telephone to be used anywhere at affordable prices. Link it to a lap-top computer and a portable fax and a car or train seat becomes an office.

Monoclonal antibodies

These genetically engineered bacteria which work to prevent particular diseases already exist and their number will expand. Blood-clotting and anti-clotting agents can now be manufactured to prevent major coronary diseases. 'Scavenger Proteins' are under investigation, designed to locate undesirable substances in the bloodstream, such as excess cholesterol. Cures for most cancers, and possibly AIDS, will be available by the end of the century. Senile dementia is now understood and drugs to combat it are under development. Life could go on, if not forever, for a lot longer than before when most diseases can be cured or prevented.

The transgenic pig

The possibility of using animal organs in humans has been under investigation for some time. The pig is biologically similar to humans and experiments are under way to engineer embryos to produce the transgenic pig, an animal with organs more manlike than piglike. Pig farms may one day mean something quite different from what they do today and replacement organs could be available on demand.

Water fields

Crops can now be genetically engineered to grow on poor quality soil or even in water (without tasting like seaweed!). Under development is an idea to engineer crops which can take their nitrogen directly from the air instead of from the ground, reducing the need for fertilizer. Any country could one day grow all the food it needs.

Enzyme catalysts

Microbes can now be used as catalysts in many chemical manufacturing processes. Some microbes can even be used to extract minerals from low-grade areas which were previously uneconomic. There are bugs which can be trained to devour and break down waste materials and can even thrive on cyanide. Rubbish disposal is now part of the chemical industry. Indeed, waste can now be converted into methane as one contribution to the energy problem. We shall see, too, self-cleaning ships which will biologically repel barnacles from sticking to their hulls.

Expert GPs

Computers programmed with up-to-date medical knowledge will be available to all GPs. These medical expert systems will not replace the doctor but will allow every doctor to be a better doctor, to make fewer demands on specialists and so release them to be better specialists. This example of 'expert systems' to enhance the work of professionals and technicians will be copied in all types of occupations, from the solicitor's office to the supermarket purchasing department.

The hearing computer

Voice-sensitive computers which can translate the spoken word into written words on a screen will be on every executive's desk one day, turning everyone into their own typist whether they can use a keyboard or not.

Irradiated food

Irradiation, once we are convinced that it is safe, will make it possible to buy 'fresh' food from all round the world at any time of year. There will also be appetite-reducing drugs for those who find the new foods too tempting, and even health-increasing foods for those who want it both ways.

Telecatalogues

Teleshopping, already in existence in experimental situations, will one day be commonplace. Every store will display its wares and prices on your home television teletext, with local pick-up centres available for those unwilling to pay the extra delivery charge. Personal shopping in the High Street will become a leisure activity rather than a necessity, with all the frills and fancies that go with something done for pleasure not for duty.

Smart cards

These cards, already in use in France, replace cash, keys, credit, debit and cash cards. They will not only let you into your home or your car but will automatically update all your bank account balances for you.

Genetic fingerprints

Instead of Personal Identification Numbers (PINs) which are easy to discover and replicate, we shall each have a fingerprint on our personal cards which cannot be reproduced by others.

Genetic fingerprinting can be used to detect criminals from remains of tissue left behind at the scene of a crime, and also to diagnose hereditary and latent diseases. A national data-bank of genetic fingerprints seems possible one day.

Soon, everything we know about ourselves, and some things we do not know, will be available to anyone with the right number or fingerprint. What price privacy then, many will ask.

Windscreen maps

Computerized autoguidance screens will become commonplace, telling you the best way to get to where you want to go and projected onto the windscreen, as in fighter aircraft, so that you need not take your eyes off the road. These systems can take weather, traffic density and roadworks into account and give you the best available route, turning the whole country, one suspects, into a constant traffic jam.

Mileage bills

Cables laid under the roads of our cities can trigger a meter inside a car programmed to charge different parts of the city at different rates, presenting you with the equivalent of a telephone bill at the end of the month for the use of your car on the city roads. Already designed for Hong Kong this system is potentially available now, although special licences for inner-city use are a more likely first step.

The technology we shall undoubtedly take in our stride. Hole-in-the-wall banking caused hardly a flutter of an eyelid when it appeared and video-recorders are now part of the furniture in nearly half of British homes. It is not the technology itself that is important but the impact which, without conscious thought, it has on our lives. Microwave ovens were a clever idea, but their inventor could hardly have realized that the effect, once they were everywhere, would be to take the preparation of food out of the home and into the, increasingly automated, factory; to make cooking as it used to be into an activity of choice, not of necessity; to alter the habits of our homes, making the dining table outmoded for many, as each member of the family individually heats up his or her own meals as and when they require them.

Whether these developments are for good or for ill must be our choice. Technology in itself is neutral. We can use it to enrich our lives or to let them lose all meaning. What we cannot do is to pretend that nothing has changed and live in a garden of remembrance as if time had stood still. It doesn't and we can't.

Thinking upside-down

Discontinuous change requires discontinuous thinking. If the new way of things is going to be different from the old, not just an improvement on it, then we shall need to look at everything in a new way. The new words really will signal new ideas. Not unnaturally, discontinuous upside-down thinking has never been popular with the upholders of continuity and the status quo. Copernicus and Galileo, arch-exponents of upside-down thinking, were not thanked for their pains. Jesus Christ, with his teaching that the meek should inherit the earth, that the poor were blessed and the first should be last in the ultimate scheme of things, died an untimely and unpleasant death. Nonetheless, their ideas live on, as good ideas do, to release new energies and new possibilities. In the long perspective of history it may seem that the really influential people in the last 100 years were not Hitler or Churchill, Stalin or Gorbachev, but Freud, Marx and Einstein, men who changed nothing except the way we think, but that changed everything. Francis Crick is not today a household name, yet he, with James Watson and Maurice Wilkins, discovered the genetic code, DNA, and so created the science of microbiology and the industry of biotechnology on which much of our economic future may depend.

The creative upside-down thinking of such people is the premise on which this chapter is built. New ways of thinking about familiar things can release new energies and make all manner of things possible. Upside-down thinking does not have to aspire to the greatness of Einstein or the all-embracing doctrines of Marx. It has its more familiar variants. The person who decides to treat every chore as an opportunity for learning discovers that cooking can be a creative art, chopping wood a craft, childminding an educational experience and shopping a sociological expedition. The organization which treats people like assets requiring maintenance, love and investment can behave quite differently from the organization which looks upon them as costs, to be reduced wherever and whenever possible. Upside-down thinking changes nothing save the way we think, but that can make all the difference.

Thirty years ago Donald Schön, an American writer on organizations and now on learning, was arguing that creativity, particularly scientific creativity, comes from the 'displacement of concepts' – from taking concepts from one field of life and applying them to another in order to bring fresh insights. Einstein's Theory of Relativity is the great example. It applies equally well, if not more so, to the field of human activities. New imagery, signalled by new words, is as important as new theory; indeed new theory without new imagery can go unnoticed. Most of what is said here is not new, nor is it being said for the first time, but much of it has gone unnoticed.

Upside-down thinking invites one to consider the unlikely if not the absurd. If Copernicus could stand the solar system on its head and still be right nothing should be dismissed out of hand in a time of discontinuity.

- Upside-down thinking suggests that we should stop talking and thinking of employees and employment. They are words, after all, which only entered the English language some 100 years ago. If work were defined as activity, some of which is paid for, then everyone is a worker, for nearly all their natural life. If everyone were treated as self-employed during their active years then by law and logic they could not be *unem-*ployed. They might be poor but that can be put right. The words 'retirement' and 'unemployment' used only as a contrast to 'employment' would cease to be useful.
- Upside-down thinking suggests that if we put *everyone* on welfare it would no longer be invidious to receive it. That would not mean that no one was expected to work, only that everyone, as of right, got an initial 'social dividend', to be repaid progressively as one earns.
- Upside-down thinking wonders what magic it is that determines that forty hours spread over five days should be the working week for most people. Why cannot one choose to distribute the 2000 hours per year of normal work in a wide variety of chunks?
- Upside-down thinking notices that marriages in Victorian times lasted fifteen years and today also for fifteen years. In Victorian times it was the

death of a partner which ended the marriage, now it is divorce. Should all relationships as well as employment contracts have a fixed term?

- Upside-down thinking suggests that it might be desirable to reward some experts for *not* using their skills. At present dentists in Britain are paid per treatment. There is an inevitable temptation to diagnose the need for treatment. If rewards were related to the number of healthy mouths in the practice not the bad ones, we might need fewer dentists and have better teeth. Similarly, upside-down thinking observes that a national health service is run and rewarded as a national sickness service and wonders why it cannot be reversed.

- Upside-down thinking suggests that instead of a *National* Curriculum for education what is really needed is an *individual* curriculum for every child, within common guidelines maybe, but given expression in a formal contract between the home and the school.

- Upside-down thinking questions whether more money for more effort is always the right way to reward all people all the time, or whether at certain stages in life more time might be as welcome as more money.

- Upside-down thinking wonders why one career or one type of job should be the norm. Why not three careers, switching progressively from energy to wisdom as the years roll on?

- Upside-down thinking wonders why assistants are always younger than their principals or superiors. Why could not people retrain in mid-life to be part-time assistants to doctors, teachers, social workers and lawyers, para-professionals leaving the full professionals to do the more special-ized work.

And so it can go on. At first sight impossible, or ludicrous, many of these ideas have already been canvassed as practical possibilities in some quarters.

It is a time for new imaginings, of windows opening even if some doors close. We need not stumble backwards into the future, casting longing glances at what used to be; we can turn round and face a changed reality. It is, after all, a safer posture if you want to keep moving.

Some people, however, do not want to keep moving. Change for them means sacrificing the familiar, even if it is unpleasant, for the unknown, even when it might be better. Better the hole they know rather than the one not yet dug. Sadly for them a time of discontinuous change means that standing still is not an option, for the ground is shifting underneath them. For them, more than for the movers and the shakers, it is essential that they understand what is happening, that they begin to appreciate that to move and to change is essential, and that through change we learn and grow, although not always without pain.

This chapter is written particularly for those who live in the midst of change and do not notice it or want it. It is not for would-be leaders, not a political tract; more a guidebook to a new country.

It is, however, only one man's view. In an age of unreason there can be no certainty. The guidebook is a guide to a country in which few have yet travelled, a country still to be explored. It is not my purpose to convince anyone that all forecasts are inevitable or that all my prescriptions are right. Rather I am concerned to persuade people that the world around them is indeed changing, with consequences yet to be understood. An age of unreason is an age of opportunity even if it looks at first sight more like the end of all ages.

If this chapter helps at all to look at things in a different way, if it sometimes creates an 'Aha' effect, as when people say 'Aha, of course, that is the way it is', if people start to think 'unreasonably' and try to shape their world the way they think it ought to be, then I shall be content.

Bibliography

Cookham Group (1988) *Headlines 2000*. Hay Management Consultants. A look at the world ahead by a group of young executives, sponsored by the Hay Group. Readable and thought-provoking.

Jones, B. (1982) *Sleepers Wake!* Wheatsheaf Books. A warning directed at Australia to re-think her ways of work and life. Very pertinent to Britain.

Olsen, M. (1982). *The Rise and Decline of Nations*. Yale University Press. A penetrating study of how and why societies freeze up or change.

21

Emerging waves and challenges: the need for new competencies and mindsets

Gareth Morgan

Imagine a long, open Hawaiian beach. The surf is rolling in, and the waves are speckled with surfers and surf-boards. Some surfers are riding the waves with flowing determination. Others are flying high into the air and plunging deep into the foam. The image provides a metaphor for management in turbulent times. For like surfers, managers and their organizations have to ride on a sea of change that can twist and turn with all the power of the ocean.

We live in times of change. And the complexity of this change is as likely to increase as to decrease in the years ahead. Numerous technological, social, and information revolutions are combining to create a degree of flux that often challenges the fundamental assumptions on which organizations and their managers have learned to operate. Managers of the future will have to ride this turbulence with increasing skill, and many important competencies will be required.

These competencies are the focus of this chapter, which draws on the results of an action-learning project designed to investigate the impact of changes in the world economy on the future of organization and management. Figure 1 gives an overview of the issues that lie at the center of attention.

Scenario: An increasingly turbulent environment.

The pace and complexity of change are as likely to increase as to decrease in the years ahead. Few, if any, organizations can be sure of a secure future, as scientific and technological developments can transform the very ground on which they have learned to operate. Changes can come from 'out of the blue.' Traditional competencies or market niches can be challenged by new technologies, generating new skills and new products. Slumbering giants can be shaken to life and left staring at new competitors, who have new ideas and new approaches and will carry developments into new realms. More than

Adapted from *Riding the Waves of Change: Developing Managerial Competencies for a Turbulent World* (San Francisco: Jossey-Bass, 1988), pp. 1–15. Reproduced with permission of the publisher

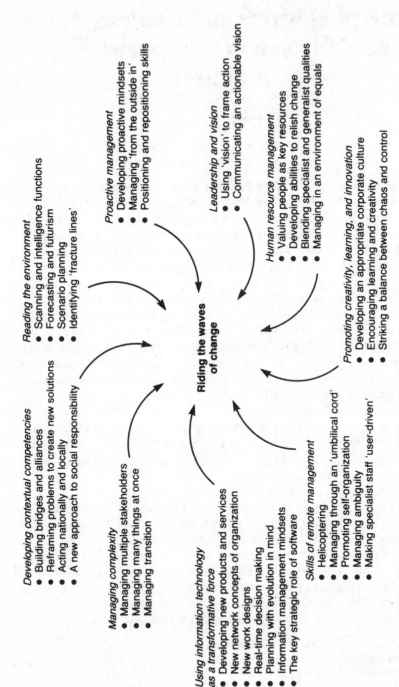

Developing contextual competencies
- Building bridges and alliances
- Reframing problems to create new solutions
- Acting nationally and locally
- A new approach to social responsibility

Reading the environment
- Scanning and intelligence functions
- Forecasting and futurism
- Scenario planning
- Identifying 'fracture lines'

Proactive management
- Developing proactive mindsets
- Managing 'from the outside in'
- Positioning and repositioning skills

Leadership and vision
- Using 'vision' to frame action
- Communicating an actionable vision

Human resource management
- Valuing people as key resources
- Developing abilities to relish change
- Blending specialist and generalist qualities
- Managing in an environment of equals

Promoting creativity, learning, and innovation
- Developing an appropriate corporate culture
- Encouraging learning and creativity
- Striking a balance between chaos and control

**Riding the waves
of change**

Managing complexity
- Managing multiple stakeholders
- Managing many things at once
- Managing transition

*Using information technology
as a transformative force*
- Developing new products and services
- New network concepts of organization
- New work designs
- Real-time decision making
- Planning with evolution in mind
- Information management mindsets
- The key strategic role of software

Skills of remote management
- Helicoptering
- Managing through an 'umbilical cord'
- Promoting self-organization
- Managing ambiguity
- Making specialist staff 'user-driven'

Figure 1   *An overview of some emerging managerial competencies*

ever, the world is in flux. And organizations and their managers must recognize the necessity of developing the mindsets, skills, and abilities that will allow them to cope with this flux.

Managers of the future will have to develop their ability to 'read' and anticipate environmental trends. They will need to develop antennae that help them to sense the critical issues and identify the emerging 'fractures' that will transform their organizations. At present these skills are largely intuitive and the preserve of exceptionally astute individuals who have a 'good nose' for new developments. One important challenge will be to find ways of developing these skills more explicitly.

Scenario: Increasing turbulence and change will require organizations and their managers to adopt a much more proactive and entrepreneurial relationship with the environment, to anticipate and manage emergent problems, and to create new initiatives and new directions for development. This proactive philosophy will be essential for empowering and energizing organizations to keep abreast of the challenges they face and will need to be dispersed throughout an organization. It will be particularly important at senior levels, especially in relation to the generation and implementation of corporate strategy.

Managers of the future will have to develop the attitudes and skills that facilitate proactive management, in particular, 'proactive mindsets,' an ability to manage 'from the outside in,' and positioning and repositioning skills that allow the pursuit of new opportunities.

Proactive mindsets are necessary if people are to approach challenges actively rather than passively. Many organizations and their managers drive toward the future while looking through the rearview mirror. They manage in relation to events that have already occurred, rather than anticipate and confront the challenges of the future. A proactive approach requires managers:

- To 'look ahead.'
- To identify problems and opportunities.
- To find ways of reframing problems so that negatives become potential positives, opening new avenues for development.
- To grasp, shape, and develop these opportunities so that they can be implemented.

This approach requires a 'we can make it happen' philosophy that empowers people to envisage and realize desirable futures, rather than wait for the future to unfold.

Outside-in management keeps an organization in close contact with its evolving environment and enhances its capacity to rise to challenges and opportunities in an ongoing way. This outside-in philosophy contrasts with the 'inside-out' philosophy so common today, where managers relate to the environment in terms of what they and their colleagues *want* to do, rather than what is necessary to meet the challenge of new technologies and the evolving demands of external stakeholders, especially customers and potential customers.

An outside-in philosophy can be developed:

- By focusing on potential transformations in production technologies and in the market to provide early warning signs of the transformations that will be required in one's organization.
- By assessing the appropriateness of current strengths and distinctive competencies and transforming them when necessary.
- By seeing the strengths and weaknesses of one's organization through the eyes of key external stakeholders, with the aim of strengthening and developing key competencies.

Positioning and repositioning skills allow an organization to adjust to new opportunities. A number of these skills are likely to become increasingly important, including:

- An ability to manage tensions between present and future, so that one can position for the future while avoiding collapse in existing operations. This ability is particularly important in achieving major strategic transformations, and requires the development of managerial attitudes and structures that aid rather than hinder transition.
- An ability to develop 'change experiments' that can test the feasibility of different lines of development and thus create a range of opportunities for large-scale change through an incremental 'trial-and-success' approach that does not place the entire organization at risk.
- An ability to balance creativity and discipline, so that imagination and flair are always backed by the disciplined effort necessary to make good ideas good realities.
- An ability to achieve 'good timing' in relation to the introduction of new technologies and entry into new markets, because in times of rapid change timing often spells the difference between success and failure.

Scenario: First-rate leadership will increase in importance at all levels of organization, but it will not necessarily be highly formalized or hierarchical. Increasingly, the leadership process will become identified with an ability to mobilize the energies and commitments of people through the creation of shared values and shared understandings.

Managers of the future will have to develop their leadership skills. In particular, they will have to view leadership as a 'framing' and 'bridging' process that can energize and focus the efforts of employees in ways that resonate with the challenges and demands posed by the wider environment. This process requires many competencies, especially those that enable the leader to create or find the vision, shared understanding, or sense of identity that can unite people in pursuit of relevant challenges; and to find means of communicating that vision in a way that makes it actionable.

Managers of the future must pay special attention to skills that increase their power to communicate, to create shared understanding, to inspire, and to empower others to take on leadership roles. The leader of the future will not always lead from the front; in times of uncertainty, a significant part of a leader's role rests in finding ways of unlocking the ideas and energies of others. He or she must articulate a relevant sense of direction, while broadening ownership of the leadership process so that others are also encouraged to bring forward their ideas and thus influence the direction that the organization actually takes.

Scenario: In an information society the management of an organization's human resources will become increasingly important. Managers will have to find ways of developing and mobilizing the intelligence, knowledge, and creative potential of human beings at every level of organization. Traditional economics has taught us that the important factors of production are land, labor, and capital. But in the modern age, knowledge, creativity, opportunity seeking, interpersonal skills, and entrepreneurial ability are becoming equally important.

The process of human resource management will thus become an important function of every manager's job, rather than the preserve of personnel specialists. Managers will have to become increasingly skilled in placing quality people in key places and developing their full potential.

It will become increasingly important to recruit people who enjoy learning and relish change and to motivate employees to be intelligent, flexible, and adaptive. Special attention will need to be devoted to finding ways of motivating people to make contributions that have long-term benefits, not just those that become visible in the short run. New ways of balancing and integrating the interests of shareholders and employees will also have to be developed.

As organizations become more aware of the importance of their human resource base and increase the quality of their human resources, the nature of the manager's role will also change. The manager will no longer be able to function as a technical specialist who is also responsible for managing people, as is so often the case today. He or she will have to become much more of an all-round generalist who is able to achieve good integration between technical, human, operational and creative sides of management. The skill of integrating short- and long-term perspectives will become of increasing importance as a means of integrating today's learning with future activities. Every manager will be required to think of tomorrow as well as be effective today.

Increasingly, managers of the future will have to be able to manage in an environment of equals and will have to prove their worth by being a resource to those being managed, as troubleshooters, resources, idea generators, problem solvers, team builders, networkers, orchestrators, facilitators, conflict managers, and motivators. The concept of manager will be transformed as organization structures become flatter through the removal of traditional supervisory roles.

The new managerial qualities will initiate new realms of opportunity for women in organizations because women have a much stronger record than men in developing many of these key people-management skills.

Scenario: The demands of an information society will require organizations and their members to promote creativity, learning, and innovation. They will have to find the key to unleashing individual creativity and learning, and develop organizational processes and structures that promote this.

Organizational hierarchies tend to stifle debate and risk taking. Managers interested in promoting learning and innovation thus have to find new ways of structuring relations to promote the creative process, especially through the values defining corporate culture. The ability to foster an appropriate culture will become increasingly important, especially one permeated by attitudes that encourage openness, self-questioning, a proactive entrepreneurial approach, an appreciation for the importance of 'adding value,' and a general optimism and orientation toward learning and change that energizes people to rise to challenges.

Managers will also need to promote innovation through brainstorming, creative thinking, and experimentation and by developing reward structures that sustain innovative activity. They will have to develop more open managerial processes that flatten hierarchies and improve lateral interactions. The ability to manage and work within multidisciplinary teams will be essential. Communications, meeting, and project-management skills will become increasingly important.

Scenario: The flattening of organization structures will require new approaches to management and control. With the props of hierarchy removed, managers will have to coordinate through the development of shared values and shared understanding and find the right balance between delegation and control.

Managers will become responsible for coordinating the work of people who want to work with a minimum of supervision. Managers will need to learn to 'let go,' and to develop skills of 'remote management,' such as 'helicoptering' and 'managing though an umbilical cord.' Managers will have to promote decentralization and become skilled in designing and managing systems that are self-organizing.

The 'hands-off' style demands a very different philosophy and approach from that required of managers working in hierarchical situations. Managers must become adept at handling the uncertainty and ambiguity that accompany remote management and at reading the early warning signs suggesting when intervention in needed. Management will become much more concerned with empowerment than with close supervision and control.

Innovation is likely to become more 'line driven,' and managers of specialist 'service' departments, such as R&D and MIS, will have to develop more 'client-oriented' approaches that tailor professional skills and standards to the requirements of users. In many cases, their departments will develop into autonomous entrepreneurial businesses serving clients outside as well as inside the parent organization.

The pace of change and the required evolution of skills will place a high premium on continuous learning. Managers will have to become finely tuned to their own learning needs and those relating to the education and development of their staff. In many cases, they will have to become exceptional educators in 'on-the-job' activities.

Scenario: Information technology – in the form of microcomputing, electronic communication, and robotics – has the capacity to transform the nature and structure of many organizations and the nature and life cycles of their products and services. Organizations that fail to get 'on board' and to reap the potential benefits will find the competition passing them by. The technology is leading us into a new age in which completely new styles of organization and new managerial competencies will come into their own.

Managers of the future will have to become increasingly skilled in understanding how computer-based intelligence can be used to develop new products and services and to redesign existing ones. Products and services that are 'smart,' 'multipurpose,' 'user driven,' and capable of evolving in design point toward the future of many industries and services. The trends are already evident in many areas of the economy; for example, in how microcomputing has transformed products like typewriters into word processors and banking and other financial services into automated transactions.

The rapid pace of technological change will require important management skills, especially in relation to the management of short product life cycles with short payback periods and in relation to the timing and scale of technological innovation and change.

The new technology can be used to reinforce bureaucratic 'top-down' styles of organization. But its true potential rests in promoting decentralization, network styles of management, and capacities for self-organization. The technology has a capacity to dissolve organizational hierarchies by creating smaller-scale, loosely coupled organizational units coordinated electronically, where work units can remain separate yet integrated. The technology facilitates new work designs that are flexible and self-organizing, where the network rather than the pyramid is the primary organizational form.

The technology will also transform interorganizational relations, dissolving rigid boundaries between separate organizations and creating more open patterns of interaction. This trend is vividly illustrated in the 'Just in Time' (JIT) management systems, which, supported by sophisticated information technology, create new connections among suppliers, subcontractors, manufacturers, unions, retailers, and customers. Organizations of the future are much more likely to form elements of a loosely coupled network of subcontracted relations, where boundaries are intermeshed rather than discrete.

All these changes will have important consequences for managers of the future. Management of interorganizational relations will become as important as management of intraorganizational relations, and skills in achieving nonbureaucratic modes of coordination, especially through development of some sense of shared purpose and identity and through the use of first-rate communications systems, will need to be acquired. Extensive use will be made of such electronic modes of coordination as electronic mail and video conferencing and of other management information systems.

The speed of communications fostered by computer technology will exert a major impact on decision-making systems. Managers will have to cope with an increased pace of work, where key decisions must be made 'on-line' in 'real time.' Bureaucratized systems of decision making have often created, and have been used to create, time for decision makers. Electronic communications will speed information exchange and force tighter deadlines that will not allow procrastination. 'Real-time decision making' will become an important skill, and will become an important criterion for judging the effectiveness of managers in key operational roles.

The new modes of electronic communication will increase the amount of data available in decision making, creating the problem of information overload. Managers will have to learn to overcome paralysis, or clouding of issues, that can result from having too much information and develop 'information management mindsets' that allow them to sort the wheat from the chaff. Skills in the design of information systems, data management, and data analysis and interpretation will become increasingly important. Managers will also have to be more computer literate and learn to dialogue electronically – with both people and data – with a high degree of skill.

The new technology will also demand new planning mindsets, so that the development and implementation of the technology can evolve along with the advances and the learning that occur with use. The nature of the technology favors small-scale, experimental, 'step-at-a-time' projects. The approach to planning must reap the benefits of this incremental, learning-oriented approach, while keeping the 'bigger picture' – the need for wider modes of integration and system compatibility – clearly in mind. Rather than developing large-scale, 'total systems engineering' approaches based on clear 'predesigns,' organizations will develop 'user-driven' approaches that achieve consistency and integration of technical and data management systems, for example, through identification and management of critical parameters. This approach will place users in the driving seat, and place MIS and other technical experts in a supportive rather than directive role.

The new technology will create great opportunities for the software industry, which is in the position to link the developments in hardware to cutting-edge implementation. At present, many organizations delegate the development of cutting-edge management systems to software engineers, both those within the software industry and their own MIS department staff, in effect saying: 'We want this, and we'd like you to do it for us.' To achieve this task, those developing software must have a thorough understanding of the new managerial and organizational principles underlying the systems that they will be expected to design. The software industry and MIS departments will have to recruit some of the best managerial minds, and people skilled in the new approaches to organizational design. Effectiveness here will be a critical factor influencing the future competence of management in general.

Scenario: Complexity is the name of the managerial game: many managers may want simplicity, but the reality is that they have to deal with complexity. The complexity of organizational life is increasing rather than decreasing, as manifested in the conflicting demands posed by multiple stakeholders, the need for managers to deal with many things at once, and the almost continuous state of transition in which organizations exist.

To manage ambiguity and paradox, managers of the future will have to develop managerial philosophies and techniques that allow them to cope with messy, ill-defined situations that do not lend themselves to clear-cut interpretation, and have no ready-made recipes for action.

Shareholders, employees, unions, customers, collaborating firms, government agencies, the local community, and the general public will be active stakeholders in the organization, imposing their own demands on management. The situation is even more complicated for senior executives in conglomerates, where different businesses falling under the same corporate umbrella may each have a complicated set of stakeholders. Managers of the future will be faced with the 'stakeholder concept of organization,' as opposed to the present 'shareholder concept,' and will have to recognize the multiple sets of interests that must be served and reconciled. They will require many political and networking skills to blend the contradictory demands.

Managers will have to be adept at managing many things simultaneously. They will have to combine specialist and generalist skills and learn to achieve excellent performance in many areas simultaneously. They will have to find ways of reframing contradictory situations so that new opportunities and problem solutions become apparent. And they will have to recognize that any situation typically has multiple meanings (to different stakeholders) that have to be managed or integrated in some way.

Managers of the future will also have to become increasingly skilled in managing transition. They will have to recognize flux as the norm and develop mindsets and skills that allow them to cope with the continuous flow of new ideas, products, technologies, skills, information, and interpersonal and interorganizational relations. In some cases, they will have to deal with crisis as a norm, for example, where product life cycles are so short that routine product development and production must be managed with the speed and precision typically required of emergency situations. Managers of the future will have to learn to ride these and other turbulent conditions by going with the flow, recognizing that they are always managing *processes* and that flux rather than stability defines the order of things.

Scenario: In addition to reading about and dealing with emerging trends, managers of the future, especially those at a senior level, will have to find ways of reshaping those trends so that they become more manageable. The proactive approach to management will have to embrace an ability to reshape the socio-economic environment and not just treat it as a given.

Many of the most important problems facing our organizations are contextual, in the sense that they are rooted in the socioeconomic environment. American, British, Canadian, French, Japanese, Scandinavian, and other nationally based organizations face particular sets of problems that are vitally linked with the national and international context in which they are operating. For example, issues relating to a country's competitive position in the world – such as the effects of government regulation, the climate of labor–management relations, the 'national psyche,' the growing problems associated with youth, unemployment, and unsatisfied social expectations, national and local politics, the quality of the educational system, and the globalization of trading relations – exert a major impact on the performance of organizations within the country. Future managers in all nations face the challenge of influencing and reshaping these problems and relations through the development of 'contextual competencies' that mobilize action from key actors in different sectors of society.

Skills in 'bridge building,' and other forms of collaborative activity uniting diverse stakeholders in attacks on shared problems, will be at a premium. Partnerships and other joint ventures, and new understandings between organizations in different sectors of the economy – such as business, education, government, labor, human services, and voluntary sectors – will be needed to attack unemployment, illiteracy, skills training, pollution, and a variety of social issues. All sectors have a stake in these problems, and novel ways of addressing them must be found. In particular, resources will need to be rechannelled to critical areas, and organizational activities will require new methods of regulation that rely on the development of shared values and understanding, rather than bureaucratic rules that hamper effective action. New ways of combining local and national attacks on problems are also necessary to avoid the inaction that often arises when stakeholders wait for broad national initiatives to emerge, rather than try to operate on both fronts simultaneously.

Finally, managers of the future will have to develop a much greater sense of social responsibility – not just for lofty moral reasons, but because in a complex, interdependent society, a high degree of responsibility needs to be integrated into the way managers *think about* their relationship with the wider context. Indifference to the social implications of organizational action scares the public, undermines confidence, and almost always backfires, especially in the long run. A greater understanding of the importance of developing along with the wider context will lead to creative solutions to many socioeconomic problems. The interdependence of economy and society means that socially responsible action is not just a luxury. In the long term, it is a necessity. Managers of the future will recognize this and approach their activities in ways that allow their organizations to evolve along with society.

Development of these contextual competencies will require a form of corporate statesmanship that uses skills of 'outside-in management' to help create the conditions through which society can flourish. These skills will help managers to shape the waves of change that they eventually ride.

22

Transnational economy – transnational ecology

Peter Drucker

Everybody talks about the 'world economy'. It is indeed the new reality. But it is quite different from what most people – businessmen, economists, politicians – talk about. Here are some of its main features, its main challenges, its main opportunities.

- In the early or mid seventies – with OPEC and with President Nixon's 'floating of the dollar' – the world economy changed from being international to transnational. The transnational economy has become dominant, controlling in large measure the domestic economies of the national states.
- The transnational economy is shaped mainly by money flows rather than by trade in goods and services. These money flows have their own dynamics. The monetary and fiscal policies of sovereign national governments increasingly react to events in the transnational money and capital markets rather than actively shape them.
- In the transnational economy the traditional 'factors of production', land and labour, have increasingly become secondary. Money too, having become transnational and universally obtainable, is no longer a factor of production that can give one country a competitive advantage in the world market. Foreign exchange rates matter only over short periods. Management has emerged as the decisive factor of production. It is management on which competitive position has to be based.
- In the transnational economy the goal is not 'profit maximization'. It is 'market maximization'. And trade increasingly follows investment. Indeed trade is becoming a function of investment.
- Economic theory still assumes that the sovereign national state is the sole, or at least the predominant, unit, and the only one capable of effective economic policy. But in the transnational economy there are actually *four* such units. They are what the mathematician calls 'partially dependent variables', linked and interdependent but not controlled by each other. The national state is one of these units; individual countries – especially the major developed non-communist ones – matter, of

Adapted from *The New Realities* (London: Heinemann, 1989), pp. 109–33 course. But increasingly decision-making power is shifting to a second unit: the region – the European Economic Community; North America; tomorrow perhaps a Far Eastern region grouped around Japan. Third there is a genuine – and almost autonomous – world economy of money, credit and investment flows. It is organized by information which no longer knows national boundaries. Finally there is the transnational enterprise – not necessarily a big business, by the way – which views the entire developed non-communist world as one market, indeed as one 'location', both to produce and to sell goods and services.

- Economic policy is increasingly neither 'free trade' nor 'protectionism', but 'reciprocity' between regions.
- There is an even newer transnational ecology. The environment no more knows national boundaries than does money or information. The crucial environmental needs – the protection of the atmosphere, for instance, and of the world's forests – cannot be met by national action or national law. They cannot be addressed as adversarial issues. They require common transnational policies transnationally enforced.
- Finally: while the transnational world economy is reality, it still lacks the institutions it needs. Above all it needs transnational law.

The transnational ecology

Concern for the ecology, the endangered habitat of the human race, will increasingly have to be built into economic policy. And increasingly concern for the ecology, and policies in respect of it, will transcend national boundaries. The main dangers to the human habitat are increasingly global. And so increasingly will be the policies needed to protect and to preserve it. We still talk of 'environmental protection' as if it were protection of something that is outside of, and separate from, man. But what is endangered are the survival needs of the human race. Until the nineteenth century, the never-ending challenge was the protection of mankind and its habitat against the forces of nature: epidemics, predators, floods, hurricanes. These forces are still as powerful as ever. The recent eruption of AIDS, the new plague, should have stilled all the prattle about 'the conquest of nature'. But in this century a new need has arisen: to protect nature against man. Indeed awareness of the problem hardly existed until after the Second World War. Since then the threat has grown explosively. And it has totally changed character.

Most people still see the problem as it originally moved into our field of vision, that is as a series of local, isolated, specific events: the smog over Los Angeles, or Mexico City, the extinction of this or that animal species, the oil spill on a beach. But as has become abundantly clear, even purely local environmental events are not 'local' in their consequences. We now know that pollution knows no boundaries. Sulphur emissions from steel mills in America's midwest become acid rain blighting Canadian forests. Toxic effluents discharged into the Rhine by chemical plants in Switzerland, or in France's Alsace, poison Holland's drinking water. Radioactive particles from a nuclear accident in the Ukraine contaminate Sweden's vegetables and make undrinkable the milk of Scottish cows.

It is still generally believed that the threat to environment and ecology is confined to the developed countries and is, indeed, a result of industrialization, of the automobile, of affluence. But the great ecological catastrophe in the making – and the one most difficult to contain, let alone to reverse – is the destruction of the world's tropical forests by the least advanced, the least developed, the poorest inhabitants of the earth: destitute peasants using primitive methods and age-old tools. And no one voices any longer the dogmatic assertion that 'pollution' is a product of capitalism and cannot happen under socialism; it was an article of the communist faith only a few years ago. The greatest ecological disaster so far has been the near-destruction of the world's largest body of fresh water, Lake Baikal in Siberia; and Beijing and Budapest are fully as polluted as Mexico City, and do as little to solve the problem.

The destruction of the ecology on which humankind's survival depends is thus a common task. To tackle it as a national task is futile – though obviously a good deal of national, and indeed of local, implementation will be needed. It is futile too to try to tackle it adversarially, with one country accusing its neighbour of befouling the environment – the Dutch accusing the French, the Swedes accusing the British, the Canadians accusing the Americans. The accused country then inevitably will proclaim its innocence and deny that there is a problem. No effective action will be taken until we accept that serious environmental damage anywhere is everybody's problem and threatens all of us.

This will require a major change in the way we think about the economy. Economists have been wont to consider pollution and environmental damages as 'externalities'. The costs are borne by the entire community rather than by the activity itself. But this will no longer do for environmental damage. There is no incentive not to pollute. On the contrary, to pollute without paying for it confers a distinct competitive advantage on those who pollute the worst. To treat environmental impacts as 'externalities' can also no longer be justified theoretically. During the last century every developed country has converted industrial accidents from an externality into a direct cost of doing business. Every developed country has adopted workmen's compensation, under which the employer pays an insurance premium based on its own accident experience, which makes the damage done by unsafe operations a direct cost of doing business. Workmen's compensation assumes that industrial activity is inherently dangerous. Accidents are thus bound to happen. This was bitterly fought at the time – as a 'licence to kill' – by reformers dedicated to making the workplace safe. Workmen's compensation has done more, however, to reduce the incidence of industrial accidents than safety regulations or factory inspection.

Making environmental threat or damage a direct cost of doing business –

for example by levying a heavy fee on traffic in and out of a city during the rush hours – would have a substantial psychological effect. It would also spur work on finding substitutes for ecologically unsafe substances or practices. Such substitutes might for instance cut sharply America's worst pollution – the runoff from toxic or non-degradable pesticides, herbicides, and ferti- lizers from the farms. Substances that do serious harm and cannot be replaced by harmless ones can be forbidden – the way fluorocarbons are in the process of being outlawed.

Environmental action has to be local. Cleaning up the most polluted oceans – the shallow inland seas like the Baltic, the Mediterranean, the Sea of Cortez – requires that the riparian states clean up the biggest polluters, the municipal sewers. But the notion has to be based on common, trans- national commitment. Transnational agreements alone can halt, and perhaps reverse, the environmental destruction in and by the developing countries. That is where the damage is greatest – simply because what threatens the ecology the most is population pressure rather than industry.

Protection of the environment requires international ecological laws. The nineteenth century offers a precedent. When steamship and railway began to make possible large-scale travel, contagious diseases formerly confined to the tropics – such as yellow fever and cholera – invaded the countries of the temperate zone and threatened to become pandemics. They were contained by quarantines which kept out people from infected areas. A century later, during the New Deal period of the 1930s, the United States government abolished child labour despite stubborn opposition by a number of southern states, by forbidding shipment across state lines of goods produced by underage youngsters. We might similarly 'quarantine' polluters and forbid shipment in international commerce of goods produced under conditions which seriously pollute or damage the human habitat – such as by polluting the oceans, by raising the temperature of the atmosphere, or by depleting its ozone. This will be decried as 'interference with sovereign nations' – and it is. It will probably require that the developed rich countries compensate the developing poor ones for the high costs of environmental protection – sewage treatment plants, for instance. In fact, environmental protection might well be the most productive purpose of foreign aid and far more successful than the development aid of the last four decades. Major problems would still remain even then. Foremost among them is the rapid destruction of the tropical forests by the pressure of land-hungry subsistence farmers which threatens permanently to make arid and infertile large areas, including parts of the temperate zones.

The nineteenth century cured two of mankind's oldest scourges by trans- national action – the slave trade and piracy on the high seas. It declared both to be common enemies of humanity, the suppression of which was in the interest of any country at any time. The threat to the human habitat, the ecology, is a recent threat. But it is a greater threat than the slave trade or piracy ever were, and a threat to everyone. If it can be averted at all, it can be averted only by transnational commitment and joint action.

23

IT in the 1990s: managing organizational interdependence

John F. Rockart and James E. Short

For the past two decades, the question of what impact information technology (IT) will have on business organizations has continued to puzzle academics and practitioners alike. Indeed, in an era when the business press has widely disseminated the idea that IT is changing the way businesses operate and the way they relate to customers and suppliers, the question of technology's impact on the organization itself has gained renewed urgency.

The literature suggests four major classes of impact. First, there is the view that technology changes many facets of the organization's *internal structure*, affecting roles, power, and hierarchy. A second body of literature focuses on the emergence of *team-based*, problem-focused, often-changing work groups, supported by electronic communications, as the primary organizational form.

Third, there is the view that organizations today are '*disintegrating*' – their borders punctured by the steadily decreasing costs of electronic interconnection among firms, suppliers, and customers. Companies, it is believed, will gradually shift to more market-based organizational forms, with specialized firms taking over many functions formerly performed within the hierarchical firm.

Finally, a fourth view of organizational change arises from a technical perspective. Here, it is argued that today's improved communications capability and data accessibility will lead to *systems integration* within the business. This, in turn, will lead to vastly improved group communications and, more important, the integration of business processes across traditional functional, product, or geographic lines.

While each of these four 'IT impact' perspectives offers important insights, there are significant and unresolved questions about each. There is clear evidence for a fifth viewpoint that draws on and expands these perspectives, providing a more integrated, managerial view with important implications.

We will argue that information technology provides a new approach to

Reprinted from *Sloan Management Review*, 30 (Winter) (1989), pp. 7–17 by permission of the publisher. Copyright 1989 by the Sloan Management Review Association

one of management's oldest organizational problems: that of effectively *managing interdependence*. Our fundamental thesis is that a firm's ability to continuously improve the effectiveness of managing interdependence is the critical element in responding to new and pressing competitive forces. Unlike in previous eras, managerial strategies based on optimizing operations *within* functional departments, product lines, or geographical organizations simply will not be adequate in the future.

By 'effective management of interdependence,' we mean a firm's ability to achieve concurrence of effort along multiple dimensions of the organization.[1] Companies have historically been divided into subunits along several dimensions such as functional departments, product lines, and geographic units. It has long been understood that the activities in each of these dimensions, and in each of the subunits *within* these dimensions (e.g., branch offices, manufacturing locations), are far from independent. Many approaches have been devised to manage this evident interdependence. Each approach has the goal of producing the concurrence of effort necessary to allow the organization to compete effectively in the marketplace. Information technology has now been added to these approaches – and it is in this role that it will have its major impact on the firm.

Competitive forces driving the need to manage interdependence

The need to effectively coordinate the activities of individual organizational subunits is vastly greater in 1989 than it was even a few years ago. Competitive pressures are now forcing almost all major firms to become global in scope, to decrease time to market, and to redouble their efforts to manage risk, service, and cost on a truly international scale (see Figure 1).

- *Globalization.* In a world linked by international communication networks and television, global competition stresses the firm's ability to innovate, to capture global levels of manufacturing efficiency, and to understand international marketing and the diversity of the world's markets. All require increasing knowledge and coordination of the firm's operations throughout geographically dispersed subunits.
- *Time to market.* Black & Decker now brings new products to market in half the time it took before 1985. Xerox and Ford have claimed similar improvements in key product lines. 'Time to market' refers to the firm's ability to develop new products quickly and to deliver existing products effectively. In either case, compressing time to market requires increased integration of effort among functional departments such as design, engineering, manufacturing, purchasing, distribution, and service.
- *Risk management.* Market volatility and competitive pressures can easily overwhelm a firm's ability to track and manage its risk. In one

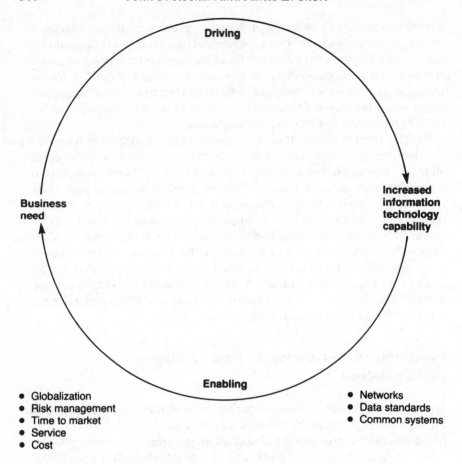

Figure 1   *What is pushing the need to manage interdependence?*

highly publicized incident, Merrill Lynch lost more than $250 million when it failed to adequately oversee an employee trading a complex form of mortgage backed securities.[2] Whatever the industry, the globalization of markets and global market volatility increase the need for effective risk management across once independently managed operations.

- *Service.* 'The excellent companies really are close to their customers,' Peters and Waterman wrote in *In Search of Excellence.* 'Other companies talk about it; the excellent companies do it.'[3] Of course, service is based not only on the effectiveness of a single repairperson, but also on management's ability to have organizationwide knowledge of customer's and equipment's status and problems.
- *Cost.* For nearly all organizations, cost reduction is always a concern. In industries where foreign competitors are becoming dominant, reductions in workforce are an increasing reality.

In sum, global competition risk, service, and cost today require firms to tightly couple their core internal and external business processes. As firms begin to draw these processes together, slack resources (e.g., inventory, redundant personnel) are being reduced.

It is here that information technology plays a major role. Vastly improved communications capability and more cost-effective computer hardware and software enable the 'wiring' together of individuals and suborganizations within the single firm, and of firms to each other. It is this multifunctional, multilevel, multiorganizational, coordinative aspect of current technology that provides managers with a new approach to managing interdependence effectively.

Technology's major impacts on the organization

Several decades of work have produced conflicting perspectives on technology's impacts on the organization. Here we briefly review the four approaches noted above.

Major changes in managerial structure, roles, and processes

In an early, celebrated article, Leavitt and Whisler argued that information technology would lead to a general restructuring of the organization, ultimately eliminating middle management.[4] In their view, IT moved middle managers out of traditional roles, and allowed top managers to take on an even larger portion of the innovating, planning, and other 'creative' functions required to run the business.

Others were quick to comment on these predictions. Some speculated that IT would lead to greater organizational centralization, greater decentralization, reduced layers of middle or upper management, greater centralization of managerial power, or, alternatively, decentralization of managerial power.[5] Others developed contingency-based models of organizational impact.[6] While it is clear that IT has affected organizations in many ways, it is also clear that this often conflicting literature has produced very little insight into how managers should plan for IT-enabled role or structural changes within their firms. Three newer perspectives begin to address this issue.

'The team as hero'

According to this second view, teams and other ad hoc decision-making structures will provide the basis for a permanent organizational form. Reich, for example, argues that a 'collective entrepreneurship,' with few middle-level managers and only modest differences between senior managers and junior employees, is developing.[7] Drucker speculates that the symphony orchestra or hospital may be models of future team-based organizations.[8]

The relationship between teams and technology in much of this work appears based on a technical dimension. On the one hand, this view stresses technology's role in enabling geographically dispersed groups to better coordinate their activities through enhanced electronic communications.[9] On the other hand, some authors stress the importance of 'groupware' in facilitating teamwork through better decision-making aids and project and problem management.[10]

Unfortunately, the team-based literature to date is highly speculative. As a general model of organizational structure, it leaves many questions unanswered. Primary among these are the long-term implications of organizing in a manner that moves primary reporting relationships away from the more usual hierarchical functional, geographic, or product structures. These structures work to immerse employees in pools of 'front line,' continually renewed expertise. Team members separated too long from these bases tend to lose this expertise.[11]

Corporate 'disintegration': more markets and less hierarchy

A third perspective argues that today's hierarchical organizations are steadily disintegrating – their borders punctured by the combined effects of electronic communication (greatly increased flows of information), electronic brokerage (technology's ability to connect many different buyers and suppliers instantaneously through a central database), and electronic integration (tighter coupling between interorganizational processes). In this view, the main effect of technology on organizations is not in how tasks are performed (faster, better, cheaper, etc.), but rather in how firms organize the flow of goods and services through value-added chains.

There are two major threads to this argument. Malone, Yates, and Benjamin state that new information technologies will allow closer integration of adjacent steps in the value-added chain through the development of electronic markets and electronic hierarchies.[12] Johnston and Lawrence argue that IT-enabled value-adding partnerships (VAPs) are rapidly emerging.[13] Typified by McKesson Corporation's 'Economist' drug distribution service, VAPs are groups of small companies that share information freely and view the whole value-added chain – not just part of it – as one competitive unit.

These proposals, however, are very recent and have only small amounts of sample data to support them. And the opposite case – the case for increased, vertical integration of firms – is also being strongly propounded.[14]

Systems integration: common systems and data architecture

A fourth, more technically oriented view is that business integration is supported by systems and data integration. Here the concept of IT-enabled organizational integration is presented as a natural outgrowth of two

IT properties: improved interconnection and improved shared data accessibility.[15] In this view, 'integration' refers to integration of data, of organizational communications (with emphasis on groups), and of business processes across functional, geographic, or product lines.

The need to manage interdependence

While each of these four approaches offers important insights, there is a need for a fifth perspective that expands these views into a more active managerial framework. Our research suggests that the concept of 'managing interdependence' most clearly reflects what managers *actually do* in today's business organizations.

Managers, of course, oversee innumerable large and small interdependencies. What happens in one function affects another. Although companies maintain 'independent' product lines, success or failure in one product line casts a long shadow on the others. Individual specialists are also highly interdependent. Surgeons, for example, cannot operate without nurses, technicians, and anesthetists. And even the simplest of manufacturing processes requires the precise interconnection of hundreds of steps. Other examples include:

- Production engineers rely on product designers to design parts that can be easily and quickly fabricated. Conversely, designers depend on product engineers to implement design concepts faithfully.
- Sales representatives for a nationwide or a worldwide company are also interdependent. The same large customer may be served by many sales offices throughout the world. Common discounts, contract terms, and service procedures must be maintained. Feedback can be important.
- Companies themselves rely on other companies to supply parts or services. The current shortage of memory chips, and the resulting shortage of some types of computer hardware, is a good example of intra-company interdependence.

In sum, interdependence is a fact of organizational life. What is different today, however, is the increasing need to manage interdependence, as well as technology's role in providing tools to help meet this need.

How do companies today manage interdependence? Several approaches have been proposed: Mintzberg, for example, argued that firms coordinate work through five basic mechanisms: mutual adjustment, direct supervision, standardization of work process, standardization of work output, and standardization of worker skills.[16] Lawrence and Lorsch found that successful companies differentiated themselves into suborganizations to allow accumulation of expertise and simpler management processes driven by shared goals and objectives.[17] Conversely, these same successful firms adopted integrating mechanisms to coordinate work activity across suborganizations. Lawrence and Lorsch postulated five mechanisms to manage the needed integration: integrative departments, whose primary activity was to coordinate effort among *functional* departments; permanent and/or temporary cross-functional teams; reliance on direct management contact at all levels of the firm; integration through the formal hierarchy; and integration via a 'paper-based system' of information exchange.

Galbraith later expanded the intellectual understanding of managing integration through people-oriented mechanisms.[18] He noted that direct contact, liaison roles, task forces, and teams were used primarily for lateral relations, permitting companies to make more decisions and process more information without overloading hierarchical communication channels. He also introduced the concept of computer-based information systems as a vertical integrator within the firm.

Five examples of managing interdependence

Today, Galbraith's vision of computer-based information systems as a *vertical* integrator appears prescient, if incomplete. Given pressures from the 'drivers' noted earlier, major aspects of information technology (networks, for example; see Figure 1) serve increasingly as mechanisms for both horizontal and vertical integration. In particular, our work has uncovered six organizational contexts where IT-enabled integration efforts strikingly improved a company's ability to manage its functional, product, or geographic subunits. We focus here on five of the six contexts, as illustrated in Figure 2. (A sixth area of interest, interorganizational integration, is well documented in the literature, and can be viewed as carrying intra-organizational integration into the multifirm context.)[19]

Value-chain integration

Lawrence and Lorsch noted the use of 'human integrators' to manage concurrence of effort between adjacent functions in the value-added chain (e.g., between manufacturing, distribution, and sales) more than twenty years ago. Today this integration is performed increasingly by using electronic networks, computers, and databases. Firms attempt between-function integration for at least one of three reasons: to increase their capacity to respond quickly and effectively to market forces; to improve the quality of conformance to customer requirements; or to reduce costs.[20]

We have found that successful between-function integration collapses the multistage value-added chain into three major segments: developing new products, delivering products to customers, and managing customer relationships (see Figure 3).[21] In manufacturing companies, for example, interdependence revolves around these three macro-organizational activities. In the insurance industry, discussions with five major companies revealed that the same three segments were targets for functional integration.

Turning to the two 'ends' of the modified value-added chain – the product

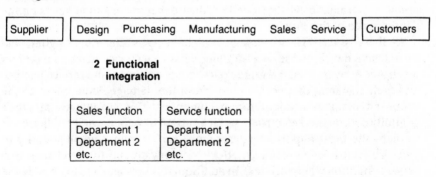

Figure 2   *Managing interdependence in five organizational contexts*

design segment on the one end, and the customer service segment on the other – the effects of technology-enabled integration are clear. To speed *product development*, companies such as Xerox, Lockheed, and Digital are introducing CAD/CAM and other design aids that provide integrated support to product designers, product engineers, materials purchasing, and manufacturing personnel involved in the design-to-production process. This compression has resulted in joint 'buy-in' for new product designs, elimin-

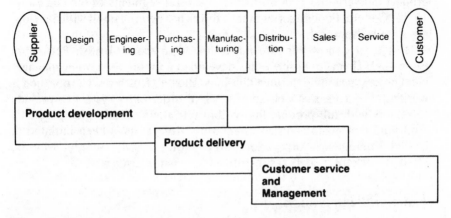

Figure 3   *Product development, product delivery, and customer service and management: collapsing the value-added chain*

ating a lengthy iterative development process (which occurred because designers did not take the needs and capabilities of other departments into account). Dramatically shortened product development time has been the consequence of this buy-in.

At the *customer service* end of the chain, Otis Elevator, Digital, and Xerox have developed service strategies and new service markets based on electronic networks, an integrated database of customer and service history, and fault signaling that goes directly from the damaged equipment to the supplier's maintenance-monitoring computer. The advantages of Otis's centrally coordinated electronic service system have been well publicized.[22] Perhaps the most important advantage is senior management's ability to view the status of maintenance efforts nationwide and to direct sales and service attention where needed. In addition, it is now feasible to provide the company's design, engineering, and manufacturing personnel with direct access to fault data.

In many ways the most interesting stage of the collapsed value chain is *product delivery*, which requires integrating several different information systems: order entry, purchasing, materials resources planning, and distribution management. The critical business issues are to provide customers with information about when orders will be completed, and to forecast and manage outside supplier, product manufacturer, and product distribution processes.

No company has yet accomplished the large-scale integration of functions and systems required to fully manage product delivery. A division of the Norton Company, however, pioneered efforts in this direction in the mid-1980s. Norton initiated a set of major IT projects, ranging from the 'Norton Connection' (a computer-based telecommunications link between the company and its distributors), to a more effective order-processing system, to a series of manufacturing technologies targeted at flexible manufacturing and automated materials control.[23] More recently, Westinghouse initiated a product delivery integration process in several segments of the company. And at General Foods a series of task forces has been charged with developing a similar approach.

Most efforts, however, are more limited in scope. British Petroleum Company's chemical business has developed an integrated order management process spanning thirteen divisions. Baxter Healthcare Corporation is working to enhance its well-known ASAP order entry system to provide customers with full product line visibility to their 125,000-plus products. And a host of manufacturing integration projects have been initiated at Digital Equipment Corporation, Ford Motor, IBM, General Motors, Hewlett-Packard, and Texas Instruments, to name just a few.

Functional integration

Many companies are also recognizing the interdependence of multiple units *within* the same function. This recognition has led to several actions designed to improve coordination across subunits – for example, centralization of functions, central management of geographically separate units, and (in some firms) the development of common systems and/or standard data definitions to facilitate coordinating organizational units.

At Sun Refining and Marketing Company, for example, senior management identified crude oil trading as one of the most critical business activities in the firm three years ago. At that point Sun's traders were dispersed worldwide, each acting relatively autonomously. Sun began developing a centralized, on-line trading function supported by integrated market information from Reuters and other trade data sources. Today Sun recognizes the importance of its integrated trading function in managing risk exposure and in developing effective pricing strategies for the volatile crude market.

At Chemical Bank in New York, foreign exchange trading has become the largest profit generator. To improve management of its worldwide trading operations, Chemical's information technology efforts have ranged from advanced trader workstations to more effective integration of the 'front end' (booking a transaction) with the back office (transaction clearance and settlement). The bank has also improved capital markets auditing through the use of expert systems support.

And finally, while OTISLINE can be viewed as an application enabling integration across stages of the value-added chain, it is also an integrating mechanism within the field maintenance organization itself. Customers with difficult problems can immediately be directed to a specialist, not left to the limited resources of a remote branch office. Frequent trouble from a specific type of elevator can be observed as the pattern develops, and corrective action taken on a nationwide basis. In addition, the quality of telephone responsiveness to anxious customers can be closely monitored.

Similarly, a number of other companies are working aggressively to coordinate the efforts of subunits within a single function, whether it be manufacturing, maintenance, purchasing, sales and marketing, or others. Kodak has developed an executive support system to assist in the worldwide scheduling of manufacturing plants. Digital is installing common MRP systems throughout all of its manufacturing plants. And so it goes. The business drivers underscoring each of these efforts range from service to cost to time-to-market to global responsiveness – but they all recognize that no single unit in a major function is truly independent.

IT-enabled team support

Ken Olsen, chairman of Digital Equipment Corporation, believes that the ability to bring teams together electronically is one of the most important features of the company's IT capability. Ford Motor has claimed that the 'Team Taurus' approach, much of it IT-enabled, shaved more than a year off the time needed to develop, build, and bring to market the new Taurus/Sable model line. In the future, as Drucker points out, many tasks will be done primarily by teams.[24]

Teamwork, of course, is not a new way to coordinate interdependent activities among separate units in an organization. What *is* new is that electronic mail, computer conferencing, and video conferencing now facilitate this process. Today it is feasible for team members to coordinate asynchronously (across time zones) and geographically (across remote locations) more easily than ever before.

The development and use of computer software to support teams is also moving into an explosive phase. There is a growing body of software labeled 'groupware,' a generic name for specialized computer aids designed to support collaborative work groups. As Bullen and Johansen point out, 'Groupware is not a thing. Rather it is a perspective on computing that emphasizes collaboration – rather than individual use.'[25] Several companies, including Xerox, General Motors, Digital, Eastman Kodak, IBM, and AT&T, are experimenting with state-of-the-art meeting and conferencing aids in addition to more 'routine' communications systems such as electronic mail or voice mail systems.

Planning and control

For the past two or three decades, the managerial control process has looked much the same across major companies.[26] Before a new fiscal year begins, an intense planning process culminates with an extended presentation to senior management of each small business unit's (SBUs) proposed activities. Agreed upon plans are then monitored on a monthly basis. Parallel to this formal control process is an informal system of 'keeping in touch,' by which senior management assures itself that 'all is going well' in key areas of the business in the interim between formal reports.

Volatility in the business environment, coupled with technology's ability to provide management with efficient communication and information, is radically changing this traditional planning and control scenario. The major issue is how best to use IT for coordination and control of the firm's activities.

At Xerox, chairman David Kearns and president Paul Allaire have implemented an executive support system that now makes the annual planning and control process a more on-line, team-based, communication- and coordination-based process. The system requires all of Xerox's thirty-four business units to submit their plans over an electronic network in a particular format. Doing this allows the staff to critique the plans more effectively and to reintegrate these plans when looking for factors such as competitive threats across all SBUs, penetration into particular industries by all SBUs, and so forth.

More important, each SBU's plans can be reviewed not only by senior executives and corporate staff but also by other top officers in the firm. Each officer receiving an SBU's plans is encouraged to send corporate headquarters an electronic message raising the issues he or she sees in the plan. The officer may also be asked to attend the review meeting. There is no

'upfront' presentation at this meeting. Only the issues raised by th
tives, the staff, or the other officers are discussed.

In short, Allaire's planning and control process is a computer-age process.
Through the network, it draws on the entire executive team for input.
Understanding of the important issues facing each SBU is deeper and its
activities are therefore sometimes subtly, sometimes more precisely, coordinated with those of the other SBUs.

A team-based, network-linked approach to the senior executive job of
managing the business is also in evidence at Phillips Petroleum Company's
Products and Chemicals Group. There, executive vice president Robert
Wallace is linked to his other top nine executives through an executive
support system that provides on-line access not only to one another, but also
to varying levels of daily sales, refinery, and financial data. External news
summaries relevant to the business are entered into the system three times a
day. Unlike Allaire, who limits his input to planning and review meetings,
Wallace has used the system to take operating command of a few critical
decisions for the business. In the volatile petroleum pricing arena, Wallace
believes that he and his top executive team can confer with the advantage of
data access and can make better pricing decisions than those further down
the line. He cites increased profits in the tens of millions as a result of the
system.

By far the majority of senior executives today do not use their systems in
nearly as dramatic a manner as Allaire and Wallace do.[27] Yet the technology
provides the capability for better coordination at the senior management
level. It also provides opportunities to move decisions either up or down in
the organization. Team decision making is a growing reality, as geographically separated executives can concurrently access and assess data and
communicate in 'real time.' Vertical on-line access to lower levels of data
and text, however, violates some established management practices. Yet
informal telephone-based systems have always provides some of this information. In an era where management is seen more as a cooperative,
coaching activity than as an iron-fisted one, vertical as well as horizontal
networking may come of age.

Within the IT organization itself

Line managers and information technology managers are also finding themselves more mutually dependent than ever before. Today, there is a small
but rapidly growing number of senior line and staff executives who are
taking responsibility for significant strategic projects centered on computer
and communication technologies in their companies, divisions, or departments. We have described elsewhere the full extent and importance of 'the
line taking the leadership.'[28]

As the line role is growing with regard to innovative systems, the role of
the information systems group is becoming more complex, more demanding, and more integrated into the business. Our sample of companies

included several firms whose IT planning efforts involved significant degrees of partnership between the line businesses and their IT organizations in designing and implementing new systems.[29] This necessary degree of partnership places four major demands on the IT organization.

First, with regard to systems development, even those systems in which the line is heavily involved require greater competence and skills on the part of the IT organization. The technical design, programming, and operation of business-critical, complex systems present a far greater challenge than do systems of previous eras. Today's integrated, cross-functional product delivery systems require database, project management, telecommunications, and other skills not previously demanded of IT personnel.

Second, today's new systems require the development and implementation of a general, and eventually 'seamless,' information technology infrastructure (computers, telecommunications, software, and data). The challenge to IT management is to provide leadership for this vital set of 'roads and highways' in a volatile competitive environment.

Third, there is a need for IT management to help educate line management to its new responsibilities. And fourth, IT executives must educate themselves and their staffs in all significant aspects of the business. Only if this happens will IT personnel be able to knowledgeably assist line management in creating effective, strategy-enhancing systems.

The concomitant demand on line management is twofold: the need to learn enough about the technology to incorporate its capabilities into business plans, and the need to select effective information technology personnel and to work closely with them.

The new managerial agenda: think interdependence

Tomorrow's successful corporations will require increasingly effective management of interdependence. IT-enabled changes in cross-functional integration, in the use of teams, or in within-function integration will force individual managers' agendas to change as well. In short, what managers do now and what they will do in the future is in the process of important change.

Dimensions of change

What areas of emphasis for senior managers stem from the increasing interdependence of organizations? In our view, there are five.

- *Increased role complexity*. The typical manager's job is getting harder. One dimension of this difficulty is in the increased pace of organizational change. As companies seek new business opportunities by aggressively defining and executing 'new ways of doing things' – for example, new strategies, new products and services, new customers – managers must adjust more rapidly and frequently to new situations. Similarly, companies must also respond to heightened competitive pressures by improving internal processes. Again, managers must respond quickly to these new situations.

A second dimension of increased role complexity is the manager's need to cope with unclear lines of authority and decision making. As interdependence increases, sharing of tasks, roles, and decision making increases. Managers will be faced with making the difficult calls between what is local to their function and what is global to the business. Moreover, as planning and control systems change, line managers must work more effectively with a wider range of people in the firm.

- *Teamwork*. Teams are real. A vastly increased number of space- and time-spanning, problem-focused, task-oriented teams are becoming the norm. This growth in peer-to-peer (as opposed to hierarchical) activities requires new managerial skills and role definitions.

- *A changing measurement process*. Measurement systems are also changing. Measuring individual, team, or suborganizational success is difficult in an environment where cooperative work is increasingly necessary. New measurement approaches will have to be devised. A transitional period, during which people will need to adjust both to a changing work mode and to a changing measurement process, will result. As new measurement systems evolve, they will almost surely lag behind the changed organizational reality.

- *A changing planning process*. Information technology is enabling the new planning approaches required to meet new competitive conditions. Our research underscores two major new capabilities. First, better information access and information management allow firms to target what is most critical to the organization. Second, organizations now have the ability to conduct 'real-time,' stimulus-driven planning at all levels – in short, to bring key issues to the surface and react to them quickly. The technology provides both the conduit for moving critical data to all relevant decision makers and, more important, the capability to disseminate changes in direction to all parts of the firm.

- *Creating an effective information technology infrastructure*. People-intensive, integrative mechanisms are limited in what they can accomplish. Accessible, well-defined data and a transparent network are, therefore, the keys to effective integration in the coming years. Developing these resources, however, is not easy. Justifying organization-spanning networks whose benefits are uncertain and will occur in the future, and whose costs cannot be attributed clearly to any specific suborganization, is in part an act of faith. Developing common coding systems and data definitions is a herculean job. This task increases short-term costs for long-term gain – a practice not encouraged by most of today's measurement systems.

Notes

The authors wish to acknowledge the contributions of colleagues Christine V. Bullen, J. Debra Hofman, and John C. Henderson, Center for Information Systems Research, MIT Sloan School of Management, to the research on which this article is based.

1 A precise definition of 'interdependence' has generated considerable disagreement among students of organizational behavior. An early and influential view is contained in J.D. Thompson, *Organizations in Action: Social Science Bases of Administrative Theory* (New York: McGraw-Hill, 1967).

   Also see critiques of Thompson's work by:

   J.E. McCann and D.L. Ferry, 'An Approach for Assessing and Managing Inter-Unit Interdependence – Note,' *Academy of Management Journal* 4 (1979): 113–119; and

   B. Victor and R.S. Blackburn, 'Interdependence: An Alternative Conceptualization,' *Academy of Management Journal* 12 (1987): 486–498.

2 'The Big Loss at Merrill Lynch: Why It Was Blindsided,' *Business Week*, 18 May 1987, pp. 112–113.

   See also 'Bankers Trust Restatement Tied to Trading Style,' *New York Times*, 22 July 1988, p. D2.

3 T.J. Peters and R.H. Waterman, Jr., *In Search of Excellence* (New York: Harper & Row, 1982), p. 156.

4 H.J. Leavitt and T.L. Whisler, 'Management in the 1980s,' *Harvard Business Review*, November–December 1958, pp. 41–48.

5 For more on organizational centralization, see:

   M. Anshen, 'The Manager and the Black Box,' *Harvard Business Review*, November–December 1960, pp. 85–92;

   T.L. Whisler, *The Impact of Computers on Organizations* (New York: Praeger, 1970);

   I. Russakoff Hoos, 'When the Computer Takes over the Office,' *Harvard Business Review*, July–August 1960, pp. 102–112.

   Also see D. Robey, 'Systems and Organizational Structure,' *Communications of the ACM* 24 (1981): 679–687.

   On organizational decentralization, see:

   J.F. Burlingame, 'Information Technology and Decentralization,' *Harvard Business Review*, November–December 1961, pp. 121–126.

   Also see J.L. King, 'Centralized versus Decentralized Computing: Organizational Considerations and Management Options,' *Computing Surveys* 15 (1983): 319–349.

   On reduced layers of middle or upper management, see C.A. Myers, ed., *The Impact of Computers on Management* (Cambridge, MA: MIT Press, 1967), pp. 1–15.

   On greater centralization of managerial power, see:

   A.M. Pettigrew, 'Information Control as a Power Resource,' *Sociology* 6 (1972): 187–204;

   J. Pfeffer, *Power in Organizations* (Marshfield, MA: Pitman, 1981); and

   M.L. Markus and J. Pfeffer, 'Power and the Design and Implementation of Accounting and Control Systems,' *Accounting, Organizations and Society* 8 (1983): 205–218.

   On decentralization of managerial power, see:

   S.R. Klatsky, 'Automation, Size and the Locus of Decision Making: The Cascade Effect,' *Journal of Business* 43 (1970): 141–151.

6 Carroll and Perin argue that what managers and employees *expect* from technology is an important predictor of the consequences observed.

   See J.S. Carroll and C. Perin, 'How Expectations about Microcomputers Influence Their Organizational Consequences' (Cambridge, MA: MIT Sloan School of Management, Management in the 1990s, working paper 90s:88–044, April 1988).

   Similarly, Invernizzi found that the effectiveness of the process used to introduce technology into the organization strongly influenced its ultimate impact. See E. Invernizzi, 'Information Technology: From Impact on to Support for Organizational Design' (Cambridge, MA: MIT Sloan School of Management, Management in the 1990s, working paper 90s:88–057, September 1988).

7 R.B. Reich, 'Entrepreneurship Reconsidered: The Team as Hero,' *Harvard Business Review*, May–June 1987, pp. 77–83.

8 P.F. Drucker, 'The Coming of the New Organization,' *Harvard Business Review*, January–February 1988, pp. 45–53.

9 M. Hammer and G.E. Mangurian, 'The Changing Value of Communications Technology,' *Sloan Management Review*, Winter 1987, pp. 65–72.

10 C.V. Bullen and R.R. Johansen, 'Groupware: A Key to Managing Business Teams?' (Cambridge, MA: MIT Sloan School of Management, Center for Information Systems Research, working paper No. 169, May 1988).

11 O. Hauptman and T.J. Allen, 'The Influence of Communication Technologies on Organizational Structure: A Conceptual Model for Future Research' (Cambridge, MA: MIT Sloan School of Management, Management in the 1990s, working paper 90s:87–038, May 1987).

12 T.W. Malone, J. Yates, and R.I. Benjamin, 'Electronic Markets and Electronic Hierarchies,' *Communications of the ACM* 30 (1987): 484–497.

13 R. Johnston and P.R. Lawrence, 'Beyond Vertical Integration – The Rise of the Value-Adding Partnership,' *Harvard Business Review*, July–August 1988, pp. 94–104.

14 T. Kumpe and P.T. Bolwijn, 'Manufacturing: The New Case for Vertical Integration,' *Harvard Business Review*, March–April 1988, pp. 75–81.

15 R.I. Benjamin and M.S. Scott Morton, 'Information Technology, Integration, and Organizat¹onal Change' (Cambridge, MA: MIT Sloan School of Management, Center for Information Systems Research, working paper No. 138, April 1986).

   Also see S. Kiesler, 'The Hidden Message in Computer Networks,' *Harvard Business Review*, January–February 1986, pp. 46–60.

16 H. Mintzberg, *The Structuring of Organizations* (Englewood Cliffs, NJ: Prentice-Hall, 1979).

17 P.R. Lawrence and J.W. Lorsch, *Organization and Environment: Managing Differentiation and Integration* (Homewood, IL: Richard D. Irwin, 1967).

18 J. Galbraith, *Organization Design* (Reading, MA: Addison-Wesley, 1977). Galbraith also introduced the concept of the organization as information processor in this work. He distinguished computer-based, vertical information systems from lateral relations and emphasized the division of organizations into suborganizations because of the need to minimize the cost of communications.

19 S. Barrett and B.R. Konsynski, 'Inter-Organization Information Sharing Systems,' *MIS Quarterly* 4 (1982): 93–105; R.I. Benjamin, D.W. DeLong, and M.S. Scott Morton, 'The Realities of Electronic Data Interchange: How Much Competitive Advantage?' (Cambridge, MA: MIT Sloan School of Management, Management in the 1990s, working paper 90s:87–038, February 1988).

   See also N. Venkatraman, 'Changing Patterns of Interfirm Competition and Collaboration' (Cambridge, MA: MIT Sloan School of Management, Management in the 1990s, working paper, forthcoming).

20 On quality process management, see G.A. Pall, 'Quality Process Management' (Thornwood, NY: The Quality Improvement Education Center, IBM, 16 February 1988).

21 Although our three collapsed segments in the value chain are integral units, data does flow from one to another. The three segments are also interdependent, but less strongly so than the functions within each segment.

22 'Otis MIS: Going Up,' *InformationWEEK*, 18 May 1987, pp. 32–37;
   J.F. Rockart, 'The Line Takes the Leadership – IS Management in a Wired Society,' *Sloan Management Review*, Summer 1988, pp. 57–64;
   W.F. McFarlan, 'How Information Technology Is Changing Management Control Systems' (Boston: Harvard Business School, Case Note No. 9–187–139, 1987).

23 Rockart, see note 22.

24 Drucker, see note 8.

25 Bullen and Johansen, see note 10.

26 R.N. Anthony, *Planning and Control Systems: A Framework for Analysis* (Boston: Harvard University Press, 1965).
27 J.F. Rockart and D.W. DeLong, *Executive Support Systems: The Emergence of Top Management Computer Use* (Homewood, IL: Dow Jones-Irwin, 1988).
28 Rockart, see note 22.
29 T.J. Main and J.E. Short, 'Managing the Merger: Strategic I/S Planning for the New Baxter' (Cambridge, MA: MIT Sloan School of Management, Center for Information Systems Research, working paper No. 178, September 1988).

Index

Index